Animal Care From Protozoa to Small Mammals

F. Barbara Orlans

Addison-Wesley Publishing Company
Menlo Park, California • Reading, Massachusetts
London • Amsterdam • Don Mills, Ontario • Sydney

Dedication

To Christine Stevens, who can turn humanitarian ideals of compassion for all living creatures into a practical reality

This book is in the
ADDISON-WESLEY INNOVATIVE SERIES

ISBN 0-201-05484-1
GHIJK-ML-89

Library of Congress Catalog Card Number: 77 - 72384

Foreword

This book offers a sound moral and ethical framework for principles of animal care appropriate for students. In so doing, it fosters a true reverence for life which is all too lacking today in science education and especially in the use of living creatures in research and teaching.

These guidelines for the care and maintenance of a wide variety of life forms will enable the teacher to introduce a more diverse selection of organisms for study which can only help enrich the learning process. The book gives even further value and applicability to the classroom by offering suggestions for a number of experiments that may be performed humanely on living creatures, including man.

A high quality of animal care not only improves the quality of student research, it brings with it an enhanced awareness of the needs and intrinsic rights of living creatures. This leads naturally to sensitization of the student, through understanding of the moral responsibilities and ethical framework which underlie mankind's relationship with all of creation. Humane values and responsible compassion towards all life can not only humanize science teaching but more importantly, as the author shows in this book, they are the essential ingredients for a truly balanced and integrated education. Other living creatures then will be seen not merely as tools to satisfy intellectual curiosity or, through needless experimental repetition, simply to be used to improve the students' manipulative abilities. Backed by soundly documented principles of animal care the student will become more involved with scientific topics, thus enhancing the total learning experience.

The author is to be congratulated on this book, which is a major stepping stone to the new age of awareness and respect for all creatures great and small.

JOHN A. HOYT, *President*

The Humane Society of the United States

2100 L Street, N.W., Washington, D.C. 20037

Acknowledgements

I must thank many persons for their direct and indirect contributions to the preparation of this book. The principles of protecting animal rights and welfare and of setting boundaries on student use of animals in biology education, which underlie every part of this book, have been developed by three national humane groups with whom I have worked closely. Three persons from these groups have profoundly influenced my personal philosophy and professional work: Mrs. Christine Stevens, President of the Animal Welfare Institute; Dr. Harry Rowsell, Executive Director of the Canadian Council on Animal Care; and Mr. John Hoyt, President of the Humane Society of the United States. I list them in the order in which I met them. They have contributed abundantly, in different ways, to the writing and publication of this book and I am most grateful to each of them.

Authorities who kindly read portions of the manuscript and provided helpful comments include: Dr. Krystina Ansevin, Rice University, Houston; Mr. Raymond E. Barrett, Oregon Museum of Science and Industry, Portland; Professor Kenneth J. Boss, Museum of Comparative Zoology, Harvard University, Boston; Professor Philip S. Callahan, Dept. Entomology, University of Florida, Gainesville; Dr. Richard E. Coggeshall, Division of Comparative Marine Neurobiology, University of Texas, Galveston; Dr. Penny Connell, Dept. Invertebrates, The American Museum of Natural History, New York; Dr. Stuart J. Coward, Dept. Anatomy, Harvard Medical School, Boston; Dr. Clarence Danhof, Sangaman State University, Springfield, Ill.; Mr. Harold Feinberg, Dept. Invertebrates, The American Museum of Natural History, New York; Dr. Ira H. Fritz, Dept. Biological Sciences, Wright State University, Dayton, Ohio; Ms. Alice Gray, Dept. Entomology, The American Museum of Natural History, New York; Ms. Marguerite D. Hainsworth, Borough Rd College, London, England; Professor Earl D. Hanson, Biology Dept., Wesleyan University, Middletown, Conn.; Mr. Richard Headstrom, Aiken, South Carolina; Dr. Harold M. Kaplan, Dept. Physiology, Southern Illinois University, Carbondale; Mr. Carl Kauffeld, Staten Island Zoo, New York; Lt. Walter E. Kilroy, Massachusetts

Society for the Prevention of Cruelty to Animals, Boston; Dr. Frank Loew, Dept. Veterinary Physiology, University of Saskatchewan, Saskatoon; Professor William Farnsworth Loomis, Oxfordshire, England; Dr. Hulda Magalhaes, Dept. Biology, Bucknell University, Lewisburg, Pa.; Dr. James V. McConnell, Mental Health Research Inst., University of Michigan, Ann Arbor; Professor Jerome Metzner, Biology Dept., John Jay College, New York; Dr. George W. Nace, The Amphibian Facility, University of Michigan, Ann Arbor; Mr. Robert Norman, Dept. Veterinary Microbiology, University of Saskatchewan, Saskatoon; Mr. Samuel Poiley, formerly of the National Institutes of Health, Bethesda, Md.; Mr. Robert E. Redfern, United States Dept. Agriculture, Beltsville, Md.; Dr. Christina M. Richards, The Amphibian Facility, University of Michigan, Ann Arbor; Mr. L.D. Schmeltz, Reptile Division, National Zoological Park, Washington, D.C.; Dr. Victor Schwentker, Tumblebrook Farm Inc., Brant Lake, N.Y.; Dr. David C. Secord, Health Sciences Animal Center, The University of Alberta, Edmonton; Ms. Helen Simkatis, Wheaton, Md.; Mr. Harold Wiper, Newton High School, Newtonville, Mass.; Dr. Richard G. Zweifel, Dept. Herpetology, The American Museum of Natural History, New York.

Among those who provided photos for the book, I want to give special thanks to Mr. Gabriel Cooney, Mr. Jeffrey Georgia, Dr. Leonard Krause, Dr. Hulda Magalhaes, and Dr. Tony Mead. Many librarians, zoo officials, museum workers, and biology teachers extended help in diverse ways.

I especially thank my husband Harold and my sons Andrew and Nicholas for their forebearance and encouragement during the demanding time when this book was being written.

Finally, I gratefully acknowledge the generous support for this publication made by the Humane Society of the United States.

Contents

1

Humane Care of Animals

One never learns to understand anything but what one loves.

J. W. von Goethe (1749–1832)

It is the intention of this book to stimulate teachers and students to keep classroom animals, to enjoy them, and to learn by studying their biological characteristics how to appreciate animal life. Biology teaching should mesh together the teaching of humaneness, kindness, and respect for life, with the pursuit of objective inquiry. Students normally show a natural interest in and fondness for animals. It is the responsibility of biology teachers to foster that normal curiosity and affection and broaden it into serious study of the understanding of life processes.

Maintaining living organisms, from protozoa to small mammals, is an ideal way to achieve this end. Among the objectives of keeping classroom animals are an appreciation for all forms of life, an opportunity to observe and perceive, and the challenge to develop a spirit of inquiry and reasoning based upon a sound sense of values. All of these pursuits are compatible with the thesis that scientific inquiry and respect for life go hand in hand.

SELECTION OF SPECIES FOR CLASSROOM CARE

Care in the initial selection of an appropriate species for classroom study is of prime importance. All species of living organism that enter a classroom must be safe, free from transmittable disease, and present no problems of allergy or other health problem to the student or teacher. Wild animals, for instance, are frequent carriers of lice and disease and are therefore not suitable. For conservation reasons, species which are becoming depleted in their natural ranges should not be kept in the classroom. The following characteristics are desirable. The living organism should:

- be hardy and able to thrive in captivity (unlike many delicate reptilians).
- have natural habitats which can be readily duplicated.
- be able to withstand the temperature range and other environmental features of a classroom.
- be fairly simple to care for and not present insurmountable problems for weekend and vacation care.
- not require extensive housing space (such as is needed for monkeys), or difficult food requirements.
- be tolerant to handling.

All animal species described in this book have been carefully selected to fulfill these requirements. Since a wide range of animal phylla is covered in this text, it should be possible to select a suitable species for particular needs of study, and to fit any limitations of budget, classroom size, or equipment available.

The animal kingdom is diverse, and the selection of species for classroom study should reflect this diversity. Too often teachers rely on a limited range of species, but hopefully, this book, by providing information on the care of a broad spectrum of species, will enable teachers to introduce a more diverse selection.

The members of some species need more care and attention than others. Select a species that can thrive in the environment present—taking into account the time available, and the skills and interest of the persons whose responsibility it will be. If in doubt, choose an "easy" species, such as one of the insects, and see that they can be maintained with success before attempting some of the more demanding animals such as small mammals.

QUALITY OF ANIMAL CARE

The quality of animal care, as young people observe it, may form a lasting impression. What they see, they tend to regard as standard and to imitate. Therefore, establish high criteria. Each classroom animal should be well looked after, not only for its own comfort, but also for the wholesome effect an example of humane animal care will have on the class. Explain the principles of culture techniques and animal husbandry to your students and give them the responsibility of daily care of protozoa, worms, mice, or whatever species are being maintained. Regular feeding and watering, and cleanliness of the animal enclosures are important to the continued good health of the species and to the development of disciplined habits and a sense of responsibility in the students. However, the final responsibility for the daily check on food, water, cleanliness, space requirements for housing, the health of each animal, and the performance of any task that is left undone, must remain with the teacher.

Inadequate animal care can occur because proper information is not available. Brief information sheets can be attached to the outside of cages or culture bottles listing the feeding, watering and cleaning schedules and, where appropriate, the names of persons whose responsibility it is to perform these tasks.

Students should not be invited to provide material for dissection or experimentation from any pet which they may possess. Furthermore, bringing any dead animal into the classroom involves risk of infection. Precautions and legal restrictions relative to conservation needs in collecting species from the wild are described in the relevant sections within the book.

LAWS ON ANIMAL USE

In support of the ethical and social implications involved with animal care and study, all states have anticruelty laws which prohibit abuse of animals. Appendix A (page 341) contains pertinent passages from these laws in both the United States and Canada. However, nothing in these laws can reasonably be construed to mean that well cared for animals cannot be kept in the classroom as pets and for observation. Animal anticruelty laws mean that standards of treatment and use of animals are not private matters for individual discretion but are of public concern and conscience.

A number of states have laws similar to that of Illinois, which says, "In every public school . . . one-half hour each week during the whole of each term . . . shall be devoted to teaching the pupils kindness and justice to and humane treatment of birds and animals and the part which they fulfill in the economy of nature." An admirable way to meet this requirement is to keep animals which readily evoke the affections of students in the classroom. Small mammals are well loved and are an obvious choice for helping to teach kindness, understanding, and respect for life. However, avoiding other animals as classroom pets—especially reptiles—may indirectly promote aversion to these animals by the students. Personal identification with non-mammalian animals is understandably more difficult. However, a desirable objective is to teach an all-encompassing respect for diverse forms of life.

The philosophy of respect for all forms of life is embraced in guidelines for the use of animals in biology education issued by the Humane Society of the United States and the Canadian Council on

Animal Care. Guidelines of both of these organizations are similar in their objectives and outlook. The essence of these guidelines is that animals shall be given optimal care appropriate for that species and that no pain shall be inflicted on any vertebrate animal used for educational purposes in elementary or secondary schools. The care and maintenance and experimental procedures described in this book are in compliance with these guidelines which are as follows:

The Humane Society of the United States

GUIDING PRINCIPLES FOR USE OF ANIMALS
IN ELEMENTARY AND SECONDARY SCHOOLS*

1. In biological procedures involving living organisms, species such as plants, bacteria, fungi, protozoa, worms, snails, or insects should be used wherever possible. Their wide variety and ready availability in large number, the simplicity of their maintenance and subsequent disposal makes them especially suitable for student work. In mammalian studies, non-hazardous human experiments are often educationally preferable to the use of species such as gerbils, guinea pigs or mice.
2. No procedure shall be performed on any warm-blooded animal that might cause it pain, suffering, or discomfort or otherwise interfere with its normal health. Warm-blooded animals include man, other mammals such as gerbils, guinea pigs, mice, rabbits, hamsters and rats. It also includes birds, such as hens, quail, and pigeons. This means that a student shall do unto other warm-blooded animals only what he can do to himself without pain or hazard to health.
3. No surgery shall be performed on any living vertebrate animal (mammal, bird, reptile, amphibian or fish).
4. No lesson or experiment shall be performed on a vertebrate animal that employs microorganisms which can cause disease in man or animal, ionising radiation, cancer producing agents, chemicals at toxic levels, drugs producing pain or deformity, extremes of temperatures, electric or other shock, excessive noise, noxious fumes, exercise to exhaustion, overcrowding or other distressing stimuli.
5. Animal observations must be directly supervised by a competent science teacher who shall approve the plan before the student starts work. Students must have the necessary comprehension and qualifications for the work contemplated. The supervisor shall oversee all experimental procedures, shall be responsible for their non-hazardous nature and shall, personally, inspect experimental animals during the course of the study, to ensure that their health and comfort is fully sustained.

---

*Copies of guidelines available from: The Humane Society of the United States, 2100 L Street N.W., Washington, D.C. 20037, USA.

6. Vertebrate studies shall be conducted only in locations where proper supervision is available: either in a school or an institution of research or higher education. No vertebrate animal studies shall be conducted at a home (other than observations of normal behavior of pet animals such as dogs or cats).
7. In vertebrate studies, palatable food shall be provided in sufficient quantity to maintain normal growth. Diets deficient in essential foods are prohibited. Food shall not be withdrawn for periods longer than 12 hours. Clean drinking water shall be available at all times (and shall not be replaced by alchohol or drugs).
8. Birds' eggs subjected to experimental manipulations shall not be allowed to hatch; such embryos shall be killed humanely no later than two days prior to normal hatching time. If normal egg embryos are to be hatched, satisfactory arrangements must be made for the humane disposal of chicks.
9. In the rare instances when killing of a vertebrate animal is deemed necessary, it shall be performed in an approved humane (rapid and painless) manner by an adult experienced in these techniques.
10. Projects involving vertebrate animals will normally be restricted to measuring and studying normal physiological functions such as normal growth, activity cycles, metabolism, blood circulation, learning processes, normal behavior, reproduction, communication or isolated organ techniques. None of these studies requires infliction of pain.
11. The comfort of the animal observed shall receive first consideration. The animal shall be housed in appropriate spacious, comfortable sanitary quarters. Adequate provision shall be made for its care at all times, including weekend and vacation periods. The animal shall be handled gently and humanely at all times.
12. Respect for life shall be accorded to all animals, creatures and organisms that are kept for educational purposes.

Canadian Council on Animal Care

GUIDING PRINCIPLES GOVERNING THE USE OF ANIMALS IN THE CLASSROOM AT THE PRE UNIVERSITY LEVEL*

I. *Purpose*

These guiding principles have been prepared by the Canadian Council on Animal Care. They are recommended for use by Departments of Education and Boards of Education across Canada in order to ensure adequate safeguards

---

*Revised May, 1975. Copies of guidelines and information on the care, housing and management for individual species, as well as suitable experiments for use at the pre-university level, may be obtained from the Canadian Council on Animal Care, 151 Slater St., Suite 1105, Ottawa, Ont. K1P 5H3.

exist for the proper care and use of animals in experimentation in the classroom, in the schools, in their jurisdiction.

These guidelines are not for use by students preparing projects for exhibit in Science Fairs. Students preparing projects for Science Fairs must adhere to the Youth Science Fair Regulations for Animal Experimentation, as prepared and distributed by the Youth Science Foundation, Suite 302, 151 Slater St., Ottawa, Ontario K1P 5H3.

II. *Philosophical Considerations*

Biological experimentation involving animals in the classroom is essential for an understanding of living processes. Such studies should lead to a respect for all living things. All aspects of the study must be within the comprehensions and capabilities of the student undertaking the study.

Lower orders of life are preferable subjects for experimentation at the pre university level. Such lower orders as bacteria, fungi, protozoa, and insects can reveal much basic biological information; they should be used for experimentation wherever and whenever possible.

III. *Care of Experimental Animals*

The care of experimental animals in the school should embody the principles laid down in the *Care of Experimental Animals, a Guide for Canada,* as prepared and distributed, by the Canadian Council on Animal Care. (address below)

The following principles are necessary in order to provide optimal animal care:–

a) The maintenance of animals in a classroom shared by students on a long term basis, is not recommended. Therefore, animal quarters specifically for housing of animals should be provided.

b) All experimental animals used in teaching programs must be properly cared for. Animal quarters should be made comfortable by provisions for sanitation, protection from the elements and have sufficient space for normal behavioural and postural requirements of the species. The living quarters shall have surfaces that may be easily cleaned, good ventilation and lighting, well regulated temperatures and cages of sufficient size to prevent overcrowding. Animals must be protected from direct sunlight or other environmental factors which may disturb the well-being of the animal.

c) Food should be palatable, of sufficient quantity and balance to maintain a good standard of nutrition. Animals shall not be allowed to go below the maintenance level of nutrition. *Clean drinking water shall be available at all times.* Containers for food and water should be of a design made specifically for that purpose.

d) Colonies and animal quarters shall be supervised by a science teacher experienced in animal care. The students and other animal care staff shall be trained and required to handle the animals gently and humanely.

e) All animals must be disposed of in a humane manner. If euthanasia has to be carried out, an approved humane method must be used and carried out by an adult experienced in the use of such procedures.
f) The use of animals must comply with existing local, provincial or federal legislation.
g) The procurement and use of wild animals and birds must comply with the Migratory Birds Convention Act of Canada, the Convention on International Trade on Endangered Species of Wild Fauna & Flora (ratified by Order in Council July 3/75) as well as any existing legislation at the Provincial level concerned with wild animals and exotic species.

IV. *Experimental Studies*

1. All experiments should be carried out under the supervision of a competent science teacher. It is the responsibility of the qualified science teacher to ensure the student has the necessary comprehension for the study to be undertaken.
2. Students should not be allowed to take animals home to carry out experimental studies. All studies involving animals must be carried out in a suitable area in the school.
3. All students carrying out projects involving *vertebrate animals* must adhere to the following guidelines:–
   A. No experimental procedures shall be attempted on a vertebrate animal that should subject it to pain or distinct discomfort, or interferes with it's health.
   B. Students shall not perform surgery on vertebrate animals.
   C. Experimental procedures shall not involve the use of:–
      a. microorganisms which can cause diseases in man or animals.
      b. ionizing radiation.
      c. cancer producing agents.
      d. drugs or chemicals at toxic levels.
      e. alcohol in any form.
      f. drugs that may produce pain.
      g. drugs known to produce adverse reactions, side effects, or capable of producing birth deformities.
   D. Experimental treatments should not include electric shock, exercise until exhaustion, or other distressing stimuli.
   E. Behavioural studies should use only reward (positive reinforcement) and not punishment in training programs.
   F. If egg embryos are subjected to experimental manipulations, the embryo must be destroyed humanely 2 days prior to hatching. If normal egg embryos are to be hatched, satisfactory humane considerations must be made for disposal of the young birds.
4. The use of anaesthetic agents, by students, is not recommended and in the case of some anaesthetics not permitted by law.

The above guidelines of the Humane Society of the United States and the Canadian Council on Animal Care apply to projects undertaken in biology classes, and not to science fair projects. The extracurricular nature of science fair projects is unfortunately often associated with a lack of qualified supervision, inadequate facilities, and lack of enforcement of rules. The result, all too frequently, is animal abuse. More restrictive rules are therefore required for science fairs than are needed for classroom projects.

Both in Canada and the United States, major secondary school competitions prohibit completely the use of vertebrate animals except for observations of normal living patterns of wild animals or of pets. The excellent rules used in Canadian Science Fairs are given in full in Appendix A, page 347. Somewhat similar prohibitions are strictly enforced in the Westinghouse Science Talent Search of the United States.

It may be helpful to amplify some aspects of the classroom guidelines. Both the USA and Canadian guidelines stress the importance of using plants, bacteria, fungi, and invertebrate species (animals without backbones) such as protozoa, worms, snails, or insects—in preference to using vertebrate species. The advantages of using plants and invertebrate species are their wide variety, ready availability in large numbers, inexpensive and simple care, and the relative lack of problems over subsequent disposal at the end of the investigation. Furthermore, use of plants and invertebrate species avoids potential ethical problems of inflicting pain and killing sentient creatures. Invertebrate organisms are eminently suitable for biological study. They display all the basic characteristics of life (that is, metabolism, response to environment, reproduction, genetic continuity, and variability). Refined analysis of these processes is possible with micro-organisms in ways not possible with more complex systems such as mammals.

The guidelines state that vertebrate animal studies shall be painless. Vertebrate species are singled out for preferential treatment because the nervous system of a vertebrate animal is more complex than that of an invertebrate animal; thus, vertebrate animals are more capable of perceiving pain and are thereby more likely to suffer abuse.

The reasons why it is recommended that elementary and secondary school projects adhere to this "painless rule" are that:*

1. MORALLY, it is indefensible to hurt or kill animals unless original contributions which will advance human health and welfare can be

*From "Rules Governing Treatment of Animals by High School Biology Students" Animal Welfare Institute, P.O. Box 3650, Washington, D.C. 20007.

expected. Elementary and secondary school studies do not meet this test.

2. PSYCHOLOGICALLY, it can be emotionally upsetting for youngsters to participate in harming or killing animals, or even worse, it may be emotionally desensitizing or hardening to immature minds.
3. SOCIALLY, in these days of widespread violence fostering personal aquaintance with inflicting pain on lesser creatures should be avoided.
4. EDUCATIONALLY, teaching about abnormal states before the student has a sound grasp of normal physiology is against common sense and does not advance scientific education.
5. SCIENTIFICALLY, promoting teenage animal surgery or induction of painful pathological conditions (which are very often poorly done in the unsanitary conditions of a student's home and have no scientific value) fosters an improper regard for animal life and an unbalanced view of biology which will rebound adversely when the next generation of scientists comes of age.

The ethical problems inherent in the use of animals or biology teaching should not be dismissed lightly. Teachers and students are strongly recommended to read the references on the ethics of student experimentation at the end of this chapter. Consideration of what should or should not be asked or permitted of students in their beginning experiences with animals should not be confused with the separate problem of what professional scientists with long years of training should do.

SUGGESTED STUDIES

Investigations for students should be selected which are appropriate to their educational levels and comprehension. At the pre-college level, emphasis should be on understanding the basics of normal functioning and natural life processes, not abnormal or diseased states. Options for investigation of these normal processes are so many, that experimentation with a pathological state and animal death is either alien or premature, or both. Small mammalian studies of normal behavior, normal physiology, reproduction (including genetic studies), nutrition and digestion, respiratory and excretory processes, sense perception, and learning will yield information to the beginning biologist. All of these studies can be pursued without inflicting pain on animals.

Many suitable investigations on invertebrate and vertebrate animals are described in this book and many others are regularly cited as references. Often experiments are explained only briefly and fuller details should be sought in the references cited. Care has been taken to review all these studies for their usefulness, value, and humaneness. A bibliographic listing of books describing experiments with living organisms which are in compliance with humane standards is found in Appendix B, page 351.

REFERENCES CLASSIFIED BY ABILITY LEVEL

References are classified into three categories indicated by the inclusion of (Advanced), or (Intermediate) at the end of the citation. "Advanced" indicated that this reference is suitable for superior high school students and college level students. "Intermediate" indicates suitability for junior high school level. All additional references, for which no designation appears, are suitable for high school level students.

AVAILABILITY OF REFERENCES CITED

Public lending libraries will usually be able to obtain photocopies by interlibrary loan of articles from the standard scientific literature which is cited in this book. Also, college libraries often carry these journals. Reprints of articles published in *The American Biology Teacher* are available from University Microfilm, Ann Arbor, Michigan 48106. Alternatively, microcard volumes of *The American Biology Teacher* are available from J.S. Canner and Co., 49-65 Landsdowne St., Boston, Mass. 02215.

A number of historical references are used in the sections at the ends of chapters dealing with suggestions for animal experiments. Do not dismiss these references as being too hard to obtain. They are well worth the effort of finding. They are normally available at local medical schools or colleges. Sometimes public libraries will help. These references are to classical work of early investigators, such as Darwin and Pasteur, and represent major contributions to the science of their day. The experiments they describe are practical for a student to repeat.

FURTHER READING

ANSEVIN, K. D. 1970. Animal Experimentation in High Schools. *School Sci. and Math.* 70(2):139–42.

Bibliography of Texts Describing Humane Experiments with Living Organisms. See Appendix B, page 351.

BRYANT, J. J. 1970. *Biology Teaching in Schools Involving Experimentor Demonstration with Animals or with Pupils: A Handbook of Guidance and Information.* Assoc. for Science Education, College Lane, Hatfield, Herts, England.

GODLOVITCH, S. and R. GODLOVITCH, eds. 1972. *Animals, Men and Morals: An Inquiry into the Maltreatment of Non-Humans.* Taplinger Publishing Co., New York 10003.

Guiding Principles for Animal Experimentation at the Pre-University Level. 1975. Youth Science Fdn., Animal Care Comm., 151 Slater Street, Ottawa (free).

Guiding Principles for Use of Animals in Elementary and Secondary Schools. Humane Society of the United States, 2100 L Street, N.W., Washington, D.C. 20037 (free).

LEAVITT, E. S. 1970. *Animals and Their Legal Rights.* 2nd ed. Animal Welfare Institute, P.O. Box 3650, Washington, D.C. 20007.

MAYER, W. V. 1973. Biology: Study of the living or the dead? *The American Biology Teacher* 35 (1): 27–30.

ORLANS, F. B. 1968. The Boundaries of Use of Animals in High School Biology. *Sci. Teacher* 35 (7): 44–47.

ORLANS, F. B. 1970. Painless Animal Experimentation for High School Students. *Scholastic Teacher* April 6, S4-7.

ORLANS, F. B. 1972. Live Organisms in High School Biology. *The American Biology Teacher* 34 (9): 343–345, 352.

ROBERTS, C. 1967. *The Scientific Conscience.* George Braziller Publisher, New York.

ROWSELL, H. C. 1974. *Canada's Experience with Student Use of Living Animals.* The American Biology Teacher 36 (1):31–36.

ROWSELL, H. C. 1971. Experimental Animal Use—Your Responsibility. *Science Affairs* 4 4:88–90. Youth Science Fdn., 151 Slater Street, Ottawa, Ontario K1P 5H3.

RUSSELL, G. K. 1973. Vivisection and the true aims of education in biology. *The American Biology Teacher* 35 (1):254–257.

SECORD, D. C. and H. C. ROWSELL 1974. Proper Use of Animals in Schools: An Educational Program. *Canadian Veterinary Journal,* 15, 42–47.

SCOTT, W. N. 1967. Live Animals in School Teaching. *J. Biol. Educ.* 1:319–23. Reprint from Universities Fed'n. for Animal Welfare, 230 High Street, Potters Bar, Herts, England.

STEVENS, C. 1970. Attitudes toward Animals. *Amer. Biol. Teacher* 32 (2):77–79.

Suggestions for Experiments Involving Animals at the Pre-University Level. Canadian Council on Animal Care, 151 Slater Street, Ottawa, Ontario K1P 5H3.

2

Protozoa and Rotifers

"The Microbe is so very small
You cannot make him out at all,
But many sanguine people hope
To see him through a microscope."

Hillaire Belloc (1870-1953)

PROTOZOA: GENERAL INFORMATION

Protozoa—which we usually cannot see—are all around us. They are among the most adaptable and novel creatures in the animal kingdom and are encountered in almost every environment which supports life at all: in both hot and cold climates, in soils and sands, in fresh and salt water, at high altitudes and below sea level, and within and on many other animals and some plants.

Protozoa are far from being simple animals. Each protozoan contains, within a single cell, one or more nuclei and the facilities and organelles for performing all the major bodily functions carried on by the organs and organ systems of the larger animals, including vertebrates.

To study them alive is exciting and more meaningful than merely viewing them as histological specimens. Studying live creatures enhances appreciation and understanding of our environment and of basic biological processes. Instead of treating live protozoa as "animals for a day," discarding them after cursory microscopic study, your class should maintain and culture them for weeks or months. Too many students have little or no understanding of where protozoa come from (other than in vials from biological supply houses), what their impact is on other organisms, or how they relate to humans. Keeping samples of pond water and observing the fluctuations and complexities of protozoan activity brings home to students more of the significance of protozoan life. If protozoan cultures are maintained, the range of observations increases enormously, and interest in these animals can be stimulated. Cultures are useful not only for observation and experimentation, but are valuable food supplies for newly hatched fish.

Because of their wide variety, ready availability in large numbers, and simplicity of maintenance and subsequent disposal, protozoan cultures are ideal for student experimentation. Furthermore, experiments with protozoa involve no ethical problems. Guidelines used widely in the United States and Canada on the role of animals in biology teaching at the pre-college level recommend the use of protozoa in preference to other species such as small mammals.[1, 2*]

Once a culture is started, it can be maintained with very little attention for as long as you want. Some school districts maintain "culture centers" in which a variety of organisms are cultured by the students and distributed to other schools. The students enjoy it, costs are cut, and more schools are provided with living organisms.

Discovery of Protozoa

The pioneer microscopist Leeuwenhoek was the first person to see protozoa. In the year 1675, he wrote, ". . . about half-way through September . . . I discovered living creatures in rain, which had stood but a few days in a new tub." These were *Vorticella*, which he described in considerable detail. Over the years, great numbers of protozoan species were discovered, and the famous Linnaeus attempted to classify them. Today, 45,000 different species—some free-living and some parasitic—have been identified and classified.

Attempts to grow free-living protozoa in mass cultures were made in the late 19th century. As with other animals, the successful laboratory rearing of protozoa depends upon the exactness with which the species' natural living conditions are duplicated. All culture methods begin with finding individuals of the desired species in material collected from the field and maintaining them by providing their natural foods. Many free-living protozoa eat bacteria and other protozoa. For research, the simplest type of culture to grow is a "mass" culture, which consists of a mixture of organisms including various protozoa and bacteria. A more specialized culture, a "clonal" culture, is a group of organisms derived asexually from a single organism. For some research, a third type, an "axenic" culture, is used, in which only one species is grown and its nutritional requirements are met by the chemical composition of the medium.

---

*Numbered references are listed at the close of a chapter. The United States and Canadian *Guiding Principles* are the first-listed references for Chapter 2 (see pages 34-35).

In this chapter, culturing of free-living protozoa will be described for *Euglena, Paramecium, Amoeba, Vorticella, Stentor,* and *Chilomonas,* as well as for Rotifera. Mass culturing techniques are described on page 17, and clonal culturing on page 29. Considerable latitude is taken by including *Euglena,* which is more plant than animal, and rotifers, which are not protozoa at all. *Euglena* is included because growing these organisms makes an ideal starting point for novice culturists; rotifers are included here because methods of culturing these organisms are similar to those of culturing protozoa.

Equipment Suggestions

Suitable containers for culturing include finger bowls, Syracuse dishes, watch glasses, and petri dishes. Plastic transparent furniture casters from hardware stores are an adequate substitute for Syracuse dishes. Containers which can be stacked are particularly convenient.

Capillary pipettes are useful for isolating single organisms to be transferred for microscopic observation. To make your own pipettes, melt the center of a 15 to 20 cm length of glass tubing approximately 6 mm in diameter over a Bunsen burner and draw it out until the center is narrow enough for your purpose. (This requires considerable practice.) Break the tube at the center of the drawn-out portion, and you will have two pipettes. When they have cooled, fit rubber suction bulbs over the larger ends.

Clean glassware is essential for the successful culture of protozoa. Ideally, all equipment should be autoclaved. If this is not practical, wash the glassware with 10 percent nitric acid solution and rinse thoroughly several times with distilled water. (Take care in handling nitric acid—strong solutions burn.) Be sure to use glassware that has never had contact with strong chemicals, such as chromate cleaning solutions, or with fixatives or formalin. Soap and most detergent residues are also harmful to protozoa. Grow the cultures in rooms that are free from toxic fumes such as acid, ammonia, or formalin.

Observation of Protozoa

Careful observation of protozoa cannot be undertaken without a microscope, preferably stereoscopic. A compound microscope with an oil immersion objective is necessary for really serious investigations.

Direct microscopic observation of protozoa is easier if their movements are slowed down. To do this, place a drop of water containing the organisms in the center of a ring of two percent methyl cellulose on

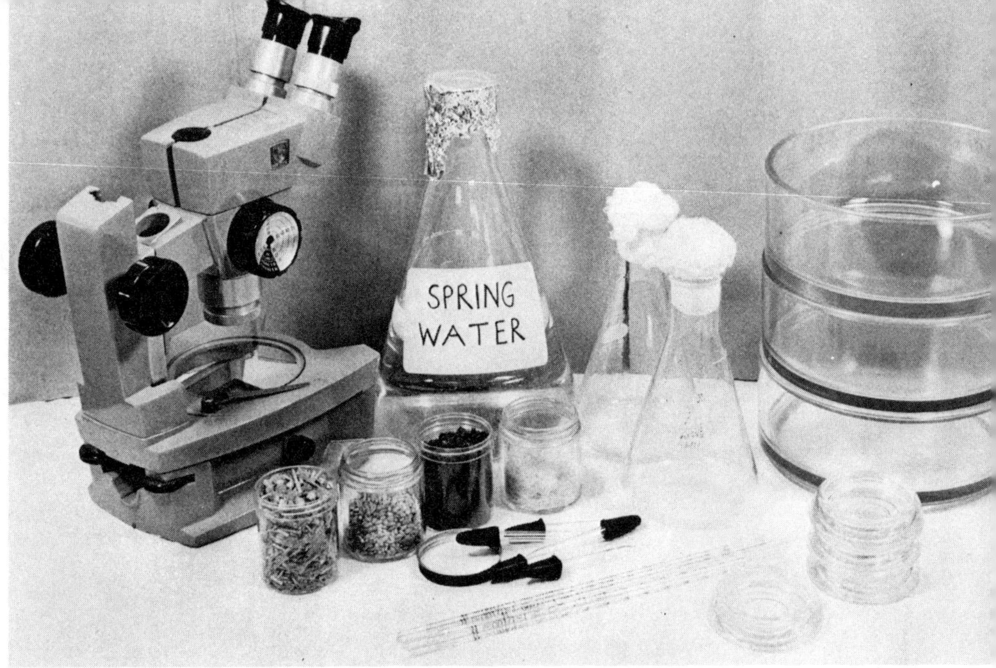

Figure 2-1. Apparatus for culturing protozoa includes binocular microscope, spring water, timothy hay, wheat grains, manure, and rice (in the four small bottles), eye droppers, pipettes, Erlenmeyer flasks, large Syracuse dishes, and furniture casters (for use as small containers for cultures).

a glass slide, and carefully cover the slide with a cover slip (see FILMS, *Protozoan*, page 36). Methyl cellulose, which is sometimes marketed under trade names, is readily available from biological supply houses.*

Sources of Protozoa

Collecting samples from the field is challenging and fun to do; but this method is often unreliable, especially if a particular species is sought, and the yield may be poor. It may be easier to purchase a pure culture of selected species from a biological supply house. *Euglena, Paramecium, Amoeba, Vorticella, Stentor,* and *Chilomonas* and Rotifera can be obtained from supply houses.** The organisms from a shipment can be used for class study and to start a mass culture.

---

*See Appendix C, pages 355-356.

**CBS, CON, MOG and NAS. See Appendix C for explanation of these abbreviations. Some of these organisms also can be obtained from BIC, CAR, CCM, CES, TIM and WAR.

Figure 2-2. A typical habitat of protozoa.

Figure 2-3. Students collecting water samples from a stream.

For those who enjoy studying their own environment, the best natural sources of protozoa are ponds and streams containing abundant plant and organic life. (See Film Reference 1, *Collecting Protozoans*, page 36.) Stagnant farmyard puddles, slow-flowing rivers, and open lakes all contain protozoa. Take samples of water, bottom mud, and vegetation from several sources and label each sample with the date and location. The quality or nature of the water will determine what organisms are found. (See Films, *Recognizing Bottom Dwelling Protozoans*, page 36.) *Euglena* are abundant in stagnant contaminated pools near manure piles, or in duck ponds. Particularly in June, July, and August, the presence of large numbers of *Euglena* sometimes turns the water brilliant green. Such aggregations are called *surface blooms*. *Paramecium* occur in freshwater ditches, in garden pools rich in decaying matter, and in neglected flower vases. *Amoeba*, *Vorticella*, and *Stentor* are found in clean ponds.

Search for amoebae on aquatic plants such as water lily, *Elodea*, and *Cabomba*. Both amoebae and stentors are frequently abundant around sphagnum. Since many crustaceans are competitors of amoebae for food, pools containing crustaceans will usually not contain amoebae.

One or another of the 200 species of *Vorticella* can be seen throughout the year as white fluffy patches on dead sticks, on submerged stones, on the undersides of duckweed, and on the bodies of water insects and crustaceans. *Vorticella* is not parasitic but appears to use other organisms merely as a form of attachment.

Stentors are large enough to be seen with the naked eye. Identification of the blue and green stentors is facilitated by viewing them against a white background, such as a white collecting bowl. Springtime is a good time to look for them. Unless disturbed, only a few of these animals will be found swimming freely; most will remain attached to their foothold on the stems of aquatic plants.

Mass Culturing

In the classroom, let the pond samples stand in jars or enamel bowls in diffuse light (away from direct sunlight). Leave the lids of the jars loose for needed aeration. Add a few grains of boiled rice or wheat; bacteria produced by this organic material as it ferments are food for protozoa. Some experience and some luck will determine what organisms are encountered and which will survive.

From time to time, make up water evaporation loss by adding distilled water, or spring, pond or well water; drying of the medium will kill large numbers of protozoa. Do not add freshly drawn tap water, as this kills certain protozoa. In most parts of the country, tap water from city mains can be used after it has been allowed to stand for several days, or after air is bubbled through it for 24 hours to remove harmful chlorine.

After one day, inspect the samples with a 10× or higher power lens. Use a coarse pipette or an eyedropper to transfer a few drops of bottom sediment onto a slide. Examine the sediment for the presence of amoebae and other organisms. Similarly, examine the upper and middle layers of the sample. Don't be concerned if you cannot identify most of the organisms present. To be able to distinguish just one is commendable. Usually, ciliates distribute themselves throughout the whole sample, except for *Paramecium* which accumulates at the top.

Figure 2-4. Checking pond sample for presence of protozoa.

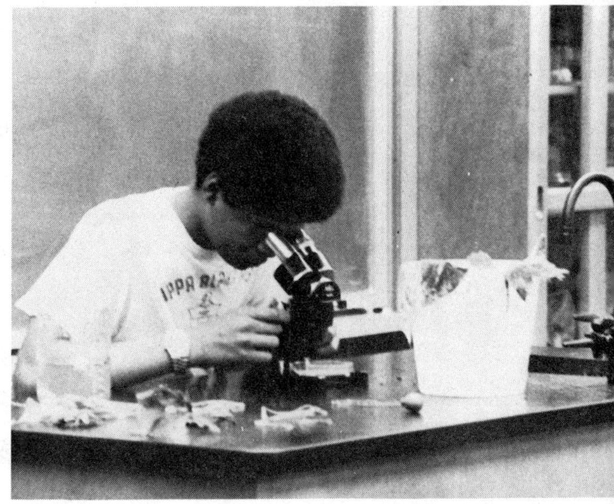

Chlorophyll-bearing flagellates, such as *Euglena*, also accumulate on the surface, as they are attracted toward the light. Paramecia are among the easiest organisms to find, since they tend to accumulate in a surface ring. As you draw them off for observation, handle the container carefully. Jarring it will disperse a ring of paramecia, and you will have to wait for it to form again. (Starved paramecia do not form surface rings.)

Isolate selected organisms from a mixed group of protozoa in the following manner. Using a binocular microscope, examine a few drops of the sample on a glass plate. When desired organisms are encountered, dilute with spring water and break up the drops until several isolated drops are formed, each with a single specimen. Use a capillary pipette to transfer these single organisms into containers for culturing. Avoid drawing up organisms other than the species you desire to culture.

Keep the samples for several weeks and examine them every few days. Note particularly that dominant species in the culture change often. Species which are more numerous one day may be absent the next. The frequency of the change in dominance depends on the kind and amount of decaying plant material, temperature, amount of sunlight, and other factors. *Amoeba* species, if present, will appear in greatest numbers after about two weeks.

If only a few organisms are available for starting a culture, it is important to begin by using small containers (Syracuse dishes or plastic casters), although you must carefully offset evaporation. A small number of organisms placed in a large volume of fluid will not repro-

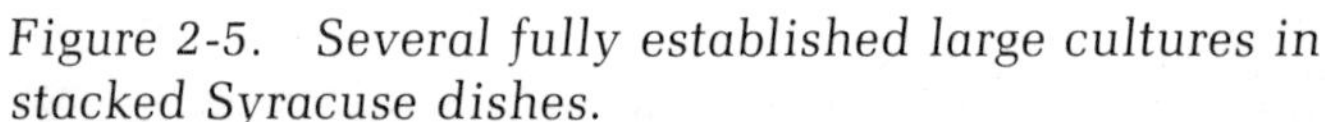

Figure 2-5. Several fully established large cultures in stacked Syracuse dishes.

duce well. As the culture increases in population, gradually increase the fluid volume and size of the container. (See *Amoeba* Method 1, page 24, which can be adapted for other organisms and media.)

EUGLENA

The order Euglenida consists of both green and colorless flagellates. When kept away from light, some species, like *Euglena gracilis,* will lose their chlorophyll and change from a plantlike pattern of nutrition to a funguslike state. *Euglena* culturing is relatively easy and makes a good starting point for those who have not grown protozoa before. The cultures can be used both for study and as food for newly hatched fish.

Appearance

Harris, in 1696, was the first person to see and describe *Euglena.* He tells of seeing in ". . . some Puddle-water which stood in my yard . . . Animals of several Shapes and Magnitudes; but the most remarkable were those which . . . gave the water that Green Color, and were oval creatures, whose middle part was Grass Green, but each end Clear and Transparent. They would contract and dilate themselves, tumble over and over many times together, and then shoot away like fishes."

The grass-green middle parts described by Harris are chloroplasts. What sort of microscope he used is not clear, but some magnification was necessary, as Euglena are only 30 to 60μ long, depending upon the species. Perhaps the most common species is *E. viridis,* but it has limited use for classroom study. Other species are preferred, such as *E. gracilis* which, although having no advantage over *E. viridis* in size, is easier to grow. It has an elongated body about 30 to 40μ long and is cigar-shaped when actively swimming, but can become shorter and broader when less motile. Usually, it is seen in motion, gracefully moving in a spiral, propelled by the constant lashing of a single long flagellum. *E. oxyuris* is larger and even easier to observe.

Culturing

A mixture of *Euglena* species may be obtained from natural sources or from biological supply houses. If only one species is required, it is easier to obtain it from a supply house. *Euglena* thrive best in water having considerable organic material. Three methods of cul-

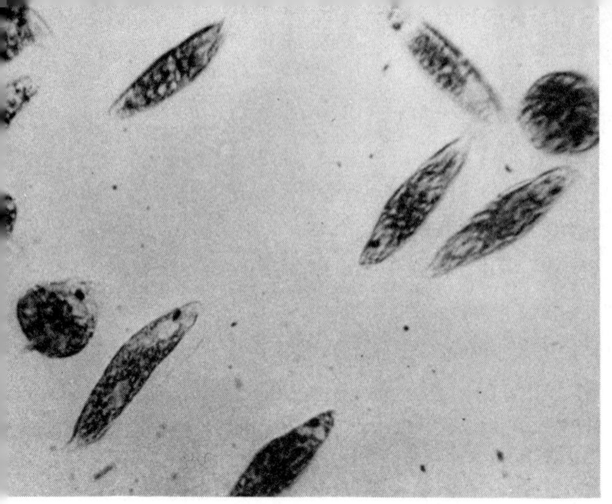

Figure 2-6. Euglena *swimming.*

turing are suggested, but Method 1 is preferred, as it results in less encystment of the organisms.

METHOD 1: MANURE-WHEAT INFUSION. Boil six rabbit or sheep pellets plus three wheat grains, (obtainable from livestock grain stores or, more expensively, from biological supply houses), in 250 ml of spring, rain or pond water for 15 minutes. An equivalent weight of cow manure, (obtainable from CON),* or horse manure may be substituted for the pellets. Allow the mixture to stand for one or two days, and then add *Euglena.* Deep culture vessels, or mayonnaise or jam jars are the preferred containers. Exclude airborne contaminants with cotton plugs, or stack the culture vessels and cover the top one with a glass lid. Stand the cultures on a window ledge in diffuse light at room temperature. Usually, after about two weeks, the culture will become green, which should indicate a profuse growth of *Euglena,* but contaminants such as other green protozoa or algae may be present.

It should be possible to maintain cultures, with little attention, for a year or more. From time to time, make up the volume of water lost through evaporation. Subculture if the organisms become congested or if the green color fades. To subculture, divide the culture and make up each half to the original volume with a new manure-wheat infusion. Some authorities recommend routine subculturing every month.

METHOD 2: WHEAT-RICE-MILK INFUSION. Mix and boil for five minutes 20 wheat grains, 15 rice grains (from a grocery), 5 ml of skim milk, and 500 ml of spring water. Let the mixture stand overnight, then add *Euglena.* Keep it on a window ledge and proceed as in Method 1. Subculture by dividing and making up the volume with more wheat-rice-milk medium.

---

*See Appendix C, pages 355-356.

METHOD 3: RICE INFUSION. Simplest of all methods for *Euglena* is to boil, for about one minute, seven or eight grains of rice in 475 ml of distilled water, spring water, or old aquarium water. Pour the broth into a broad dish and allow it to stand for a week or so until a bacterial scum has formed on top. Then add *Euglena*, place on a window ledge, and allow six to eight weeks for a good thick culture to form. Subculture as necessary.

Encystment

After a time, free-swimming *Euglena* may undergo a change and become encysted. The green color will fade. The organism will become spherical, lose its flagellum, secrete an outer cell wall, and enter a resting stage, which can last for several months. Changing the water and raising or lowering the temperature may induce encysted organisms to revert to the free-swimming stage again. However, you may wish to keep the cultures encysted, especially over a school vacation, and revive them afterward by adding fresh culture medium.

PARAMECIUM

Appearance

Paramecia are just large enough (120 to 180μ) to be seen with the naked eye. Size varies according to species. They appear as white, rapidly moving specks, or they may collect and form a white edge or ring on the waterline. The success of a culture can thus be easily assessed by observing the surface film of the dish when held up to the light. Common species of *Paramecium* are the colorless species *P. aurelia* and *P. caudatum*, and the green *P. bursaria* (inhabited by the symbiotic green algae *Chlorella paramecii*).

Paramecia feed on bacteria and other small particles, and are selective feeders, rejecting many particles that are too large. Certain *Paramecium* species, along with many other protozoa, aid in natural purification of polluted waters. Untreated sewage water contains *Escherichia coli*, a common colon bacillus; a single *P. caudatum* may devour 2 to 5 million *E. coli* in 24 hours.

Paramecia are oval-shaped organisms; their surface is covered with cilia with which they swim. They rotate as they travel forward—keeping a fairly straight course unless they meet an obstacle. Using some method of slowing down this motion makes them easier to observe under a microscope. (See page 14 for instructions on observation of protozoa.)

Reproduction takes place asexually by transverse division. There is also a sexual process called conjugation. *P. aurelia* divides asexually about five times a day under favorable conditions, whereas *P. caudatum* divides about three times a day. Because of rapid division and the ease of providing paramecia with food, this species is easier to culture than amoebae. (For suggestions on feeding *Paramecium* cultures to newly hatched fish, see page 172.)

Culturing

METHOD 1: LETTUCE INFUSION. This is the preferred method for experimental studies on paramecia. A lettuce infusion can be used to grow several species of protozoa including all freshwater species of *Paramecium;* it is particularly good for *P. bursaria.* Separate the leaves of head lettuce (or obtain discarded outer leaves free from a supermarket) and dry them slowly in an oven until brown and crisp. Reject burned black leaves and grind up the rest using a mortar and pestle. (The dried, roasted leaf bits will keep indefinitely if stored in a stoppered jar.) Add 1.5 gm of desiccated leaves to one liter of boiling distilled water in an Erlenmeyer flask and continue to boil for five minutes. Filter the hot brew into smaller Erlenmeyer flasks and either stopper the flasks with cotton or seal them with Parafilm®.* (Cotton or Parafilm will reduce evaporation but will not prevent growth of contaminating organisms.) These techniques will produce satisfactory results; but, for best results, you can prevent growth of contaminating organisms by autoclaving the flasks before sealing, or sterilizing them in a pressure cooker at 15 lbs. pressure for 15 minutes. Also autoclave or sterilize some spare flasks filled with distilled water, and some pipettes; then stopper all equipment with cotton immediately.

Allow the prepared medium to stand overnight; then, using sterile or well-cleaned flasks and pipettes, mix two parts of medium with one part of distilled water to obtain the right dilution. Introduce a small volume of concentrated *Paramecium* culture, stopper the flasks, and maintain in diffuse light at room temperature. Maximum growth is obtained after about one to two weeks. Subculture every month or so by preparing fresh infusion and adding to it a small volume of *Paramecium* culture pipetted from the old culture.

METHOD 2: HAY INFUSION. (See Film Reference 11, *Setting Up and Observing a Hay Infusion,* page 36.) Boil 6 gm of hay (spikes and stems, cut into 2 cm segments) in one liter of distilled water for 20 minutes, or

*Obtainable from CBS, Appendix C, pages 355-356.

until the water becomes brown. This medium is good for *P. caudatum*, but for *P. aurelia* or *P. bursaria* use only 4 gm of hay per liter. When the medium is cool, pour it into one or more shallow dishes and immediately add a pipetteful of concentrated paramecia. (Paramecia tend to aggregate where bacteria are growing. To obtain your own concentrates, withdraw fluid from the surface of the medium or from the area around the hay of old cultures.) After adding the paramecia concentrate, stack or cover the vessels immediately and keep them at room temperature in indirect light. Avoid dark places, window ledges, and bright sunlight (which encourages growth of other protozoa in the culture). Bacterial growth can be controlled by diluting the medium; otherwise too many bacteria may crowd out the paramecia. If a film of bacteria forms on the surface of the culture (where paramecia also congregate), it should be broken up.

In 10 to 14 days, the concentration of paramecia will be at a maximum level. Once every three to four weeks, add more hay or a few grains of wheat. Subculture every six weeks by preparing fresh hay infusion and adding it to some concentrated paramecia obtained from the old culture.

METHOD 3: EGG YOLK AND *Chilomonas*. *P. caudatum* will eat *Chilomonas* and will thrive if added to a flourishing *Chilomonas* culture. Make a solution of egg and water as described on page 29. When the *Chilomonas* is well established, add paramecia obtained either from a dealer or from another culture. Keep the cultures as in Method 2. Paramecia can be maintained for substantial periods of time if additional egg medium is added every few weeks.

AMOEBA

Appearance

Of all the species of freshwater *Amoeba*, *A. proteus* is probably the one most commonly used for biological study. Particularly large specimens of *A. proteus* measure up to 600μ. Against a black background, they can be seen with the naked eye as white specks about the size of pinheads. Other species can be seen only with a microscope.

Amoebae can be differentiated from other organisms microscopically by their granular endoplasm containing a nucleus, contractile vacuole, and various food vacuoles. The most obvious feature is that the whole organism constantly changes shape as it forms pseudopodia. This is readily observed with 400× magnification.

The staple foods of *A. proteus* are *Chilomonas*, *Tetrahymena*, and *Colpidium*. If problems are encountered in culturing amoebae by the

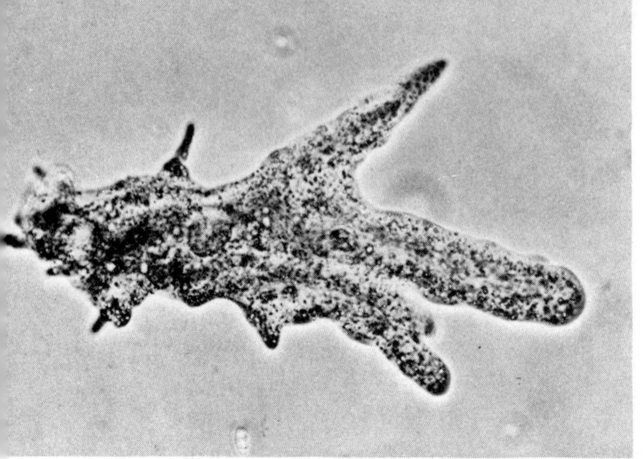

Figure 2-7. Amoeba.

methods recommended below, adding a few ml of a flourishing *Chilomonas* culture may be beneficial. (For culture of *Chilomonas*, see page 29.)

Culturing

METHOD 1: CHALKLEY'S MEDIUM AND RICE. This method utilizes a special salt solution which is not difficult to prepare and which yields more reliable results than hay infusions. Prepare several liters of Chalkley's culture medium for stock in the following proportions:

NaCl	0.1 gm	KCl	0.004 gm
$CaCl_2$	0.006 gm	Distilled water to 1 liter	

Place 200 to 250 ml of this medium into each finger bowl or similar container (a large jar). To each container add four or five grains of polished rice (from grocery stores). Optionally, add a few ml of *Chilomonas* culture. Immediately, put in 50 to 100 amoebae and stack the dishes or cover them with loosely fitting lids. Leave in a dark place at room temperature. After two to four weeks, most of the cultures should show an abundant increase in amoebae, but some will probably fail.

Chalkley said that he gave no attention to his cultures, once started, other than occasionally adding a few grains of rice. He also added water to compensate for evaporation, but with no attempt at regularity. Thus treated, his cultures survived in very good condition for 11 months or more. However, Chalkley was an expert. Most people will need to feed amoebae a supplemental pipetteful of *Chilomonas* or *Colpidium* every four days, and subculture them once a month.

METHOD 2: HAY INFUSION. This simple method gives variable results but may be quite satisfactory for some purposes. Prepare timothy hay (from biological supply houses) by heating a few slips, each 15 to 20 mm long, in a dry test tube immersed in boiling tap or other water for 15 minutes. Place amoebae in a Syracuse dish or similar container, along with 5 ml of the solution in which they have grown, and at once add one slip of the preheated hay. Prepare several such dishes to ensure success, as some of the amoebae will die. Either stack or cover the dishes and keep them at room temperature, 15 to 25°C (59 to 77°F); best growth is obtained at 17 to 19°C (63 to 66°F). Place the culture dishes in a cupboard or in cardboard boxes, because direct sunlight encourages the growth of other more vigorous protozoa such as *Euglena* and *Paramecium*. Other protozoa usually are present in the cultures, and some of these may serve as food for the amoebae. Small crustaceans or rotifers, however, will eat the amoebae. Too much decaying timothy hay is detrimental to the culture.

Over the next few days, gradually add a total of 5 ml distilled water to each dish. Inspect the cultures under a microscope after one or two weeks and retain only those cultures that show profuse growth of *Amoeba*. Transfer each successful culture into a large container, such as a finger bowl or jar. Make up the volume to about 30 ml with distilled water and add three more slips of preheated hay. At intervals of five to ten days, add 10 ml of distilled water and three slips of hay until there are about 70 ml of liquid present. When established, the culture will live at least a month without further attention.

To subculture, pour off and discard about half the liquid. Enough amoebae remain at the bottom of the container to seed the new culture. Using a stream of distilled water, dislodge the attached amoebae and mix them into the remaining solution. Divide this, retaining both halves. Gradually make up these volumes to about 70 ml as described before. Leave them for one month; then repeat the procedure.

Figure 2-8. Preparation of hay infusion for culturing Amoeba.

A more professional way to subculture is to pour off most of the liquid; allow the remainder to settle; then pick up the amoebae individually using a narrow-bore pipette and a 10× lens. If the water is shallow enough, amoebae on the bottom of the dish can be seen quite readily when black paper is placed under the dish. Collect a number of amoebae, one by one; transfer them to another dish; and make up the volume as before.

VORTICELLA

Appearance

Vorticella can be fairly large organisms, each measuring up to 150μ, depending on the species. *Vorticella* look most attractive under the microscope. Each organism is like an inverted bell held on a stalk. The bell part is ciliated around its broad end and contains inclusions and food vacuoles. The whole organism is strongly contractile and can quickly clench into a tight ball in response to danger. The bell part may become detached from the stalk during transportation, making identification difficult, especially if other pond organisms are present.

Supplying food for *Vorticella* in culture is no problem. The bacteria produced by fermenting wheat or hay provide adequate nutrition. The common method of reproduction is asexual by longitudinal division; sexual reproduction also occurs.

Culturing

METHOD 1: WHEAT INFUSION. Very briefly boil 20 wheat grains in one liter of water. Allow the infusion to stand for a few days, then pour it into shallow dishes and add some *Vorticella*. To ensure success, start several cultures at the same time. Stack or cover the dishes to retard evaporation and keep them at room temperature. *Vorticella* need more light than paramecia and will grow well if kept directly under a fluorescent light. Growth of *Vorticella* is slow. After several weeks, when significant increase is observed in the number of organisms present, divide the solution and make up each half to the original volume with more infusion.

METHOD 2: HAY INFUSION. Hay infusions are used for culturing many organisms, but for *Vorticella* it must not be too strong. Boil 2 gm of chopped-up timothy hay in 100 ml of spring or filtered pond water. Make up to 200 ml and wait two to three days, so the bacterial growth is well established, before adding the vorticellae. Leave the cultures undisturbed at room temperature in fairly strong light. Subculture as in Method 1, when necessary.

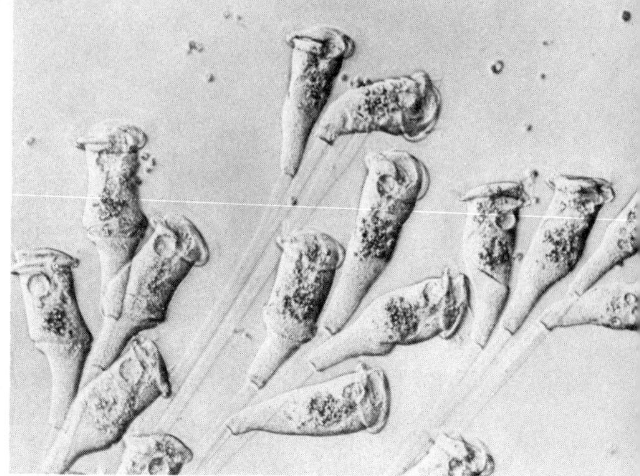

Figure 2-9. Vorticella. *(Courtesy Carolina Biological Supply House)*

STENTOR

Appearance

The cone-shaped bodies of these relatively large protozoa can be seen clearly with the naked eye. When fully extended, they can measure as much as 1 to 2 mm, but the normal size of *Stentor coeruleus* (blue stentor) is 100 to 500μ. The narrow posterior end of the cone attaches to some foothold, such as an aquatic plant stem. The broad anterior end is a disk encircled with special cilia (as in *Vorticella*) which beat the water, producing a whirlpool current that sweeps particulate food into the mouth. Stentors eat a variety of food—bacteria, flagellates, ciliates, and rotifers. If stentors are alarmed, they quickly contract, fold in the crown cilia, and assume a spherical shape; they may detach themselves and swim away. Reproduction in stentors is usually by asexual division; conjugation also occurs.

An ideal medium for growing stentors contains small protozoa, such as *Chilomonas* or *Paramecium,* in an infusion rich in bacteria. Protozoa and bacteria should both be present as food; stentors will grow, but less well, on bacteria alone.

Culturing

METHOD 1: CHALKLEY'S SOLUTION, WHEAT AND *Chilomonas.* This method provides a more favorable medium than Method 2 and should promote more rapid increase of the culture. (To prepare Chalkley's solution see Method 1 for amoebae, page 24.) Use 100 ml Chalkley's solution and add five or six wheat grains which have been boiled for one minute. Then add about 5 ml of a heavy *Chilomonas* culture (page 29). After one or two days, introduce 10 to 20 specimens of *Stentor.*

Stack or cover the culture containers and keep them in a cool room where the temperature does not fluctuate widely. A window location is fine if there is no bright sunlight. Add distilled or boiled spring water regularly to compensate for evaporation loss. Stentors attached to the sides of the vessel do not seem able to loosen their hold, and they will die if exposed. Stentors become abundant in two to three weeks. Add one wheat grain every month. The culture should keep for six months without subculturing.

To transfer stentors, agitate the vessel to make them fall to the bottom where they can be sucked up into a pipette. Collect them in a small volume of solution. Alternatively, add a large pinch of absorbent cotton to the culturing vessel; stentors will attach them themselves to the fibers and the cotton can be transferred.

When the stentor population starts to decrease, gently pour off the old medium. Since stentors attach themselves mainly to the sides of the vessel and to the cotton fibers, retain the cotton and immediately add fresh water, *Chilomonas* and wheat.

METHOD 2: WHEAT INFUSION AND *Chilomonas*. Split 20 grains of wheat* in half and add to one liter of water. Add approximately 5 ml of a heavy *Chilomonas* culture (obtained from a dealer or cultured, see page 29), and let it stand for a few days. This solution can be kept in a single vessel or divided into several containers. Distribute 100 to 200 stentors into the solution and keep as in Method 1. Within a few weeks, rich cultures should develop which will last for months. Once a month, add 10 to 20 wheat grains for every liter of water used; do not over-nutrify.

CHILOMONAS

Often it is beneficial to add a few ml of a flourishing *Chilomonas* culture as food for *Amoeba, Paramecium, Vorticella, Stentor,* and *Daphnia.*

Appearance

Chilomonas must be identified under the microscope. Each organism has an oval body about 15μ long from which two flagella protrude at the anterior end, making a total length of about 30μ. They are colorless, and are bounded by a relatively thick cuticle.

Chilomonas grow readily from cysts present in the air. Alternatively, they can be collected from almost any pond where there is decomposing vegetation, or can be purchased from biological supply houses. Frequently, they can be taken from established *Paramecium* cultures.

---

*Rice grains or hay can be substituted for wheat.

Culturing

EGG MEDIUM. Mix 0.5 gm hard-boiled yolk of a fresh hen's egg and a small amount of distilled water into a smooth paste. Add this to 500 ml of distilled water and allow the mixture to stand for several days at room temperature. Leave the dishes uncovered to permit spontaneous inoculation from the omnipresent *Chilomonas* cysts, which will encyst and multiply rapidly in the egg medium. Within a week or two, the culture should become cloudy with *Chilomonas*. To be certain of producing a rich culture, some free-swimming *Chilomonas* from an established culture can be added, but this is not really necessary.

Clonal Cultures

Genetically uniform specimens of protozoa, needed for certain experiments, are obtained by deriving cultures asexually from single individuals. For clonal cultures, it is necessary to develop a separate culture of food organisms, such as *Chilomonas*, to feed the selected organisms. Isolate a single organism, such as an amoeba, paramecium, vorticella, or stentor, in a drop of fluid and place it in a deep depression slide. Check under the microscope to see that only a single animal is present. Add five drops of medium (hay, wheat, or similar infusion) and five drops of *Chilomonas* culture. Place the slide in a moist chamber (plastic sandwich box with moist blotting paper) and add more food organisms as needed. Start several isolated individuals in this manner to ensure success. When about 25 organisms have developed in one slide, transfer them to a slightly larger container and add more medium and food. Continue to increase the capacity of the culture vessel as described in Method 1 for amoebae. Finally, a flourishing culture can be obtained.

EXPERIMENTS USING PROTOZOA

In performing protozoan investigations, do not experiment on (alter the condition of) the main colony, but remove organisms for the experiment and keep them separate from the main colony. In this way, stock animals will always be available for more experiments. A great many experiments can be done with protozoa to reveal basic biological principles of living creatures. Here are a few suggestions.

SPONTANEOUS GENERATION. Many years ago, it was believed that algae and protozoa appeared magically in a mixture of hay and water. Is there any basis in fact for this idea? Repeat Pasteur's classic experiments. What explanations account for the apparent "spontaneity" of generation? (See FILMS, *An Experiment of Louis Pasteur,* page 36.)

EFFECT OF TEMPERATURE ON LIFE PROCESSES. What effect does lowering the temperature have on culturing protozoa? What factors cause encystment? Do stentors lose their food organelles when subjected to low temperatures?[3]

Slowly change the temperature and measure the frequency of pulsation of contractile vacuoles in a paramecium at different temperatures.[4] At temperatures of 20 to 22°C (68 to 72°F), pulsations of vacuoles occur about once every ten seconds but at 1 to 2°C (34 to 36°F) the contractions stop almost completely.

What are the effects of freezing on protozoa?[5] Is it possible to culture organisms from samples of pond ice collected in subzero weather? Which is more injurious, a sharp drop in temperature or a moderate rise? Raising the temperature only a few degrees beyond the optimum can be fatal to some species, unless the increase is made very gradually over a period of several days. In 1887, certain flagellates were acclimated to withstand temperatures as high as 70°C (158°F) by gradually increasing the temperature over several years. Some amoebae can survive at 50°C (122°F). Try to repeat this experiment.

ENVIRONMENTAL PREFERENCES OF PROTOZOA. Study the effects of changes in the environment such as pH, presence of inorganic salts,[6] gravity, and temperature.[3] For a description of suitable methods which can be used for such studies, see Goldstein, et al.[7a] *Euglena* can withstand pH changes from 4.5 to 8.5. What are the ranges for each species?

The lithium ion affects developmental processes in stentors, causing structural changes and formation of doublets. What are the effects of longterm, low concentrations of lithium?[8]

SENSORY PERCEPTION. What is the response of stentors to light,[7b] carmine particles, salt solutions, and weak electric currents? Compare with other organisms such as *Euglena,* planaria, and earthworms. Test the response to light of *Euglena* from several cultures which have been kept in (a) sunlight, (b) diffuse light, and (c) darkness. Are there similar responses in all types?[9] Can *Euglena* of a photopositive type be made photonegative by increasing the intensity of light? Explain a particular species' response to light. Why would you expect various species to respond differently?

Where is sensory perception localized in stentors? Alverdes found that stentors failed to respond to heat if their anterior end was cut off.[10a] His conclusion that warmth perception in stentors is localized in the anterior end has been challenged, because he tested only the posterior end and did not report retesting the anterior end. Reinvestigate this problem.

ACTIVITY CYCLES. Demonstrate whether protozoa are as active by night as they are by day. For several weeks, take population counts of one or several species at the end of 12 hours of light and again after 12 hours of darkness to determine whether asexual reproduction is affected by light. Compare the activity cycles of protozoa with animals of other phyla.

WATER BALANCE. Protozoa maintain an osmotic balance between the surrounding medium and their cytoplasm by constantly discharging water from their contractile vacuoles. Measure the rate of vacuolar discharge in media of differing osmotic pressures. This gives an indication of the animal's ability to adapt to changing environmental conditions, an important concern of ecologists.

RESPONSE TO ULTRAVIOLET IRRADIATION. Study the effects of ultraviolet irradiation on cell division in various protozoa.[11] What is the effect of irradiation on algae living inside *P. bursaria*? (**Caution**: Ultraviolet light is invisible to humans but can cause bodily damage, especially to the eyes. Protect your body from this light.)

SEX REACTIONS OF PROTOZOA. What is the relation of body size to sexual activity? Measure the body lengths of stentors just before they divide and just before conjugation.[10b] Make direct observations to show that food vacuoles are absent in sexually conjugating stentors. What are the optimal temperatures for reproduction?

RELATION OF HOST TO ALGAE IN *P. bursaria.* Demonstrate whether the nature of the relationship between *P. bursaria* and its enclosed zoochlorellae is symbiotic or parasitic. It is possible to get rid of the algae in *P. bursaria* by making the protozoa multiply more rapidly than the algae. This is achieved by providing a rich nutritive solution for the paramecia, or by irradiation.[12] Do paramecia reproduce as actively when rid of their enclosed algae?[13]

REGENERATION IN PROTOZOA.[14,15] Some protozoa have a remarkable capacity for regeneration and are widely used to investigate the still unsolved mechanisms of this phenomenon. There are reports of complete regeneration of stentors from fragments as small as 1/120 the volume of an adult. Use a soft glass rod pulled out to form a needle and perform the microsurgery at a magnification of about 150×. A glass rod with an eyelash attached with epoxy glue is useful for manipulating the stentor during surgery. What are the minimal parts necessary for regenerating the whole cell?[7c]

Compare the ability of stentors to regenerate when well fed and when underfed. Do both portions of a transversely bisected stentor regenerate at the same rate? Investigate the nature of polarity. Will the anterior portions regenerate only posterior parts? Does the size of a portion affect its rate of regeneration?

Simply squash stentors in solutions containing varying concentrations of calcium. Does regeneration take place equally well in all calcium concentrations? If not, what possible explanations can be presented to account for the results?

DIGESTION. Demonstrate by means of biochemical tests that food vacuoles of *P. caudatum* contain starch and that living paramecia produce a starch-splitting enzyme which can be extracted from the organisms.[16]

ROTIFERS

These microscopic animals are not protozoa, being more complex; but they grow in similar environments and are considered here for convenience. Old protozoan cultures will sooner or later become populated with rotifers, especially the common *Rotaria rotatoria.* (See Figure 2-10.) An abundance of rotifers in a general culture is a certain indication that the culture is unfit for further protozoan study. Rotifers are usually classified with the roundworms in Phylum Aschelminthes. They have been called "wheel animalcules," because members of many species have ciliated crowns which beat, giving the appearance of rotating wheels.

They live most commonly in freshwater, but some species occur in salt water. They are very widely distributed and can be collected from almost any body of freshwater—shallow ponds and bogs, puddles, damp soil, mosses and vegetable debris. They are often found in *Daphnia* ponds, sometimes attached to the *Daphnia,* giving them a rusty sheen. A very handsome rose-pink rotifer *Philodina roseola*, similar to *Rotaria* species, is found in such places as bird baths. Rotifers also are available from biological supply houses.*

Very few rotifers are visible to the naked eye, most being the size of ciliate protozoa. Some species eat other microscopic animals such as

---

*BIC, CBS, CCM, CES, CON, MOG, NAS, TIM and WAR, Appendix C, pages 355-356.

amoebae; but larger, slower-moving species are vegetarians and eat filamentous algae. Observations of rotifers are best made on living specimens, as it is difficult to preserve them in a lifelike condition. Because study can be hampered by their rapid movements, it is best to slow them down with methyl cellulose (see page 14).

Culturing

For some common rotifers, such as *Philodina, Monostyla,* and *Euchlanis,* use the same culture methods as for *Paramecium.* For instance, start a *Chilomonas* culture with egg yolk as described on page 29 and inoculate with rotifers on the fourth, sixth, and eighth days thereafter. Rotifers will grow indefinitely, in either dark or light, and a dense population should be achieved within a few weeks. Subculture about once a month. The boiled wheat grain method (see *Vorticella* Method 1, page 26) is also suitable for culturing common rotifers.

EXPERIMENTS WITH ROTIFERS[17]

Many of the experiments on ciliated protozoa are suitable for rotifers. For instance, study the effects on life processes of changes in temperature and other environmental conditions. Determine the extremes of cold and drought which can be withstood by encystment. What factors influence the production of males in the species in which males occur? Collect information on the distributión and habits of various species in the wild.

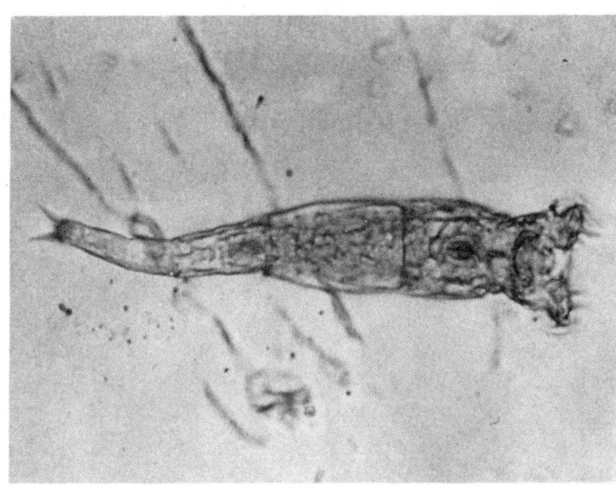

Figure 2-10. Freshwater rotifer.

Figure 2-11. Collecting water sample from a bird bath for possible source of rotifers.

REFERENCES

1. *Guiding Principles for Use of Animals in Elementary and Secondary Schools.* 1973. Reprinted on page 4 and available from the Humane Society of the United States, 2100 L St., NW, Washington, D.C. 20037.

2. *Guiding Principles for Animal Experimentation at the Pre-University Level.* 1975. Reprinted on page 5 and available from the Canadian Council on Animal Care, 151 Slater St., Suite 1105, Ottawa, Ont K1P 5H3, Canada.

3. GREELEY, A. W. 1901. On the Analogy between the Effects of Loss of Water to Lowering of the Temperature. *Am. J. Physiol.* 6:112–28. (Advanced)

4. HANCE, R. T. 1917. Studies on a Race of Paramecium Possessing Extra Contractile Vacuoles. *J. Exp. Zool.* 23:287–333. (Advanced)

5. HOLM-HANSEN, O. 1976. Effects of Low Temperature on Living Cells. *Research Problems in Biology,* Series 3. Second Ed. Biological Sciences Curriculum Study. Oxford University Press, New York. pp. 108–112.

6. PACE, P. 1933. The relation of Inorganic Salts to Growth and Reproduction in *A. proteus. Arch. Protistol.* 79:133. (Advanced)

7. GOLDSTEIN, P. and J. METZNER. 1971. *Experiments with Microscopic Animals.* Doubleday & Co., Garden City, N.Y. a. pp. 100–115, b. pp. 33–43, c. pp. 47–52.

8. TARTAR, V. 1957. Reactions of *Stentor coeruleus* of Certain Substances Added to the Medium. *Exp. Cell Res.* 18:317–32.

9. WELSH, J. H., R. I. SMITH and A. E. KAMMER. 1968. Orientation Responses to Light. *Laboratory Exercises in Invertebrate Physiology.* 3rd ed. Burgess Publishing Co., Minneapolis, Minn. pp. 95–96. (Advanced)

10. TARTAR, V. 1961. *The Biology of* Stentor. Pergamon Press, New York. a. p. 24, b. pp. 323–25. (Advanced)

11. DUCOFF, H. C. 1976. Responses of Algae or Protozoa to Ultraviolet Irradiation. *Research Problems in Biology.* Series 1, Second Ed. Biological Sciences Curriculum Study. Oxford University Press, New York. pp. 16–19.

12. SIEGEL, R. W. 1960. Hereditary Endosymbiosis in *Paramecium bursaria. Exp. Cell Res.* 19:239–52. (Advanced)

13. KARAKASHIAN, S. J. 1963. Growth of *Paramecium bursaria* as Influenced by the Presence of Algal Symbionts. *Physiol. Zool.* 36:52–68. (Advanced)

14. MANWELL, R. D. 1961. *Introduction to Protozoology.* Dover Publications, New York. p. 213. (Advanced)

15. TARTAR, V. 1970. Experimental Techniques with Ciliates. PRESCOTT, D. M., ed. *Methods in Cell Physiology.* Academic Press, New York. pp. 109–125.

16. BERMAN, W. 1968. *Experimental Biology: Road to Research.* Sentinel Books Publishers, New York. pp. 106–110.

17. GARNETT, W. J. 1965. *Freshwater Microscopy.* 2nd ed. Dover Publications, New York. p. 240 *et seq.*

FURTHER READING

AARONSON, S. 1970. *Experimental Microbial Ecology.* Academic Press, New York. (Culturing methods) (Advanced)

BUETOW, D. E., ed. 1968. General Biology and Ultrastructure. *The Biology of* Euglena. Vol. 1. Academic Press, New York. (Advanced)

CURTIS, H. 1968. *The Marvelous Animals—An Introduction to the Protozoa.* Natural History Press, Garden City, N.Y.

DOBELL, C. 1960. *Anthony Van Leeuwenhoek and His "Little Animals."* Dover Publications, New York.

HALL, R. P. 1964. *Protozoa—The Simplest of All Animals.* Holt, Rinehart & Winston, New York.

JAHN, T. L. and F. F. JAHN. 1949. *How to Know the Protozoa.* W. C. Brown, Dubuque, Iowa.

KUDO, R. R. 1966. Protozoology. 5th ed. Charles C. Thomas Publisher, Springfield, Ill. (Advanced)

MACKINNON, D. L. and R. J. S. HAWES. 1961. *An Introduction to the Study of Protozoa.* Clarendon Press, Oxford, England. (Culturing methods) (Advanced)

MORGAN, A. H. 1930. *Field Book of Ponds and Streams.* G. P. Putnam's Sons, New York.

NEEDHAM, J. G., ed. 1937. *Culture Methods for Invertebrate Animals.* Dover Publications, New York.

PATENT, D. H. 1974. *Microscopic Animals and Plants.* Holiday House, New York.

PENNAK, R. F. 1953. *Fresh-Water Invertebrates of the United States.* Ronald Press Co., New York.

REID, G. K. 1967. *Pond Life—A Guide to Common Plants and Animals of North American Ponds and Lakes.* Golden Nature Guide. Golden Press, New York.

SCHWARTZ, G. I. 1970. *Life in a Drop of Water.* Doubleday & Co., New York.

SOLDO, A. T. and W. J. VAN WAGTENDONK. 1970. Methods Used in Axenic Cultivation of *Paramecium aurelia. In* Prescott, D. M., ed. *Methods in Cell Physiology,* Vol. IV. Academic Press, New York. pp. 117–30.

SONNEBORN, T. M. Methods in Paramecium Research. *In* Prescott, D. M., ed. Methods in Cell Physiology. Vol. IV. Academic Press, New York. pp. 241–339.

VICKERMAN, K. and F. E. G. COX. 1967. *The Protozoa.* Houghton Mifflin Co., Boston, Mass. (Advanced)

WELLS, T. A. G. 1962. *Invertebrate Types.* Heinemann Educational Books, London, England.

WHITTEN, R. H. 1973. *Use, Care and Culture of Invertebrates in the Classroom.* Carolina Biological Supply Company, Burlington, North Carolina 27215.

FILMS

Collecting Protozoans. Super 8 mm, cartridge, silent, 5 min., color. Encyclopaedia Britannica Films, Encyclopaedia Britannica Educational Corp., 1150 Wilmette Ave., Wilmette, Ill 60091

Euglena—*A Green Flagellate.* Film loop, super 8 mm, cartridge, color. Encyclopaedia Britannica Films, Encylopaedia Britannica Educational Corp., 1150 Wilmette Ave., Wilmette, Ill 60091

An Experiment of Louis Pasteur. Film loop, super 8 mm, 2½ min. International Communication Films, NASCO, Fort Atkinson, Wis 53538

The Living Cell: An Introduction. 20 minutes. Encyclopaedia Britannica Educational Corp., 425 N. Michigan Ave., Chicago Ill 60611

The Paramecium. Film loop, super 8 mm, cartridge, color. Encyclopaedia Britannica Films, Encyclopaedia Britannica Educational Corp., 1150 Wilmette Ave., Wilmette, Ill 60091

Paramecium. Super 8 mm cartridge, silent, 4 min., one of set of six. American Cancer Society, 219 East 42nd St., New York, N.Y. 10017

Protozoa: Structures and Life Function. 16 mm 16 min, b/w or color. Coronet Films, Coronet Building, 65 E. South Water St., Chicago, Illinois 60601

Protozoan. (Includes *Euglena, Amoeba, Stentor, Paramecium,* and how to slow down protozoans). Set of 19 film loops, super 8 mm, color, 2 min. 13 sec. and 4 min. 45 sec. Thorne Films Inc., 1229 University Ave, Boulder, Colo 80302

Raising Microscopic Water Animals. Film loop, super 8 mm, 3 min. International Communication Films, NASCO, Fort Atkinson, Wis 53538

Recognizing Bottom Dwelling Protozoans. Film loop, super 8 mm, cartridge, color. Encyclopaedia Britannica Films, Encyclopaedia Britannica Educational Corp., 1150 Wilmette Ave., Wilmette, Ill 60091

Setting Up and Observing a Hay Infusion. Film loop, super 8 mm, silent. BFA Educational Media, 2211 Michigan Ave., Santa Monica, California 90404 (Intermediate)

Stentor—*A Large Ciliate.* Film loop, super 8 mm, cartridge, color. Encyclopaedia Britannica Films, Encyclopaedia Britannica Educational Corp., 1150 Wilmette Ave., Wilmette, Ill 60091

Vorticella—A Stalked Ciliate. Film loop, super 8 mm, cartridge color. Encyclopaedia Britannica Films, Encyclopaedia Britannica Educational Corp., 1150 Wilmette Ave., Wilmette, Ill 60091

3

Hydras

A microscope.
  I looked through
A little Hydra,
  With a baby
A bud on her side.
  She raised her tentacles
    And lowered them on one side
Beautiful thing.
  Over she goes . . .
A perfect handstand . . .
  How else could I see you
But through this marvel,
  Microscope?

J. W. Chisholm (age 12 years)

The Phylum Coelenterata is predominantly a marine group of jellyfish, sea anemones, and corals. Hydras, almost the only freshwater representatives, are related to the hydroid stage of the marine coelenterates and have around 100,000 cells differentiated into two layers, an ectoderm and an endoderm (or gastrodermis).

Hydras are soft, transparent animals measuring about 12 mm when fully extended. They can be seen with the naked eye and look like a piece of string frayed out at one end. The frayed strands are the tentacles which surround the mouth. When contracted, hydras look like pinheads. In nature, they live in sunlit pools and attach themselves to plant stems and to the undersides of leaves. They do not form colonies. They eat small fish and crustaceans, but they, in turn, are eaten by larger fish.

Among several species, the most common are the brown and green hydras. Their color is derived from ingested food or from organisms

Figure 3-1. Hydra. (Courtesy Carolina Biological Supply House)

living inside them in a symbiotic relationship. (The green algae *Chlorella* live within the body cells of the hydras *Chlorohydra viridissima*, which are consequently green.) Students will learn much more about hydras if living rather than preserved specimens are observed.

COLLECTION

To collect hydras, gather a generous quantity of water plants and some pond water from pools, small lakes, or slow-flowing streams. If possible, take several samples from different locations. Place the weeds and pond water in large, white-enamel bowls or similar containers and keep these undisturbed in a sunny, but not hot, indoor location. After a few hours, examine the bowls. Any hydras present soon detach themselves from the weeds and can be picked out clearly against the white background of the bowl. Some hydras may collect on the surface of the water; you can gently dislodge others from the sides of the bowl with your finger tips. If the water is then swirled around, hydras will collect in the center where they can be pipetted up. (Use a coarse pipette, oven baster, or medicine dropper.) You can then transfer them to another vessel.

If you have difficulty locating hydras in pools, you may obtain them from biological supply houses.* As soon as the shipment arrives, open the bottle containing hydras and aerate the liquid with a clean pipette. Some hydras can be used immediately for class study and the remainder (say 6 to 12) can be kept for culturing.

For simple maintenance, fill a 1–gallon tank with pond, spring, or well water; add two or three different plants such as *Elodea, Vallisneria, Nitella, Sagittaria,* or *Myrophylla,* and let it stand for several days before adding the hydras. A well-established aquarium will pro-

---

*BIC, CAR, CBS, CON, TIM and WAR. See Appendix C, pages 355-356.

vide sufficient nutrient for *green* hydras to survive several weeks with little attention—providing fish are not present.

For experiments requiring linear growth curves (see EXPERIMENTS WITH HYDRAS, page 41), it is more practical to omit the water plants and keep hydras in small glass containers, such as finger bowls. A petri dish will suffice for growing up to about 100 hydras.

City tap water can kill the hydras.* If possible, use only spring, well, or pond water. (Spring water can be obtained from supply houses.) Keep the temperature around 20 to 25°C (68 to 77°F), never above 30°C (86°F). Medium light to semi-darkness will prevent detrimental algae growth.

CLASSROOM MAINTENANCE

FEEDING. Considerable patience and care are needed if hydras are to flourish. Providing food for them can be something of a problem, as they are strictly carnivorous, eat only live food, and have hearty appetites. Among the easiest foods to obtain are: tiny crustaceans, such as brine shrimp larvae (page 101); *Daphnia* (page 95); *Cyclops*, copepods, *Cypris* or *Gammarus;* annelid worms such as *Tubifex;* or the small white worms *Enchytraeus albidus* (page 71). Chop worms into small pieces. For maximal growth, feed hydras once a day. They will grow, however, if fed every other day or even less frequently.

If you use *Daphnia* as food for hydras, you must maintain enough for daily mass feedings that provide about two per hydra. As the hydra population increases, you must supply hundreds of *Daphnia* at a time, daily. Except for the problem of supply, the feeding procedure is simple: Take the *Daphnia* from stock cultures with an aquarium net, and add them directly to the hydras' aquarium or vessel. Only if organic debris is heavy in the *Daphnia* culture should these food organisms be washed (with spring water) before being fed to the hydras.

If you find it difficult to maintain a constant supply of *Daphnia*, supplement the hydras' diet with larvae of the brine shrimp *Artemia*. The eggs are readily obtainable from biological supply houses and will keep almost indefinitely. Set up a serial hatching schedule for the eggs, in salt water, and after 48 hours separate the first larvae from the unhatched eggs (see pages 102–105 for hatching and separating techniques). Hydras will eat only the larvae. Wash the salt off the separated larvae with pond or spring water, and add them to the hydras' vessel. Every day, start new batches of brine shrimp eggs.

---

*If tap water is used, it *must* be modified by the addition of versene and various salts to neutralize the toxic traces of copper. For details, see Galen or Goldstein and Metzner.[1, 2a]

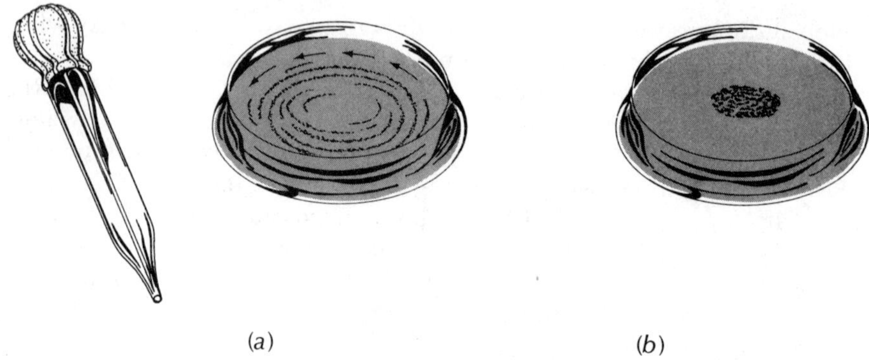

Figure 3-2. Swirling a decanted solution of hydras will cause them to mass in the center, so that they may be removed with a pipette and placed in a clean solution.

CLEANING. Hydras will flourish only in clean, frequently-changed water. Uneaten brine shrimp larvae will accumulate and foul the water; therefore, 30 minutes after each feeding, decant the solution in the hydra vessel into a round bowl and replace it with new spring water. Most of the hydras will adher tenaciously to the bottom and sides of the aquarium. The few hydras that are decanted can be recovered by swirling the solution in the bowl. The hydras will collect in the center and can be pipetted off and placed in the new solution. (See Figure 3-2.)

Hydras that are raised on foods other than brine shrimp larvae also need to have their water changed daily, but the timing of feedings and water changes is less important. You may change the water before or after feeding.

About once a week, you should clean the culture vessel to minimize accumulation of slime. Loosen attached hydras with your finger tips or dislodge them with a jet of water, then pour them off into a series of round bowls. When the culture vessel has been cleaned and rinsed well, collect the hydras by swirling and centering, as described before, and return them to the culture vessel. They recover quickly from any mechanical injury suffered during this procedure.

DEPRESSION. Even with excellent care, hydras will pass into a stage of depression from time to time, and it may be impossible to prevent them from dying out. Depression is characterized by continuous contraction, followed by loss of tentacles, leading often to final disintegration. This state may be caused by incorrect temperature, insufficient oxygen, excessive fermentation, or an unsuitable culturing medium. At the first sign of diminishing in tentacle size and failure of the tentacles to expand properly, transfer all the specimens into a clean tank of fresh spring or pond water with weeds. Sometimes the hydras will recover. More frequent changing of the water may prevent depression.

REPRODUCTION. Hydras reproduce asexually by budding and, under certain circumstances, will also reproduce sexually. When well fed they will develop asexual buds very rapidly; the buds detach and begin an independent life. Spontaneous sexual differentiation will also occur as the population of hydras increases with regular feeding and cleaning. Usually the sex organs (testes and ovaries) are found on different animals, but occasionally both occur on the same individual. The eggs remain attached to the parents during fertilization and early development.

Sexual reproduction in green hydras occurs more frequently in the spring and summer; in brown hydras it is more likely to occur in the fall and winter.

MAINTAINING HYDRAS OVER VACATIONS. When active increase is not desired, hydras may be left in covered containers with clean spring water, at room temperature, for several weeks without feeding, or for several months in a refrigerator at a temperature above 10°C (50°F). Usually they will bud again within 48 hours of being returned to room temperature and a daily routine of feeding and water change.

SLOWING DOWN OR KILLING SPECIMENS FOR OBSERVATION. Drop a crystal of chloretone on the surface of the water to anesthetize the hydras if you need them immobilized for certain experiments. An ice cube will work as well; rest the microscope slide containing a hydra on the cube of ice. The animal will be slowed down by the cold, and sectioning a live animal for regeneration experiments becomes easier.

To kill and preserve hydras, heat 95 percent alcohol (ethanol), and drop the animals in it. Hydras are usually preserved in the elongated state and may be left in the alcohol. Alcohol is highly inflammable, so heat it only in a double boiler on an electric hot plate—never in an exposed container over an open flame.

EXPERIMENTS WITH HYDRAS

FEEDING BEHAVIOR. Study the way hydras eat. Use an overhead projector to demonstrate the behavior to the class. (See FILMS, *Feeding Behavior of* Hydra, page 45.) A hungry hydra will work for its meal if necessary; it may even begin ingesting a living *Tubifex* worm several times its size.

Loomis investigated the role of reduced glutathione (GHS)* in eliciting the feeding response of hydras.[3] Reduced GHS is present in the body fluids of all living organisms, and Loomis suggested that hydras respond to it in their prey. In dead organisms, GHS becomes oxidized, suggesting a reason why hydras might not eat dead food. The GHS hypothesis is not accepted by all scientists, however, and the subject is still under investigation. Forrest, for instance, found that hydras do, in fact, normally eat dead organisms; and she concluded that feeding is regulated by means other than GHS.[4]

Try to make hydras feed on *Daphnia* or brine shrimp that have been dead for several hours. Then moisten these long-dead animals with the juice of freshly killed creatures, and offer them to the hydras again. Are they now ingested? See if hydras will accept other dead foods such as bits of beef, pieces of hard-boiled egg white and yolk, and pieces of washed filter paper in the absence of GHS or fresh tissue juice. Are dead foods more readily accepted in the presence of reduced GHS?* (Use concentrations of 0.0001 M, about 0.03 gm/liter.)[3,4,5a,6] Try to determine what factors influence the response of hydras to reduced GHS.

Loomis challenges Forrest's conclusions and offers a "Loomis prize" of $100 for any proven method of growing hydras on dead material—on condition that 100 hydras are obtained from one parent while using the feeding method, and that the method be repeatable by two other experimenters. His rationale is that if hydras can eat dead material, the organisms should be able to grow and reproduce on it, as they do on living material. He offers the prize whether or not GHS is used, although to match Forrest's findings GHS should *not* be used. Any takers?

Many other interesting and well described hydra-feeding experiments that are suitable for students are available.[2]

INFLUENCE OF ENVIRONMENT ON BEHAVIOR. Changes in the environment, such as lightness or darkness, presence of various chemicals, and vibration, evoke certain behavioral responses (contraction and withdrawal, or feeding response) in hydras.[7] If hydras are given a choice of living under light of different wavelengths, where do most of them congre-

*Reduced glutathione is obtainable from Aldrich Chemical Co., Inc., 10 Ridgedale Ave., Cedar Knolls, New Jersey 07927; or Schwarz/Mann, Mountain View Ave., Orangeburg, New York 10962.

gate? Cover the culture dish with several sections of cellophane paper of different colors, leaving one section open to white light. Does a certain colored light promote asexual budding? Other experiments include the responsiveness of different regions of the hydra's body to touch and to habituation—lack of responsiveness with repeated stimulus.[5b]

INFLUENCE OF ENVIRONMENT ON POPULATION. Population growth can be studied by starting with five hydras, each having a bud. Place them in a petri dish with 30 ml of culture solution. Arbitrarily designate the earliest indication of a bud as a "hydranth" (food-catching portion of a hydra); five hydras with buds are recorded as "ten hydranths." Count the number of hydranths each day for a week or so. Record each bud on the day the first evidence of it occurs.

To make a graph of the results, use semilog paper and plot the number of hydranths on the logarithmic scale against the number of days since the start of the experiment.[8] The graph should be a straight line if the hydras have been kept under satisfactory conditions with adequate feeding. Calculate from the graph the number of days required for the hydranth population to double.

When you are sure the normal growth rate has been established, you can study the long-term effects of environmental factors on growth rate by altering one factor at a time. How is growth rate affected by changes in temperature, frequency of feeding, light intensity, pH, osmotic pressure, oxygen tension, calcium concentration, or the presence of poisons?[9] In each instance, compare the time required for the number of hydranths to double with the normal rate.

INFLUENCE OF POTASSIUM IONS ON TENTACLE LENGTH. Lenhoff discovered that hydras grown in a medium rich in potassium ions develop tentacles two to three times larger than normal.[9] For experimental details of a student project based on this work, see Goldstein and Metzner.[2c]

REGENERATION. Study the ability of hydras to regenerate. Working under a dissecting microscope, cut a hydra horizontally into four segments: base, bud, upper body tube, and mouth and tentacles.[10] Do all the segments regenerate, and if so, do they do so at the same rate?

What is the effect of over-crowding on regenerative processes?[11] What are the effects of chemicals such as ammonia, caffeine, riboflavin, or lysine?

Advanced students may wish to consult Goss for a general account of regeneration in the animal kingdom.[12]

SEXUAL REPRODUCTION. What factors influence sexual maturation? Try to prevent production of sexual forms by frequent changes of water, by overcrowding, and by extreme shallowness of the water. Development of sexual forms will be stimulated by keeping hydras in deep bowls in a refrigerator and feeding them daily.[13, 14]

Determine the influence of reduced oxygen tension on sexual reproduction. Make use of the fact that, with the volume of culture medium held constant, the amount of dissolved oxygen will decrease with surface area. Grow hydras in containers of different shapes to vary their surface-to-volume ratios. For instance, grow cultures of 25 hydras in 25 ml of culture medium in four beakers, each with a different diameter. Feed the cultures each day for 30 mintues with brine shrimp larvae, and daily remove all newly hatched buds (the products of asexual reproduction). Examine all the animals in each vessel under a microscope for the presence of testes or ovaries. Look for small nodules on the body column between the hypostome (mouth area) and the budding zone.[13] What is the shape of the culture vessel in which the greatest rate of sexual reproduction occurs? How does this relate to the oxygen tension in the culture medium?

REFERENCES

1. GALEN, D. F. 1969. Culturing Methods for *Hydra*. *Amer. Biol. Teacher* 31:174-77.

2. GOLDSTEIN, P. and J. METZNER. 1971. *Experiments with Microscopic Animals.* Doubleday & Co., New York. a. pp. 126–28. b pp. 116–52, c. pp. 143–52.

3. LOOMIS, W. F. 1955. Glutathione Control of the Specific Feeding Reaction of *Hydra*. *Ann. N.Y. Acad. Sci.* 62:211–27. (Advanced)

4. FORREST, H. 1962. Lack of Dependence of the Feeding Reaction in *Hydra* on Reduced Glutathione. *Biol. Bull.* 122:343–61. (Advanced)

5. HAINSWORTH, M. D. 1967. *Experiments in Animal Behaviour.* Houghton Mifflin Co., Boston. a. pp. 28–32, b. pp. 21–28.

6. WELSH, J. H., R. I. SMITH and A. E. KAMMER. 1968. Feeding Behavior of Hydra. *Laboratory Exercises in Invertebrate Physiology*. 3rd ed. Burgess Publishing Co., Minneapolis, Minn. pp. 5–7.

7. LENHOFF, H. M. 1976. *On the Behavior of Hydra.* Research Problems in Biology, Series 1. Second Ed. Biological Science Curriculum Study. Oxford University Press, New York. pp. 24–28.

8. LOOMIS, W. F. 1954. Environmental Factors Controlling Growth in *Hydra*. *J. Exp. Zool.* 126:223–34.

9. LENHOFF, H. M. 1966. Influence of Monovalent Cations on the Growth of *Hydra littoralis*. *J. Exp. Zool.* 163:151–55. (Advanced)

10. Hechtlinger, A. 1971. *Handbook of Modern Experiments for High School Biology*. Parker Publishing Co., Inc. West Nyack, New York. pp. 157–158.

11. Davis, L. V. 1966. Inhibition of Growth and Regeneration in *Hydra* by Crowded Culture Water. *Nature* 212:1215–17. (Advanced)

12. Goss, R. J. 1968. *Principles of Regeneration*. Academic Press, New York. (*Hydra*, page 36 *et seq.*) (Advanced)

13. Loomis, W. F. 1957. Sexual Differentiation in *Hydra*. *Science* 126:735–39. (Advanced)

14. Loomis, W. F. and H. M. Lenhoff. 1956. Growth and Sexual Differentiation of *Hydra* in Mass Culture. *J. Exp. Zool.* 132:555–74. (Advanced)

FURTHER READING

Chalkley, H. W. and H. D. Park. 1947. Methods for Increasing the Value of Hydra as Material in Teaching and Research. *Science* 105:553.

Garnett, W. H. 1965. *Freshwater Microscopy*. 2nd. ed. Dover Publications, New York.

Lenhoff, H. M. and W. F. Loomis, eds. 1961. *The biology of* Hydra *and of Some Other Coelenterates*. Univeristy of Miami Press, Coral Gables, Florida. (Advanced)

Loomis, W. F. 1953. The Cultivation of *Hydra* under Controlled Conditions. *Science* 117:565–66. (Advanced)

Wells, T. A. G. 1967. *Invertebrate Types—A Practical Guide*. Heinemann Educational Books, London. Available from Dover Publications, New York.

FILMS

Feeding Behavior of Hydra. Super 8 mm, cartridge, silent, color. B.S.C.S. Single Topic Inquiry Films, Rand McNally and Co., Box 7600, Chicago, Ill 60680

Hydra. Film loop super 8 mm, 1 min. 28 sec. Thorne Films, Dept 17–SL, 1229 University Ave., Boulder, Colo 80302

Hydra. Film loop, super 8 mm, color or b/w. Hubbard Scientific Co., Dept B–3, Box 105, Northbrook, Ill 60062

Microscopic Water Animals. (Rotifer, Stentor, hydra). Film loop, super 8 mm, 3 min. 14 sec. International Communication Films, NASCO, Fort Atkinson, Wis 53538

Sponges and Coelenterates: Porous and Sac-Like Animals. 16mm,b/w or color, 11 min. Coronet Films, Coronet Building, 65 E. South Water St., Chicago, Ill 60601

4

Flatworms and Roundworms

"The apparent simplicity of the [planarian] and its intriguing biological properties have attracted the efforts of diverse types: the modern and the antiquarian; biologists and psychologists; Charles Darwin and high school students. One conclusion, at least, is shared by all of these; that simplicity is paradoxical and more common in the mind of the investigator than the behavior of the planarian."

Stuart J. Coward (b. 1936)

FRESHWATER FLATWORMS—PLANARIANS

Planarians are famous not only because they are the lowest animal with bilateral symmetry, a rudimentary brain, and a true synaptic type of nervous system; but also because they possess enormous powers of regeneration. For years physiologists, psychologists, and biochemists have investigated their regeneration and their amazing behavior, learning and memory capabilities. These beguiling creatures are ideal classroom animals. They are very easy to care for and can be used for a great variety of biological experiments.

Planarians inspire not only scholarly investigations, but humor; a journal called *The Worm Runner's Digest* reveals the lighter side of planarian research and provides much useful information.[1]

In their natural habitats, these inconspicuous animals live in freshwater streams, ponds, and rivers almost anywhere—from mountaintops to tidal basins. They are one of the few animals with virtually no enemies. Planarians are carnivorous and eat *Daphnia*, other small crustaceans, and any other meat they can scavenge.

They belong to the phylum called Platyhelminthes (Greek for *flatworm*). Of the 600 species in this phylum, some are parasitic, such as the *Taenia* tapeworms which infects man; but some, like the planarians, are free-living. Planarians belong to the Turbellaria class, which consists of freshwater, marine, and terrestrial species; but few studies have been made of the marine and land species.

Freshwater planarians may be gray-brown, brown, white, velvety black, plain, or spotted. They commonly measure 12mm or less, have flattened bodies, and look like very small leeches. In many species, there is a definite triangular-shaped head with a point facing forward. There are two eyes near the base of the head on the dorsal side. One entertaining feature is that the *Dugesia* species has a cross-eyed appearance because of dark spots at the inner edges contrasting with colorless eye cells elsewhere. Planarians' eyes have no lenses and cannot form an image, but they are sensitive to light. A planarian can probably see about as well as a human with eyes closed against a strong light.

Planarians can be collected at any time of the year from most streams, rivers, and lakes. They avoid light, and in swifter portions of a stream, they are usually found underneath large rocks. To collect them, attach a bait of liver or beef to a string and throw it into the water. Within an hour or so, planarians will gather on the underside of the meat, and you can shake them off into a container of water. A white enamel collecting bowl makes observation of the captured planarians easy. Those worms which respond to baiting usually belong to the species most easily raised in a classroom. If you are in the field without

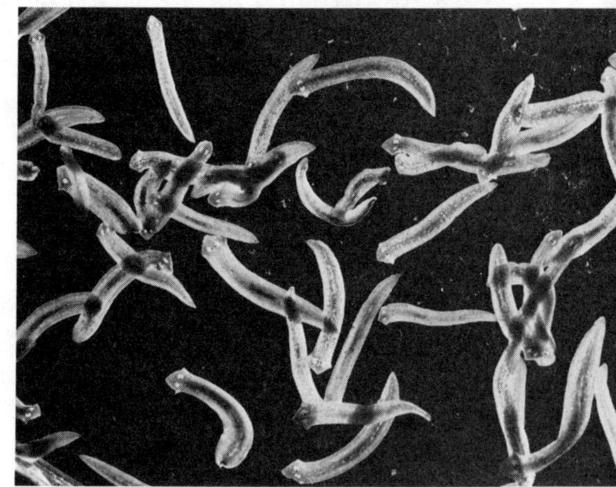

Figure 4-1. Planaria. (Courtesy Carolina Biological Supply House)

Figure 4-2. *Collecting planaria from under rocks in a stream.*

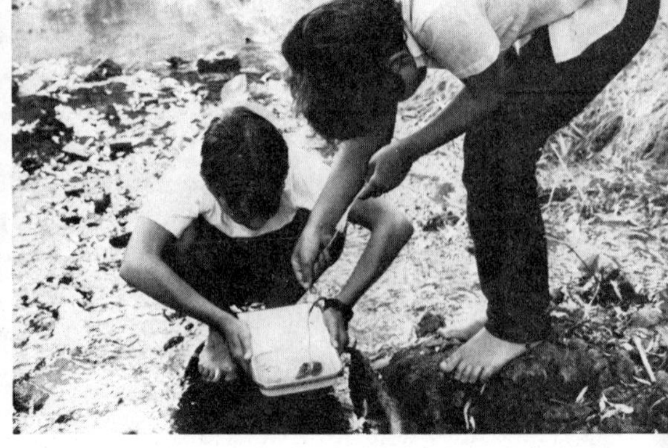

Figure 4-3. *Liner on a string makes good planaria bait.*

the suggested bait, collect large amounts of aquatic vegetation, such as *Elodea* and filamentous algae, place it in containers of water, and cover the mixture with a lid to keep out the light. When the oxygen content decreases, the planarians will rise to the surface where they are easily seen and removed.

The larger species *Dugesia dorotocephala*, which can be up to 5 cm in length, is found most commonly in rapidly-moving streams. *Dugesia tigrina* (Figure 4–4) is a light brown, somewhat transparent, spotted species of 2 cm maximum length; it commonly occurs in slower-moving rivers and lakes. A third common species, which is recognized easily by its square head and dark color, is *Phagocata gracilis* (Figure 4–5).

D. tigrina is the species of choice for psychological conditioning experiments, but *D. dorotocephala* is best for maze training and regeneration studies, as well as for experiments involving cannibalism. These species and sometimes several others are available from biological supply houses.

Housing

Planarians can be kept successfully in almost anything that will hold water, including shallow baking trays, jars, bottles, and culture dishes. Shallow pans help to ensure adequate oxygen in the water. Cut-off milk cartons lined with plastic wrap make satisfactory homes. A glass soup bowl is large enough to house a dozen or more planarians. Glass custard cups will house animals individually during training experiments.

Cover the containers with aluminum foil to retard evaporation and to provide a dark environment. Planarians are not comfortable in bright light. Locate them away from radiators, and try to maintain the water temperature around 20°C (68°F). A cool temperature is needed for successful regeneration experiments.

If you wish, you can set up a balanced aquarium with some hundreds of planarians, water plants, and aquatic animals such as snails and *Daphnia*; but note that fish, frogs, and other amphibians do not make suitable companions. Add some stones under which the planarians can hide. If they creep up and form a line along the water's edge, their oxygen supply is low and more plants are needed. Keep the tank covered with a lid to retard evaporation. Every few days, add water to the original level, and add a small amount of rolled oats to feed the snails. The *Daphnia* feed on bacteria and algae that are formed, and the planarians feed on young snails and *Daphnia*. Do not crowd the animals, particularly the planarian species which are cannibalistic (*D. dorotocephala*, for example). Do not mix the species.

CHANGING THE WATER. Planarians, like protozoans, are extremely sensitive to changes in their environment. If the water becomes even slightly contaminated, the worms are likely to die. If the animals were collected from a nearby stream or pond, it is best to obtain water regularly for them from the same source. Alternatively, spring water (from biological supply houses) or distilled water (from supermarkets) is satisfac-

Figure 4-4. Dugesia dorotocephala.

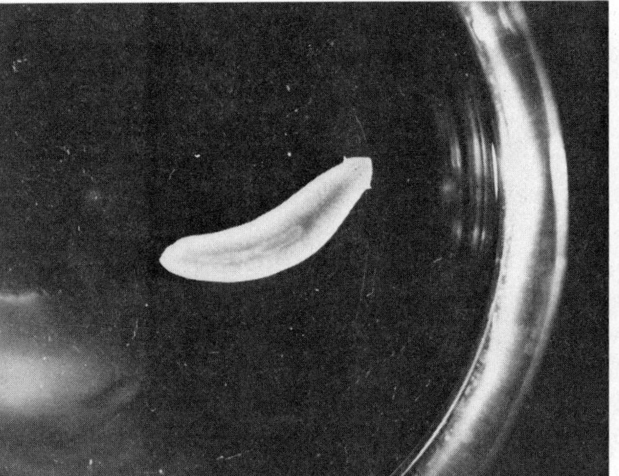

Figure 4-5. Phagocata gracilis.

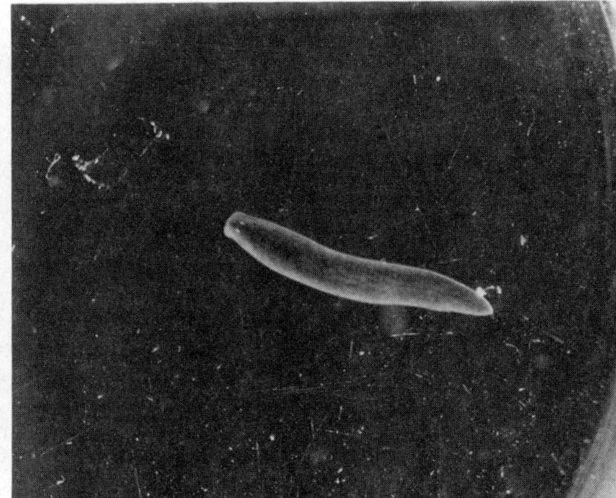

tory. Tap water is not recommended; but if it is used, it *must* be aerated with a bubbler or let stand for one or two days to allow any chlorine, which is lethal to planarians, to escape.

Change the water at least once a week, two or three times if the container is small. This should be done whether or not food has been added. From time to time, clean the container. To do this, transfer the planarians and their water to a temporary container, scrub the original container thoroughly and wipe it with paper towels to remove the mucus which planarians secrete. Avoid using soap or detergent. Rinse very well and refill with fresh water. To return the planarians to the container, handle them with a soft paint brush or, less desirably, pick them off with a pipette.

During an experiment, the *type of water used* should not be changed, as even the slightest difference in chemical composition of the medium may be enough to alter the worms' behavior radically.

A technique used by professional scientists is to keep the animals routinely in artificial pond water, which is just a dilute salt solution. The formula for this solution follows. First, make up two stock solutions:

Stock Solution A	*Stock Solution B*
133.0 gm NaCl	3.8 gm $NaHCO_3$
26.6 gm CaCl	1.0 liter distilled H_2O
1.0 liter distilled H_2O	

Then, add 10 ml of each stock solution to every gallon of distilled water used in the aquarium.

Feeding

Planarians are carnivorous and will grow and thrive if fed thin strips of fresh calf or beef liver once or twice a week. Frozen liver is not ideal but will suffice; pork liver should not be used because it is too fatty. Other red meats and eggs are not particularly suitable. The juices of liver rapidly contaminate the water in which the planarians are kept. It is *essential*, therefore, to *change the water within two to three hours* after liver has been put in. Other satisfactory foods that produce less contamination include freshly hatched brine shrimp (page 101), chopped-up bits of white worms (page 72), or *Tubifex* worms (for some planarian species). After several hours, excess food should be removed with a pipette.

Remember that a large, healthy planarian can live for three or more months without any food whatsoever. The more food they receive, the more likely they are to undergo spontaneous asexual fission—"dropping tails," as it is called, after the manner in which the animal divides between the head and tail.

Asexual fission is usually undesirable during an experiment. Stop feeding the animals several days before beginning regeneration or psychological experiments; it is best not to feed them during the entire experiment. Planarians kept without food become smaller, using up their bodies to sustain life.

Reproduction

Planarians can reproduce both asexually and sexually. Asexual methods include fragmentation with subsequent regeneration of the parts, and spontaneous "dropping tails." Both of these methods can be observed readily in the classroom. Typically, spontaneous division starts with a transverse constriction just behind the pharynx, which increases until the two parts separate and move away from each other. The head soon grows a new tail, and the tail grows a new head. Planarians kept in stale water will drop tails very frequently and will not grow sufficiently between divisions. This produces planarians which remain pigmies as long as bad conditions exist.

Planarians also reproduce sexually, most species producing thin-shelled, transparent "summer eggs," as well as thick-shelled "winter eggs," or cocoons. Planarians are hermaphroditic; each animal possesses complete male and female systems. During copulation, each animal fertilizes the other and, later, both produce eggs. The cocoon of *D. dorotocephala* is about 1 mm in diameter and is typically orange-red

Figure 4-6. Planaria cocoon. (Courtesy Carolina Biological Supply House)

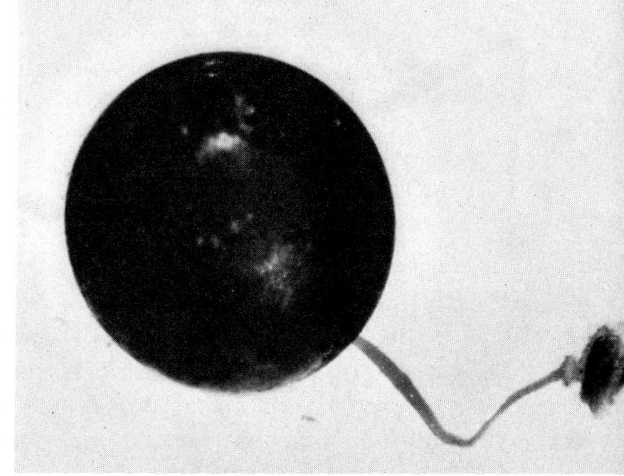

when laid, but within a few hours it turns jet black. Each cocoon contains approximately 16 eggs which hatch in about 14 days. Cocoons will have a better chance of survival in the classroom if they are removed from a communal tank and housed in individual containers with water. Adult planarians will eat both cocoons and young planarians if hungry enough. The cocoon should be left in the bowl for several days after the eggs hatch, since it provides food and shelter for the offspring. Hatchable planarian cocoons are available from some biological supply houses in early spring.

Anesthetizing and Killing Planarians

Microscopic examination of live planarians will be easier if you slow down the animals' movements by lowering the temperature of the surrounding water with ice. Anesthetize planarians before making incisions for regeneration studies. Again, as with hydras, ice is the method of choice. The anesthetizing procedure is as follows: Place water in a petri dish or any shallow dish, cover with aluminum foil so that the water touches the foil, and freeze. The foil should adhere tightly to the ice. Prepare a dissecting microscope with illumination from above (reflected light). Place a planarian on a small piece of fluffy paper towel or filter paper soaked with water. Now act quickly! Place the dish with ice and foil under the microscope and focus onto the aluminum foil. Then place the worm on the paper towel on top of the foil, and focus on the animal. When the animal stops moving, but *not* before, quickly make the desired incisions. Use single strokes with a sharp razor blade, tenotomy knife, or 00 cover slip. Then, with forceps, immediately lift the paper with the cut-up planarian and place the animal in its individual dish. If the paper freezes to the aluminum foil, the animal will die.

All other methods (commercial preparations for slowing down planarians, chloretone, TMS, menthol, or Epsom salts) are much inferior to using ice.

To humanely kill planarians, slowly lower the temperature of the surrounding water to freezing.

Vacation Care

Planarians can survive without food or attention for periods such as the long summer vacation if the temperature is lowered to around 10°C (50°F) to decrease their metabolism. Try keeping them in covered containers in a basement room, or on a shelf of a refrigerator adjusted to the highest temperature setting.

EXPERIMENTS WITH PLANARIANS

Planarians can be used for a wide variety of experiments in three major areas: study of taxes, learning and other psychological behavior, and regeneration. There are two good books which provide instructions for the planarian experiments on all three of the topics listed above, interpreted for the secondary school level.[2,3] Several review articles, which give abstracts of published works and extensive bibliographies, will be helpful to advanced students who wish to understand the current status of planarian research.[2a,4,5]

Study of Taxes

A versatile technique for studying several environmental preferences of planarians requires a Y-shaped Plexiglas® tube. Prepare contrasting environmental conditions in two of the arms (for instance, one arm may contain warm water and the other cold, or one arm may be lighted and the other dark); introduce a planarian into the system in the third arm and observe its movements and behavior.[6a,7] The following experiments describe other techniques for studying planarians' responses to their environment.

RESPONSES TO TEMPERATURE CHANGE. Build a rectangular trough, at least 15 cm wide, around a tank filled with pond water. The tank should contain at least 20 planarians. Mark the tank off into equal sections and provide a thermometer in each section. Pack ice around one end of the trough and add hot water to the other at a temperature not higher than 32°C (90°F). After a short time, a temperature gradient will be established. For at least 30 minutes, record the number of planarians in each section at 5–minute intervals. What is the temperature of greatest activity? When this has been established, keep the water at this temperature and test the effects of other stimuli.[3]

RESPONSES TO LIGHT. Little or no special apparatus is required for experimenting on planarians' responses to light. There are many experiments that are suitable.[8–11] Observe responses to directional illumination by lighting a planarian from above with a flashlight and noting the direction in which the worm turns. In 20 trials does the animal show a preference to turn to the right or to the left? In an otherwise dark room, fatigue one eye's sensitivity to light by turning the dish as the planarian wanders about—keeping the left eye continuously exposed to light for ten minutes. Now repeat the experiment of illuminating the animal from directly above. Does the tendency for turns to one side increase or decrease? After a period of rest in the dark, fatigue the other eye and repeat the experiment.

Does a planarian respond to red light? It is easy to find out. For another experiment, try testing the ability of planarians to respond to differences in background or non-directional illumination.[11] Using tape or paint, color half of the outside surfaces of small, clear glass dishes black and the other half white. Place a planarian in each dish. Compare the number of animals which come to rest on the dark side with the number on the white side. For still another experiment, compare the sensitivity of regenerating eyes with fully-formed eyes.

EFFECTS OF MECHANICAL AGITATION. Subject the planarians' vessel to vibrations by placing it in contact with a striker from an electric bell, or rock the animals' vessel gently by hand a given number of times per second. What is the effect on the planarians?[3]

EFFECTS OF WATER DEPTH. Construct a series of sloping steps from Plexiglas® or other material to fit exactly inside the planarians' container, which should be at least 15 cm deep. At what depth do you find the most planarians? Relate these findings to the ecological distribution of these animals in the wild[3]

RHEOTAXIC RESPONSES. Planarians exhibit rheotaxis; they tend to move *against* the current of the water in which they live. In nature, apart from migrations which planarians undertake from time to time, the simple maintenance of position in a flowing stream demands some form of rheotactic response. In the classroom, test this response by using a jet of water from a fine pipette to produce a stream down a slightly inclined plane. Or create a stream in a trough of water. (Use a fine filter at each end to prevent loss of planarians.) The base of the trough should be marked off with cross lines so that the animals' movements can be measured. To find out if other factors affect the rheotactic response, experiment with starvation and change of water temperature. Make comparative field studies of planarian migrations in a segment of a stream.[12]

Social Behavior

Do planarians show preference for forming social groups rather than remaining isloated? Do planarians produce a chemical that attracts others of the same species? To test these possibilities, use a fine screen to confine a group of planarians at the outer edge of one arm of a Y-shaped tube, and in the control arm place a fine screen but no planarians.[6a,6b] Then release a number of individual planarians into the third arm of the Y tube and observe their movements. Do the free planarians locate the confined group and attempt to join them? If so, does this indicate the production of an attractant chemical? Plan other experiments to find out, and to investigate whether conditions of illumination affect the production of an attractant chemical or whatever else occurs.

Learning

It takes a long time to train planarians; 200 or more trials are not unusual to train many species. Do not attempt these experiments if you want quick results. Much patience is needed.

1. Use simple T and Y mazes, or, preferably, modified T mazes formed in the curve perimeter of a crystallizing dish, to train planarians to turn to the right or to the left. Provide food as a reward. Statistical analysis can be made of the results. The references include instructions for building suitable mazes and for the training techniques.[2b,3]
2. Other types of training, such as associative learning, can be investigated. To do so, subject planarians to weak electric shocks, and after a suitable number of trials, switch on a light each time the animals receive the shock. Eventually, omit the shock and observe the reaction of the animals when light alone is turned on. Many variations of this classical conditioning experiment can be tried; for instance, the shock stimulus can be paired with food or with a chemical stimulus instead of the light stimulus.[1b,2c,13,14]
3. Anesthetize trained planarians using the foil and ice technique, then bisect them crosswise and allow both the head and tail ends to regenerate the missing segments in pond water. Retest the regenerated animals to determine whether the presence of the brain in the head end affects the ability to retain a learned response.[15]
4. Using cannibalistic species, train and feed conditioned planarians to naive ones. For controls, keep some naive planarians on a diet of beef liver. Test the two groups of planarians to see if those which ate their trained fellows learn more quickly than the naive controls.[1a]

Regeneration

These experiments are not easy. Bissecting planarians requires considerable skill; often mortality rates are high. In addition, these studies are quite lengthy because time is needed for regeneration to take place.

Use the anesthetizing procedure described on page 52 for dissecting living planarians. If you wish, you may remove each anesthetized animal quickly from the paper towel and place it on a piece of wax or wood under the dissecting microscope before making the incisions. Make cuts in different directions on different animals; for instance, cut one animal transversely to form two equal halves, cut another transversely into three equal parts, and cut another longitudinally to partially split the tail end.

Where does regeneration begin? How does new growth differ in appearance from the original part of the planarian? How large a piece of planarian must be present to produce a new head, a new tail, or both? Do normal animals result from the regeneration process? Compare the rates of regeneration of pieces from different regions. Do environmental factors, such as light, temperature, or oxygen content of the surrounding water, influence planarian regeneration?[3] (See FILMS, *Planaria—Cutting for Regeneration, Regeneration in Flatworms,* and *Regeneration in Planaria,* page 63.)

Digestion—the Planarian Pharynx

The mouth of a fresh-water planarian is on the end of a short muscular tube, the *pharynx*, located in the middle of the body and protruded through an opening in the underside. Wastes must go out through the mouth just as they do in *Hydra*. To watch an animal extend its pharynx to feed, place a small piece of beef liver on a slide and use a second slide to make a liver smear, as in making a blood smear. Invert the smeared slide (be sure it is transparent) on two small chips of wood, 5 mm thick, and place the chips and the slide in 6 mm of water in a petri dish. With a dissecting microscope, focus on the smear suspended in the water. Introduce two planarians that have been deprived of food for several days. Within a few minutes, the planarians will migrate to the liver smear to eat, and the distended pharynx, like a miniature elephant's trunk, can be observed.

ROUNDWORMS—VINEGAR EELS AND SOIL NEMATODES

The roundworms (Phylum Aschelminthes) are mostly very small with long cylindrical bodies tapering almost to a point at each end. They can be fresh-water, marine, or terrestrial animals, but are predominantly aquatic. Some are free-living. Others are parasitic, (such as the hookworms, pinworms, and trichinae which infect man), and are generally larger than the free-living worms. The nematodes—

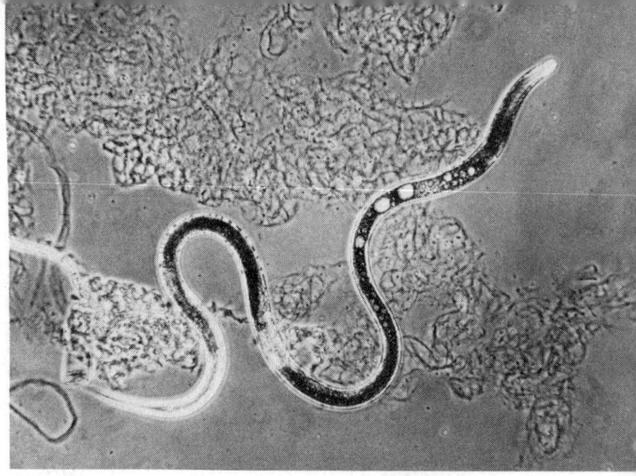

Figure 4-7. *Vinegar eel.*

nonsegmented roundworms such as vinegar eels and their relatives, and soil nematodes—are of interest for type study, although experimentation with them is somewhat limited.

Vinegar Eels

These harmless, nonparasitic roundworms are variously called *Anguilla aceti* or *Turbatrix aceti*. They occur, usually in profusion, in bulk cider vinegar and feed upon the fungus "mother of vinegar" which forms in the bottom of the barrel. Bottled vinegar is pasteurized to prevent growth of these worms.

Vinegar eels are small, transparent worms about 1.5 to 2 mm long, the females being larger. They can just be seen with the naked eye if viewed with a bright light against a dark background, but a strong magnifying glass (about 4×) or a hand lens makes viewing easier. To see anatomical details, a microscope is necessary. They move continuously with rapid powerful movements.

They can be obtained from biological supply houses* or purchased inexpensively from local cider mills or vinegar manufacturers by asking for pure bulk vinegar which contains "mother of vinegar." For those who object to keeping vinegar eels because of the strong smell, a good nonodiferous substitute is *Anguilla silusiae*** which has a different but very simple method of culture (see next page).

CULTURING. In addition to a beginning supply of worms, the following items are necessary: bulk vinegar, apple, or "vinegar eel medium" (the latter available from several biological supply houses); and unadulterated cider vinegar which has no chemical preservatives added (from grocery stores).

---

*CAR, CBS, CON, MOG, NAS and WAR. See Appendix C, pp. 355-356.

**Obtainable from CON, Appendix C.

Use finger bowls or other appropriately-sized glass or plastic containers. Place worms in 200 ml of unadulterated cider vinegar and add *either* four medicine droppersful of bulk vinegar *or* "vinegar eel medium." A 2.5 cm cube of raw peeled apple can be used in place of the bulk vinegar. Cover the cultures loosely, to admit some air yet retard evaporation, and keep cultures away from strong lights and contaminants. Wide variations in temperature are tolerated by vinegar eels. No further care is necessary except to subculture about every three months by adding some of the old culture to fresh cider vinegar. The life span for individual worms is ten months or more, but with normal reproduction the cultures will continue indefinitely.

CULTURE OF *Anguilla silusiae.* Make a thick paste of Pablum® with cool tap water and add a pinch of dry yeast. Stir the mixture until it is smooth and pour it into a small bowl to a depth of 6 mm. Add a small amount of water to the beginning supply of *A. silusiae* and pour them onto the Pablum mixture. Cover the container with a sheet of glass and place in semidarkness at 24 to 27°C (75 to 80°F). After one week, the nematodes should be visible on the surface and on the sides of the container. Subculture every two weeks by removing a few worms and adding them to a new Pablum-yeast mixture. These creatures are excellent to use as the first food for offspring of live-bearing fish, such as young guppies.

Experiments with Vinegar Eels and A. silusiae

1. Since these worms are transparent, all the stages of development can be examined *in utero*. For detailed microscopic observations, slow the worms down by mixing a drop of culturing medium with a drop of thick solution of polyvinyl alcohol or methyl cellulose. To stain the tissues for better observation, add a small drop of 0.2 percent neutral red stain to the drop of worm culture on the slide. (Prepare the stain by dissolving 0.2 gm of the powdered stain in 1 ml of alcohol; bring the volume up to 100 ml with distilled water.) Eggs are fertilized internally and are surrounded by a thin membrane during development. The membrane eventually ruptures, releasing the young, which are born in an active condition. About 40 young are born at one time, in approximately equal numbers by sex. Try to identify various stages of the reproductive process.
2. Compare the survival rates of vinegar eels over a range of pH values. Set up a series of small jars containing vinegar, and add HCl to some of the jars to lower the pH, and NaOH to others to raise the pH. Transfer an equal number of vinegar eels to each jar and determine

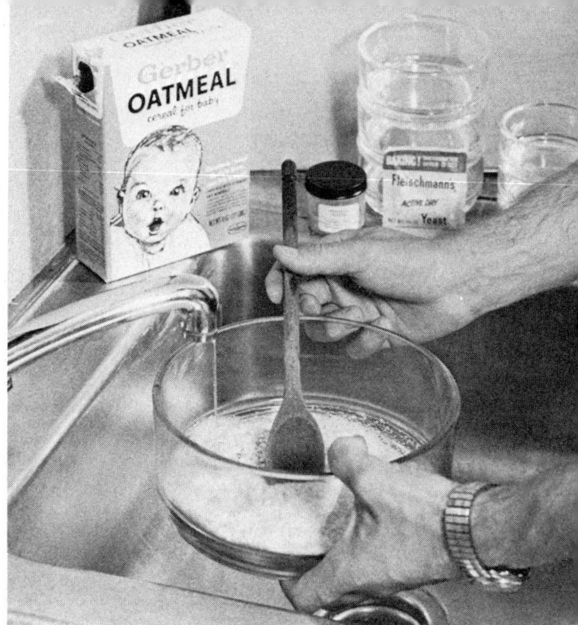

Figure 4-8. Preparation of medium for culturing Anguilla silusiae.

their survival rates.[16] Make a graph of the results by plotting the pH on the horizontal axis and the number of surviving worms on the vertical axis.

3. Determine the optimal temperature for the culture of vinegar eels or *A. silusiae.* Keep the cultures in a variety of situations—out-of-doors, in a basement, in the classroom, under electric light bulbs of different wattage, or in incubators—to provide different environmental temperatures.[6c]

Ideas for other experiments on vinegar eels can be found in References 17 and 6d.

Soil Nematodes[18]

Somewhere between 1,000 and 10,000 nematodes live in every cubic centimeter of soil. They usually settle in the upper layers. If this layer dries out, they enclose themselves in cysts or capsules and can survive in this manner for long periods of time. When the environment improves, the tiny worms reappear.

Collect soil nematodes by weighing small quantities of soil (say, 100 gm); wrap each sample in two layers of cheesecloth to make a bag, and secure the wrapping with a rubber band. Place the bag in an ordinary funnel containing a circle of fine mesh screen, so that the soil in its bag rests in the upper half of the funnel.[6e] (See FILMS, *Collecting Nematodes–Baermann Funnel,* page 62.) Place the funnel upright in a ring clamp on a ringstand. Attach a short piece of rubber tubing to the neck of the funnel and close this off with a pinch clamp. Pour water into the funnel until it is almost filled. Leave it undisturbed for 24 hours. During this time the nematodes will work their way out of the soil, through the cheesecloth and screen, and into the reservoir of water in the lower half of the funnel. To harvest the worms, open the pinch clamp and run a measured amount of the water (say, 10 ml) into a small test tube or beaker held underneath.[19]

Population counts can be made by examining such samples under a microscope, on slides ruled off for blood cell counts. (If the number of worms is small, centrifuge the sample to concentrate the nematodes into a smaller volume of fluid.)

CULTURING. Many nematodes will thrive and reproduce in sterilized potato slices. Cut a piece of fresh, uninfected potato about 12 mm long; remove the skin; and place in a bacteriological test tube. Add spring water to fill the space between the potato and the tube, plug the tube with cotton, and sterilize in an autoclave or pressure cooker at 15 lbs. pressure for 30 minutes. Remove the tube and let it cool, then inoculate the potato in the tube with nematodes collected from a Baermann funnel, or from a small piece of potato which has been buried several inches deep in garden soil for two to three weeks. (Do not add the garden sample of potato.) Replace the cotton plug to maintain sterile conditions. Keep at room temperature.

Experiments with Soil Nematodes

1. Will nematode populations vary according to the type of soil? Take several core samples of the same size by boring down into the earth a few inches with a hollow tube (such as a piece of piping or a cork borer). Take samples from a garden bed, lawn, vacant lot, compost pile, manure pile, compacted barren path, and a potato field. Compare populations by counting the numbers of nematodes in a set of measured samples obtained from Baermann funnels. Are nematodes more numerous in acid, alkaline, or neutral soils? In loamy, sandy, or clay soils?
2. How long can soil nematodes withstand drying? A certain plant nematode is reported to have revived after 28 years in dry storage. Prepare several vials of soil nematodes and dry them out, preferably in a desiccator containing a dehydrating agent such as calcium chloride. When the vials are very dry, plug them with rubber stoppers and leave them undisturbed for weeks, months, or years. Periodically check to see if they require any further drying. To test for revival, add a few ml of *sterile* water and a small cube of *sterile* potato (heated in a pressure cooker for 30 minutes at 15 lbs. pres-

sure). During the undisturbed rest period, the effects of some extremes of temperature can be examined. Can encysted nematodes withstand greater temperature fluctuations than the free-living worms? Other experiments on plant nematodes, parasitic nematodes, and the microfauna of the soil are described in References 6f and 20.

REFERENCES

1. *The Worm Runner's Digest—The Journal of Biological Psychology.* J. V. McConnell, ed. P. O. Box 644, Ann Arbor, Mich. 48107.
   a. McConnell, J. V., R. Jacobson and B. M. Humphries. 1961. The Effects of Ingestion of a Conditioned Planarian on the Response Level of Naive Planaria: A pilot Study. 3(1):41–47.
   b. Zelman, A., L. Kabat, R. Jacobson and J. V. McConnell. 1963. Transfer of Training through Injection of "Conditioned" RNA into Untrained Planarians. 5(1):14–21. (Advanced)
2. McConnell, J. V. 1967. *A Manual of Psychological Experimentation on Planarians.* 2nd ed. J. V. McConnell, P. O. Box 644, Ann Arbor, Mich. 48107. (Advanced)
   a. Mosler, U., M. L. Clay and J. V. McConnell. An Annotated Bibliography of Research on Planarians. Sec. 9, pp. 75–128. b. pp. 37–42; c. Jacobson, A. L., S. D. Horowitz and C. Fried. An Apparatus for Training Planarians en masse. Sec. 7, pp. 68–70.
3. Hainsworth, M. D. 1967. Behaviour of Planaria. *Experiments in Animal Behaviour.* Houghton Mifflin Co., Boston, Mass. 02107. pp. 33–46.
4. Jacobson, A. L. 1963. Learning in Flatworms and Annelids. *Psychol. Bull.* 60:74–94. (Advanced)
5. Jacobson, A. L. 1965. Learning in Planarians: Current Status. *Animal Behavior.* Sup. 1, Learning and Associated Phenomena in Invertebrates. pp. 76–82. (Advanced)
6. Goldstein, P. and J. Metzner. 1971. *Experiments with Microscopic Animals.* Doubleday & Co., Garden City, N.Y. a. pp. 103–108 and 213–17, b. pp. 111–14; c. pp. 164–65; d. pp. 161–64; e. pp. 154–61; f. pp. 153–95.
7. Laszlo, P. T. 1967. An Apparatus for the Demonstration of Taxes in Small Aquatic Animals. *Turtox News,* 45(11).
8. Taliaferro, W. H. 1920. Reactions to Light in *Planaria maculata;* with Special Reference to the Function and Structure of the Eyes. *J. Exp. Zool.* 31:59–116. (Advanced)
9. Ullyott, P. 1936. The Behaviour of *Dendrocoelum lacteum.* Responses at Light-and-Dark Boundaries. *J. Exp. Biol.* 13:253–64. (Advanced)

10. WALTER, H. E. 1907. The Reactions of Planarians to Light. *J. Exp. Zool.* 5:35–162.(Advanced)

11. WELSH, J. H., R. I. SMITH and A. E. KAMMER. 1968. Orientation Responses to Light; Planarians. *Laboratory Exercises in Invertebrate Physiology*. 3rd. ed. Burgess Publishing Co., Minneapolis, Minn. pp. 97–99. (Advanced)

12. BEAUCHAMP, R. S. A. 1933. Rheotaxis in *Planaria alpina*. *J. Exp. Biol.* 10:113–29. (Advanced)

13. MCCONNELL, J. V., R. R. CORNWELL and M. CLAY. 1960. An Apparatus for Conditioning Planaria. *Amer. J. Psychol.* 73:618–22. (Advanced)

14. THOMPSON, T. and J. V. MCCONNELL. 1955. Classical Conditioning of the Planaria, *Dugesia dorotocephala*. *J. Comp. Physiol. Psychol.* 48:65–68. (Advanced)

15. MCCONNELL, J. V., A. L. JACOBSON, and D. P. KIMBLE. 1959. The Effects of Regeneration upon Retention of a Conditioned Response in the Planarian. *J. Comp. Physiol. Psychol.* 52:1–5.

16. BEHRINGER, M. 1967. Use of the Vinegar Eel. *Amer. Biol. Teacher* 29(7):515–22.

17. GALEN, D. F. 1971. Culturing and Using the Vinegar Eel. *Amer. Biol. Teacher* 33(4):237–38.

18. SCHALLER, F. 1968. *Soil Animals*. University of Michigan Press, Ann Arbor, Mich.

19. PRAMER, D. 1965. *Life in the Soil*. BSCS Laboratory Block. D. C. Heath Co., Lexington, Mass.

20. *Control of Plant-Parasitic Nematodes*. Vol. 4 of *Principles of Plant and Animal Pest Control*. Subcommittee on Nematodes. Publ. No. 1696, National Academy of Science, Washington, D. C.

FILMS

Collecting Nematodes—Baermann Funnell. Super 8 mm. cartridge, color, silent, 3 min. Biological Techniques Series. Encyclopaedia Britannica Films, Encyclopaedia Britannica Educational Corp., 1150 Wilmette Ave., Wilmette, Ill 60091

Planaria. Film loop, super 8 mm, cartridge, color or b/w, approx. 4 min. Holt Biology Filmloops, Holt, Rinehart and Winston, Inc., Media Dept. 383, Madison Ave., New York, N.Y. 10017

Planaria. Film loop, super 8 mm, color or b/w. Hubbard Scientific Co., Dept. B-3, P.O. Box 105, Northbrook, Ill 60062.

Planaria. Film loop, super 8 mm, color 2 min. 17 sec. Thorne Films, Dept 17-SL, 1229 University Ave., Boulder, Colo 80302

Planaria Behavior. Super 8 mm, cartridge. B.S.C.S. Single Topic Inquiry Films. Hubbard Scientific Co., Dept. B-3, P.O. Box 105, Northbrook, Ill 60062

Planaria—Cutting for Regeneration. Super 8 mm, cartridge, color, silent, 4 min. Biological Techniques Series, Encyclopaedia Britannica Films, Encyclopaedia Britannica Educational Corp., 1150 Wilmette Ave., Wilmette, Ill 60091

Regeneration in Flatworms. Film loop No. 53, super 8 mm, 1 min. 52 sec. Thorne Films Inc., Dept 17-SL, 1229 University Ave., Boulder, Colo 80302

Regeneration in Planaria. Laboratory Experiments Filmstrip. Silver Burdett Co., 250 James St., Morristown, N.J. 07960.

5

Earthworms and White Worms

". . . the organization of the [earthworm's] nervous system is quite different from ours. An earthworm has only a limited number of ways to respond to a wide variety of external stimuli (such as light and touch), . . . [and] we do not know and cannot know how much 'pain' we are inflicting. So treat your earthworm . . . with respect; it's alive, and it may hurt."

Steven Vogel (b. 1940)

Darwin made detailed observations of earthworms for many years, and he remarked that their "degree of intelligence. . . surprised me." He often showed visitors an experiment designed to demonstrate the earthworms' sensitivity to vibrations. On his piano stood a row of flower pots, each containing earthworms. At night they would come out to fetch leaves. Whenever he struck certain low notes, they would suddenly withdraw into their burrows; other notes would not affect them in the least.

Earthworms are invaluable animals for studies of behavior and learning. They make ideal classroom animals, as they are inexpensive, easy to care for, and have many experimental uses. Observations of the living animal should be used in preference to dissection studies whenever possible.

Earthworms are also useful as food for *Hydra*, crayfish, fish, tadpoles, toads, frogs, small salamanders, lizards, and snakes. White worms, also described in this chapter, provide an excellent source of food for these animals, but are less useful for experiments.

Earthworms and white worms belong to the Phylum Annelida. They have long, tubular digestive tracts, open at both ends, and blood which circulates within a closed system. They are segmented, Thus, their anatomy is more complicated than that of either the flatworms or roundworms. Earthworms and white worms are terrestrial; but most members of this phylum are aquatic, for example, the *Tubifex* worms and leeches.

EARTHWORMS (LUMBRICIDAE)

Depending upon species, earthworms are from 7.5 to 15 cm long, have 100 or more segments, and are brown, red, or yellow. At sexual maturity, a light band called a *clitellum* forms from segment 32 to 37 making these segments less obvious.

There are many species of earthworms. *Lumbricus* species form casts within the soil. The large *Lumbricus terrestris* (10 to 15 cm), commonly used for dissection, is less hardy than other species for rearing in the classroom. The many smaller species include the pale *Allolobophora,* which usually forms surface casts and frequently lives in lawns. *Eisenia foetida,* which lives in manure piles, is very hardy and is good for experimental purposes. The smaller species can be fed to other animals, except *E. foetida,* which many fish will not eat.

The best source of earthworms is the earth. Late spring or early summer are the best times to collect them. If winters are cold, the worms burrow so deeply they may be hard to find. Dig for them in likely places: garden areas, manure piles, barnyards, or moist woodlands. Press the face of a ringing alarm clock to the surface of the ground. The vibrations will disturb the earthworms, and they will emerge from their burrows to be collected by hand. It is also possible to

Figure 5-1. Searching for earthworms in a compost pile.

Figure 5-2. A picnic cooler makes a good earthworm container.

collect worms merely by lifting stones or old planks lying on top of the soil. (It may take years for conditions under logs and stones to reach a point at which life is possible for some organisms, so be sure to return all overturned objects to their original positions.) In the spring, a search in composted fall leaves will usually yield an abundant supply of earthworms. Or, search for them on the surface with a flashlight on warm, moist nights during spring or summer, especially after a rainfall. For best results, cover the flashlight with red tissue paper to dim the light.

Live earthworms can be purchased from fish bait stores or earthworm farms where they are often called "night crawlers,"* or from biological supply houses.**

Housing

Prepare a container of earth at least a day before obtaining the earthworms. The size will depend upon how many earthworms are to

---

*AQU, DBI and CWF. See Appendix C, pp. 355-356.

**CAR, CBS, CON, MOG, NAS and WAR, Appendix C.

be kept. Almost any wooden, plastic, or glass container will do. A wooden cigar box is satisfactory for one or two worms; a Styrofoam® picnic cooler or wooden box about 30 × 30 × 45 cm will accommodate 75 to 100 worms. Oak barrels or large wooden kegs with holes punched in the bottom for drainage can be used for even larger quantities. As a rough guide, allow approximately 145 cu cm of soil per worm for large species and about half this volume for small species. For certain experiments it is useful to keep worms between two parallel sheets of glass. (See Figure 5-3 for construction details.)

To prevent escape, use a container with sides extending 30 cm above the soil level, or one that has a lid made of muslin, close wire, or even a piece of cardboard (with a hole about 5 × 15 cm covered with wire mesh or thin cloth for ventilation). A light shining on the surface of the soil can be used to prevent the worms from crawling out. A lid, however, retards evaporation and helps maintain an even temperature. If the worm box is kept outdoors, a meshwork or solid lid placed 15 cm or more above the soil level will deter hungry birds.

Fill the container with at least 5 cm of soil from the same site the earthworms were gathered from, or use a mixture of very light loam (never use clay) and partly rotted leaves. Place some of the leaves on the surface. For *E. foetida,* use a half-and-half mixture of loam with well-rotted cow or horse manure. Keep the soil mixture slightly moist by sprinkling with water as needed. A weekly check is usually sufficient, if the humus content is high. Always test for dampness prior to watering. Use your fingertips or squeeze a bit of the earth in your hand. Do not add water if the earth is already damp—overwatering is a common mistake.

Before introducing the earthworms into their container, discard any injured ones. After placing the worms on the soil surface of their new home, wait 15 minutes and then remove as unsuitable any which have not burrowed into the soil.

Keep the earthworms in the coolest part of the room. Avoid radiators and furnaces. Ideally, the temperature should be as near 4.5 to 14°C (40 to 57°F) as possible. High temperatures can be fatal. *E. foetida* are easier to keep at higher temperatures than *L. terrestris.* Indoor room temperatures are tolerated, but the reproduction rate will be retarded. Basement rooms are ideal if fast reproduction is required. Worms kept outdoors will survive cold weather if their bedding does not freeze solid. To prevent this, cover the boxes with hay or a tarpaulin during extreme conditions. If too cold, earthworms will not breed, but will coil up in masses at the bottom of their burrows.

Change the soil every six months.

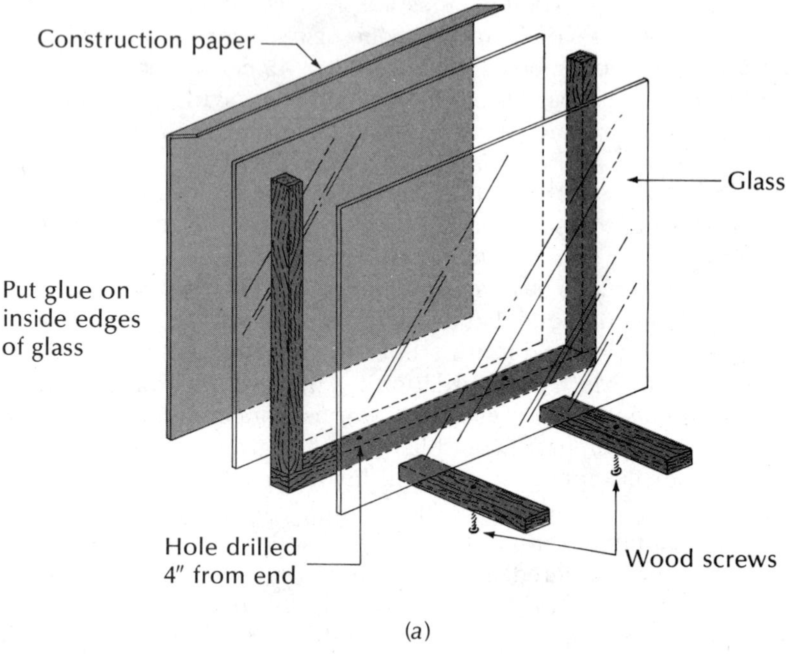

(*a*)

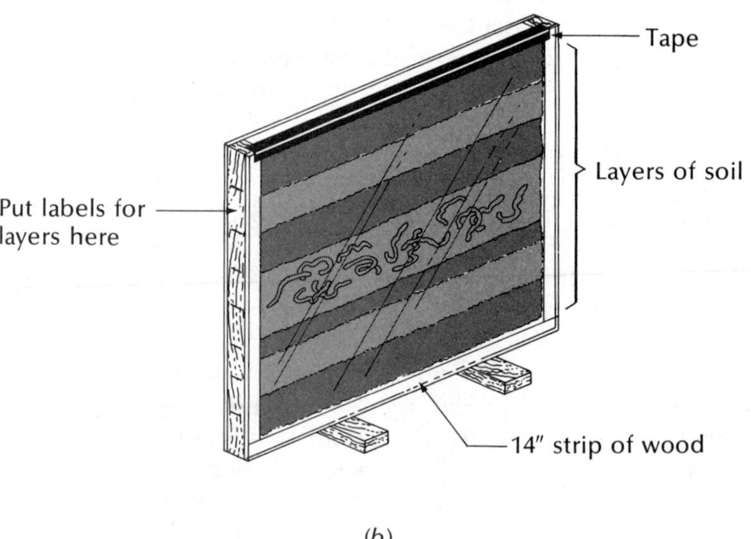

(*b*)

Figure 5-3. An earthworm vivarium.

Feeding

Worms eat decaying organic matter which can be provided entirely by the humus content of the soil. However, it is a good precaution to see that some dead leaves are always present on the soil surface. Renew this supply from time to time. Earthworms gather bits of dead leaves from the surface and drag them underground to eat them. They also extract nutrients from the soil and discard the remainder, forming burrows as they eat.

If the humus content of the soil is low, add a very small amount of bread, cornmeal, Pablum®, or oatmeal every two or three weeks. Mix this gently into the top of the soil. Excessive addition of these foods causes mold.

Reproduction

Worms reach sexual maturity, indicated by a well-developed clitellum, when they are 60 to 90 days old; but they continue to grow in body size until about six months of age.

Earthworms are bisexual; a single worm contains both eggs and sperm. When mating, the two worms face in opposite directions and are held together by bands of mucus. The eggs from each worm are fertilized by the sperm from the other. Both worms then lay brown, orange, or yellow egg cocoons (the color depends on the species) about the size of a rice grain. Hatching time for different species varies from a few days to a month. Each cocoon may produce 2 to 20 young worms (average is 4 to 6). Maintain the cocoons separately from the adults if

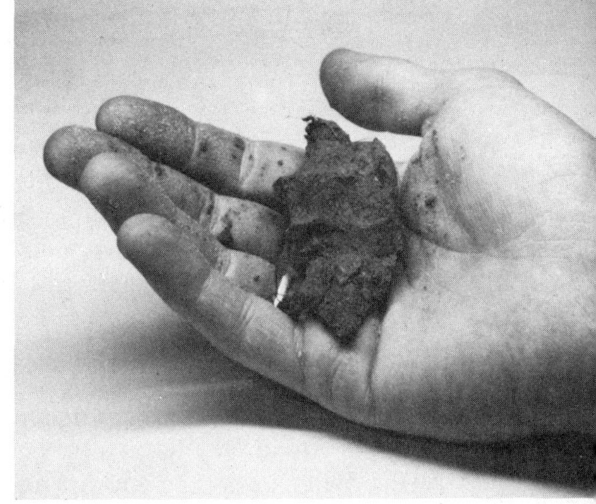

Figure 5-4. Testing for moisture of earth prior to watering. If earth clings together in a ball, do not water since there is sufficient moisture already.

Figure 5-5. Earthworm egg capsules. (Courtesy Carolina Biological Supply House)

you wish to observe the hatching; keep them in covered petri dishes containing moist filter paper. Commercially grown worms will usually arrive with cocoons and young worms mixed in with adults, but hand-collected specimens may take several weeks to reproduce. Once established, a healthy earthworm will produce a cocoon every seven to ten days and will continue to reproduce at all seasons in favorable temperatures. After some months, if the worms become crowded, transfer half of them to a new box or release them in a suitable location outdoors. With proper care, your earthworms will thrive and multiply for an indefinite period.

Earthworms as Food

Rinse the worms in water and, if they are too large, cut them into segments with scissors or a razor. Larger fish will eat whole worms. If the worms are to be chopped up, place them on damp sphagnum moss for a few days prior to killing them. They will eat the moss and deposit previously consumed soil which may otherwise cloud the aquarium.

Killing Earthworms

Earthworms mix and aerate the soil and are beneficial animals. Do not kill them unnecessarily. Disband a wormery by emptying the worms and soil in a favorable location.

A freshly killed earthworm is far superior to a preserved one for dissection. Select large worms. Two satisfactory methods for killing earthworms are as follows:

METHOD 1. Place the worm in a wide-mouthed jar and suspend a wad of cotton, damp with chloroform or ether, from the stopper. Do not let the chloroform or ether touch or drip on the animal, as this causes violent reactions which may be painful and may damage some of the internal organs. When the worm appears dead, place it in a warm solution of 0.7

percent sodium chloride to relax the tissues for immediate dissection. Immersing the dead animal in 70 percent alcohol will preserve it in a pliable condition for several months.

METHOD 2. Shake up a few drops of chloroform in a flask of water. Allow this chloroform-water to drip slowly from an aspirator into a dish containing the worm. Adjust the rate of drip so the worm at no time shows any violent reactions. When it becomes relaxed, usually after about 30 minutes, place it either in sodium chloride solution or alcohol as in Method 1.

Caution: Chloroform and ether are dangerous substances. Only use them in well-ventilated areas. Ether must not be used near open flames as it is highly inflammable.

WHITE WORMS, ENCHYTRAEUS ALBIDUS

White worms, also known as threadworms, look like pieces of fine thread about 12 mm long. They can be collected from cool, moist locations where there is plenty of decaying matter. Search for them on the underside of rotting boards. If you do not find them, they can be purchased from dealers* or from pet or tropical fish stores.

Culture methods for white worms are similar to those for earthworms. Metal or glass pans filled to a depth of 10 to 15 cm with a mixture of good garden loam and decaying leaves (not hard or sandy earth), make suitable homes. If a constant source of white worms is needed, use several small pans rather than one large one, as the cultures usually go through cycles of population abundance and scarcity. Cultures can be maintained indefinitely with no further attention than feeding and watering. Every year or two, add some new soil.

To encourage breeding, add the worms to the container in small, thick groups. Do not scatter them throughout the soil. Cocoons will be laid near sources of food. Rest a glass pane lightly on the surface of the soil, or cover the surface with plastic wrap to retain moisture. White worms grow best at temperatures between 10 and 16°C (50 to 60°F); they will die at 24°C (75°F) and will not breed if the temperature falls to 2°C (35°F).

Feed the worms sparingly once or twice a week. Make small depressions in several locations in the soil surface and push in a few bread crumbs, crackers soaked in milk, or cooked oatmeal, then cover with soil. Vary the diet from time to time. Do not bury too much food or

---

*AQU, CBS, CON, MOG and WAR. See Appendix C, pp. 355-356.

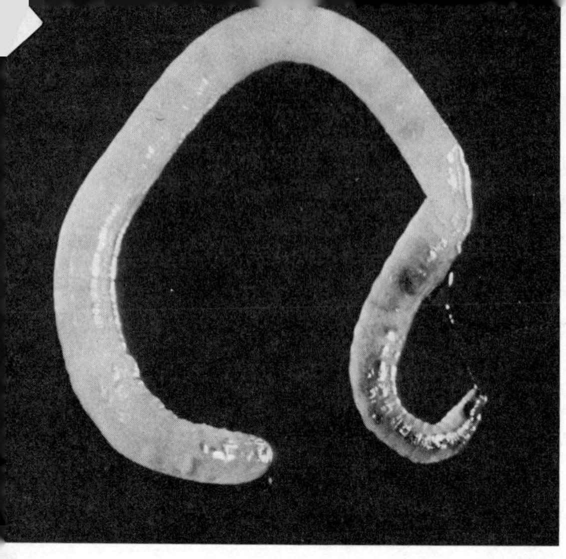

Figure 5-6. White worm, highly magnified.

some of it will mold. Remove old food each time fresh food is added, or wait until all the old food is consumed.

Occasionally, moisten the soil with a laundry sprinkler. However, too much water will drown the worms. If many worms congregate on the underside of the glass lid, the moisture content is too high. Prop the container at an angle and drain off some of the water.

For microscopic study, kill white worms by the same methods described for earthworms.

White Worms as Food

Leave a new culture for six weeks before removing any worms to feed to other animals. White worms collect in balls on the undersides of food and can be removed by hand or with forceps. To free the worms of soil, place them in a paper cup filled one quarter full with water. Within 30 minutes, the worms will have crawled up the sides of the cup where they can be collected, free of all soil. Pet shops sell small glass feeders that float on the surface of aquariums. The fish can see the worms more easily in the feeder.

EXPERIMENTS WITH EARTHWORMS

The following experiments involve earthworm behavior in response to various stimuli (light, heat, touch, moisture, acids); their feeding behavior; their relationships with the environment (burrow system, soil preference); and regeneration. To identify individual worms during experiments, house them singly in labelled plant pots.

Handle earthworms gently and as little as possible. Heat from human hands can anesthetize and even kill a much-handled worm. Wet your hands before picking up a worm. During any experiment, sprinkle the worm, your hands, and the crawling surfaces freqently with water. Never allow a worm to dry up.

White worms usually are not suitable for most of these experiments.

Responses to Various Stimuli

REACTIONS TO LIGHT. Partially cover an enamel dish so that half is in darkness and half is in light. Record the earthworms' reactions when placed with posterior ends in the dark and anterior ends in the light. Then retest them in the reverse position.

Place other earthworms in a box, each half of which has a different level of illumination and, after 30 minutes, determine the distribution of the worms.[1] Repeated tests with decreasing differences in light intensity will demonstrate the earthworms' threshold of sensitivity to light.[2]

Use photographic and other light filters to show whether earthworms can discriminate between light of different wavelengths; try to keep the intensity constant. What is the regional sensitivity of earthworms to light? Use a narrow pencil beam of light to demonstrate which area of the body is most sensitive to light stimulation.[3a] How do low temperatures and depressant drugs affect an earthworm's responsiveness to light?

Figure 5-7. Feeding bread to white worms.

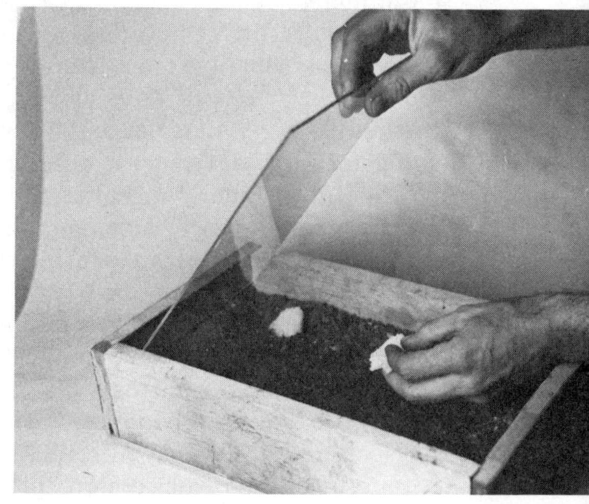

EFFECT OF TEMPERATURE. To study the effect of temperature on the circulatory system, induce an earthworm to enter a narrow plastic or glass tube approximately the same diameter as that of the animal, then plug the ends with cotton. Immerse the tube in water of different known temperatures.[4] Experiment only with cool and warm water; hot water will kill the worm. Under a binocular microscope, count the number of pulsations in the dorsal blood vessel and compare the rates for different temperatures.

RESPONSES TO DIFFERENT SURFACES AND TO MOISTURE. Arrange a series of equal strips of different materials, such as soil, gravel, sawdust, soot, and rock (or use cardboard, wood, linen, blotting paper, bond paper, cheesecloth, and stiff gauze), and provide a small, vertical wall along one end. Be sure all the surfaces are at the same level. Place a worm on the first strip of material, near the wall. The worm will keep close to the wall as it moves along. It may (a) cross over all the strips continuously, (b) turn at the edge of a new material and remain in that one, or (c) turn around and move back. Conduct at least 100 trials, keeping a record of behaviors (a), (b), and (c) to determine surface preferences.

A variation on this investigation employs two strips of soil (or filter paper), one of which is moist and the other dry. Will an earthworm cross the dry region?[5] Is this a common characteristic of all earthworms? Does the width of the dry strip affect the result? Can the preference for wet surfaces be attributed to the greater harshness of the dry surface? Retest the animals on surfaces that remain rough whether they are dry or wet, such as brick and tile. Which is more important for the animal to avoid, roughness or dryness? Will worms draw back from a *dry smooth* surface to go onto a *wet rough* one? Is the posterior end of the worm as sensitive to moisture as the anterior end? Make the animal move backwards onto a dry strip by gently and repeatedly touching its front end. Does it move onto the dry surface about as far as it would if going forward? From these results, what can be deduced about the position of the neural receptors of moisture?

Pour water over a patch of earth and, from soil analysis, determine the critical moisture content which induces worms to leave their burrows and come to the surface. Why do they not burrow further into the earth? Scientists disagree concerning what causes earthworms to leave their burrows after heavy rain. One theory is that the burrows become sealed with water and that this causes a build-up of either gaseous carbon dioxide or carbonic acid solution (to which the worms respond negatively) within the burrows. This, however, seems unlikely in base-rich soils; so what other explanations can there be?

Other experiments on the response of earthworms to contact with water are described by Hainsworth.[1]

RESPONSES TO SALTS AND ACIDS. Compare the ability of earthworms and humans to discriminate between low concentrations of acetic, sulphuric, and nitric acids, and of salts. To test earthworms in weak concentrations of acids, pass a fine thread through the tail end of each worm and lower the animal into various test solutions.[6,7,8] Start a stopwatch and measure the time it takes for the worm to withdraw. Or, divide a small, rectangular glass tray into two compartments with a paraffin partition. Cut a notch 6 mm wide to within 12 mm of the bottom of the partition.[8] Place a different test solution on either side of the partition, and put the test worm across the notch with its anterior end in one solution and its posterior end in the other. Record the response of the worm to various concentrations of solutions—it will enter one solution, withdraw from it into the other, or stay on the notch. Similar solutions could be tested with humans, for discrimination in taste.

Feeding Experiments

Darwin reported that earthworms are able to distinguish between food substances and to demonstrate various preferences[9] Devise experiments to reconfirm Darwin's findings. A simple feeding experiment is to place 100 leaves of a species known to be eaten (lime, beech, willow, poplar, dandelion, groundsel, apple) on the surface of an outdoor container housing 100 earthworms. As leaves of each kind are eaten or carried underground, replace them to keep the number constant. A weekly check suffices. Continue the experiment for several months, recording the types and amounts of leaves eaten or buried in different months of the year, and correlate this with the mean temperature.[1]

Boil pine needles to remove the flavor, which is not attractive to earthworms, and coat the needles with gelatin containing a fine-powdered litter of other leaves. Pine needles are easily drawn into burrows. Investigate the rate at which these prepared foods are eaten, and determine which species of leaves are most favored. Are the results influenced by whether fresh or decaying leaves are used? It has been suggested that accumulation of polyphenols may be important in determining earthworms' selection of decaying leaves. Can the earthworms' selection of certain leaves be attributed to other chemical constituents of plants such as glucose, saccharose, citric or oxalic acids?

Learning Experiments[10]

Worms show daily fluctuation in their learning abilities; they have good and, sometimes, bad days.

A SIMPLE MAZE. Learning experiments can be performed with a simple maze.[3b, 11, 12, 13] Use a plastic T or Y maze 15 cm long. Place a plant pot filled with moistened soil at the end of one of the side arms and a small strip of sandpaper at the end of the other arm. Keep the worm's possible pathways moistened. Place an earthworm in the long arm of the maze. Record the worm's choices between the two pathways, and determine how much time and how many trials it takes before the worm makes 10 consecutive, errorless trials. Usually, after about 20 to 100 trials, the worm will learn to turn consistently toward the favorable side arm.

Since worms are normally more active at night than during the day, perhaps they would learn better if they were trained at night. Test this hypothesis by comparing the rate of learning for night-trained worms with day-trained worms.

HABITUATION. Does a worm learn not to respond when it is repeatedly exposed to a harmless stimulus such as light or touch? Keep a worm in a narrow glass tube in semidarkness on a piece of graph paper. Repeatedly measure the withdrawal response to light (the reduction in body length as measured on the graph paper). Use a 100 watt bulb at a distance of 20 cm, kept on for four seconds[1] Keep a record of the number of trials required before the animal's response finally ceases. At this point, the animal has become accustomed to the stimulus—habituated. After a one-hour rest, repeat the series of tests to see if the worm learns more quickly the second time.

A similar experiment can be performed using touch as the stimulus. The apparatus consists of a ring (about 30 cm diameter) of clear plastic tubing (a Tygon® tube) that has many holes drilled along the top.[14] Place the worm and several drops of water in the tube and tape the tube together to make a circular pathway. After 30 to 60 minutes (for acclimation), touch the worm through one of the holes in the tube with a piece of bell wire 5 to 8 cm long. Use dim lighting of constant intensity for all trials. Each time, stimulate the worm at the same point in the posterior third of its body by touching it for *one second*. Observe and record the animal's response. Repeat at 20-second intervals—recording the number of trials needed until the response has stopped for five consecutive trials. Compare the number of trials needed to habituate the worm on the first and on subsequent days. Are fewer trials needed on subsequent days? Make a graph of the results, plotting the number of trials needed to produce habituation on the vertical axis and the days of the test on the horizontal axis. What is the pattern?

Does habituation of responses to stimulation in the posterior region affect habituation in the anterior region of the animal? How do these results relate to the structure of an earthworm's nervous system?

Environment Relationships

EXCRETORY SYSTEM. Analyze surface casts made by *Allolobophora* species of earthworm for nitrate, calcium, potassium, and phosphate content, and for pH, and compare with the composition of surrounding soil.

BURROW SYSTEM. Between two parallel glass plates, establish a new vivarium with good soil to house the worms. (See Figure 5-3.) Make a sketch of the vivarium to scale, and record daily changes in burrows and in the location of the worms. Try to determine how many openings each burrow has on the surface. Do several worms share one burrow? How closely do individuals come to each other in the burrows or on the surface?[14]

SOIL PREFERENCE. Collect different types of soil: yellowish soil near rock, hard-packed soil along the road, good loam, and sandy soil. Keep each sample in a separate plastic bag. Place the different kinds of soil in a vivarium (Figure 5–3) in layers at least one inch deep.[12b] Use leaves as one layer. Put the "worst" soil, for instance the hard-packed soil, on the top. Mark the layers on the side of the vivarium. Pour in some water (not too much) to moisten the soil. Which layer holds the most water? Add the worms and cover the top and one side of the vivarium with construction paper to provide a dark and a light environment. Watch the development of the burrow system. Are there more burrows on the dark side than on the light side? Do certain layers have more burrows than others? In which layers do the worms spend most of their time? Is this due to the worms' preference for that particular soil or for that depth? Change the order of the layers in another vivarium to find the answer. Do the worms mix the layers by moving the soil?

REACTION TO SOIL. What influence does soil acidity or alkalinity have on earthworms? Make field studies to determine the best soil pH for natural colonization by different species. It is reported that earthworms do not occur either in gardens or agricultural land in Egypt because the soil has a pH above 7.5. Test the pH of different soil types, such as peat moss, acid sphagnum, or limey regions, by stirring a few grains of the sample in water and determining its reaction to pH paper or pH testing solution. (Kits for these tests are available at gardening stores.) Relate the incidence of earthworms to the pH of the soil.

Alternatively, set up a series of identical pots containing good garden soil treated with varying quantities of 0.1 N sulphuric acid or 0.1 N potassium hydroxide solution to produce a pH range from 2 to 11.[15] Add an equal number of worms to each pot and check daily for survival time.

REFERENCES

1. HAINSWORTH, M. D. 1967. Behaviour of Earthworms and Bristleworms. *Experiments in Animal Behaviour.* Houghton Mifflin Co., Boston, Mass. 02107. pp. 47–67.
2. WELSH, J. H., R. I. SMITH and A. E. KAMMER. 1968. Orientation Response to Light; Earthworms. *Laboratory Exercises in Invertebrate Physiology.* 3rd ed. Burgess Publishing Co., Minneapolis, Minn. pp. 100–101.
3. SIMON, S. 1968. *Animals in Field and Laboratory: Science Projects in Animal Behavior.* McGraw-Hill Book Co., New York 10017. (Intermediate) a. pp. 15–17; b. pp. 104–106.
4. SMITH, A. C. 1902. The Influence of Temperature, Odors, Light and Contact on the Movements of the Earthworm. *Amer. J. Physiol.* 6:459–86. (Advanced)
5. PARKER, G. H. and H. M. PARSHLEY.. 1911. The Reactions of Earthworms to Dry and Moist Surfaces. *J. Exp. Zool.* 11:361–64. (Advanced)
6. HURWITZ, S. H. 1910. The Reactions of Earthworms to Acids. *Proc. Amer. Acad. Arts Sci.* 46:67–81. (Advanced)
7. PARKER, G. H. and C. R. METCALF. 1906. The Reactions of Earthworms to Salts: A Study of Protoplasmic Stimulation as a Basis of Interpreting the Sense of Taste. *Amer. J. Physiol.* 17:55–74. (Advanced)
8. SHOHL, A. T. 1914. Reactions of Earthworms to Hydroxyl Ions. *Amer. J. Physiol.* 34:384–404. (Advanced)
9. DARWIN, C. 1898. *Formation of Vegetable Mould through the Action of Worms.* D. Appleton & Co., New York. (Advanced)
10. JACOBSON, A. L. 1963. Learning in Flatworms and Annelids. (Review article.) *Psychol. Bull.* 60:74–94. (Advanced)
11. BHARUCHA-REID, R. P. 1956. Latent Learning in Earthworms. *Science* 123:222.

12. PRINGLE, L., ed. 1970. *Discovering Nature Indoors: A Nature and Science Guide to Investigation with Small Animals.* Natural History Press, Garden City, N.Y. 11530. (Intermediate) a. pp. 91–94; b. pp. 87–89.

13. SCHMIDT, H., JR. 1955. Behavior of Two Species of Worms in the Same Maze. *Science* 121:341–42. (Advanced)

14. RATNER, S. C. and L. E. GARDNER. 1968. Behavior of Earthworms. Stokes, A. W., ed. *Animal Behavior in Laboratory and Field.* W. H. Freeman & Co., San Francisco. 94104. pp. 53–56. Or, Separate No. 807 from the publisher.

15. ARRHENIUS, O. 1921. Influence of Soil Reaction on Earthworms. *Ecology* 2:255–57. (Advanced)

FURTHER READING

ASHBY, G. J. 1972. Earthworms. *The UFAW Handbook on the Care and Management of Laboratory Animals.* 4th ed. Churchill Livingston, Edinburgh, England. pp. 610–613. Section IV available from Universities Fed'n. for Animal Welfare, 230 High St., Potters Bar, Herts, England.

EDWARDS, C. A. and J. R. LOFTY, 1973. *Biology of Earthworms.* Halsted Press, New York. (Advanced)

GADDIE, R. E. SR. and D. E. DOUGLAS, 1975. *Earthworms for Ecology and Profit:* Vol. 1 Scientific Earthworm Farming. North American Bait Farms, Inc., 1207 S. Palmetto Ave., Ontario, Ca. 91761.

LAVERACK, M. S. 1962. *The Physiology of Earthworms.* Pergamon Press, MacMillan Co., New York. (Advanced)

MORGAN, C. *The Worm Farm.* Shields Publications, Box 472, Elgin, Ill 60120

NESPOJOHN, K. V. 1972. *Worms,* Franklin Watts, New York.

SCHALLER, F. 1968. *Soil Animals.* University of Michigan Press, Ann Arbor, Mich.

FILMS

Earthworm. Film loop, super 8 mm cartridge, color or b/w, approx. 4 min. Holt Biology Filmloops, Holt, Rinehart, and Winston, Inc., Box 3670 Grand Central Station, New York, N.Y. 10017

Earthworm. Film loop, super 8 mm, color or b/w. Hubbard Scientific Co., B-3, P.O. Box 105, Northbrook, Ill 60062

Earthworm. Film loop, super 8 mm 3 min. 8 sec., Thorne Films, Dept 17-SL, 1229 University Ave., Boulder, Colo 80302

Life Story of the Earthworm. 16 mm, color or b/w, 10 min. Encyclopaedia Britannica Films, Encyclopaedia Britannica Educational Corp., 1150 Wilmette Ave., Wilmette, Ill 60091

Segmentation–the Annelid worms. 16 mm, color or b/w, 16 min. EBE Biology Program, Encyclopaedia Britannica Films, Encyclopaedia Britannica Educational Corp., 1150 Wilmette Ave., Wilmette, Ill 60091

Worm: Flat, Round and Segmented. 16 mm, b/w or color, 16 min. Coronet Films, Coronet Building, 65 E. South Water St., Chicago, Ill 60601

The Worm Family. (annelids) Film loop, super 8 mm, cartridge, color. Encyclopaedia Britannica Films, Encyclopaedia Britannica Educational Corp. 1150 Wilmette Ave., Wilmette, Ill 60091

Worms—the Annelida. 16 mm, color or b/w. 13 min. Encyclopaedia Britannica Films, Encyclopaedia Britannica Educational Corp., 1150 Wilmette Ave., Wilmette, Ill 60091

6

Pond Snails, Land Snails, and Freshwater Mussels

At sunset, when the night-dews fall,
Out of the ivy on the wall
With horns outstretched and pointed tail
Comes the grey and noiseless snail.

James Reeves (b. 1909)

The second-largest animal phylum has few land and freshwater representatives. The principal ones are land snails (*Helix*) and garden slugs, pond snails (*Lymnaea, Physa,* and *Planorbis*), and freshwater mussels (*Anadonta*). But the sea is rich in mollusks—snails, clams, oysters, mussels, whelks, nudibranchs, squid, octopus, and many more. Mollusks are soft-bodied animals (in Latin *mollis* means "soft"), many of which secrete hard protective shells. With or without the protection of shells, however, they are food for the world.

Sea gulls fly with clams to a height and drop them to break them open. Starfish spend up to half an hour prying open a clam or an oyster. Oyster drills attack still more mollusks, and fish eat numerous species that are unprotected by a shell. Humans eat clams, oysters, mussels, slugs, snails, whelks, abalone, squid, and octopus. Smaller parasitic animals attack the mollusks, completing a picture that is the opposite of the adventure movie theme showing a giant clam, squid, or octopus attacking other animals and men. Some mollusks do present moderate risks to divers and swimmers, but not as voracious predators.

SNAILS

Freshwater and land snails are readily available, easy to keep in a classroom aquarium, and useful for studies of development (embryol-

Figure 6-1. White-lipped land snail.

ogy) and behavior. Snail eggs are much easier to care for than hen eggs, which must be carefully incubated. Also, it is possible to watch the same embryo throughout its complete development, which is impossible with the chick embryo. (Breaking open the shell to observe the embryo will kill it.)

A pond snail has an appearance often copied in science fiction for "beings" from outer space. It has two tentacles, each with a small black eye at its base. Land snails have four tentacles, the upper two tipped with eyes and the lower two equipped with organs of smell. Also, land snails can draw in their tentacles for protection; pond snails cannot.

Among land snails, any of the native *Helix* species can be kept in the classroom. They are good for behavioral experiments. Native pond snails, such as *Physa* and *Lymnaea*, as well as some imported varieties of *Planorbis*, are also good classroom animals. The little brown *Physa* is the most active of all pond snails. It has a pointed shell, coiled to the left, and is extremely common in eastern and midwestern states. *Lymnaea* is a near relative of *Physa*. It, too, is brown to blackish in color with a spiral shell, but the shell whorls to the right. The imported *Planorbis* has a shell coiled in one plane, like a watch spring, and is larger—up to 2.5 cm in diameter. The decorative red *Planorbis corneus* has no pigmentation in its shell but derives its color from its blood. Both red and black *Planorbis* snails are useful for demonstrating changes in color under environmental influences; and because their distinctive coloring is a hereditary trait, they are ideal for crossbreeding experiments.

Planorbis, Lymnaea, and *Physa* species lay eggs, breed easily, and are very good for embryological studies. They are hermaphroditic; a single individual produces both eggs and sperm. They usually mate, however, so that two snails fertilize each other's eggs.

In contrast to these egg-laying species, some snails are live-bearing; the eggs develop within the body, and the young are born already hatched. These snails—for example, the species *Viviparus* and *Campeloma*—make an interesting addition to any collection. Some are native and some are imported. One member of this group is the "trap door" snail (*Viviparus viviparus*); it can close the mouth of its shell by folding over a door on the back of its foot. Many pond snails have this "door" feature, which is a thick, horny pad called an *operculum*. When it is sealed in place, the animal inside can withstand prolonged periods of drying (it "aestivates"). In contrast to other pond snails and to land snails which have lungs, these operculate species breathe with gills that enable the snail to renew its oxygen directly from the surrounding water. The lung snails (*Planorbis, Lymnaea,* and *Physa*) come to the surface of the water from time to time and breathe enough air directly into their lungs, or mantle cavities, to last for long periods of time underwater.

Land Snails

Land snails are easy to catch. Choose a drizzly night or very early morning after heavy showers, and look for them in woodlands and gardens. Search in dark damp places under leaves, stones, or rotting logs. Sometimes they can be "tracked" if you keep an eye out for their

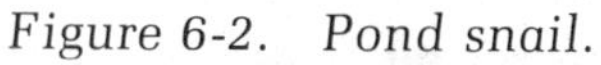

Figure 6-2. Pond snail.

Figure 6-3. Terrarium for land snails.

silvery trails of mucus. The mucus they secrete protects their soft bodies from injury as they move along. Collect some of the leaves, plants, and earth near where the snails are captured to include in their terrarium. Several species of *Helix*, including the common garden snail *Helix aspersa*, are likely to be found among your captives.

In the eastern United States, some of the *Helix* species are relished as gourmet delicacies and can be obtained from food markets. Commercial suppliers of food snails sometimes ship and store them refrigerated alive. If you obtain snails in this dormant state, place them on damp paper in a container; the healthy ones will soon become active.

Land snails also can be obtained from biological supply houses.*

CARING FOR LAND SNAILS. Set up a terrarium in any suitable container; an unused or leaking aquarium is excellent. Use soil, a few stones, and rotted leaves, and place a pan of water in one corner to keep the atmosphere humid. Do not overwater; keep the soil just moist. Snails climb well, so cover the terrarium with a piece of fine screen to prevent their escape.

The common garden snail is hermaphroditic and lays from 40 to 100 eggs in a little hollow at the base of a plant. The tiny snails, when hatched, eat the same foods as adults—lettuce and leaves. Snails have filelike tongues, or *radula*, which shred the leaves into tiny pieces the animal can swallow. Snails gnaw many things, including limestone (which provides calcium for shell growth). The radula can be observed through a hand lens as the animal eats.

Pond Snails

Pond snails are usually found in abundance in lakes, canals, rivers, and streams, especially in spring and early summer. Scoop them up in

---

*AQU, BIC, CBS, CCM, CES, CON, MOG, NAS and WAR, Appendix C, pp. 355-356.

Figure 6-4. Aquarium for pond snails. (Courtesy Carolina Biological Supply House)

a large kitchen strainer tied to the end of a stick; or hand collect them from under lily pads; or collect some weeds and later search for snails hiding among the leaves. If the snails are to be put into an aquarium with fish, scrub their shells with a toothbrush, warm water, and soap; and immerse them for several minutes in a solution of potassium permanganate (of such strength that the water is pale pink) to destroy any external parasites and organisms that could be harmful to fish. Catches in fishermen's nets may yield interesting species. Pond snails also can be purchased from biological supply houses.* However, they are much less expensive if you can find them at aquarium suppliers, tropical fish stores or pet shops.

CARING FOR POND SNAILS. Pond snails will live in a glass of water for a short time. Add a little fresh water occasionally and some scrapings of algae for food. For a more permanent arrangement, house pond snails in an aquarium of any size (about one snail per gallon of water) with gravel or sand at the bottom and some water plants such as *Vallisneria* and *Sagittaria* (see SETTING UP THE AQUARIUM, page 169.) Use spring or well water, or aged tap water, and avoid metal containers. Every so often, replace one quarter of the water.

In an established aquarium, pond snails usually find enough algae to satisfy their food needs; but when they increase in number, they will eat water plants. If the algal population is inadequate, as in newly established aquariums or those which are kept extremely clean, add bits of lettuce leaves or small quantities of dried fish foods. The large pond snail *Lymnaea stagnalis* is a greedy plant-eater, but its appetite can be satisfied if snails of this species are fed a few slices of carrot and, occasionally, a little meat. If the water has a low calcium content, add calcium carbonate (plaster of Paris), crushed limestone, or powdered cuttlefish bone (from pet stores) to ensure proper shell growth.

---

*AQU, BIC, CAR, CBS, CCM, CES, CON, MOG, NAS and WAR. See Appendix C, pp. 355-356.

Figure 6-5. Pond snail eggs.

From time to time, search for jellylike masses of eggs on the glass aquarium sides and on the stems and leaves of plants. A strip of ground or sanded glass 5 cm wide makes a good breeding place. Lean it against the side of the tank, rough surface up, with 5 to 10 cm sloping out of the water. The snails will crawl up the strip and lay their eggs near the top—cementing them to the glass. Whenever possible, transfer snail eggs to a separate jar of water of similar temperature for hatching; otherwise, they may be eaten by fish or by adult snails. The eggs take one to two weeks to hatch. Dried, powdered lettuce leaves and finely powdered tropical fish food are suitable for young snails. When the snails hatch, they have a shell with only one whorl. Usually the pattern is a miniature of the adult shape. As the young snail grows, material is added to the edge of the shell to form a spiral. Adult snails are ready for breeding about eight months after they hatch.

Anesthesia

Anesthetize land and freshwater mollusks by keeping them overnight in a tightly closed jar filled with cooled boiled water (from which air has been excluded). The increased carbon dioxide acts as an anesthetic. Another convenient anesthetizing method for freshwater snails is to sprinkle a few crystals of menthol on the surface of the water in a covered container; then leave the snails in this water overnight. TMS, tricaine methanesulfonate is also a suitable anesthetic.*

---

*TMS is available from Crescent Research Chemicals, Inc., 7050 Fifth Ave., Scottsdale, Ariz. 85251, and, under the trade name of Finquel®, from Ayerst Laboratories, Veterinary Medical Division, 685 Third Ave., New York 10017.

EXPERIMENTS WITH SNAILS

During certain experiments you may need to mark individual snails or mussels for identification. Use a tiny spot of quick-drying oil paint or colored nail polish on the shell.

Egg Development

POND SNAILS When eggs are laid, remove the adult snails and house them in another container. Maintain the eggs in aged water of constant temperature. Each day, until they hatch, place some eggs on microscope slides and examine them under a dissecting microscope. Make measurements of the developing embryos.[1,2] If maintained at 20°C (68°F), the eggs will hatch in about ten days. Does the temperature affect the number of eggs produced? What effect does acidity or alkalinity of the water have on hatching? Does aeration of the water benefit hatching? How does the heartbeat of the embryo change with age? What comparisons of embryological development can be made among different species of pond snails, such as *Lymnaea*, *Physa*, and *Planorbis* species?

LAND SNAILS. The eggs of land snails also can be used for developmental studies. Look for the eggs buried under bark or logs. They are larger than pond snail eggs. They do not adhere to each other, so a single egg can be picked up. Sometimes land snails respond to handling by laying eggs for about 20 minutes thereafter. This may be a response to the warmth of the hands, or it may involve some more complicated reaction. Examine individual eggs microscopically, as described for pond snails.

Breeding Experiments

Crosses between red and black varieties of ram's horn snails are convenient and instructive. Use the *large* ram's horn snail *Planorbis corneus* for these experiments (not the smaller Brazilian type *Helisoma nigricans*). The snails which are to be used for breeding must be isolated when young so their eggs are not fertilized by their own kind. Keep the water temperature between 23 and 25°C (73 and 77°F); in this range the color differences are more clearly defined and development is more rapid. Cross one black with one red snail and follow the coloration of several succeeding generations. The first generation will be all black; the next should be divided into a ratio of three blacks to one red.

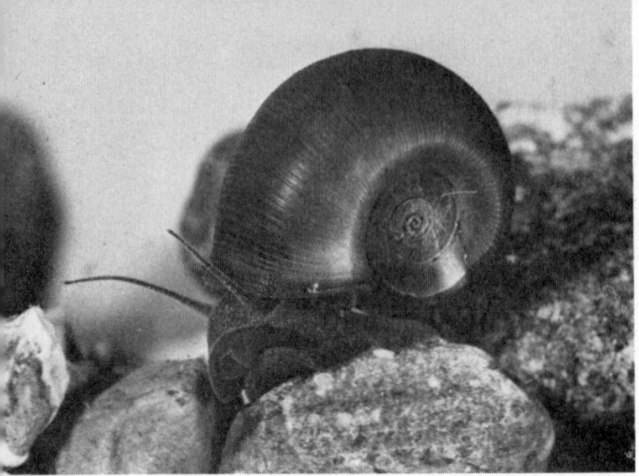

Figure 6-6. Ram's horn pond snail.

Pigment Formation

Again using black and red ram's horn snails (*P. corneus*), observe the effect of temperature on shell pigmentation. The coloration is highly temperature-dependent. When kept at 23 to 25°C (73 to 77°F), red snails develop even if the parents were brownish. In contrast, at 15°C (59°F), the developing snails tend to be a brownish-red. If young, bright red snails are transferred to colder water, they become darker; older specimens will not make this change.

Respiration

To determine the ability of aquatic snails to survive underwater, fill two vessels—one with untreated water, and the other with water that has been boiled to expel contained air and then cooled to room temperature. Put three or four marked pond snails (*Lymnaea*, *Physa*, or *Planorbis* species) into each vessel (without water plants), and count the number of times each comes to the surface to breathe during one hour. Compare individuals of different species for surfacing behavior. Which snails can stay the longest underwater? Vary this experiment by using different water depths or by raising the water temperature. Do not exceed 27°C (80°F), as this would harm the snails.

Sensory Perception

1. Try to test the sense of smell of land snails.[3a] Will snails respond to food placed several inches away? At what distance is there no response? Remove the lower pair of tentacles using forceps with sharpened tips (see ANESTHESIA, page 86). Is perception of smell then reduced, abolished, or unaffected? Watch for regeneration of these tentacles.

2. What is the response of snails to a vibratory stimulus? What is their response to gravity? Do they have a righting reflex? (Will they turn over and right themselves if placed on their backs?)

3. Do snails show any preference for rough or smooth surfaces—sand, mud, rocks with sharp points, or earth? With a feather or the blunt end of a glass rod, test various areas of a snail's soft body and hard shell for tactile response.[3b] Are all areas equally sensitive?

4. Immerse *Physa* snails in water of different temperatures. What is the effect on activity?

5. Set up the terrarium or aquarium so that one end is dark and the other light. Where do most snails congregate? Experiment with light of different wavelengths (colors) by using photographic filters. Do snails prefer red or blue light, or can they not tell the difference?

Defense Behavior

Physa species rotate their shells as a type of alarm response in the presence of leeches, which are their enemies. The leech *Glossiphonia complanata* will attack *Physa fontinalis* and related species of snails. If a suitable snail and leech are placed together in a dish, the snail will twirl its shell. With a stopwatch time this movement and record the number of rotations.[4a] Record the frequency of contact between the two animals and relate this to the frequency of shell twirling. Does the duration of twirling shorten with frequency of meeting?

Is it direct contact that induces the snail's response, or could chemical factors be involved? To test this, place the snail in a dish by itself. Stroke the leech with a brush and bring the brush close to the snail. Does the snail respond with shell twirling? If so, how far is the brush from the snail when this response first occurs? As a control to check the occurrence of the response, use another brush that has not been in contact with a leech. If no response to the control brush occurs, but if a shell-twirling response to the experimental brush does occur consistently, it can be concluded that the snail responds to a chemical substance secreted by the leech and diffused through the water. As a further experiment, test the snail's response to water that has been inhabited by leeches.

In a similar manner, test the closure and withdrawal responses to leeches of operculate species, for instance, *V. viviparus* or *Bithynia tentaculata* (the faucet snail found in the Great Lakes and throughout the northeastern and central United States).

Homing Behavior

Mark certain land snails or, if you are near a seashore, marine mollusks (limpets, for instance) in their natural habitat and check on their movements from day to day. With land snails, try to start with a colony on a bush; then, check on their dispersal in wet weather. With marine mollusks, observe their movements during several high tides. How far do they travel? Do they return to the same resting place?

Aestivation (Resting Stage)

Induce aestivation by crowding snails into a confined space; for instance, pack land snails in a cardboard box so they cannot move. Allow an air space or make air holes; otherwise they will die without air. In this way, snails will aestivate for weeks or months. To remove snails from aestivation, place them in a dish of warm water. Within ten minutes to an hour or so, those that have survived will become active again. What are the factors which cause snails (land, pond, and marine mollusks) to aestivate? How long can various species survive in a "dry" condition? Can operculate species, those with a horny door to close the shell, survive aestivation for longer periods and withstand greater temperature variations than nonoperculate species?

Locomotion

1. Measure the top speed at which pond and land snails can travel.[3c] Prepare a bull's eye chart with concentric circles 5 mm apart (immerse the chart in the aquarium for pond snails). Start a snail in the center and time its travel for one minute. Do this several times, rounding off the figure to the nearest millimeter. Is there much variation in the distance traveled? With aquatic snails, stir a few ice cubes in the water and measure their speed again.
2. Set up four razor blades to fit exactly around the four sides of a small wooden block. Fasten the blades with an elastic band or tape so that the edges of the blades protrude about 2 mm above the edges of the block. Set a snail in the middle of the wooden block. If the snail moves off, it will have to go over a razor edge. How does it do this? Does the snail's foot remain free from injury? Why?
3. Devise a method to determine the weight a land snail can pull. It is reported to be able to pull 200 times its own weight, which is equivalent to a man pulling eight full-sized automobiles. Place varying loads directly on the snail's back and determine the maximum load it can carry. How much weight can it pull up an inclined surface?[4b]

When a land snail is placed on a sloping surface, it will usually creep uphill, not down. If, as it moves uphill, the surface is rotated (from a central pivot) so the snail's body becomes horizontal and begins to point downward, the snail will reorient itself and resume an upward course. This is called a *geotactic response*. Conduct an experiment to show whether this response is due to air currents on the animal's tentacles or to other factors.[5a]

FRESHWATER MUSSELS

Bivalve mollusks have two shells clamped together. Freshwater mussels, called Swan mussels or *Anodonta*, belong to this group and should be considered as possible inhabitants for an aquarium, although they are not very active. Their life span is the longest of all mollusks—about 30 years. (Garden snails live up to 5 years.) Freshwater mussels are available from biological supply houses.*

Freshwater mussels thrive in established aquariums where the plankton content is high. To collect plankton from a lake, river, or stream, tie a knot in the foot of a nylon stocking and insert a tightly fitting jar down the stocking leg so the bottom rests on the knot. Hold the top of the stocking open and net the plankton into the jar.

Be even more careful with mussels than with snails to remove those which have died, because they quickly foul the water. (Mussels are dead if their shells are open more than about 1 mm.)

EXPERIMENTS WITH MUSSELS

Study the burrowing habits of freshwater mussels; their withdrawal response to light;[5b] the closure of the shell in response to chemical stimulation; the effects of cigarette smoke on gill cilia;[6] the activity of the adductor muscles which close the two shells;[5c] and the reproduction of the mussels. These animals also are useful for dissection.

Egg Development

Anodonta species of freshwater mussels provide unusual material for the study of development. Eggs are retained and develop after fertilization in the gills of female mussels. Open a few adult specimens and examine the gills for eggs and larvae. The sexes are separate, but it is difficult to tell which are females unless they are opened. The larvae are small, bivalve creatures about ½ mm in length and occur in enor-

---

*CAR, CON and EVA. See Appendix C, pp. 355-356.

Figure 6-7. Freshwater mussel.

mous numbers. In nature, these larvae are shed and attach themselves to stickleback fish, which act as hosts during the next stage in the mussel's life history. Eventually, the young mussels assume a free-living state again. (In captivity, the host stage usually does not occur.)

REFERENCES

1. DAVIS, H. T. 1969. *Projects in Biology*. Science Publications, Normal, Ill. pp. 123–33.
2. DAVIS, H. T. 1969. The Study of Aquatic Snail Embyros. *Amer. Biol. Teacher* 31(3):165–67.
3. JENKINS, M. M. 1972. *The Curious Mollusks*. Holiday House, New York. a. pp. 208–10; b. pp. 210–11; c. p. 207.
4. HAINSWORTH, M. D. 1967. *Experiments in Animal Behavior*. Houghton Mifflin Co., Boston, Mass. a. pp. 112–24; b. 54–55.
5. WELSH, J. R., R. I. SMITH and A. E. KAMMER. 1968. *Laboratory Exercises in Invertebrate Physiology*. 3rd ed. Burgess Publishing Co., Minneapolis, Minn. a. Geotaxis in Helix, pp. 89–90; b. Light Stimulation of Mya, pp. 102–104; c. Adductor Muscles of Bivalve Molluscs, pp. 120–23. (Advanced)
6. GOSSELIN, R. E. 1965. Effects of Cigarette Smoke on Molluscan Gill Cilia. *Research Problems in Biology*, Series 4. BSCS, Anchor Books, Doubleday & Co., Garden City, N.Y. pp. 57–62.

FURTHER READING

ABBOTT, R. T. 1972. *Kingdom of the Sea Shell*. Crown Publishers, New York.

ABBOTT, R. T. 1968. *Seashells of North America*. Golden Field Guide. Golden Press, Western Publishing Co., New York.

BARTSCH, P. 1968. *Mollusks*. Dover Publications, New York.

BEHRINGER, M. P. 1973. *Techniques and Materials in Biology*. McGraw-Hill Book Co., New York. pp. 65–70.

BURCH, J. B. 1962. *How to Know the Eastern Land Snails*. Wm. C. Brown Co., Dubuque, Iowa.

Garnett, W. J. 1965. *Freshwater Microscopy*. 2nd ed. Dover Publications, New York. pp. 260–68.

Morton, J. E. 1968. *Molluscs*. 4th ed. Hutchinson University Library, Biological Sciences Series, Humanities Press, New York.

Solem, G. A. 1974. *The Shell Makers: Introducing Mollusks*. John Wiley and Sons, New York.

Webb, W. F. 1962. *United States Mollusca*. Lee Publications, Wellesley Hills, Mass.

FILMS

Characteristics of the Garden Snail. Film loop, super 8 mm, color, 3 min. 30 sec. NASCO, Ft. Atkinson, Wis. 53538.

Characteristics of the Water Snail. Film loop, super 8 mm, color, 3 min. NASCO, Ft. Atkinson, Wis. 53538.

Characteristics of Water Snails. Film loop, super 8 mm, color. BFA Educational Media, 2211 Michigan Ave., Santa Monica, Cal. 90404.

Echinoderms and Mollusks. 16 mm, b/w or color, 16 min. Coronet Films, 65 E. South Water St., Chicago, Ill. 60601.

Garden Snail. Film loop, super 8 mm, b/w or color. Hubbard Scientific Co., Dept. B–3, P.O. Box 105, Northbrook, Ill. 60062.

Land Snail. Film loop, super 8 mm, 2 min. 26 sec. Thorne Films, Dept. 17–SL, 1229 University Ave., Boulder, Colo. 80302.

Mollusks. (Clam, sea slug, nudibranch.) Standard 8 mm or super 8 mm, 2 min. 31 sec. Doubleday & Co., Garden City, N.Y. 11530.

Mollusks. (Snail, mussel, octopus.) 16 mm, color or b/w, 14 min. Encyclopaedia Britannica Films, 1150 Wilmette Ave., Wilmette, Ill. 60091.

Mollusks. (Chiton, snail, squid, clam). Film loop, super 8 mm, cartridge, color 3 min. 40 sec. Oceanography Unlimited, 91 Delaware Ave., Paterson, N.J. 07503.

Mollusks: A Story of Adaptation. 16 mm, color, 28 min. McGraw-Hill Films, 330 W. 42 St., New York 10036.

Pond Animals, Parts I and II. (Pond snail, great ram's horn snail, *Hydra*, water beetle, water spider and stickleback.) Super 8 mm, cartridge, color, optical sound, 4 min. Gateway Educational Films, 470–472 Green Lanes, Palmers Green, London N. 13, England.

The Snail. Film loop, super 8 mm, cartridge, color. Encyclopaedia Britannica Films, 1150 Wilmette Ave., Wilmette, Ill. 60091.

Snails. (How they move, eat, hibernate and mate.) 16 mm, color, 11 min. ACI Films, 35 W. 45 St., New York 10036.

Unusual Mollusks. 16 mm, b/w, sound, 11 min. Library Films, 723 Seventh Ave., New York 10019.

7

Arthropoda: Crustacea and Arachnida

"It detracts nothing from the splendor of the human consciousness to recognise that myriad lower forms of life have much of the same biochemistry as does man and that they have perhaps retained superior features of certain common systems."

Donald S. Frederickson (b. 1924)

Arthropods have adapted successfully to every available habitat. There are more species in this great phylum than in any other. Adult arthropods have jointed bodies and legs and an external skeleton that supports the muscles and inner organs. This exoskeleton may be thick and limy, as in crayfish, or delicately transparent, as in *Daphnia*; it is molted and replaced as the animal grows.

Arthropods are divided into many classes, among which are the crustaceans, centipedes, millipedes, insects and spiders. This chapter will be concerned mainly with the care of four common species of crustaceans—*Daphnia*, brine shrimp, sowbugs and crayfish; a concluding section deals with spiders. Insects form such an important class and are so valuable for biological investigations that they are dealt with separately in the next chapter.

Most crustaceans live in water, usually the sea, and breathe with gills. Typically, the young develop from fertilized eggs. Crustaceans are divided into two main groups: the small ones, such as *Daphnia*, brine shrimp and fairy shrimp; and the large ones, such as sowbug, crayfish, lobster and crab.

DAPHNIA

Water fleas are important in nature because of their enormous reproductive capacity. They are the basic food of many fish, both marine and freshwater, and are therefore of considerable economic significance. One *Daphnia* produces a brood of eggs every two or three days and is reported to have 13 billion descendants within 60 days. Great masses of *Daphnia* collect as brown plankton on sea and inland waters. They eat all types of small nonfilamentous algae and some bacteria and protozoa.

Freshwater *Daphnia* thrive especially on *Bacillus coli, Euglena,* and *Chilomonas* and on the smaller green algae which sometimes invade established aquariums. A tank can soon be cleared of unwanted algae by introducing a few of these little crustaceans, which then serve as food for fish, *Hydra*, tadpoles, and larval salamanders.

An aquarium of plants and *Daphnia*, rather than fish, generates much interest in a classroom. A wide variety of physiological, pharmacological and biochemical experiments can be performed with *Daphnia*. Some species, such as *Daphnia magna*, measure up to 4 mm and are visible to the naked eye. Others, such as *D. pulex*, are microscopic. *D. magna* is the preferred species for culturing.

Daphnia have transparent oval bodies enclosed in a bivalve carapace. They have single compound eyes. A vigorous downward beat

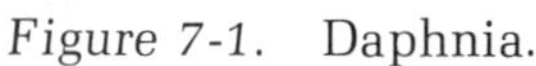
Figure 7-1. Daphnia.

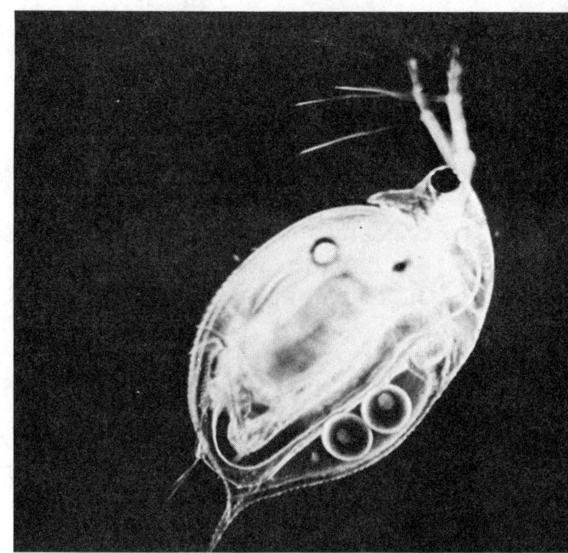

of their antennae raises them in the water. They slowly sink until the antennae beat to raise them again. They appear to move up and down constantly in the water, in rapid jerks. The marvelously intricate arrangement of the internal structure is readily seen with a 10× hand lens or a microscope. The steadily beating heart can be observed in live mounts, in depression slides or welled slides.

Egg cases and developing young embryos are visible in the brood pouches situated above the rear of the abdomen. *Daphnia* produce two kinds of eggs: thin-shelled ones, which are produced all summer and develop parthenogenetically (i.e., without fertilization), and thick-shelled, "winter eggs," produced in the fall, which require fertilization by male *Daphnia* to remain viable over the winter. Dormant winter eggs resume development as soon as warmer conditions prevail.

Cultures of *Daphnia* maintained at room temperature normally consist of only females, but adverse conditions cause them to produce male *Daphnia* as well, and dark winter eggs. Males can be recognized by the straightness of their intestinal tubes.

Sources

Daphnia can be collected at almost any time of the year, but late spring and early fall are the most favorable. They live in the shallow water of most small ponds, lakes, or streams. Ponds fed by barnyard drainage are ideal, but pools on the fringes of city dumps and swamps are also good. Usually, *Daphnia* are found close to the surface around some type of vegetation, away from strong currents. In favorable areas, thousands of them can be dipped up in a cup or jar, but in less populous areas it may be necessary to collect them in round-bottomed (not conical) plankton nets (about 170 mesh per inch), or use fine nylon or cheesecloth. Winter samples of pond water should be matured in the classroom to allow *Daphnia* eggs to hatch. The *Daphnia* can be identified by their jerky movements and can be isolated by means of a capillary pipette (page 14) or eyedropper. They also are available from biological supply houses* or from fish hatcheries and aquarium supply stores.

Culture Methods

It is fairly simple to keep a few *Daphnia* alive in glass jars all year round, but it is not so easy to maintain thick cultures for feeding large populations of *Hydra*. If *Daphnia* are to be raised as food, start with a

*BIC, CAR, CBS, CCM, CES, CON, MOG, NAS, TIM and WAR, Appendix C, pp. 355-356.

Figure 7-2. Materials needed for preparation of stable tea, in which Daphnia *may be maintained.*

pure culture from a laboratory or biological supply house. A collection from the wild would inevitably contain contaminant organisms. All of the methods described below should yield large enough populations to feed other organisms. For some tips on general culturing techniques, see Chapter 2. (Fairy shrimp, *Gammarus,* are cultured by the same methods as *Daphnia.*) The three methods described are about equally satisfactory.

METHOD 1. STABLE TEA. A surprisingly nonmalodorous method of keeping *Daphnia* is a simple mixture of cow, sheep, or horse manure with water—known as "stable tea." Large glass, plastic, or wooden containers of at least one gallon capacity are preferred. Plastic food containers from school cafeterias are ideal. Galvanized metal or copper vessels are toxic and should not be used. Allow farm manure to age seven to ten days. Keep a small supply outdoors, sheltered from the rain in a wooden or cardboard container. Very fresh, dry, or moldy manure is usually not satisfactory.* Use about one tablespoon of manure for each gallon of spring, well, or aged tap water. Do not use freshly drawn tap water; the contained chlorine is toxic. Do not make the mixture too strong.

---

*Suitable animal manure is available from CON, See Appendix C, pp. 355-356, and from large garden supply outlets.

Figure 7-3. Stable tea culture of Daphnia *in large bottle at right. Use a large-diameter dropper for transferring the organism. A translucent light box provides a bright field background for observation of* Daphnia.

Let the stable tea stand for two to three days to produce bacteria. Then pour off a small volume (about 2.5 cm deep) and add some *Daphnia*. Gradually increase the volume to one gallon as the organisms reproduce. Partly cover the culture with a glass plate to retard evaporation, and keep it at room temperature, 21 to 27C° (70 to 80F°). Some cultures flourish in diffuse sunlight; others thrive better in poor light. Try several cultures in varying conditions to see which is best. In one or two weeks, a good population of *Daphnia* should develop, and some can be strained off to feed other organisms.

Every few weeks, strain off or discard about half the culture and make up the original volume with fresh medium. Maintain an adequate fluid volume, as crowded *Daphnia* will not do well. Do not remove the bottom sediment; this often contains viable eggs. It also contains old moltings of exoskeletons which the *Daphnia* cast off as they grow. Microscopic inspection of the moltings will show the outline of the limbs. Markings on the shed carapaces will aid in identification of the species.

METHOD 2. LIVER WATER. Stir about one teaspoon of ground-up liver in three or four teaspoons of water and feed the cloudy emulsion to the *Daphnia*. Start with *Daphnia* in one inch of spring, well, or aged tap water and add a tiny amount of liver water. Gradually, over several weeks, build up the volume by adding water. Every few days, add liver water in very small amounts—too much will foul the water and too little will inhibit *Daphnia* reproduction. Plenty of sunlight is needed. Maintain the culture at room temperature and, when the *Daphnia* become crowded, subculture as described for Method 1.

METHOD 3. *Chilomonas* OR *Euglena*. Either purchase or grow *Chilomonas* (page 28) or *Euglena* (page 19). Keep *Daphnia*, uncrowded, in spring, well, or aged tap water. Add about 200 ml of flourishing *Chilomonas* or *Euglena* culture per gallon of water. Do not overfeed. A few sprigs of *Elodea, Spirogyra*, or other water plant and some mud sediment are desirable additions. Keep the containers at room temperature in good light.

Healthy cultures with sufficient food are slightly green. To increase the population of bacteria and provide food for *Daphnia*, from time to time add a few rice grains, a little yeast suspension, or several ml of egg yolk mashed into a paste with a little culture medium. The secret of success lies in achieving a balance between producing bacteria and maintaining adequate oxygen. Be conservative when adding fermenting agents. Stir in some yeast or egg yolk paste until the water *just* starts to turn milky. Do not add any more until the *Daphnia* have completely cleared the solution, which may take several days. Prevent anaerobic conditions from developing by skimming the surface of the water with a paper tissue to remove the scum that forms. Oxygen is lacking when the normally colorless *Daphnia* become reddish- or pinkish-brown. Unless this is corrected, the *Daphnia* will die. The appearance of the male *Daphnia* indicates overcrowding. To correct this adverse condition, remove and discard about half of the *Daphnia* and medium, or use the *Daphnia* as food. Then top up the aquarium to the original volume with aged tap water and add more *Chilomonas* or other food as experience dictates. Sometimes it is possible to achieve a stable culture in which *Daphnia* reproduction and food production are held in balance. In such cultures, simply replace the water lost by evaporation.

If the culture becomes infected with *Cyclops* (recognized by twin egg pouches carried posteriorly), reculture the *Daphnia*. Select and isolate several of the better egg producers with an eyedropper, and begin again with freshly prepared medium. *Cyclops* can be cultured by the same methods as those used for *Daphnia*, but they will replace *Daphnia* if they are cultured together.

To store *Daphnia* over long vacations, induce the production of winter eggs by chilling, underfeeding, or overcrowding the *Daphnia*. Winter eggs are identified by their dark color in the brood pouch. These egg cases can be collected, dried, and stored up to several months—until it is convenient to set up the culture again. To hatch the winter eggs, place the egg cases outside a window for two weeks of October weather, so they freeze and thaw several times; then place them in water or stable tea to develop. The eggs can be hatched immediately indoors by placing approximately 30 egg cases in a pint container of fresh culturing medium. Aeration may increase the yield. Remove the young with an eyedropper as they hatch, and transfer them to larger vessels. Maintain them by one of the methods already described.

EXPERIMENTS USING DAPHNIA

Daphnia are extremely useful for studying many basic biological principles. Possibilities for laboratory exercises or individual projects are listed below.

1. Using wet mounts of *Daphnia,* determine normal heart rate. If a counting device is not available for recording the heartbeat, which, under normal conditions, is in excess of 300 per minute, use a pencil point. Tap the point on paper in time with the heartbeat, and after a measured interval of time, count the number of dots on the paper.[1] Demonstrate the effects of amphetamine, chloropromazine, tea, cocoa, coffee, carbonated beverages, and various environmental factors on the rate of heartbeat. To test the effect of a given substance, place one drop of its solution on one side of a cover slip under which there is a *Daphnia* and draw the drop through by holding a strip of filter paper at the opposite end of the cover slip.

   What is the effect of temperature change on heart rate? Hold a *Daphnia* still by placing it in the desired position in a dab of petroleum jelly on the bottom of a dry beaker. Add water. Begin with water at 0°C (32°F) and allow it to warm up to room temperature.[2a] At various temperature intervals, measure the heart rate. Make at least two determinations at each temperature and use their average. Test several *Daphnia* to determine the normal range of variation. Make a graph of the results, plotting the heart rate on the vertical axis and the environmental temperature on the horizontal axis. Repeat the experiment using *Daphnia* which have been reared and maintained at different temperatures (for instance, at 21 and 27°C (70 and 80°F). Do these two populations show different responses to temperature change and different upper and lower limits of normal activity? What physiological processes are involved in adaptations to different temperatures? How long does it take for *Daphnia* raised at 27°C (80°F) to become acclimated to 21°C (70°F), as shown by their heart rate-temperature curves?

2. Study the effects of environmental changes on population growth; variables include pH, oxygen, light, temperature, aeration, carbon dioxide, chlorine, and various minerals and chemicals.[3] To study light or temperature preference, place *Daphnia* with their medium in a Plexiglas® tube about 1 m long. Determine their vertical distribution when one end of the tube is subjected to bright light or warmth, so there are gradations in temperature or light along the tube. Use filters of colored cellophane to determine the animals' preference for light of certain wavelengths.

3. What are the effects of waste products on the growth of *Daphnia*—for example, urea, uric acid, manure, urine, and sodium chloride?
4. Plot individual longevity, growth, and reproduction rates.
5. Demonstrate that adrenaline and pituitrin cause spontaneous shedding of eggs from the dorsal brood sac.
6. What environmental factors influence the appearance of males in the culture?
7. Study the viability of winter eggs. What extremes of temperature and drying can these eggs withstand?
8. Compare salt tolerances among *Daphnia*, various algae, protists, and small aquatic worms. Compare the rate of increase in populations raised in distilled water with those raised in tap water.
9. What is the threshold of response of *Daphnia* to light intensity? Does constant light affect the reproductive rate? Compare the reproductive rate of *Daphnia* cultured in constant light with others kept on a 12-hour-light, 12-hour-darkness schedule.
10. Demonstrate the effects of various water pollutants on *Daphnia*.

BRINE SHRIMP, ARTEMIA SALINA

Brine shrimp are small, salt lake crustaceans closely related to fresh-water fairy shrimp. They are very easy to hatch and relatively easy to raise and breed in the classroom. Although newly hatched brine shrimp make excellent food for *Hydra*, small freshwater fish, planarian worms, and sea horses, they are fascinating animals in their own right and should be grown to maturity for study. They will breed in captivity, are inexpensive to keep, and are useful laboratory animals.

Figure 7-4. Brine shrimp.

In the United States, brine shrimp are found in two main regions: in Mono and Little Soda Lakes and along the coast south of San Francisco, in California; and in the Great Salt Lake of Utah. They also live in salt flats and in places where salt water is evaporated commercially. Although they grow very well in a jar of ordinary sea water, they are not found in the open ocean. Adult brine shrimp lay eggs in shallow salt-water pools, and many of the eggs are washed ashore. Collectors dry the small brown eggs to keep them dormant. If kept in cool, dry surroundings, eggs can remain viable for up to 12 years. Brine shrimp eggs are widely available. The least expensive sources are tropical fish supply houses,* local tropical fish dealers and pet stores. Other sources are biological supply houses.**

Adult brine shrimp are pale white or pinkish in color, have prominent compound eyes, and measure about 12 mm. (See Figure 7–4.) They are characterized by 10 to 30 pairs of leaflike swimming limbs which beat 150 to 200 times per minute. When swimming, they orient themselves so that the ventral surface is toward the light, which often results in an upside-down appearance, unlike most swimming creatures.

Hatching for Use as Food

Shallow glass or enamel (not metal) baking pans or trays approximately 36 × 20 × 5 cm are ideal hatching trays. When the brine shrimp larvae are used as food, it is necessary to separate them from unhatched and unwanted eggs. To build a partition in the tray, cut a piece of glass or lumber scrap (a piece of wooden yardstick will suffice) to fit snugly across the width of the pan, leaving 6–mm clearance between the bottom of the partition and the pan. (See Figure 7–5.) The partition should extend slightly above the sides. If wood is used, soak it for 30 minutes in boiling water to season it. Insert the partition about 7.5 cm from one end. Then place the pan in an area out of direct sunlight where it can be left undisturbed. Place the larger compartment nearest the light. (Another method for separating larvae from unhatched eggs is given on page 105.) The best hatching temperature is between 24 and 27°C (75 and 80°F). Lower temperatures are satisfactory, but hatching time is increased. Larvae can survive temperatures as low as 10°C (50°F) and as high as 37°C (99°F).

---

*CBR. See Appendix C, pp. 355-356.

**CAR, CBS, CES, CON, NAS, TIM and WAR, Appendix C.

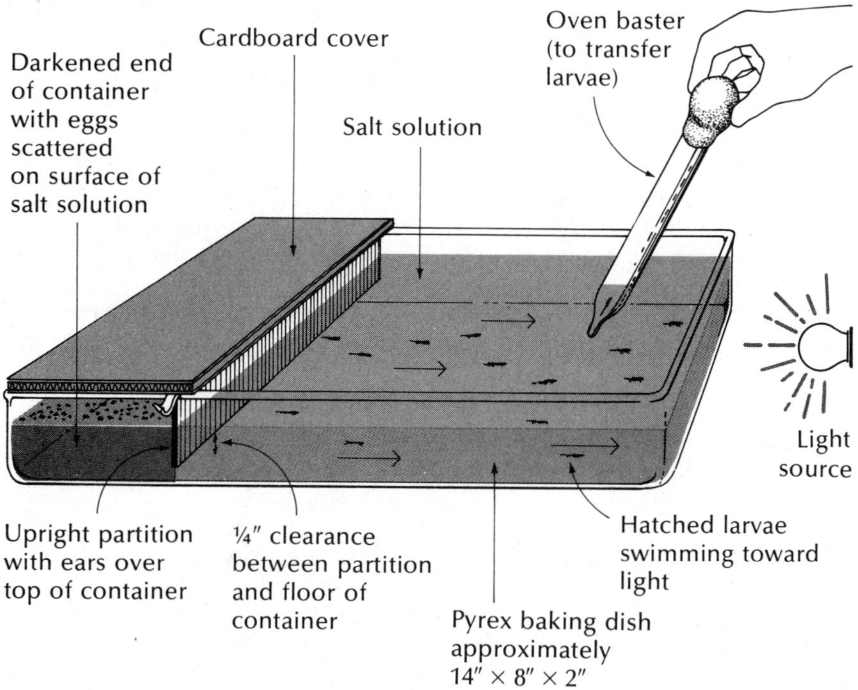

Figure 7-5. Brine shrimp hatching tray. The unhatched and unwanted eggs are separated from the larvae with a partition.

Use eight level tablespoons of noniodized salt in each gallon of water in the hatching trays. Mix well. This gives a 5.5 percent salt solution (5.5 gm NaCl per 100 ml water). (For large-scale hatching it is less expensive to use rock salt, obtained from ice cream manufacturers.) Natural or artificial sea water, with a salinity of about 3.5 to 4 percent, can be substituted. For each pan measuring $36 \times 20 \times 5$ cm, add 2.8 liters of salt water to a depth of about 5 cm. Measure 1.4 gm of dry brine shrimp eggs and spread evenly over the surface of the 7.5 cm strip of water behind the partition. This will yield thousands of larvae. (If the water is disturbed, the eggs will wash up on the sides and will not hatch.) Cover the egg compartment with a piece of cardboard or black cloth. In one or two days, the phototrophic larvae will swim under the partition into the large, lighted area of the pan. Remove them with an oven baster, bulb syringe, or pipette for feeding to other animals. Start each hatching with fresh saline solution.

Larvae will not survive more than five days in the hatching trays unless they are fed.

Salt must not be added to freshwater aquariums, so wash the shrimp larvae before you feed them to *Hydra* or fish. Pour the salt water and young brine shrimp into a small net of fine nylon, silk bolting cloth, or a linen handkerchief. Wash the trapped shrimp thoroughly under a gentle flow of water from the cold water faucet and add directly to the *Hydra* or fish tank. Brine shrimp larvae do not survive more than a few hours in fresh water, so add only enough for one feeding.

Occasionally, eggs fail to hatch due to incorrect salinity, wrong temperature, poor condition of the eggs, or improper relationship of eggs to the amount of water. Eggs that have been too moist during storage will cake together and will not hatch well. Before hatching, oven or sun dry these eggs for an hour in temperatures not above 43C° (100F°).

Detailed instruction for raising large numbers of brine shrimp for food are given in Galen.[4]

Raising Brine Shrimp to Maturity

Transfer newly hatched brine shrimp into a 1–gallon glass container, such as a small aquarium. Fill up the container with more saline solution of about the same strength as that in the hatching trays. Some authorities recommend that the strength of the salt solution in which brine shrimp are kept be gradually increased until a concentration about twice that of sea water is attained. If this is to be done, start increasing the salinity within two or three days after hatching; young shrimp can withstand changes in salinity better than mature animals.

A good solution for mature brine shrimp is made by adding 5 to 8 gm of sodium chloride to each 100 ml of natural or artificial sea water. But a wide variety of concentrations is satisfactory, ranging from four percent to saturation (360 gm per liter), providing the level of potassium is not high. (By comparison, the eggs can be hatched in salt mixtures ranging from 0.1 to 6 percent.) To avoid changes in salinity due to evaporation, mark the outside of the container with a wax crayon or masking tape at the original fluid level and add *freshwater* (not salt solution) every few days up to this mark. It may be necessary to cover the container.

Salt-water algae and bacteria are the natural foods of brine shrimp. Under artificial conditions, the best way to provide food is to add powdered yeast or "quick oats" two or three times a week to produce a good general population of bacteria. Mix a pinch of yeast or a few oats in a little water, and float a small quantity of this on the surface of the culture. Too much yeast or oats will kill the brine shrimp. A general rule is to feed no more than disappears in two days—leaving the water crystal clear. Apart from food, oxygen is an essential requirement for successful maturation of brine shrimp, so artificial aeration is desirable.

Subculture once a month by straining off the brine shrimp in a net, discarding the old solution, and adding new salt water. Mature brine shrimp will die unless the salinity remains approximately the same at each water change. Small amounts of chlorine contained in tap water can also be harmful, so use *aged* tap water or spring or pond water in making up the new solution. Prevent crowding. Return only half the brine shrimp to the original container. Either discard the other half or culture them in a similar container.

Sexing and Breeding

Under ideal conditions, brine shrimp mature in about six weeks and will begin to breed. Females can be identified by their lateral egg pouches. In males, the first pair of trunk limbs is used to hold onto the female during mating and are exceptionally large. After each molting the females are ready for mating and will lay batches of eggs every four to five days when ample food is available.

Brine shrimp larvae go through a nauplius stage (unlike *Daphnia*, which has direct development). The first batch of eggs produced by a female usually goes to the nauplius stage inside the brood pouch and then escapes. Subsequent batches from the same female are "resting eggs," which float on the surface of the water. Remove these eggs and spread them in a thin layer on a sheet of paper to dry. When the eggs are thoroughly dry, store them in a bottle until needed for hatching.

EXPERIMENTS WITH BRINE SHRIMP

Some recommended experiments using brine shrimp cultures are:

1. Compare the hatching rates of cultures kept in a constant temperature oven, in a vegetable bin or crisper of a refrigerator, and at room temperature.
2. Can brine shrimp eggs survive freezing and thawing?
3. Prove that aeration gives better results in hatching and raising.
4. What are the effects of crowding on hatching and population growth?
5. Show by experimentation why iodized salt should not be used for the culture medium. How does salt concentration affect hatching?

6. Is it possible to induce brine shrimp to adapt to fresh water? Demonstrate the range of salt concentration necessary for the survival of newly hatched and mature brine shrimp.[2b]
7. What is the approximate life span of brine shrimp? Assess this by determining when the population is greatest in a hatching tray.
8. What is the influence of salt concentration on the morphology of brine shrimp?[5]

SOWBUG, PORCELLIO

The sowbug is sometimes called "wood louse" and is closely related to the pill bug *Armadillium.* Sowbugs and pill bugs are useful experimental animals as well as food for frogs and toads. They are called *isopods* because their legs are of about equal length. They have flattened, gray-brown, oval bodies measuring about 1 cm long. (See Figure 7–6.) The young develop in brood pouches. Sowbugs and pill bugs are among the few successful land crustaceans. They live in the same ecological conditions and are cultivated in the same way.

These animals can be collected from damp, dark places in most gardens and woods, or around stables and barns. Check under logs or stones (be sure to return these to their original position), or leave a piece of burlap, rotten wood, or a garbage can lid undisturbed on the ground for several days. (See Figure 7–7.) If you live in Florida or California, look for sowbugs and pill bugs under fruit trees where there is rotten fruit. These creatures are slow-moving enough to be easily captured. Or you may purchase them from biological supply houses.*

To maintain and breed sowbugs, start with six to ten of them in an unused aquarium, tin pan, half-barrel, or other suitable container with a fine-mesh screen lid. (See Figure 7–8.) If the container is kept indoors, make sure it is escape-proof. Sowbugs flourish in the dark, so partly or completely cover the container with burlap or other cloth. Provide several inches of rich humus or friable topsoil, or use African violet soil from dime stores or supermarkets. The sowbugs will need hiding places, so add several flat stones, some rotted wood, or a piece of crumpled burlap.

Sowbugs require little attention. Water and occasional food is all they need. Their delicate gill-like breathing organs must be kept moist, so check to see that the soil remains moist (not wet) at all times. They eat decaying vegetation; provide some matted-down autumn leaves, any kitchen vegetable wastes (squash, potatoes, etc.), Pablum® or other

---

*CAR, CBS, CON and MOG, Appendix C, pp. 355-356.

Figure 7-6. *Sowbugs.*

Figure 7-7. *Searching for sowbugs. Whiteworms and earthworms may also be found here.*

cereal. Feed them only about once every two months; do not overfeed them.

Animals collected in the fall and kept at temperatures between 20 to 25°C (68 to 77°F), will bear their first brood of young in February. Mating occurs readily, and a fertilized female is recognized by the eggs carried in a ventral thoracic pouch. After about three weeks, from 10 to 200 young are hatched. Sowbugs will breed and flourish for years in a classroom colony. To dispose of them, release them anywhere outdoors on moist soil.

SOWBUG EXPERIMENTS

There is a variety of interesting experiments involving sowbugs. If necessary, sowbugs can be individually marked with Magic Marker® pens, but these colors fade after a few days. Quick-drying, acetone-base

Figure 7-8. Housing for sowbugs.

paints (used for model airplanes) are quite satisfactory also, but these marks will be lost when the animal molts.

CHOICE OF ENVIRONMENT. Offer sowbugs a choice of environments. Use a hot glass or metal rod to make four holes, evenly spaced, in the sides of a plastic petri dish. Into each hole fit one end of a 10–cm plastic tube large enough for sowbugs to crawl through. In the same manner, connect a petri dish to the other end of each tube, so that the four dishes are arranged in a circle around the original center dish. Provide variations of light and dark, moist and dry, or warm and cool, in the four satellite dishes. Place sowbugs in the center dish and determine their distribution in these environments after several hours. Do all sowbugs prefer a particular set of environmental conditions, or are there some exceptions?[6]

To determine sowbugs' preference for a certain humidity, prepare a shallow rectangular dish with a lid. Across the inside of the lid attach three broad strips of cotton. Thoroughly moisten one end-strip with water. Place 20 sowbugs (mildly refrigerated to facilitate handling) in the dish on a line bisecting the length. Cover and, after one hour, note the number of sowbugs in each half of the dish.[7] Repeat the experiment five times. What proportion of animals prefer a moist to a dry environment?

Shine a light in one half of the dish and cover the other with cardboard. Place 20 animals in the center of the dish and determine which environment they now prefer. Test combinations of variables, such as moist and light compared with dry and dark.[7] Using similar techniques, determine the temperature range that sowbugs prefer.

BIOLOGICAL CLOCK. Determine whether sowbugs are most active by day or night. Divide a dish into light and dark halves. Measure the time taken for the *majority* of sowbugs to choose between the two environments. For instance, if 20 sowbugs are used, measure the time taken for 11 to collect in one end of the dish. Compare these results with measurements made at night using artificial lighting for half the dish. What are the physiological processes responsible for greater responsiveness? Does the response to light change in sowbugs which have been kept in continuous darkness for several days?[8]

HUMIDITY RECEPTORS. Very little is known about the sensory mechanisms of sowbugs. Scientists do not even know if these animals have special nerve receptors sensitive to humidity (hydroreceptors). Cut off the antennae of some sowbugs and see if they collect in areas of high humidity just as sowbugs with antennae do. (A simple method of controlling humidity levels is described in Reference 9.) If they are still attracted to the high humidity, where else might the receptors be? Smear the mouth parts, head, or other regions of the body with petroleum jelly to block contact of that region with the air, and see if this affects their response to humidity.[10, 11]

RELATIONSHIP OF ACTIVITY TO HUMIDITY. Does sowbug activity vary according to the relative humidity? Set up several similar enclosures (such as petri dishes or shallow pans with lids). Air can be dried with calcium chloride, as used in desiccators, or moistened with dampened cotton to vary the relative humidity in the dishes from dry to very moist. (More elaborate techniques for controlling humidity levels are described in the references.)[2c, 12, 13]

Place an equal number of animals in each enclosure and allow the humidity level to stabilize. At five-minute intervals, record the number of animals that remain motionless for 30 seconds in each enclosure.

Calculate the average number of motionless animals for each level of humidity. If possible, determine the relative humidity in each enclosure. (One convenient method for determining relative humidity is to expose small strips of colbalt thiocyanate-treated paper in the test enclosure. This paper changes from clear blue in very dry air to pink at high relative humidities. Dip the exposed paper in mineral oil to preserve the color and match it against color standards for relative humidity.) Make a graph of the results, plotting the number of motionless animals vertically and the relative humidity horizontally. Do the animals become more or less active as the relative humidity increases?

CORRECTING BEHAVIOR. Block one side arm of a T maze. Demonstrate correcting behavior by placing 50 sowbugs in the long arm of the maze with the blocked side arm to the right. The sowbugs will be forced to turn left to escape the maze. Repeat. Then remove the block and immediately retest the sowbugs, recording whether the animals turn left or right. Sowbugs (and other invertebrates) tend to turn in the opposite direction from a prior forced turn. Repeat the whole experiment, forcing a right turn.[14]

CAMBARUS SPECIES

A crayfish, or "crawfish" as fishermen call it, has a typical crustacean horny shell and five pairs of legs, the first pair armed with conspicuous pincers. (See Figure 7–9.) Crayfish look and behave like small lobsters. They live in water and breathe with gills. They are widely distributed in the United States and occur in quiet streams and rivers. The most common species in the states from Tennessee north to Maine, is *Cambarus bartoni*, which is about 7.5 cm long, greenish-gray or brown, and has a smooth carapace. Members of this species mate and spawn all year, unlike those of another common, but larger species *C. limosus*, which mate only in the fall and lay eggs in the spring.

Crayfish are, to some extent, nocturnal. They usually hide during the day under stones or in burrows in the banks of streams, rivers, ponds, and marshes. At night they come out to search for food. They eat fish, water insects, and organic matter; they cannot be kept in aquariums with other creatures, except perhaps water striders which they will not attack. Crayfish are, in turn, eaten by raccoons and otters, and sometimes by campers! They can be kept in the classroom for months or years with very little attention. They are of limited use for experimentation, but their life cycle is interesting to observe. Freshly killed specimens are desirable for dissection.

Crayfish are hardy animals and show signs of disease infrequently. Occasionally, however, the shell appears fuzzy, indicating the presence of fungal growth. Treat it by bathing the animals with streptomycin on a cotton wad.

Collecting and Handling

In some states, collecting crayfish is restricted to certain seasons of the year. Check with your state Fish and Game Department about state laws (see Appendix D, page 356); they may also advise on the best collecting places. Crayfish occur in limy streams, muddy rivers, ponds, and marshes. They are easily collected on night walks with a flashlight on mud flats or stream banks. In the daytime, lift up flat stones and quickly catch them by hand. Approach the animals from the rear and grasp them with your thumb and forefinger on either side of the body just above the walking legs. (See Figure 7–9). Their front claws can pinch quite hard but will cause no serious injury. Press down gently to get a firm grasp before lifting the animal; crayfish can dart backwards at great speed to escape being caught.

Sometimes you can catch crayfish by swishing a dip net around among plants, mud, and bottom debris. The easiest way to catch many animals, however, is to set a trap, such as a minnow trap from a sporting goods store. Lay the trap in shallow water on a sloping bank and partly embed it in mud or pebbles so that the bottom of the funnel is even with the bottom of the pond. A trap set in a favorable area may

Figure 7-9. How to pick up a crayfish.

capture more crayfish in a single night than you will need. Release unwanted crayfish and take one to six back to the classroom in a covered plastic pail *without water*. If the journey takes longer than an hour, pack the crayfish loosely with pond weeds or damp grass. Covering them with water will kill them. Crayfish can live in deep water only if there is enough oxygen dissolved in it, such as from an aerator.

In some areas, state officials of the Fish and Game Department drain ponds to obtain stock fish. They often have thousands of crayfish they do not need and are usually glad to give them away to schools. Live crayfish also can be ordered from several biological supply houses.*

Housing

To replicate their natural habitat, shallow water must be provided for crayfish. Keep them in plastic wading pools at least 1.25 m in diameter. (See Figure 7–10). One to six crayfish can be kept in such a pool. Very large pools must be used if crayfish are to be housed together, as they have a strong sense of territorial rights and will fight if crowded. Cover the bottom of the pool with gravel to a depth of 2.5 cm and add tap, spring, or pond water to about 2.5 cm above the gravel. Include one or two flat stones with the tops slightly above the water level.

Crayfish need hiding places, such as inverted 3–inch plastic flower-pots. Chip out small doorways in the pots with pointed pliers or wire cutters. (See Figure 7–11.) If you wish to observe the crayfish, saw off the bottom of each pot with a hacksaw and replace it with a removable lid of aluminum foil. Provide one pot for each crayfish.

Single crayfish can be kept satisfactorily in 5– or 10–gallon aquariums, plastic sweater boxes, or large enamel dishpans. Metal containers are toxic. Make a sloping, sand bottom and add water to an overall depth of 5 cm. The crayfish should be able to walk out of the water onto the sand.

Do not keep crayfish near radiators or in the sun; high temperatures can be harmful. An air temperature between 18 and 24°C (64 and 75°F) is satisfactory.

If a crayfish loses a limb, it will regenerate it after the next molt. Isolate dismembered animals to protect them from attack by other crayfish and to observe the regeneration process, which sometimes takes weeks or months.

---

*BIC, CBS, CCM, CES, CON, MOG, NAS and TIM. See Appendix C, pp. 355-356.

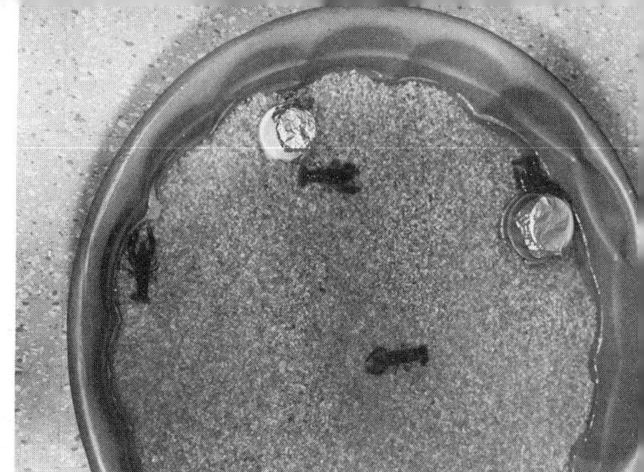

Figure 7-10. Looking down on a child's plastic wading pool set up for keeping crayfish.

Figure 7-11. Plastic flower pot converted into a crayfish home.

CLEANING THE TANK. The water in small containers should be changed every other day, not just for cleanliness but to provide enough oxygen. Water may be changed less often if an aerator is used. Sudden changes in temperature can be harmful, so allow the tap, spring, or pond water to stand at room temperature for 24 hours before using. Remove the crayfish to a temporary container. They can remain out of water for five to ten minutes without harm, but do not leave them untended on a desk or in a low dish—even a short fall can injure them. Remove as much water as possible from the tank, wipe the sides with paper towels, and add freshwater of approximately the same temperature. Do not use soap or detergent to clean the container; toxic residues are difficult to rinse away.

Large crayfish pools need not be cleaned very often if feeding is done outside the tank and dead crayfish are not left to foul the water. Considerable evaporation may take place from such a large surface area, especially in dry atmospheres, so check the water level each day. If a depth of 7.5 cm is maintained, the water level will not have to be watched so closely; but an aerator is then essential.

Feeding

Crayfish will eat almost any kind of fresh or frozen fish. If you have a freezer, one package of inexpensive frozen fish will provide food for several months. Canned fish, raw liver or beef, chopped earthworms, insects, and tadpoles also make good food. Dry or cooked Pablum® is particularly appetizing. Crayfish should not be fed to the limits of their appetites, or they will become inactive.

If crayfish are housed in portable containers that are easily cleaned, small amounts of food can be added directly to the tank, but the container must be cleaned soon after feeding. Build-up of bacteria from decaying leftovers will reduce the oxygen supply. Cleaning can be done less frequently if a mechanical aerator is used.

If, however, a container such as a wading pool is used, the crayfish must be removed for feeding. Place the crayfish in a large culture dish, enamel pan, or other suitable feeding container, in 1 cm of water. Crayfish may not eat if placed in a different temperature, so use water from the big pool. Add small pieces of food to the water. When the crayfish have eaten, return them to the stock aquarium—taking care that none of the uneaten food is returned. Discard the water and surplus food in the feeding dish. Normally, crayfish should be fed once or twice a week.

Molting

Animals with external skeletons, such as crayfish, molt in order to grow. This usually occurs in the spring, although young crayfish may molt every two or three months until they are two years old. The process of shedding an outgrown shell takes only a few minutes. Underneath, a new shell has already formed. Newly molted crayfish appear lighter in color for a few hours. They swell up with water to stretch the soft, new shell. The animal is exceedingly vulnerable before the new shell hardens and may be killed by other crayfish, especially in overcrowded conditions. A molting crayfish can survive this period housed with other crayfish only if the tank is very large and adequate hiding places are provided. It is usually better to house softshelled crayfish in isolation for four to five days until their shells harden. Old shells are often eaten by crayfish, so collect them promptly for examination. Successive molts provide an accurate visual record of the growth of the animal.

Sexing and Breeding

To determine the sex of crayfish, look at the first pair of appendages on the tail. In the male, these are long and conspicuous; but in the female they look just the same as the swimmerets. Also, the female's swimmerets are often larger and look fuzzier than the male's, and her tail is broader.

Crayfish become fertile at the end of the summer, and they usually mate during the fall or winter months. Copulation may take a few minutes or a few hours and can sometimes be observed. The male deposits sperm on the outside of the female's body near the oviduct. The sperm may remain stored there for many months. In the spring, the female finds a dark hiding place, lies on her back, and prepares a glue-lined basket on the underside of her body. About 500 eggs pour out from the oviduct and are fertilized by the sperm on the outside of her body. The fertilized eggs remain attached to the underside of her body and are carried around for up to two months.

During this period, provide an egg-carrying female with a spacious home of her own in spring or pond water. If tap water must be used, *age it* to remove harmful chlorine. It is not necessary to feed the female. If a glass bottom tank is available, elevate it on legs 7.5 cm high, and place a mirror under the tank to observe the eggs.

If the female is handled or disturbed in any way, she will eat the eggs. Eggs floating free in the water are dead; remove them and change the water. When the eggs hatch, generally around the middle of May, the offspring take a firm hold on the female's swimmerets with their pincers and are transported about and protected for a week or two. Gently handle the female during this period and examine the 20 to 30 offspring with a hand lens. The tiny crayfish grow rapidly, shed their shells several times, and finally drop their hold on the mother and lead independent lives.

Vacation Care

Weekend care presents no problems, as crayfish only need to be fed once or twice a week. Occasionally, they can be left up to a month without feeding. Students may take them home for longer vacations. Under exceptional circumstances, it is possible to keep them in cold storage for several weeks. Place them on damp filter paper in the crisper drawers of a refrigerator.

Disposing of Crayfish

At the completion of the study, release crayfish in their natural habitat on the banks of streams or rivers. Or painlessly kill them by placing them in a heat-proof vessel and *slowly* raising the temperature to about 40°C (104°F). To prevent animals at the bottom of the pot from feeling the heat, use a small wire or metal lattice to keep them from direct contact with the vessel.[15] This painless method can be used for other crustaceans, such as crabs.

Animals that die from natural causes or are killed can be preserved for dissection by placing them in closed jars containing equal parts of rubbing alcohol and water.

EXPERIMENTS USING CRAYFISH

When it is necessary to identify individual crayfish for experiments, mark the animals with coded dots applied to the carapace. (See Figure 7–12.) First wipe the shell dry; then, using a solid glass rod or felt pen, apply a very small amount of colored nail polish or indelible ink. Large amounts can be toxic and may kill the animal. Allow about ten minutes for the markings to dry before returning the crayfish to the water.

1. Build an activity cage for crayfish, and study the effects of differing light and dark periods on voluntary movement.[2d, 16, 17] Basically, the apparatus consists of a lightweight cylinder of Plexiglas® which holds the animal and some water and allows adequate ventilation. The cylinder is attached to a device which records the number of revolutions made. Inexpensive 24-hour recorders can be made from electrically-driven chart mechanisms.*
2. Observe the social order that evolves when four or five crayfish share a small territory such as a plastic wading pool. During this study, crayfish should not be handled frequently, as this affects their behavior. Use crayfish of the same sex, marked for identification. Do crayfish ever share the same hiding place? Does one crayfish ever

---

*Available from Warren Telechron Co., Ashland, Mass. 01721.

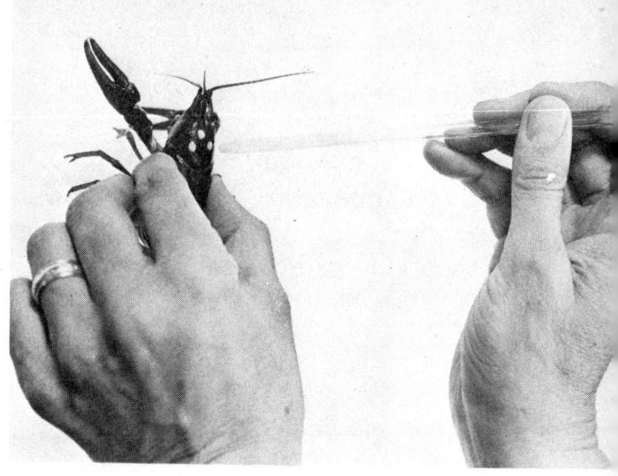

Figure 7-12. Applying a small amount of colored nail varnish to identify individual crayfish.

oust another from its hiding place? What happens if only one hiding place is provided for the whole group? If the dominant crayfish is removed? If one crayfish of the opposite sex is added to the pool?

3. Make photographic records of color changes in crayfish when different colored gravel is placed in the tank. Dramatic changes can be induced over a period of a few weeks.

SPIDERS

With black, wicked eyes, hairy thin legs and
creepy crawly movements
Black shoe polish coat shining dully.
Hairy black thin legs.
Beautiful, silky and soft web
Dew hangs like miniature diamonds on lacy
fingers.
A quick movement and this monster
disappears.

J. Jenkins (age 10)

Many spiders can be kept in captivity, as they are sedentary and have simple food requirements. Collect them indoors, or from woods, fields, or gardens, or purchase them from a biological supply house.* A large jar with a muslin lid is ideal for housing most spiders. Burrowing spiders need several inches of earth, and web-building spiders require plenty of space. Provide the largest container available.

*CBS and NAS. See Appendix C, pp. 354–355.

The garden spider *Argiope* will survive satisfactorily in a humid atmosphere on a diet of fruit flies or houseflies. Try several kinds of insects to find the spiders' preference. Some spiders can go for long periods without any food, but do sprinkle the cage and the web, if any, with water regularly.

EXPERIMENTS USING SPIDERS

Study the natural habitats of different species of spiders and their web-building techniques.[18, 19, 20]

Take web prints and compare the different web patterns of various species. To make a print, remove the spider, and coat both sides of the web by spraying white paint sparingly from a side angle. Use either enamel paint or Grumbacher Tuffilm® plastic spray from art supply stores. Lean a sheet of construction paper against the web, gently touching the paper to the whole web at once. Snip off the guy lines at the paper's edge, and set aside to dry.

REFERENCES

1. Allen, D. 1968. The Use of *Daphnia* in High School Biology. *Amer. Biol. Teacher* 30:397–98.

2. Welsh, J. H., R. I. Smith and A. E. Kammer. 1968. *Laboratory Exercises in Invertebrate Physiology*. 3rd ed. Burgess Publishing Co., Minneapolis, Minn.
   a. Q_{10} of Heart Rate and Respiratory Movement in *Daphnia*, pp. 32-34.
   b. Osmotic and Ionic Relations in *Artemia*, pp. 65-66.
   c. Determination of Atmospheric Humidity, pp. 188-90.
   d. Diurnal Rhythms, pp. 159-60.

3. Goldstein, P. and J. Metzner. 1971. *Experiments with Microscopic Animals*. Doubleday & Co., Garden City, N.Y. pp. 103-108.

4. Galen, D. F. 1969. Hatching Techniques for *Artemia*—Brine Shrimp. *Turtox News* 47(3):106–110.

5. Heim, W. G. 1976. The Influence of Salt Concentration on the Morphology of the Brine Shrimp, *Artemia gracilis* Verril. *Research Problems in Biology*, Series 2. Second Ed. Biological Sciences Curriculum Study, Oxford University Press, New York. pp. 129–130 (Advanced)

6. Man and the Environment—*Life Science Investigations*. 1971. Educational

Research Council of America. Houghton Mifflin Co., Boston, Mass. pp. 169–74.

7. HAINSWORTH, M. D. 1967. Behaviour of Arthropods Other than Insects. *Experiments in Animal Behaviour.* Houghton Mifflin Co., Boston Mass. pp. 91–108.

8. CLOUDSLEY-THOMPSON, J. L. 1952. Studies in Diurnal Rhythms, II, Changes in the Physiological Responses of the Woodlouse *Oniscus asellus* to Environmental Stimuli. *J. Exp. Biol.* 29:295–303. (Advanced)

9. HEIM, W. G. 1972. Device for Controlled Humidification. *Amer. Biol. Teacher* 34(2):101.

10. EDNEY, E. B. 1954. Woodlice and the Land Habitat. *Biol. Rev.* 29:185–219. (Review article). (Advanced)

11. GUNN, D. L. 1937. The Humidity Reactions of the Woodlouse, *Porcellio scaber. J. Exp. Biol.* 14:178–86. (Advanced)

12. EDNEY, E. B. 1953. The Construction and Calibration of an Electrical Hygrometer Suitable for Microclimatic Measurements. *Bull. Entomol. Res.* 44:333–42. (Advanced)

13. SALOMON, M. E. 1951. Control of Humidity with Potassium Hydroxide, Sulphuric Acid, or Other Solutions. *Bull. Entomol. Res* 42:543–54. (Advanced)

14. HUGHES, R. N. 1966. Some Observations of Correcting Behavior in Woodlice (*Porcellio scaber*). *Animal Behav.* 14:319. (Advanced)

15. GUNTER, G. 1961. Painless Killing of Crabs and Other Large Crustaceans. *Science* 133:327. (Reprints available free from Massachusetts S.P.C.A., 180 Longwood Ave., Boston, Mass. 02115.)

16. DAVIS, H. T. 1969. *Projects in Biology.* Science Publications, Normal, Ill. pp. 100–102.

17. GUYSELMAN, J. B. 1957. Solar and Lunar Rhythms of Locomotor Activity in the Crayfish *Cambarus virilis. Physiol. Zool.* 30:70–87. (Advanced)

18. EMERTON, J. H. 1902. *Common Spiders of the United States.* Dover Publications, New York.

19. SNOW, K. R. 1970. *The Arachnids.* Columbia University Press, New York.

20. WITT, P. N. 1976. Spider Web-Building as an Example of an Innate Behavior Pattern. *Research Problems in Biology.* Series 2, Second Ed. Biological Sciences Curriculum Study. Oxford University Press, New York. pp.23–26.

FURTHER READING

Daphnia

JOHNSON, W. J. 1970. *Daphnia* in the Classroom. *Amer. Biol. Teacher* 32(6): 365–66.

MASTERS, C. O. 1970 *Daphnia* Farming. *Ward's Bull.* 66(9):1–4. Ward's Natural Science Establishment, Inc., Rochester, N.Y.

MORHOLT, E., P. F. BRANDWEIN and A. JOSEPH. 1966. *A Sourcebook for the Biological Sciences.* 2nd ed. Harcourt Brace Jovanovich, New York.

NEEDHAM, J. G., 1937. *Culture Methods for Invertebrate Animals.* Dover Publications, New York. p. 207–20.

Rearing of Daphnia *and Related Arthropods.* Culture Leaflet No. 12. Ward's Natural Science Establishment, Inc. Rochester, N.Y.

ZIEGENHAGEN, G. 1969. Sustained Culturing of *Daphnia. Amer. Biol. Teacher* 31(9): 597–99. December.

Brine Shrimp

The Brine Shrimp and How to Hatch Its Eggs. San Francisco Aquarium Society, Inc., California Academy of Sciences, San Francisco, Cal. 94118.

GANNON, R. 1960. *Live Foods for Aquarium Fishes. T.F.H. Publications, Jersey City, N.J. pp. 18–20.*

LOOMIS, W. F. and H. M. LENHOFF. 1956. Growth and Sexual Differentiation of *Hydra* in Mass Culture. *J. Exp. Zool.* 132:555–74. (Describes methods of culture of brine shrimp.) (Advanced)

PRINGLE, L., ed. 1970. *Discovering Nature Indoors: A Nature and Science Guide to Investigation with Small Animals.* Natural History Press, Garden City, N.Y. pp. 95–99. (Intermediate)

Sowbugs

SUTTON, S. 1972. *Woodlice.* Ginn and Co., Ltd., 18 Bedford Row, London WC1 4EJ, England. (Advanced)

Crayfish

CROCKER, D. W. and D. W. BARR. 1967. *Handbook of the Crayfish of Ontario.* University of Toronto Press, Toronto, Canada. (Advanced)

MOORE, C. B. 1954. *The Book of Wild Pets.* Charles T. Branford Co., Boston.

MORGAN, A. A. 1959. *Aquarium Book for Boys and Girls.* Charles Scribner's Sons, New York. (Intermediate)

SCHMITT, W. L. 1965. *Crustaceans.* University of Michigan Press, Ann Arbor. (Advanced)

STRAYER, J. L. 1969. Living Crayfish in the Laboratory. *Amer. Biol. Teacher* 31:162–64.

FILMS

Daphnia

Life Story of a Water Flea—Daphnia. 16 mm, color or b/w, 10 min; or film loop, super 8 mm, cartridge, color. Basic Life Science Series. Encyclopaedia Britannica Films, 1150 Wilmette Ave., Wilmette, Ill. 60091.

Pond Community. (Includes *Daphnia,* backswimmers, giant water bug and frog.) Film loop, super 8 mm, color or b/w. Hubbard Scientific Co., P. O. Box 105, Northbrook, Ill. 60062.

Brine Shrimp

Brine Shrimp. 16 mm, color, silent, and *Brine Shrimp I* and *Brine Shrimp II.* Film loops. Elementary Science Study Films. Holt, Rinehart and Winston, Inc., Media Department, 383 Madison Ave., New York 10017.

Brine Shrimp. Film loop, super 8 mm, cartridge, color or b/w, approx. 4 min. Holt Biology Film Loops. Holt, Rinehart and Winston, Inc., Media Department, 383 Madison Ave., New York 10017.

Brine Shrimp. Film loop, super 8 mm, color or b/w. Hubbard Scientific Co., Dept. B-3, P. O. Box 105, Northbrook, Ill. 60062.

The Story of the Brine Shrimp. (Also covers the tropical fish hobby.) 16 mm, sound, color, 30 min. San Francisco Aquarium Society, California Academy of Sciences, San Francisco, Ca 94118.

Sowbug

Isopod. Film loop, super 8 mm, 1 min. 41 sec. Thorne Films, Dept. 17–SL, 1229 University Ave., Boulder, Colo. 80302.

Crayfish

Crayfish. Film loop, super 8 mm, color or b/w, approx. 4 min. Holt Biology Film Loops. Holt, Rinehart and Winston, Inc., Media Department, 383 Madison Ave., New York 10017.

Crayfish. Film loop, super 8 mm, color or b/w. Hubbard Scientific Co., P. O. Box 105, Northbrook, Ill. 60062.

Crayfish. Film loop, super 8 mm, color, 2 min. 33 sec. Thorne Films, Dept. 17–SL, 1229 University Ave., Boulder, Colo. 80302.

The Crayfish. 16 mm, color or b/w, 15 min. McGraw-Hill Textfilms, 330 W. 42nd St., New York 10036.

Life Story of the Crayfish. 16 mm, color or b/w, 10 min. Encyclopedia Britannica Films, 1150 Wilmette Ave., Wilmette, Ill. 60091.

Spiders

Spiders. Film loop, super 8 mm, color or b/w. Hubbard Scientific Co. P. O. Box 105, Northbrook, Ill. 60062.

Spiders.—Capturing of Prey. Film-loop, super 8 mm, 3½ min. International Communications Films, NASCO, Ft. Atkinson, Wisc. 53538.

Spiders—Courtship and Mating. Film loops, super 8 mm, Part I, 3½ min., Part II, 3 min. International Communication Films, NASCO, Ft. Atkinson, Wisc. 53538.

Arthropods

Arthropods: Insects and Their Relatives. 16 mm, color or b/w, 11 min. Coronet Films, 65 E. South Water St., Chicago, Ill. 60601.

Collecting Small Arthropods—Berlese Funnel. Super 8 mm, cartridge, silent, color, 3 min. Biological Techniques Series. Encyclopedia Britannica Films, 1150 Wilmette Ave., Wilmette, Ill. 60091.

Crustaceans. (*Daphnia,* sowbug and fiddler crab.) Film loop, super 8 mm, cartridge, color, 3 min. 40 sec. Oceanography Unlimited, Inc., 91 Delaware Ave., Paterson, N.J. 07503.

8

Insects

i once heard the survivors
of a colony of ants
that had been partially
obliterated by a cows foot
seriously debating
the intention of the gods
towards their civilization

the bees got their
governmental system settled
millions of years ago
but the human race is still groping

Don Marquis (1878–1937)

GENERAL INFORMATION

There are many thousands of insect species. Some are helpful—many plants would not bear fruit without insects to pollinate them; we get silk from silkworm cocoons and shellac from Indian lac insects. Some food products also come from insects. On the other hand, insects spread malaria, yellow fever, and bubonic plague, which even today cause extensive human suffering. Insects damage agricultural crops and harass domestic animals and humans. Other species, such as gnats, flies, and mosquitos, are simply nuisances.

An insect's body is divided into three main regions (head, thorax, and abdomen), with an exoskeleton and three pairs of jointed legs. Insects are used in studies of life cycles, individual and social behavior, special senses, communication, learning, genetics, and other investigations.

Most insects grow from egg to adult by one of two schemes: *incomplete metamorphosis,* with only a pupal stage between egg and adult; or *complete metamorphosis,* with both larval and pupal stages. Grasshoppers, cockroaches, milkweed bugs, and praying mantises have incomplete metamorphosis. In these species, the young are very much like the adults, but are smaller and have no wings.

In more advanced species, which show complete metamorphosis, the eggs hatch into larvae that are quite different from adults. These species undergo a quiescent stage (called *pupa* or *chrysalis*), during which they are transformed into adults; examples are ants, fruit flies, houseflies, mealworms, and wax moths.

Where to Find Insects[1,2,3,4]

Both federal and state laws control the shipping of some insect species to prevent the spread of harmful pests. A list of some commercial suppliers who distribute insects nationally is provided in Appendix C. Permission for shipment of pest insects must be obtained from federal and/or state plant quarantine officials.*

In general, it is advisable to use local insects, which can be found almost anywhere—insects have adapted to nearly every environmental niche.

If the local insects are not suitable for your experiments, others can be obtained from supply houses.** Entomological, government or commercial testing laboratories, state extension services, or zoos (which raise insects for reptile food) frequently will help teachers and students obtain live insects.

Studying Insects in Nature

Some insects can be studied more successfully in nature than in the classroom. A muslin bag, securely fastened around an entire branch or twig infested with insects, provides an excellent outdoor cage for such leaf-mining and leaf-eating insects as tent caterpillars and bagworms. The larvae cannot escape and the insects are protected from birds. When the leaves are eaten, move the cage and insects to another branch. In time, the larvae will become fully fed and less active and are

---

*For permits and information about interstate shipment of pest insects including Lepidoptera (butterflies and moths), ants, cockroaches, crickets, and milkweed bugs, write to: Veterinary Services, Animal Plant Health Inspection Service, USDA, Federal Building, Hyattsville, Maryland 20782.

**See Appendix C, pp. 355-356.

ready to pupate. Some larvae pupate in soil, and some species pupate on the branch. For those which pupate in soil, open one end of the muslin cage and tie it around a pot of soil or peat. The larvae will move down into the soil, and, in time, the adults will emerge. Larvae of insects that do not pupate in soil will spin cocoons inside the cage. The branch on which the cocoon is developing can then be placed in a gauze cage and taken for closer observation. (See Figure 8–7.) The adult will emerge faster indoors than out. (For further details on care, see BUTTERFLIES AND MOTHS, page 131.)

Aquatic insects can be studied in local ponds, lakes, or streams. Enclose nymphs in a wire or gauze cage, part of which projects above the water. Food, of course, must be provided. A suitable diet for carnivorous forms includes fly maggots, fruit flies, ant larvae, *Daphnia* species, or mealworms. For herbivorous species, include a few stones covered with algae.

Selecting Classroom Insects

Insects are easy to maintain in a classroom and can survive weekends and week-long school vacations without daily care. They can be raised as food for crayfish, fish, frogs, lizards, and snakes.

Select a hardy species with a short life cycle. Indoor insects are the easiest to keep. Natural habitats and food should be provided for any outdoor insects that you bring into the classroom. In some regions, leaf-eating insects may be difficult to maintain in winter without a greenhouse. (Putting such insects in a greenhouse may mean sacrificing your plants.) Rearing some insects through all stages of development can be impractical—especially those species with mating swarms or long life cycles. However, one of the simplest, yet most delightful projects, is to hatch Lepidoptera pupae, releasing them after the butterflies or moths emerge.

CAUTIONS. Do *not* keep stinging or bloodsucking insects, such as wasps, bees, and mosquitoes, in the classroom. Take special care to prevent the escape of pest insects such as native roaches and termites. *All pest insects should be killed at the end of the study.*

Marking Insects

For some experiments, you may need to mark insects for identification. With a toothpick or very fine paintbrush, apply a *tiny dot* of nontoxic paint, dye, ink, or nail polish to the thorax or abdomen of adults. Mark nymphs or larvae to record the number of instars (the form an insect assumes between successive molts). The number of instars varies according to species.

Anesthesia

Many insects (but not fruit flies) show a marked resistance to ether, so other methods of anesthesia are needed. To anesthetize a cockroach, hold it under warm water for about three minutes, repeating as necessary. Most other insects can be anesthetized with carbon tetrachloride (cleaning fluid for clothes, which is obtainable from supermarkets and local stores). Simply place a wad of cotton soaked in carbon tetrachloride into a wide mouthed beaker or bottle, gently add the insect, and place a dish over the mouth of the bottle to make it relatively airtight. The fumes from the carbon tetrachloride will anesthetize the insect. Be patient. Test for responsiveness of the insect to touch. When it fails to respond, the animal is anesthetized. This anesthesia can be safely administered for up to one hour. At the completion of the experimental observation (for instance of functioning heart and blood circulation, see page 157), kill the insect without allowing it to recover.

To kill insects, administer an overdose of ether or place them in a freezer for 24 hours.

ANTS

Ants, family Formicidae, can be found anywhere—they have even been reported on top of the Empire State Building. Ants are easy to capture and maintain, making them ideal classroom animals.

All ants have a "pinched-in waistline" and six legs, but they vary greatly in size and color (black, brown, red, or yellow). Pale yellow garden ants stay in dark places, and observing them can be difficult although rewarding. For your classroom, select a larger ant species that is easy to see.

Ants undergo complete metamorphosis; egg laying typically occurs in the spring, larvae can be obtained in the early summer, and pupae from mid-summer until late autumn. This time schedule may vary depending on the climate in your region. Eggs may appear in a classroom nest as early as January.

OBTAINING ANTS. City dwellers will find black pavement ants, *Tetramorium caespitum*, between cracks in sidewalks, in grassy areas, or even indoors. House ants can be enticed into a trap such as a darkened glass jar (draped with a cloth or made of brown glass) laid on its side, baited with jam or paper soaked in syrup. Add a small piece of wet sponge to keep the air humid, and run a cardboard ramp from the floor to the lip of the jar. Leave the trap overnight where ants normally run, and by morning many ants should have moved in.

In suburban and rural areas, field ants are easy to collect. Most species that build anthills are suitable. In very early spring, look for these nests under stones in grassy meadows, on southern slopes of hills, or in wooded areas. Capture a queen first and the smaller, more numerous workers afterward. It may be possible to catch more than one queen in an ant colony. However, an interesting colony can be established without a queen. Workers will lay eggs, but all the offspring will be males.

Collect active ants by taking advantage of their propensity to seize any new object. Throw some rags on top of the mound and, when the ants have congregated on the rags, shake them into a paper bag or can. Repeat this procedure only until you capture as many ants as you need. A 30 cm square nest will hold about 50 ants. Before transferring the ants into their classroom nest, place them in a refrigerator for a short time to quiet them and make them easier to handle.

To obtain eggs or larvae, dig a 40–cm circle around the top of the nest. Dig deeply, and carefully place each spadeful of earth containing workers and eggs onto a square meter of muslin or directly into a permanent container. Tie up the ends of the muslin. Replace the earth on the nest carefully, so the remaining ants can reorganize their home.

For a small project, worker ants are available commercially.* However, mortalities in shipping are high and survivors usually do not live more than a few weeks.

HOUSING. Ant houses are available from biological supply houses, but are often expensive and more elaborate than necessary. Homemade houses are very satisfactory and easy to construct. Make a nest from two wide-mouthed jars or beakers, one of which will sit inside the other with about 12 mm to spare. Fill the narrow space between the jars with earth. You will be able to see the tunnels and chambers dug by the ants in the narrow strip of earth between the two beakers. Run a plastic drinking straw from top to bottom in the soil; drop water down the tube with a medicine dropper to keep the soil moistened but not wet. The top level of soil should remain dry. If the top rim of the inner jar is below that of the outer jar, anchor a piece of cloth tape or string in the soil and dangle it down into the inner jar. If food is placed inside the

*GIA, Appendix C, pp. 355-356.

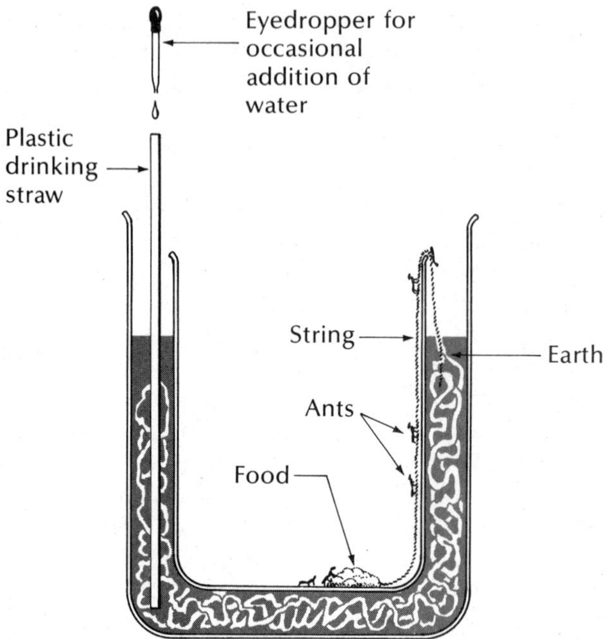

Figure 8-1. Homemade ant house made with two beakers.

inner jar, the ants will use the string as a ladder to reach the food. It is intriguing to see how quickly they establish a route—keeping to one side of the road! To prevent their escape, fasten a piece of nylon stocking or muslin over the whole nest, or place the house in a pan of water to create a moat. A moat is particularly necessary if you use the large black carpenter ants. However, the water must be changed frequently or a thin surface film will form which is strong enough to provide the ants a path to freedom.

Another simple nest can be made of two 30 cm square panes of glass or plastic set about 1 cm apart in a wooden frame. Stand the nest on two blocks of wood at right angles to the frame. Fill the nest with soil and no more than 50 ants. Seal the top of the frame with muslin or fine screen. Pierce two small holes in the muslin, one for water (as before), the other for a short, wide food tube. Drop small food morsels down the tube onto the top of the soil. Clamp the tops of both tubes when they are not in use.

Suitable foods include *very small pieces* of lettuce, potatoes carrots, bread crumbs, hard-boiled eggs, raisins, or raw ground meat. The common tendency to overfeed the ants results in harmful fermentation. Remove leftovers before they begin to mold.

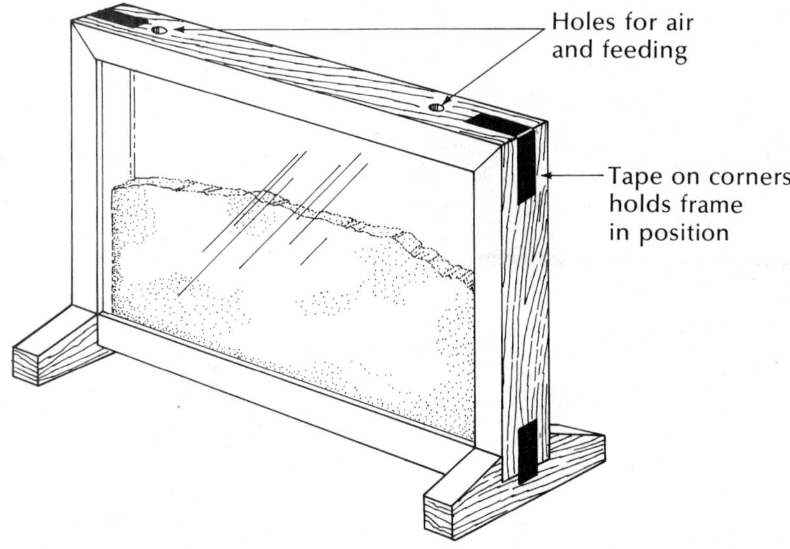

Figure 8-2. An ant house made with parallel pieces of glass held together in a wooden frame.

AQUATIC INSECTS

Most aquatic insects live in water only during their immature stages, and leave it when they reach the adult stage. Use a dip net to collect them from streams, lakes, ponds, and rivers in spring, summer or early autumn. Caddis fly larvae construct a case around themselves from stones and other bits of material. These insects can be seen protruding from their homes—feeding on small animals and plants. Look for larval aquatic forms in silt and mud; you can find eggs on submerged leaves. Many kinds of water bugs (whirligigs, water scavengers, and water striders, for example) can be captured on the surface of the water. Mayflies, perhaps the most beautiful of all aquatic insects, will survive only a short time in the classroom. If you are unable to capture aquatic insects, dragonflies and others are obtainable commercially.*

Using water from the same site, set up the collection of aquatic insects in an aquarium or large jar covered with screen netting or mus-

---

*NAS and CBS. See Appendix C, pp. 355-356. In this chapter, where several sources of supply are mentioned, they are listed in approximate order of increasing cost, based on catalog prices at the time the sources were investigated. In other chapters sources of supply are listed alphabetically.

Figure 8-3. *Collecting water insects with a dip net.*

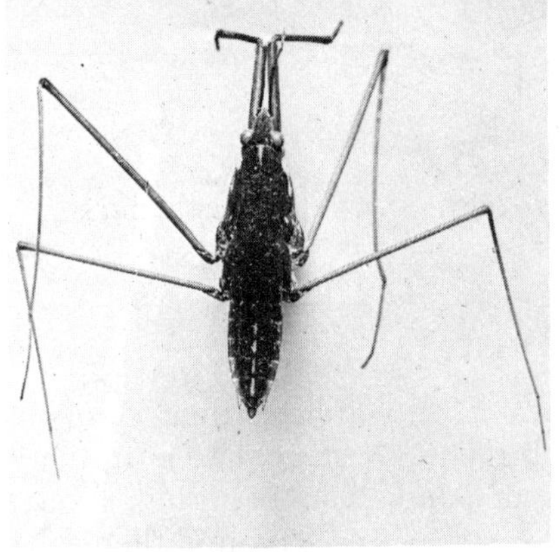

Figure 8-4. *Water strider.*

Figure 8-5. *Water scavenger.*

lin. You may include snails and water plants from their natural habitat and stones covered with algae. (Do not crowd the aquarium, as a good oxygen supply is essential for larval development.) Eggs and larval forms will develop in a week or two, and the nymph forms of stoneflies, mayflies, dragonflies, or damsel flies may emerge. However, stonefly nymphs will not survive in an aquarium unless you can provide running water.

Separate the larvae of predatory insects (such as water scavengers, giant water bugs, and electric light bugs) from the larval forms of other aquatic insects. Larvae of these carnivorous insects may be difficult to identify. As a result, they may be the only insects to survive! Paramecia and other protozoans (See Chapter 2) can be added to the aquarium as food.

Predatory species can be separated when they have reached the adult form and are more easily identified. Keep carnivorous adults in a screen cage suspended above the aquarium, with half the cage submerged in the water. Feed them mealworms (page 144), fruit flies (page 96), housefly larvae (page 143), mosquito wigglers, *Daphnia* (page 95), or small moths. A small piece of raw, lean beef suspended in the cage each day is a suitable alternative to an insect diet. Some predatory insects, such as electric light bugs, will attack tadpoles and even devour small fish, so house them separately. Unless you plan to follow their whole life cycle, release adult forms at their place of capture after a brief period of study.

BUTTERFLIES AND MOTHS[5]

The order Lepidoptera contains one of our most beautiful and well-known aerial insects (the Monarch and other butterflies), as well as some of our most common pests (army worms, clothes moths). The

Figure 8-6. Dragonfly.

Figure 8-7. *Gauze cage for butterflies and moths.*

Figure 8-8. *To make your own 18 in. high screen cage, cut a piece of 18 in. wide window screen wire to be 24 inches long. Roll the screening and lap the edges one inch. Clip the laps together at the top and bottom. Using a coarse needle and string or a wire stapler if available, secure the length of the seam (see a). Place some well-dampened soil or sand into one of the pie pans. Insert a suitable branch, the leaves of which will provide food for the insect. Set the screen cylinder in this pan and use the other pan as a lid (see b). The screen cage is now ready for use.*

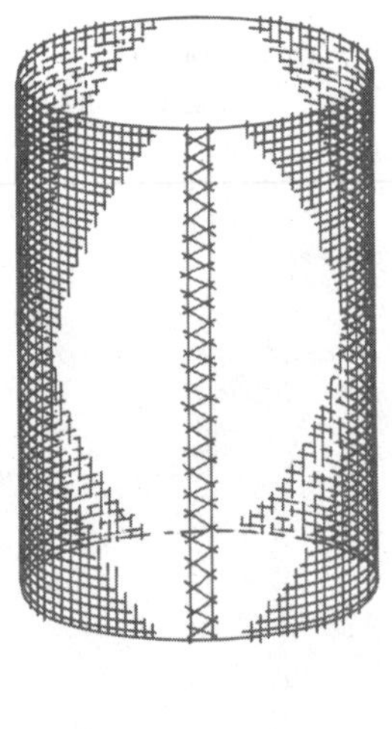

(a)

(b)

adults usually have two pairs of brightly colored wings covered with overlapping scales. Lepidoptera species show complete metamorphosis.

Lepidoptera can be raised easily from the larval (caterpillar) stage through the pupal (cocoon) stage to adulthood. Collect caterpillars from gardens and trees in summer and early fall. The caterpillar and cocoon of the cabbage butterfly *Pieris rapae* is easy to find on the underside of cabbage leaves. Caterpillars of the Painted Lady butterfly *Vanessa cardui* or of other Lepidoptera species can be purchased from biological supply houses.*

Keep caterpillars in a dry, well-ventilated jar or perforated box covered with muslin netting, or in a screen or gauze cage. (See Figures 8-7 and 8-8.) Continuously supply fresh leaves such as those on which the caterpillars were found. Provide freshly picked leaves or a live potted plant. A branch of leaves can be kept in water in a broad-based container. Wrap the base in cloth or paper toweling to provide a rough surface for an insect to crawl up, should it fall from a leaf. Pack the neck of the vase above the water with cotton to prevent the insects from falling and drowning.

When caterpillars are fully grown they will stop eating and settle down to pupate. Broken-up egg cartons or cellulose packing material provide good surfaces for cocoons. The caterpillars also may pupate on twigs or on the sides or top of the cage. Some spin beautiful silken cocoons; others develop into naked pupae which may be buried underground. If in doubt about your species, provide a complete choice of pupating sites: 2 to 5 cm of soft damp earth, egg cartons, and twigs. No food is required until the adults emerge.

Raising Lepidoptera from cocoon to adulthood is even easier than starting with a caterpillar. You will find cocoons in nooks and crevises of windows, under logs or fallen leaves, or on the underside of leaves of growing plants (such as cabbage). Sets of Lepidoptera cocoons also can be purchased.**

An important factor for successful hatching is control of humidity. If the cage is too dry the pupae will die. To prevent this, fill bottle caps with water and place them in the cage. On the other hand, too much humidity leads to mold and fungus formation and the pupae become diseased. Sprinkle the soil with water only when it begins to feel dry—be conservative.

---

*ILO, CBS and CAR. See Appendix C, pp. 355-356. Federal laws control interstate shipment of certain species. See footnote 1, page 124.

**BUB, CBS, CCM and MOG, Appendix C.

When the adults emerge after several weeks or months in the cocoons, they will need a twig to crawl onto to shake their soft wings, and plenty of room to fly. Release butterflies in the wild shortly after they emerge. For most species, to initiate a complete life cycle in the classroom (from production of fertile eggs from adults to a new adult generation) is not feasible.

COCKROACHES AND CRICKETS

i am going to start
a revolution
i saw a kitchen
worker killing
water bugs with poison
hunting pretty
little roaches
down to death
it set my blood to
boiling

i thought of all
the massacres and slaughter
of persecuted insects
at the hands of cruel humans
and i cried
aloud to heaven
and i knelt
on all six legs
and vowed a vow
of vengeance

Don Marquis (1878–1937)

Two very common household insects, cockroaches and crickets (order Orthoptera), are fine subjects for many behavioral, genetic, and physiological experiments. Nymphs (young adults that are still molting) provide excellent food for some reptiles and amphibians.

Three species of roaches are commonly used for classroom purposes:[6] the relatively inactive, 2.5 cm long, almost jet black species from Asia called the Oriental cockroach, *Blattus orientalis;* the large 4 cm long, brown American roach, *Periplaneta americana,* which is common in the south; and the less common, 7.5 cm long *Blaberus giganteus,* which is ideal for the classroom because it has no odor and does not become a pest if it escapes. Strict precautions must be taken to prevent the escape of the Oriental and American roaches. The 1 cm long German roaches, *Blattella germanica,* or Croton bugs, are not recommended for classrooms. Newly hatched German roaches are so small that it is almost impossible to prevent their escape through screen cage covers.

Roaches can be trapped at night in a jar or wooden box fitted with a funnel for easy entrance but difficult exit. An exterminator or entomological laboratory may contribute a few insects to start a culture.

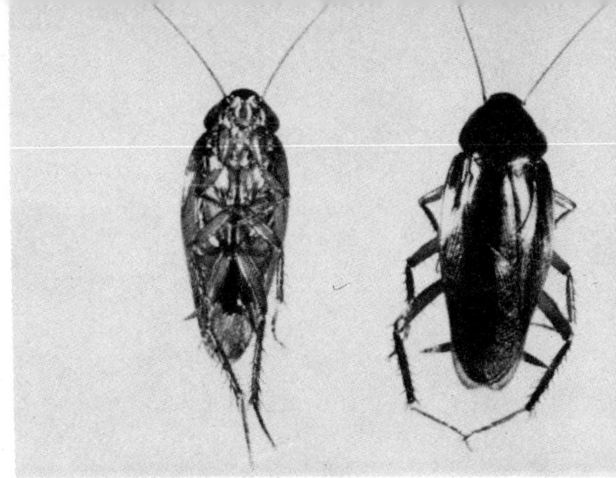

Figure 8-9. American cockroach. (Courtesy Carolina Biological Supply House)

American and Oriental roaches can be obtained from biological supply houses.* Inquire at local entomological laboratories for *B. giganteus.*

The most common species of cricket are the black field cricket, *Gryllus* species, and the European house cricket, *Acheta domestica.* The straw-colored house cricket was accidentally introduced into this country and is now most abundant in southern regions as far west as the Rocky Mountains. House crickets can be trapped readily and are easier to breed than black field crickets. Search under logs or among debris at roadside dumps for outdoor crickets. Catch them quickly with your hands or scoop them into a net. Camel, hunch-back, and wingless crickets are found in similar dark places, but are less attractive—they don't sing.

Crickets are available from commercial sources.** You may obtain unnamed species from local fish bait stores. Keep all species of roaches or crickets in separate containers and away from ants; ants will kill them.

DEVELOPMENT. Most roaches and crickets lay eggs. The egg capsules hatch into nymphs which molt 5 to 13 times as they develop into adults; this may take from five to eight months. A newly hatched nymph is the first instar, and after the first molt, it is the second instar, and so on. After the final molt the insect will develop wings—reaching the adult stage. Adult crickets live about three months. However, adult American roaches may live as long as two years—during which time a female may lay 2,600 eggs.

Some species of roaches, such as *B. giganteus*, give birth to live young. Unlike mammalian reproduction in which the young are also

---

*American roaches from INS and CBS and Oriental roaches from INS. See Appendix C, pp. 355-356.

**SEL, NAS, MOG and CBS, Appendix C.

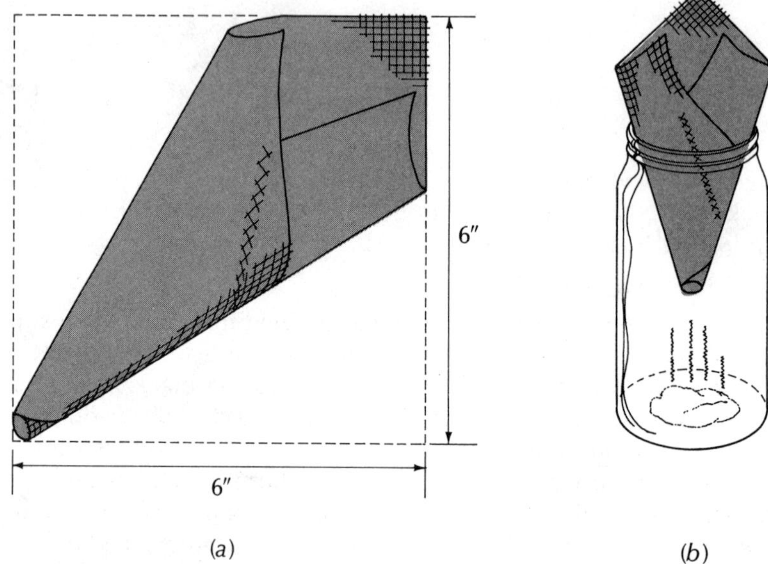

Figure 8-10. To make your own trap, cut a piece of screen wire 6 inches square. Begin at one corner and roll the wire to make a cone which is wide at one end and narrow at the other (see A). The narrow hole should be just large enough to permit entry of the insect you seek. Fit the cone tightly inside the mouth of a bottle, with no space between (see B). When the cone shape is correct, sew the overlapped sides to hold the shape. Place a piece of overripe meat in the bottle. Set the completed trap in an area known to have the insect you seek. Roaches and crickets are best caught at night with the trap lying on its side. Houseflies are best caught by day with the trap standing upright.

born alive, roach eggs do not derive any nourishment from the female during their internal development. Animals that reproduce in this manner are called *ovoviviparous*. *B. giganteus* females usually give birth to 20 or more living young at one time. Birth of the young and successive molting stages can be observed in the classroom.

Both types of reproduction represent incomplete metamorphosis. The nymph is the only intermediate stage between egg and adult.

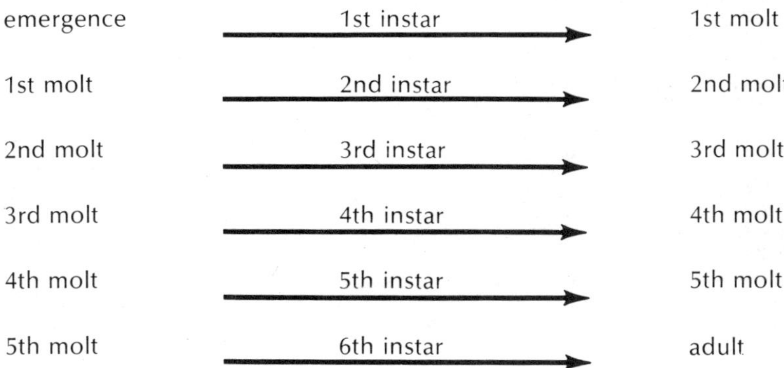

Figure 8-11. Scheme of instars for five-molt insects, such as some species of cockroach.

HOUSING. House all stages of either roaches or crickets together, in watertight, galvanized iron containers or in plastic sweater boxes (from variety or department stores) measuring approximately 45 × 35 × 20 cm (18 × 14 × 8 inches), with a lid made of 16- or 20-mesh screening.* Crickets fly at night; male American roaches occasionally fly; so be sure the lid fits tightly to prevent escape. Large glass jars, aquariums, or large metal drums can also be used. Keep the containers in a dark place, never in sunlight.

Overcrowding produces unhealthy crickets; only a single pair should be kept in a quart jar. In contrast, roaches tolerate crowding. Inverted pint cartons with V-shaped openings provide resting surfaces and dark hiding places suitable to the animals' nocturnal habits. A cage with a floor size of 45 × 35 cm containing 11 round pint cartons will accommodate up to 600 adult American roaches. Without the cartons, far fewer insects can be housed in a cage of this size.

To prevent escape, spread a band of petroleum jelly 5 cm wide around the inside of the container an inch or two below the top. Eventually this layer will need to be replaced. Take additional precautions with roaches, to prevent escape and consequent infestation, by surrounding the containers with a moat of mineral oil or water at least 4 cm deep and 15 cm wide. Or, use a container such as an aquarium with sides at least 10 inches high. Unless a separate room can be as-

---

*Suitable plastic boxes for housing insects also are available from (1) Direct Industrial Supply Division of Dynalab Corp., P. O. Box 161, Rochester, N.Y. 14601; (2) Interex Corp., 66 Woerd Ave., Waltham, Mass. 02154; or (3) Maryland Plastics, Inc., 9 East 37 St., New York 10016.

Figure 8-12. Housing for cockroaches. Lid not shown.

signed for their care, raise cockroaches on a small scale—large colonies of most species produce an unpleasant odor. Crickets do not.

Carpet the floor of the container with fine sand, earth, paper toweling, or blotting paper and keep it slightly damp, but never soaking wet. Test for dampness with your fingers and sprinkle water with a laundry sprinkler if the floor feels dry. Do not let the cage get moldy. The best relative humidity is around 60 percent. If necessary, put bottle caps filled with water in the container to increase humidity.

Roaches and crickets thrive best in temperatures of 21 to 32°C (70 to 90°F), so keep the cage near a radiator or warm air vent. At lower temperatures they are likely to be somewhat sluggish.

Twigs and crumpled paper furnish cover and climbing room and discourage cannibalism by providing hiding places. Sand or soil 2 to 5 cm deep is essential for crickets because they lay their eggs in the ground. Crickets will sit and chirp on a decayed, dampened piece of wood elevated on two stones. Females do not sing. Males sing by rubbing their wings—not legs—together and have three distinct calls: one for attracting a distant female, one for courting, and one for making angry sounds to warn off rivals.

The only required cleaning is changing the sand or soil every few months. Very occasionally wash the cage with soap and water. Sift the floor debris through ⅛–inch mesh screen. Separate unhatched egg capsules and place them in other containers to start new cultures. If the cage contains nymphs less than two months old, return the debris after sieving. It contains hatched egg cases which provide food and hiding places for young nymphs. With proper care and no overcrowding, colonies will thrive indefinitely.

FEEDING. Dry dog food pellets supplied in a small shallow container, or a stiff paste made of rolled oats ground in a mortar with a little sugar, powdered skim milk, and water, provide simple diets for both roaches and crickets. With a spatula, spread a thin layer of the paste on heavy wrapping paper and allow it to dry. A similar mixture of bran, powdered milk, and brewer's yeast may also be used. This food will last indefinitely. Five to 8 square cm per week will feed several crickets or roaches. They also will eat small pieces of stale bread, sour milk, cheese, cooked eggs, raisins, and peanut butter—neglecting other foods if these are available. Cannibalism (wing-nipping), the result of protein deficiency, can be corrected by increasing the supply of powdered milk or meat.

Fill a small test tube with water and plug it with tightly packed cotton. Place it in the cage so that the cotton is moist but the water does not leak out. Or, invert a half-pint jar of water into a shallow dish; fill the dish with cotton to provide a moist surface. (See Figure 8-13.) Roaches need a great deal of water. Check and replenish the food and water supply at least once a week.

At the end of your studies, release crickets into the wild, but roaches should be killed by freezing.

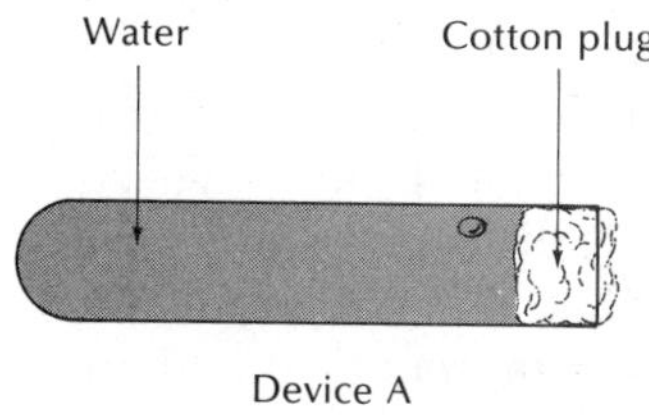

Figure 8-13. Three different kinds of watering devices that may be used in the roach cage.

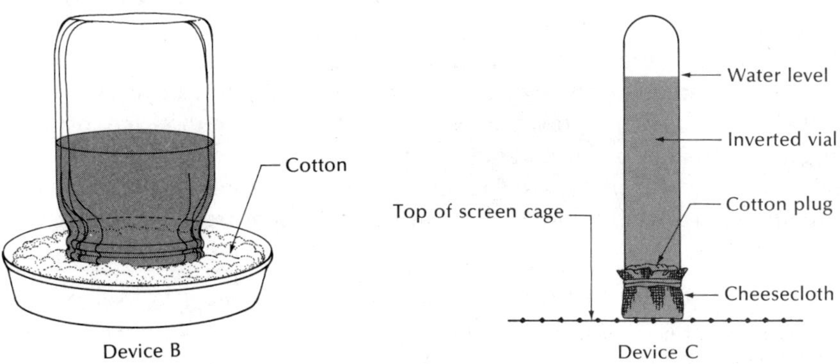

FRUIT FLIES

For most breeding experiments, the fruit fly *Drosophila melanogaster* is preferred to mammals. These insects are cheaper and easier to maintain, reproduce rapidly, and present no disposal problems. They are excellent food for carnivorous animals, such as reptiles or praying mantises.

Fruit flies are easy to find in the wild. A dish of well-ripened banana placed near a garbage can is an effective bait. One of the suppliers listed in Appendix C will furnish many stocks with different characteristics for a small service charge* and will include a guide with detailed genetic experiments.[7] You may prefer to begin with a flightless species.

Fruit flies have been used widely in research, and many cluture methods have been developed. If the flies are to be raised for food or for nongenetic studies, the simplest housing method is to keep them, with some well-ripened banana, in a small jar or disposable container.** Stopper the bottle with a cotton plug wrapped in muslin or cheese cloth. If the bottle is large enough to contain adequate oxygen for up to two weeks, cover it tightly with plastic wrap. Wild or cultured flies will lay eggs on the banana if kept at 21 to 24°C (70 to 75°F), out of direct sunlight. They need no further care.

The banana medium becomes very soft; removing the flies in a dry, clean condition may be quite difficult if the bottle has to be inverted. To avoid this, use a medium with a firmer consistency, such as canned pumpkin or reconstituted instant potato sprinkled with a little dry yeast and a pinch of sugar, or banana pulp mixed with agar.[7] Instant *Drosophila* mixtures from major biological supply houses are more expensive. Fruit flies can, in fact, be raised on any fermenting medium; plum and other fruit pulps, with or without agar, are satisfactory if sprinkled with yeast. Since yeast is present wherever fermentation occurs, it probably constitutes an important part of the fruit flies' diet. A slightly offensive fermentation odor is present with large cultures of fruit flies, but this is not a problem with small cultures.

Development from egg to adult takes about ten days. The eggs develop quickly into crawling white larvae which molt twice, producing three instars or larval stages. The larvae are intensely active and such voracious feeders that the culture medium soon becomes heavily channeled. In the final instar, the larvae may measure 4.5 mm. (Experi-

---

*CUD; also CAR, CBS, NAS, MOG and CCM. See Appendix C, pp. 355-356.

**Disposable urine-specimen bottles such as "Dispo" bottles by Scientific Products, 1210 Leon Place, Evanston, Ill. 60201, or styrofoam coffee cups, are ideal.

enced handlers can differentiate the sex of larvae by the larger male gonad.) Larvae will crawl onto a strip of dry paper toweling to pupate. The last larval skin turns brown and slowly hardens, immobilizing the pupa. About one day before the adults force their way out of the pupal cases, the folded wings and pigmented eyes are discernible through the pupal case. Twelve hours later the adults mate, eggs are laid, and the cycle begins again. (Any experiments requiring virgin females must be done within 12 hours after hatching.) At first, the adults are relatively light in color, but they darken within the first few hours.

TRANSFERRING FRUIT FLIES. Cultured fruit flies are shipped in small vials. To transfer them into a culture bottle, wrap the vial in dark cloth and hold the necks of the two containers close together. Shine a light on the culture bottle, remove the vial stopper, and quickly close together the two necks, as shown in Figure 8–14. The light attracts the flies; they should fly out of the mouth of the shipping vial into the culture bottle. Quickly stopper the bottle. Or shake the flies to the bottom of the shipping vial by rapidly tapping it on a table; then remove the stopper, shake the flies into the bottle, and cover at once. In order to save eggs that may have been laid in the vial, replace the stopper and attach the vial to the culture bottle with a rubber band. As the eggs hatch, transfer the larvae into the culture bottle. If you are conducting genetic studies, label each bottle with the date of transfer and the flies' mutant characteristics.

Under good conditions, adult flies will live for several weeks, remaining fertile as long as they live. Every three to four weeks, when the

Figure 8-14. Transferring fruit flies by attracting them to a light source.

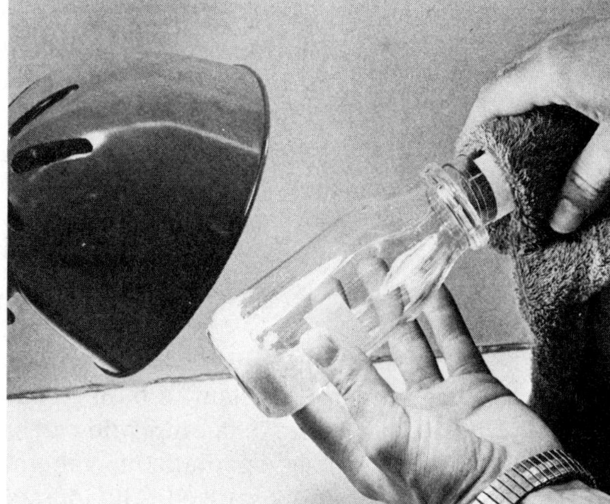

flies become crowded or need new food, transfer them into fresh culture bottles. This may need to be done more often, depending on temperature. (Clean the old bottles immediately, or they may become infested with parasitic mites.) When transferring flies from one culture bottle to another, use the principle of attraction to light. Attract the flies to the bottom of the jar, then force a test tube into the top beside the cotton plug. Reverse the bottle and drape it with a dark cloth; light will attract the flies into the test tube. Quickly withdraw the test tube and seal it with your thumb. The cotton will expand again to seal the culture bottle. Transfer the flies from the test tube to the new culture jar by reversing the method.

FRUIT FLIES AS FOOD. When fruit flies are to be fed to other insects or reptiles, the predator should be kept in a sleeve cage (Figure 8–21). Cool an entire jar of fruit flies in a refrigerator for a few minutes to make them sluggish. Cover the jar with a piece of netting, with mesh *just wide enough* to allow the flies to escape, and place it in the predator's cage. Replace the jar every week or as often as needed. Since it takes ten days or two weeks for breeding, keep three breeding jars in rotation, starting one jar each week. Thus, one jar has mature flies, one is not quite ready, and the other is just being started.

Further instructions for etherizing and sorting, as well as genetic experiments, are contained in the references.[7,8,9] At the completion of investigations, kill fruit flies by freezing them.

HOUSEFLIES AND BLOWFLIES[10]

> *St. Augustine remarked . . . "For it is inquired, what causes those members so diminutive to grow, what leads so minute a body here and there according to its natural appetite, what moves its feet in numerical order when it is running, what regulates and gives vibrations to its wings when flying" . . . To know the fly is to share a bit in the sublimity of Knowledge. That is the challenge and the joy of science.*
>
> Vincent Dethier (b. 1915)

The housefly *Musca domestica* and the blowfly *Phormia regina* have been important in biological history. The common association of fly maggots with manure and carrion led to the belief that decomposing matter caused spontaneous generation of life. Pasteur's research, published in 1862, caused fundamental rethinking by religious and scientific leaders, and was a turning point in the understanding of the origin of life. Only 70 years later, in the 1930s, these humble insects again assumed importance when Dr. William Baer of Baltimore made use of blowfly larvae in postoperative treatment of certain bone disorders and gangrene. Surgical use of maggots was superceded by penicillin and other antibiotic drugs in the 1940s. A strange reversal: first associated with manure, and then raised by the millions in elaborate sterile conditions to clean wounds.

Houseflies are pests when they occur in large numbers. They travel at almost 5 miles per hour and can walk upside down by means of the sticky hairs on two tiny pads (which ooze viscous fluid) just below the claws. Disease-causing microbes stick to the hairs and are spread far and wide by the flies. In colder regions of the world, the adult houseflies may die in the fall, leaving the pupae or larvae to survive the cold weather. In warmer regions, they breed throughout the year. Houseflies have a dull color; blowflies are a metallic blue or green.

You will need quick reflexes to capture houseflies, or you can purchase them from supply houses.* The blowflies' larvae are especially useful for feeding classroom reptiles and amphibians, and can be obtained free from LEV or purchased from CBS.**

Two or three days before obtaining the insects, prepare a mixture of dry yeast and moistened dog biscuits (broken Milkbone® or kibbled biscuits). Prepare a layer 5 to 8 cm deep in a large breaker or other open container with straight sides. Allow this mixture to ferment for a few days, then transfer the medium to the rearing jar. Four gm of dry dog biscuits will support 100 flies; 250 grams will support 1,000 flies. A 2–quart jar with about 5 cm of dog biscuit medium supports 2,000 larvae. (Greater production can be obtained only by using more jars.) If mold forms in the medium, add a layer of wood shavings to smother it, or add polypropylene glycol or a commercial mold inhibitor such as Moldex®. The best moisture content is learned by experience. Have a continuous supply of fermenting medium. Except for the smell of alcohol during fermentation, there are few bad odors with houseflies. Blowflies, however, should be housed in a well-ventilated area.

The World Health Organization reports that one female housefly laying 120 eggs in the spring will have 5,500,000,000,000 descendants by the fall! No wonder it takes only a few adult flies to start a culture. Indoor rearing can be continued all year at a temperature of 21 to 27°C (70 to 80°F). Each female will lay about 120 eggs in the medium. Within eight hours the eggs will hatch into larvae. The larvae will wander aimlessly about the jar, so be sure the lid is secure. As the

*VIT, INS, CRO and NAS. See Appendix C, pp. 355-356.

**Appendix C.

larvae develop, the medium becomes more moist, and the larvae may leave the food and crawl in the surface film of water. If this happens, add a layer of sawdust about 2 cm deep to take up the moisture and drive the larvae back into the medium. Housefly larvae tolerate wider variations in moisture content than blowfly larvae. After four or five days, when the larvae are ready to pupate, add more wood shavings or coarse sawdust, either as a layer or mixed with the dog biscuit medium. The quiescent pupal stage lasts four to five days; then the adults emerge. It takes only eight to ten days for an egg to develop into an adult.

The fly is fully grown when it emerges—small flies do not grow into large ones. When the pupae appear, the medium must remain dry. Pour the contents of the rearing bottle into a shallow tray enclosed in a fine-mesh cage. This will ensure more successful emergence of adults—especially with blowflies. Remove adults by attracting them to a light source and dividing the population into several culturing bottles. Do not crowd them.

INCREASING THE YIELD OF HOUSEFLIES. Adult flies can be kept in good health for several weeks on a sugar cube diet. However, females will not lay eggs until a protein supplement is provided. Since dog biscuits contain protein, flies will lay eggs on this medium without supplementary food, but a single feeding of red meat will increase the yield. Add a small amount of ground lean beef or a piece of beef or pork liver to a jar containing adults up to four weeks old. Remove the meat after 24 hours. Reintroduce the meat 24 hours later for the insects to lay their eggs in. Egg-laying will usually occur within hours. Liver quickly decomposes, so remove any eggs laid on the meat. Supplemental protein can also be provided by offering dry skim milk in a vial covered with cheesecloth and inverted on top of the screen lid.

Adult females live up to 60 days, but greatest egg production occurs during the first three to four weeks. To start additional cultures, either remove some of the adults, as mentioned before, or divide the visible white eggs. For each half-gallon jar use an egg mass half the size of a pea. If only one culture bottle is required, all the eggs can hatch together in the original bottle.

Upon completion of the study, kill houseflies and blowflies by freezing.

YELLOW MEALWORMS AND CONFUSED FLOUR BEETLES

The mealworm *Tenebrio molitor* and the confused flour beetle *Tribolium confusum* are common and easy to raise as food sources for

Figure 8-15. Mealworms: from left, larva, pupa, and adult.

classroom fish, amphibians, or reptiles. Yellow mealworms derive their common name from the appearance of the yellow wormlike larvae, not the handsome black adult mealworm beetle. The larvae of *Tenebrio obscurus* is similar to that of the yellow mealworm, but darker. The confused flour beetle is a small beetle which infests flour, grain, and other stored foods. The same rearing techniques can be used for both mealworms and confused flour beetles.

Mealworms are available from local aquarium dealers, fish bait stores, and pet shops. Both mealworms and confused flour beetles are available from commercial suppliers.*

A plastic sweater box, enamel vessel, or metal or glass bowl about 10 cm deep is a suitable container. Plastic sandwich boxes can be used for raising small populations. Partly cover the box to conserve moisture; the adults cannot climb the sides of the box. The adults will lay their eggs on a crumpled paper towel into the food medium (described below).

The optimum temperature for rearing mealworms is about 30°C (86°F), so place the container in a warm location (for instance, 30 cm away from a dim light bulb.)

Breakfast cereals such as uncooked Cream of Wheat®, standard CSMA fly medium,** wheat middling or bran (both available from livestock feed stores), or ready-mix *Tenebrio* nutrient*** are satisfactory food sources for mealworms. Use whole wheat flour or cornmeal for confused flour beetles. Supply *dry* food 5 to 8 cm deep and add a slice of potato, carrot, or apple. Mealworms have the amazing

---

*Mealworms from RAI, CRO, MOG, NAS, CBS, and CCM, and confused flour beetles from CRO. See Appendix C, pp. 355-356.

**CSMA fly medium from Ralston Purina, General Offices, Checkerboard Square, St. Louis, Mo. 63102.

****Tenebrio* nutrient is available from Ward's Natural Science Establishment, P. O. Box 1712, Rochester, N.Y. 14603.

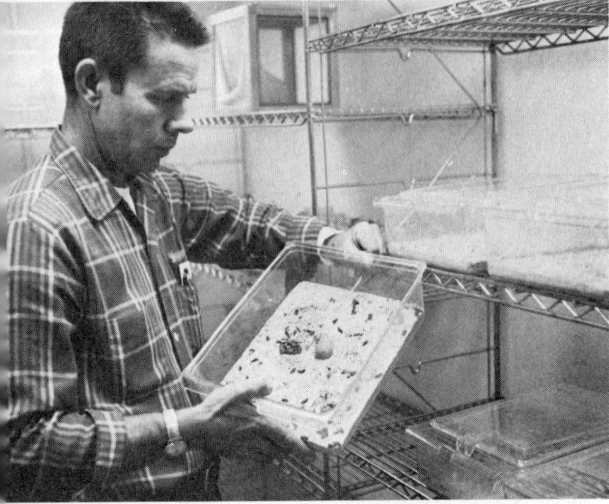

Figure 8-16. Plastic sweater boxes are suitable containers for raising mealworms.

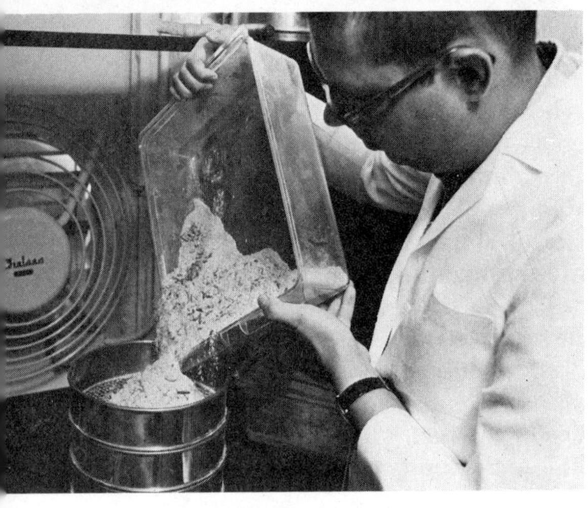

Figure 8-17. Separating mealworm larvae from the medium by sieving.

physiological attribute of making water from a carbohydrate food. Therefore, do not add water to the dry food medium or mold will form. Normally, feeding them every six months is adequate. This is also a good time to subdivide a culture. Save the old medium; it contains eggs and larvae. Divide the medium so there are eight or more adult beetles to each subculture.

Start a culture in the spring so larvae will be ready in the fall. These insects breed only once. The female of *T. molitor* lays as many as 275 eggs; the dark mealworm *T. obscurus* is even more prolific, producing as many as 475 eggs. They usually lay eggs from May until late October, the eggs hatch in four to seven days, and the 9 to 20 larval instars take three to six months to develop. After a period of activity, the larvae crawl to the top of the medium, become C-shaped and inactive. Removing the larvae from the medium at this prepupal stage and placing them in a shallow plastic tray to pupate and hatch may increase the yield. No food is required during the three to ten days of pupation. When the beetles hatch, return them to the food medium to eat and lay their eggs. All stages may be housed together.

For feeding amphibians, reptiles, and fish, a good yield of larvae can also be obtained by layering. Spread 6 mm of medium over the bottom of a container 30 × 45 cm, cover this with four layers of burlap, then spread another 6 mm of medium, more burlap, and so on. Place several hundred worms or old medium with eggs in the container. Sprinkle with water, do not soak. In three months there will be a seething mass of larvae.

Mealworms are intermediary hosts for a number of mammalian helminth parasites; keep them away from mice, rats, or other small mammals.

MILKWEED BUGS[11]

Just one container and very simple care are needed to study the whole life cycle of this pretty insect. Wherever milkweed plants grow, the attractive orange and black milkweed bug *Onocopeltus fasciatus* can usually be found eating the seeds or flying among the plants. Collect milkweed bugs in the fall, keep them in the classroom through winter, and release them in the spring or summer. They can be obtained from an entomological laboratory at a university or from biological supply houses.*

The common milkweed plant *Asclepias syriaca* is widely distributed in the United States, and any of the other species of *Asclepias*—showy, whorled, fern-leaf, or purple milkweed—may serve as hosts to the milkweed bugs. The plants grow about 1.5 meters tall, have large fleshy leaves, milky juice, and numerous pink, purple or orange flowers. You can find these plants in pastures and along railway embankments. Seeds are contained in green pods which turn brown as they ripen. Collect a generous supply of the seeds when the pods are green and just starting to open. Milkweed seeds are the bugs' primary food and are not available commercially. In the midwest, the pods reach maturity in August and September. A tuft of soft, silky hair is attached to each of the seeds; collectively these tufts are called "milkweed down." In nature these tufts aid in aerial dispersal of the seds; commercially, the down is used for lining coats. A 3–gallon pail of pods will yield about one quart of seeds, enough to support a small colony of bugs for nine months. Remove the seeds outdoors because of the down.

*SCH, CRO and BUB. See Appendix C, pp. 355-356. Federal laws control interstate shipment. See footnote 1, page 124.

Figure 8-18. Collecting milkweed bugs from milkweed plant.

To remove the down from the seeds, it is helpful to put the seeds in a deep container and stir them with the paint mixer attachment of an electric drill. You will still have to remove some of the down by hand. Place the cleaned seeds in glass screw-top jars and store them in a dry place at room temperature.

Collect the bugs at the same time you gather the seeds. Milkweed bugs are large, about 16 mm long, and colorful, with a reddish-orange background and three black splotches on the dorsal side. Try to collect 20 or 30 bugs by hand—although 10 will suffice. Transport them in an ice cream container covered with cheesecloth.

House the bugs in a plastic sweater box (from variety or department stores) or a similar container with a lid. You can keep up to 200 adult milkweed bugs in a 25 × 30 cm box. A large fish bowl of about two liters capacity could also be used. Make a lid from screen or from cheesecloth held by an embroidery hoop (from variety stores). In addition, partly cover the top of the container with a piece of glass or plastic to conserve moisture.

Spread a band of petroleum jelly around the top edge of the container to prevent the insects from crawling onto the lid. Put a wad of cotton 8 cm in diameter in the box. The bugs will lay their eggs on the cotton. Fill four small vials (test tubes are ideal) with water and plug them with cotton. Rest these on the floor of the container, so the water

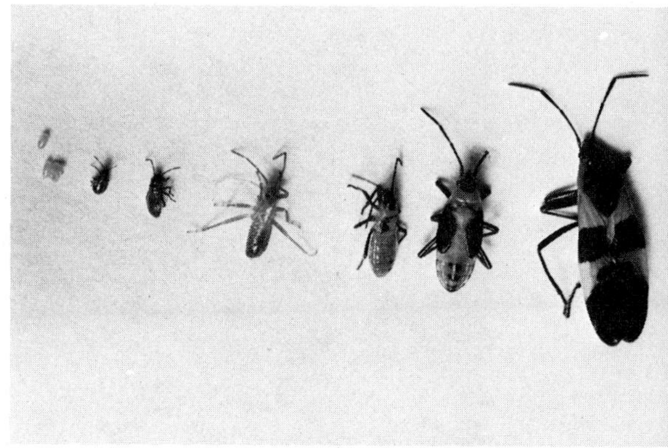

Figure 8-19. Stages of development of milkweed bugs.

will soak through the cotton but will not leak. At least twice a week, check the drinking water supply and provide a few milkweed seeds. If fresh water is not available at all times, the adults may become cannibalistic. If milkweed seeds are hard to obtain, substitute blanched raw peanuts. These are shelled, raw peanuts from which the brown seed coats have been removed by treatment with hot water.

Every two weeks remove the insects, empty the box, and wash it with soap and water. Conserve the eggs by shaking them onto a clean cotton wad. Return the bugs to the box along with the cotton. This is all the care that is required.

Milkweed bugs can thrive in temperatures from 10 to 35°C (50 to 95°F). The higher the temperature within this range, the faster the eggs will develop. There are no larval or pupal stages—milkweed bugs undergo incomplete metamorphosis. Newly emerged nymphs are bright red and about the size of a pinhead. They actively crawl about looking for food soon after they hatch. The nymphs molt four times as they grow, and thus have five instars. They shed cases and deposit excrement which will accumulate in the box. The life cycle takes about 32 days, depending on temperature, so several generations can be studied during the school year.

At the end of the study, free the insects near where they were found, or kill them by freezing.

PRAYING MANTISES[12, 13, 14]

The praying mantis *Stagmomantis carolina* is a "natural" insecticide. When established in a garden or crop-growing area, mantises can diminish populations of plant lice, caterpillars, and other enemies of vegetation.

Figure 8-20. The bulge on the stem is a praying mantis egg case.

Egg cases of praying mantises are found in tan foamlike masses securely attached to twigs or stems. Collect them in the fall or early spring, or order them (between January and June) from biological supply houses.* The Chinese mantis *Tenedera aridifolia* is also available commercially.** If you cannot get mantises, the walking stick insect *Drapheromera femorata* can sometimes be obtained and is reared in the same manner as praying mantises.

Egg masses of any of these insects will hatch readily in a warm, humid room. Plan ahead, so you can release the young mantises soon after they hatch, when outdoor temperatures are warm enough for them. If the egg cases have been ordered too early, keep them outdoors or in a refrigerator until warm spring temperatures are a few weeks away. Then speed their development by bringing them into a warm room.

Keep the egg masses in a sleeve cage (Figure 8–21), or in a terrarium or aquarium covered with cheesecloth or fine mesh screen. Secure the lid to prevent escape of the adults when they emerge. Moistened soil (with plants, if desired) will provide the necessary humidity. Place weed stems or twigs, to which the egg masses are attached, up-

---

*MOG, BUB, PYR and CBS. See Appendix C, pp. 355-356.

**BCC, Appendix C.

right in the soil. About 200 lively, miniature mantises will emerge from each egg mass. Keep them away from direct sunlight and maintain a humid atmosphere. Mantises molt and the new cases must not dry too quickly or the insects will die. Mantises mate readily in captivity, and the females deposit eggs whether fertile or not.

Mantises must have food as soon as they hatch, or the strong will eat the weak until there is only one survivor. They will not eat dead food. Their natural foods are living insects, such as fruit flies (Page 140), cockroaches (page 134), grasshoppers, spiders (page 118), caterpillars or moths (page 131). An easy method of feeding predators is described on page 142. Collect live insects in a sweep net, or bait a wire fly trap with banana and place it outside the classroom window. Do not try to feed ants to mantises—the ants will win! An adult mantis requires two or three houseflies per day but will eat more if available. For adult mantises, provide a dish of water and branches to rest on.

Release mantises into the wild soon after hatching. Otherwise, each mature adult, which will grow to a length of about 6 cm, will need

Figure 8-21. A sleeve cage makes excellent housing for mantisis.

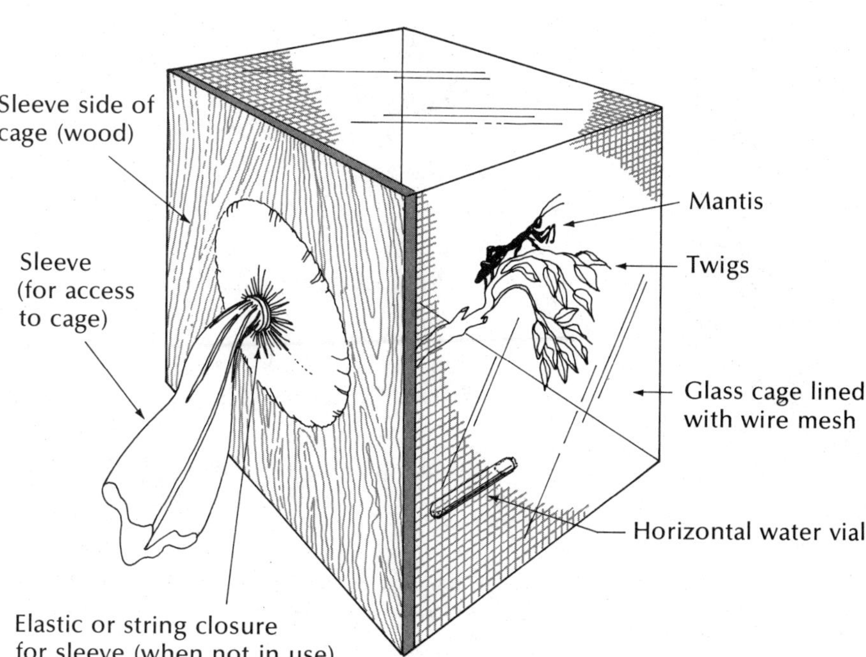

its own cage. One mantis might be retained and housed in a sleeve cage throughout the year.

Since it is always undesirable to kill beneficial insects, set them free at the completion of the study.

WAX MOTHS[15, 16]

A parasitic relationship exists between the wax moth *Galleria mellonella* and bees. Also known as bee moths, bee millers, wax worms, web worms, and wax millers, wax moths are found everywhere there are bees throughout the United States, except high in the Rocky Mountains. Adult wax moths lay their eggs in deserted beehives or in hives with small, weak bee populations. The larvae hatch and immediately start burrowing through the walls of the hives in search of food. In the process, they destroy the hives and also eat young bees. Invasions of wax moths can be responsible for large economic losses for beekeepers.

These moths are a rather undistinguished brown or gray, approximately 2 cm long, with a wingspan of about 4 cm. Although they can and do sometimes fly, they usually walk. They are completely safe to handle and will calmly walk on your hand.

You can obtain wax moths from fish bait stores (they are usually called wax worms), from entomological laboratories, or from supply houses.*

The following rearing method is advocated by the Beltsville entomological unit of the USDA. House all stages of the insect in a single 1–gallon glass jar, covered tightly with 20–mesh screening; do not use a cotton plug or airtight cover. Space requirements for rearing are minimal. To prepare the food medium, use the following recipe from the USDA:

a. 500 ml or 2 cups granulated sugar
b. 500 ml or 2¼ cups glycerine (from pharmacies)
c. 470 ml or 2 cups water
d. 0.6 ml vitamin mixture (Meads Dica-Vi-Sol® or equivalent multivitamin solution, available from pharmacies, 0.6 ml calibrated dropper provided)
e. 1200 ml or 5¾ cups dry Pablum® (mixed cereal available from food markets or pharmacies. Other baby food cereals can be substituted if necessary.)

---

*SCH and NAS. See Appendix C, pp. 355-356.

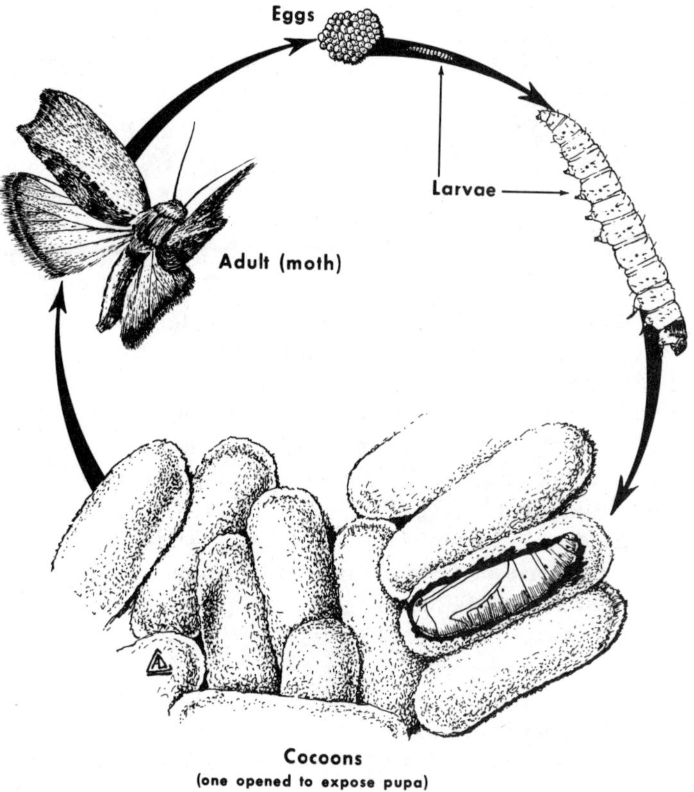

Figure 8-22. Wax moth life cycle.

In a saucepan or flask, mix together *a*, *b*, and *c*. Heat slowly, stirring often until the sugar has dissolved and the solution has become clear (about 15 minutes). Allow the mixture to cool. To prepare just one culture bottle, measure 240 ml (one cup) of this mixture and add to it the vitamin solution *d*. Place *e* in a large container and mix the *a–b–c–d* solution into it with your hands or a spoon. Try to avoid lumps. The medium is now ready for use.

Place the wax moth eggs in the insect container, pour the prepared medium on top of the eggs, and secure the lid. Keep the culture in either an incubator at 34°C (93°F) or in another warm environment, such as under a desk lamp, but not over a direct source of heat. No further care is necessary.

After 3 to 4 days, the eggs will hatch into milky white or tan caterpillars. They are very active and can crawl backward almost as well as forward. They tunnel through the food medium as they feed. Gradually, they darken, become quiescent, and leave the medium to spin white silk cocoons. About 30 days elapse from the beginning of the larval stage until the cocoon is complete. Ten days later, the wormlike creature within the stationary cocoon has developed into an adult moth. The male is generally lighter in color and the posterior edges of its forewings are notched, while those of the female are almost straight. Male antennae are shorter, and the labial palps are hooked inward; in contrast, those of the female protrude forward and upward, giving a beaklike appearance to the front of the head.

Two days after their emergence, the adult females start to deposit round, white eggs. A single female lays from 200 to over 1,000 eggs during the two or three weeks of adult life. Female wax moths never eat or drink during the adult stage. For continuous rearing of a culture, new food medium must be supplied every six months or so. The insects can be subdivided once the culture is well established. Crowding causes an adverse rise in temperature. Divide the adults and the old medium (which will contain eggs and larvae) into as many new cultures as you require. If wax moths escape, they will not establish a colony.

If the larvae are to be used as food for amphibians, reptiles, or fish, put a roll of cardboard tied to a string in the insect jar. Mature larvae will crawl into this roll to pupate. Remove it when you need the larvae. To provide a constant supply of larvae, stagger the starting days of cultures.

Do not set these insects free at the end of the study, but kill them by placing them in a freezer for 24 hours.

INSECT EXPERIMENTS

The number of biological experiments possible with insects probably exceeds that for any other group of animals. Basic principles of living organisms can be illustrated by studying insects: These include genetics, behavior (responses to temperature, light, and gravity, and territoriality and other social behaviors), diurnal rhythms, trail making, communication, learning, comparative anatomy, food chains, and interdependence of living creatures. This enormous range prohibits detailed descriptions of experimental design here. All that will be given is procedural details. Many useful books describing excellent insect experiments are listed in the references.[17, 18a, 19, 20]

GENETICS. Many student texts contain instructions for fruit fly and other insect experiments on genetic inheritance.[7, 26]

TEMPERATURE AND HUMIDITY. Determine an insect's preference for certain temperatures or humidity levels by providing it with different environments from which to choose. (Apparatus for similar experiments with sowbugs is described on page 109.)

BEHAVIOR. Ideas for experiments on insect behavior are almost as limitless as those on genetics. All the species described in this chapter can be used for study of one or another aspect of insect behavior. Use the larval and nymph stages as well as the adult; sometimes behavior changes radically during development. Although one species may be described in the references, others usually can be substituted and the experimental design retained. The total behavior pattern of an animal is made up of many aspects, such as feeding, and aggressive, social, and sexual behavior. Many ingenious experiments have been designed to study these behavioral responses.[20a-d, 20h, 22, 23, 24a, 25]

CHEMICAL SUBSTANCES. What is the nature of the response to chemical substances? Where are the receptors located?[18b, 26]

LIGHT AND GRAVITY. Various factors, such as light and the pull of gravity, influence the direction in which an insect orients itself and moves.[18c] Not all species respond the same way—adult fruit flies move toward light;[20e] adult cockroaches move away from light—and responses may vary according to the stage of maturation of a species (compare larval with adult stages of mealworms.[23a]

Shine a beam of light on an insect and observe its response. What light intensity is needed to elicit a response? Will the insect change its course if a second beam of light is introduced at right angles to the first? Is there a relationship between these responses to light and conditions needed for survival of the species?

Certain colors of flowers are known to attract pollinating insects. Set up two or more interconnecting glass chambers covered with cellophane of different colors, and determine in which chamber a certain species spends most of the time. Compare the preferences of several species.

Another orienting mechanism is the response to gravity—the "geotaxic" response.[18c] Place a nymph, larva, or adult on an inclined board that is illuminated equally on all parts, and trace the insect's movement. Does it go uphill or down? A response toward the pull of gravity is "positively geotaxic;" a response away from gravity is "negatively geotaxic." This response does not necessarily remain the same throughout an animal's life cycle. A housefly maggot migrates positively only up to the fourth instar. The more mature maggot needs to migrate negatively to pupate in a favorable position. Test different stages of a species and relate your findings to its survival.

PHEROMONES—CHEMICAL COMMUNICATION. Recent work has shown that chemical communication systems are surprisingly common in the animal world.[27] Certain mammals and insects are known to secrete substances, known as *pheromones*, that influence the behavior of other members of the same species. Thus, if an ant finds a good source of food, as it returns to the nest it lays down an invisible odor trail for other ants to follow. When the food is consumed, unrewarded ants return to the nest without laying chemical trails, and the outgoing traffic wanes. Fascinating experiments can be undertaken to study this remarkable phenomenon.[20f, 28] Do pheromones from different colonies vary? Will ants of one colony follow trails laid by ants from other colonies? (Not all species of ants lay odor trails from food.)

GROWTH. A variety of factors influence insect growth and development. Study the effects of temperature on development time from egg to adult. Raise insect cultures under different constant temperatures and measure the population densities.

Certain "juvenile" and other hormones also control insect development. Advanced students could study the balance required between hormones which inhibit and those which stimulate growth. A compound called "farnesol,"* can be used to demonstrate the inhibiting effects of hormones. Inject minute quantities into mealworms in the last larval stage (just before they are ready to pupate), and observe their maturation.[29, 30]

REPRODUCTION AND DRUGS. Certain drugs affect insect reproduction. For instance, reserpine, a tranquilizing agent, profoundly affects the reproductive processes of the confused flour bettle. Inject varying small quantities of a 1 percent solution of reserpine into adult confused flour beetles, and determine the dosage required to completely inhibit egg laying. If smaller concentrations are used (try a 0.5 percent solution), egg production will be partially inhibited but not stopped, and only a few eggs will hatch successfully. What are the possible mechanisms of action of this drug?

---

*Obtainable from Aldrich Chemical Co., 2371 N. 30 St., Milwaukee, Wis. 53201.

BLOOD CIRCULATION. Anesthetized cockroaches can be used to study the heart and circulation *in situ*. If the heart is bathed in physiological saline solution, it can be kept functional for several hours for tests with various drugs.[31, 32]

LOCOMOTION AND FLIGHT. What is the usual stride pattern for adult insects? If the legs on the right side of the body are labeled R_1, R_2, and R_3, and those on the left side L_1, L_2, and L_3, in which sequence are they placed on the ground as the animal walks forward? Does the sequence remain the same for all speeds? Compare this with the walk, trot, and gallop sequence of horses.[20i]

Highly sophisticated problems of aerodynamics are posed in studies of insect flight. Students with an interest in biophysics can construct flight chambers and photograph the insects' flight behavior.[1b] Other rather complicated experiments are described by Hainsworth and King, [18d, 20g] and simple experiments on insect locomotion are given in Pringle.[24b]

BIOLOGICAL CLOCKS. Insects show daily variations in activity, as do mammals and other animals. Everyone is familiar with gnats that appear out of nowhere in time for an evening barbecue. Where are these insects during the rest of the day? Establish by experimentation that daily fluctuations in activity do occur.[1c] Compare several species to show that peaks of activity take place at different times of day or night. Are the peaks of activity due to changes in illumination, or are they dependent also upon temperature and humidity changes? Conduct experiments in which two of these factors are held constant, while the other is varied. What variations of activity are observed under these conditions? Is it reasonable to conclude that diurnal activity in insects results from the combined effects of light, temperature, and humidity?

LEARNING. Ants,[24c] mealworms,[23a] and other species can learn simple mazes. Using a single insect marked for identification, record the number of errors it makes in successive trials in a T–maze. Mealworms can be conditioned to turn left or right at the choice point by rewarding them with darkness as soon as the desired choice is made. What rewards would be suitable for other insects? Do not punish them for incorrect choices. Animals learn best when rewarded.

FIELD STUDIES. Conduct a study of plant galls (especially oak, willow, and poplar), which are insect homes in growing plants; or collect and identify the insects that inhabit the school grounds or a local park. Study the biological balance in a pond community or other ecological site. What biological controls are operating? Study the relationships of parasites and predators to insect species.

List local plants and trees that require insects for pollination. Tie cellophane bags over clusters of buds and, after the flower petals have fallen, count the fruits and seeds that have formed. Compare these results with those of adjacent control plants to which pollinating insects have had free access.

CONTROL OF INSECT PESTS. Test a variety of nonchemical insecticides such as infrared light, ultraviolet light, ultrasonic waves, magnetic fields, and temperature variations for effectiveness on wax moths, fruit flies, houseflies, and cockroaches.

PUBLIC HEALTH. In your community, what sanitation programs involve control of insect pests? Consult your local health office about sanitation measures to control insect pests at garbage disposal dumps and in public buildings. How are agricultural pests controlled in your area?

REFERENCES

1. Callahan, P. 1970. *Insect Behavior.* Four Winds Press, New York. a. pp. 121–27; b. pp.136–41; c. pp. 130–36. (Advanced)
2. *Collection and Preservation of Insects.* 1964. USDA Misc. Publ. 601. Sup. of Documents, U.S. Govt. Printing Office, Washington, D.C. 20402.
3. *Finding Hidden Insects,* Student or Classroom Science Project No. 1; and *Trapping Insects with Light,* Project No. 2. USDA Educ. Services Branch, Agric. Res. Center, Beltsville, Md. 20705.
4. Oldroyd, H. 1958. *Collecting, Preserving and Studying Insects.* McMillan Co., New York.
5. Villiard, P. 1969. *Moths and How to Rear Them.* Funk & Wagnalls, New York.
6. Guthrie, D. M. and A. R. Tindall. 1968. *The Biology of the Cockroach.* Edwin Arnold Publishers, Ltd., London. (Advanced)
7. Demerec, M. and B. P. Kaufman. 1967. Drosophila *Guide.* 8th ed. Carnegie Institute, 1530 P St., NW, Washington, D.C. 20005. (Advanced)
8. Hechtlinger, A. 1971. *Handbook of Modern Experiments for High School Biology.* Parker Publishing Co., Inc., West Nyack, New York. pp. 179–181.
9. Novitski, E., ed. Drosophila *Information Service.* Annual publication of information on new mutants and new techniques. Dr. E. Novitski, Department of Biology, University of Oregon, Eugene 97402. (Advanced)
10. Dethier, V. 1963. *To Know a Fly.* Holden-Day, Inc., San Francisco.

11. MASTELLER, E. C. 1970. Live Insects in the Classroom and Laboratory. *Amer. Biol. Teacher* 32(7):410–14.

12. *The Care of Living Insects in the School Laboratory*. Turtox Leaflet 34. General Biological Supply House, 8200 S. Hoyne Ave., Chicago, Ill. 60620.

13. *Live Insects in the Classroom*. Audubon Nature Bulletin, part of Set NB4. National Audubon Society, 1130 Fifth Ave., New York 10028.

14. NEEDHAM, J. G., P. S. GALTSOFF, F. E. LUTZ and P. S. WELCH. 1959. *Culture Methods for Invertebrate Animals*. Dover Publications, New York.

15. *Rearing the Greater Wax Moth*. 1970. Science Study Aid No. 3. USDA, Educ. Service Branch, Agric. Res. Center, Beltsville, Md. 20705.

16. *The Wax Moth: An Ideal Laboratory Animal for All Grade Levels from Primary through College*. NASCO Teachers' Guide, NASCO, Ft. Atkinson, Wis. 53538.

17. BROWN, V. 1968. *How to Follow the Adventures of Insects*. Little, Brown & Co., Boston. (Intermediate)

18. HAINSWORTH, M. D. 1967. *Experiments in Animal Behaviour*. Houghton Mifflin Co., Boston. a. Chapter 6. Suggested Lines of Experiments with Insects, pp. 68–90; b. pp. 74–78; c. pp. 80–84; d. pp. 85.

19. KALMUS, H. 1960. *One Hundred and One Simple Experiments with Insects*. Doubleday & Co., Garden City, N.Y. 11530. (Intermediate)

20. STOKES, A. W., ed. 1968. *Animal Behavior in Laboratory and Field*. W. H. Freeman & Co., San Francisco 94104.
    a. CALDWELL, R. L. and H. DINGLE. Cyclic Reproductive and Feeding Behavior in the Milkweed Bug. pp. 61–64. Available from the publisher as Separate No. 809. (Advanced)
    b. DINGLE, H. Aggressive, Territorial, and Sexual Behavior of Crickets. pp 89–92. Separate No. 815.
    c. EHRMAN, L. Reproductive Isolation in *Drosophila*. pp. 85–87. Separate No. 814. (advanced)
    d. HAWKSLEY, O. Cockroach Behavior. pp. 57–60. Separate No. 808.
    e. JENNINGS, J. and T. H. CLACK, Jr. Optical Orientation in the Fly Larva. pp. 23–25. Separate No. 800.
    f. KANZLER, W. W. 1968. Pheromones and Trail Making in Ants. pp. 27–28. Separate No. 801. (Advanced)
    g. KING, J. A. Insect Flight. pp. 21–22. Separate No. 799. (Advanced)
    h. MARLER, P. Mating Behavior of *Drosophila*. pp. 79–83. Separate No. 813. (Advanced)
    i. MÜLLER-SCHWARZE, D. Locomotion in Animals. pp. 13–19. Separate No. 798.

21. WILLIAMS, R. D. and D. M. SMITH. 1970. Preparation of Blowfly Salivary-Gland Chromosomes. *Amer. Biol. Teacher* 32(8):491–92.

22. CUNNINGHAM, J. D. 1970. *First You Catch a Fly*. McCall Publishing Co., New York. (Feeding behavior and taste threshold of flies.)

23. Polt, J. M. 1971. Experiments in Animal Behavior. *Amer. Biol. Teacher* 33(8):472–79. a. pp. 473–74, orientation in mealworms.

24. Pringle, L., ed. 1970. *Discovering Nature Indoors: A Nature and Science Guide to Investigations with Small Animals.* Natural History Press, Garden City, N.Y. 11530. a. pp. 80–81; b. pp. 65–66; c. pp. 83–84.

25. Vogel, S. and S. Wainwright. 1969. *A Functional Bestiary: Laboratory Studies about Living Systems.* Addison-Wesley Publishing Co., Reading, Mass. pp. 87–89, 91–92.

26. Welsh, J. H., R. I. Smith and S. E. Kammer. 1968. Behavioral Study of Chemoreception in Flies. *Laboratory Exercises in Invertebrate Physiology.* 3rd ed. Burgess Publishing Co., Minneapolis, Minn. pp. 90–93. (Advanced)

27. Dröscher, V. B. 1969. *The Magic of the Senses: New Discoveries in Animal Perception.* E. P. Dutton & Co., New York. pp. 128–33. (Also, paperback, 1971, Harper & Row.) (Background information.)

28. Simon, S. 1968. *Animals in Field and Laboratory: Science Projects in Animal Behavior.* McGraw-Hill Book Co., New York 10017. pp. 18–20.

29. Pierce, R. G. 1969. Programming the Insect's Life Cycle. *Science Teacher* 36(4):23–27.

30. Witters, W. L. 1969. Hormonal Control of Insect Growth and Development. *Amer. Biol. Teacher* 31(9):585–86.

31. Davey, K. G. 1961. Substances Controlling the Rate of Beating of the Heart of *Periplaneta* (cockroach). *Nature* 192:284. (Advanced)

32. Miller, T. A. 1973. Measurement of Insect Heartbeat by Impedance Conversion. *The Physiol. Teacher* 2(1):1–4. The American Physiological Society, 9650 Rockville Pike, Bethesda, Md. 20014. (Advanced)

FURTHER READING

General

The American Biology Teacher, May 1976, volume 38, Number 5. The whole issue is devoted to various articles on uses of insects in biology teaching.

Borden, J. H. and B. D. Herrin. 1972. *Insects in the Classroom.* British Columbia Teachers' Fed'n., 105–2235 Burrard St., Vancouver, B.C., Canada.

Borror, D. J. and D. M. DeLong. 1970. *An Introduction to the Study of Insects.* 3rd ed. Holt, Rinehart & Winston, New York 10017.

Callahan, P. S. 1971. *Insects and How They Function.* Holiday House, New York.

Chauvin, R. 1971. *The World of Ants.* (G. Ordish, tr.) Hill & Wang, New York.

Dethier, V. G. 1972. *The Physiology of Insect Senses.* Harper & Row, New York. (Advanced)

Klots, A. B. and E. B. Klots. 1967. Living Insects of the World. Doubleday & Co., Garden City, N.Y. 11530. (Advanced)

MASON, H. M. 1974. *The Fantastic World of Ants*. David McKay Co., Inc., New York.

MASTELLER, E. C. 1970. Live Insects in the Classroom and Laboratory. *Amer. Biol. Teacher* 32(7):410–14.

MORGAN, A. 1930. *Fieldbook of Ponds and Streams*. G. P. Putnam's Sons, New York.

OLDROYD, H. 1970. *Elements of Entomology: An Introduction to the Study of Insects*. Universe Books, New York.

PATENT, D. H. 1975. *How Insects Communicate*. Holiday House, New York.

ROMOSER, W. S. 1973. *The Science of Entomology*. MacMillan Publishing Co., Inc. Riverside, New Jersey.

Test Your Fly's Sweet Tooth. 1975. Animal Behavior Series, Collateral Materials Booklet. No. 05091. National Geographic Society, 17th and M St., N.W., Washington, D.C. 20036.

VILLIARD, P. 1973. *Insects as Pets*. Doubleday & Co., Garden City, N.Y. 11530.

WHEELER, W. M. 1960. *Ants: Their Structure, Development, and Behavior*. Rev. ed. Columbia University Press, New York. (Advanced)

WIGGLESWORTH, V. B. 1964. *The Life of Insects*. Mentor Books, New American Library, New York.

WIGGLESWORTH, V. B. 1965. *The Principles of Insect Physiology*. 6th ed. Barnes & Noble, New York. (Advanced)

Insect Identification

BORROR, D. J. and R. E. WHITE. 1970. *A Field Guide to the Insects of America North of Mexico*. Houghton Mifflin Co., Boston.

Handbook of the Insect World. 1956. (free) Hercules Inc., 910 Market St., Wilmington, Del. 19899. (Intermediate)

HOLLAND, W. J. 1968. *The Moth Book*. rev. ed. Dover Publications, New York.

SWANN, L. A. and C. S. PAPP. 1972. *The Common Insects of North America*. Harper & Row, New York.

VESSEL, M. F. and E. J. HARRINGTON. 1971. *Common Native Animals: Finding, Identifying, Keeping, Studying*. Chandler Publishing Co., San Francisco. pp. 125–48.

ZIM, H. S. and C. COTTAM. 1956. *Insects*. Golden Nature Guide. Golden Press, Western Publishing Co., New York. (Intermediate)

ZIM, H. S. and R. MITCHELL. 1964. *Butterflies and Moths*. Golden Nature Guide. Golden Press, Western Publishing Co., New York. (Intermediate)

RECORDINGS OF INSECT SOUNDS

"Songs of Insects." 12 in. LP Record. No. 6–86828. Houghton Mifflin, Boston.

"Songs of Insects." Cornell University Records, Ithaca, New York.

9

Fish

"No human being, however great, or powerful, was ever so free as a fish."

John Ruskin (1819-1900).

Psychologists report that fish in an aquarium have a tranquilizing effect on patients waiting to see a dentist or doctor. No one has checked their influence upon students in a classroom, but certainly an almost universal pleasure attends observing their graceful swimming movements.

Of all vertebrates, fish are easiest and least expensive to care for and breed. Once an aquarium is properly set up, little further work is involved. Fish are cleaner and free of the smells that are present with mammals; but, like mammals, they can be used for a wide variety of genetic, behavioral, and learning experiments. Fish, amphibians, reptiles, birds, and mammals are all vertebrates, members of the same phylum, Chordata. All these animals, at some stage in their life cycle, have a dorsal nerve cord enlarged at the anterior end to form a brain.

Procedures for caring for goldfish, guppies, white cloud mountain fish, sticklebacks, paradise fish, and bettas are described in this chapter. However, many salt-water fish and other marine organisms are suitable for a classroom aquairum. Special procedures for maintaining marine organisms are described in several of the references (see FURTHER READING, Marine Animals, page 188).

SELECTING CLASSROOM SPECIES

Unless your choice of classroom fish is dictated by particular studies you have in mind, select a hardy species that is easy to care for and generally useful for experimental purposes. Among the best are ordinary goldfish, *Carassius auratus*. Fancy varieties of goldfish are

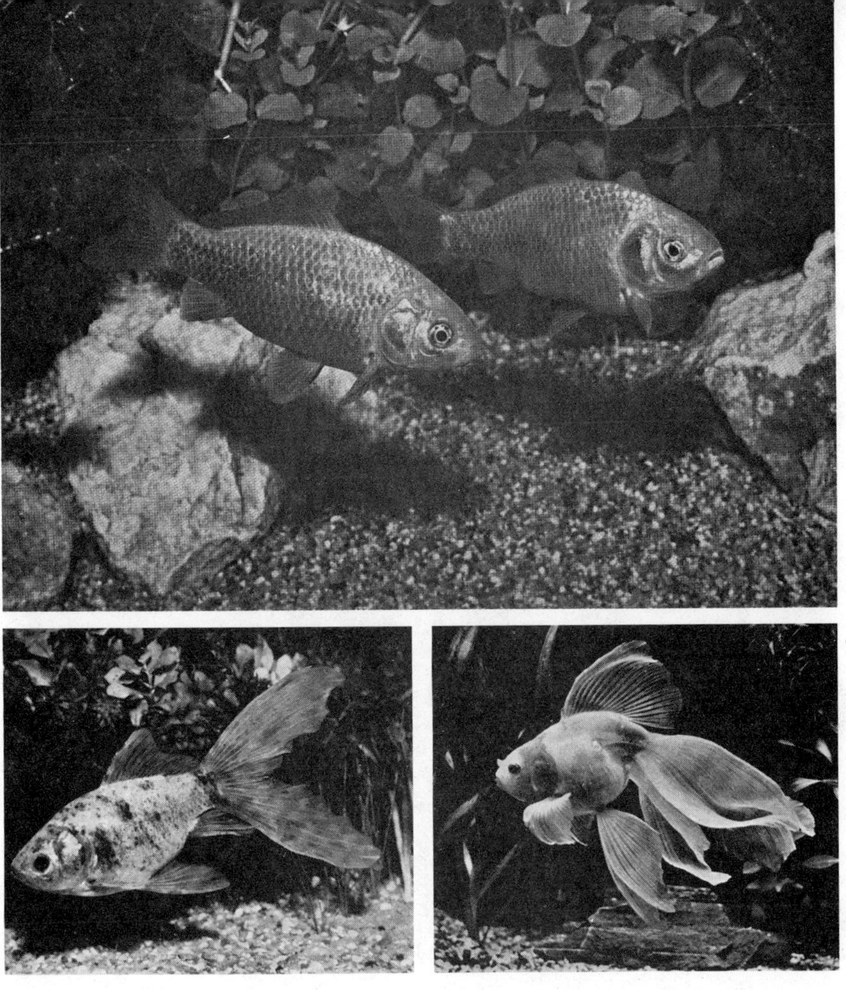

Figure 9-1. The common goldfish is shown at top. The Shubunkin (bottom left) and the veiltail (bottom right) are two fancy varieties.

less hardy and, therefore, less desirable. Other classroom species are (in approximate order of hardiness): guppies (*Lebistes reticulatus*), native to areas north of the Amazon in Brazil and Venezuela, paradise fish (*Macropodus opercularis*), white cloud mountain fish (*Tanichthys albonubes*), and bettas (*Betta splendens*), all native to China and southeast Asia. All of these are relatively easy to care for—guppies are the easiest to breed. Because bettas are the least hardy of this group, you may prefer to substitute the closely related, robust paradise fish.

Many other species of native or imported cold-water fish can be kept in the classroom. Several species of sticklebacks (*Gasterosteus*), varying in the number of upstanding back and pelvic fins, are native to

Figure 9-2. Guppies. The large female is swollen with eggs. The male makes his approach to mate. The arrow points to the male's gonopodium which is swung round 180° to a forward position.

Figure 9-3. Paradise fish.

Figure 9-4. Red betta.

the United States. The three-spined stickleback is recommended. Consult the references (FURTHER READING, page 187) for information on specific requirements for these and other native cold-water species.

Fish are generally very good for embryonic studies because they develop rapidly. White cloud mountain fish and paradise fish are particularly recommended for embryonic studies. Paradise fish and bettas are good species for breeding experiments. Paradise fish come in albino and normal color strains which breed true; therefore, the inheritance of skin colors in this species can be studied in crossbreeding experiments. Live-bearing guppies are ideal for genetic experiments and for investigating the effects of sex hormones. All fish species are suitable for general behavior studies; sticklebacks are best for observations of schooling behavior; goldfish for learning experiments. Study the brilliant courting displays, nest-building behavior, and parental care of paradise fish, bettas, and sticklebacks.

COMPATIBILITY. Many different species can be housed together in the same aquarium if you follow these general rules:

1. Do not place big fish with little fish, or the smaller ones may be eaten.
2. Do not house cold-water fish, such as goldfish and sticklebacks, with tropical fish that require warm water.
3. Do not place together members of two species that do not get along with each other, in either their natural habitats or as aquarium fish.

Figure 9-5. *Sticklebacks.*

4. *One* specimen of an aggressive species, such as a paradise fish or a betta, can sometimes be housed with fish of other species, but watch it carefully and remove it if fighting begins. Maintain paradise fish and bettas separately and individually except when breeding.

To illustrate these rules, you might try guppies, white cloud mountain fish, and possibly one paradise fish (or one betta) in the same aquarium. Check with local pet stores and the references if you have species of fish not covered here.

SOURCES. Obtain goldfish and tropical fish from pet stores. Buy only fish that appear to be healthy, active, and well fed. Look for a clean pet store—be suspicious if you see dead fish in the aquarium. But purchase the fish locally; it is better to see what you are getting, and shipping can lower resistance to disease.

Sticklebacks are not easy to acquire. You probably will have to catch them in lakes or streams. Early in the fishing season, you may obtain them free from bait collectors, since they are usually thrown away. Individuals about 5 cm long are best. Brook sticklebacks can be purchased from a few biological supply houses.*

TRANSPORTING. For short journeys, transport fish, with water, in several plastic bags placed one inside the other and secured at the top. Leave a chamber of air to maintain an oxygen supply and pack the bag in a carton for protection, insulation, and easier handling. Or use plastic food boxes or ice cream cartons half filled with water. The area of water surface exposed to the air is more important than the volume of water.

Fish can become frightened. After transferring them to the aquarium, leave them undisturbed for several days. Distract them as little as possible for another week or two, until they become accustomed to their new environment.

HOUSING

Ornamental containers, small tanks (5 gallons or less), and spherical goldfish bowls should not be used. Goldfish can live in captivity for 10 to 15 years—the record is 34. Yet, in the pet trade millions exist only a few weeks or months because of bad standards of care. One of the contributing factors is the small round goldfish bowl, still sold by most pet stores, that allows inadequate water surface for oxygen exchange.

---

*Such as MOG and NAS, Appendix C, pp. 355-356.

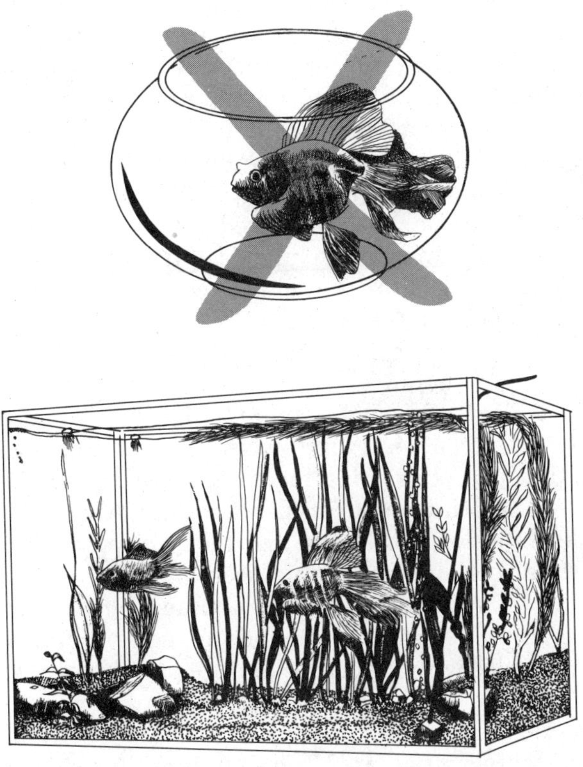

Figure 9-6. Good and bad methods of housing fish.

Manufactured aquariums are generally well made and are not easily duplicated by home construction methods. A suitable size for a classroom aquarium is 15, 20, or 25 gallons. (Divide the capacity in cubic inches by 231 to determine the volume in gallons.) Usually, a large tank is best, but several medium-sized tanks are more versatile. Although fish tanks are expensive, they will last for many years if properly maintained and not moved. Moving a tank filled with water distorts the frame and loosens the glass, causing leaks. Remove most of the water from a tank before moving it. Slight leaks along the cemented edges may be sealed with Silastic® or other aquarium sealants found in hardware or pet stores. Alternatively, fill the tank with water just hot enough *not* to burn your hand; often this procedure will soften the cement and reseal the glass. Tanks that are beyond repair make excellent terrariums, and they can house gerbils or insects.

If you wish to make your own aquarium, see Reference 1, page 185.

The number of fish that can be maintained in an aquarium will depend on the natural habitats of the fish and the temperature of the water. Generally, allow 60 sq cm of water surface for each fish 2.5 cm long (exclusive of caudal fin and tail). Fish need dissolved oxygen to breathe; the amount of oxygen dissolved in the water is proportional to the water surface area exposed to the air. If fish stay near the top of the tank, they probably lack oxygen; either reduce the number of animals or increase the plants in the tank. An artificial aerator will help correct an oxygen deficiency to some extent.

The aquarium should always be covered to reduce evaporation, keep dust out, and prevent the more active fish from jumping out. Using Silastic®, glue at least four pieces of cork to the top of the frame to prevent the lid from resting on it. A glass lid, with a *very small* corner cut out is convenient for feeding. Stainless steel hoods, often with built-in lights, are available, but they are very expensive. If improperly wired, they may be unsafe near water.

Place the aquarium on a sturdy, flat base where it will not have to be moved again. Metal aquarium stands are convenient, but not essential; movable tables with legs on casters are particularly suited to classroom use. Select a well-lighted place, such as a windowsill with a north or east exposure and strong diffuse light. (Only in winter is a southern exposure satisfactory.) The aquarium should not receive more than two hours of sunshine a day, or the water will become overheated and overgrown with algae. To limit the sunshine, shade the window side of the tank with a green cloth. If an aquarium is placed in a dark location, an overhead light will be necessary. Mount a fluorescent lamp or a small incandescent bulb in a reflector cap over the aquarium. Avoid radiators; fluctuations in temperature are harmful to the fish.

WATER. Rain, well, spring, or aged tap water can be used. If you use tap water, let it stand in a glass container for two days in a warm place to allow chlorine to escape. In some parts of the country, tap water is particularly hard (containing many dissolved salts), or has been softened over lime. In these areas, it is best not to use tap water. However, pet stores have chemical treatments for most water conditions.

TEMPERATURE AND AERATION. Fish are cold-blooded animals—their body temperatures vary according to their external environment. Fish survive in a large variety of temperatures, from cold mountain streams to warm tropical water. Usually no artificial heating is required to keep

Figure 9-7. A happy guppy with plenty of room.

goldfish at 20 to 24°C (68 to 75°F). Sticklebacks need cool temperatures, about 18°C (65°F); no artificial heating is required. If room temperature is usually 21 to 30°C (70 to 85°F) and does not go below 10°C (50°F), you can keep white cloud mountain fish without artificial heating; if room temperature falls, use a heater to maintain a constant water temperature. Paradise fish will not need a heater if the water remains from 18 to 27°C (65 to 80°F). When you buy paradise fish, check to see at what temperature they have been kept and maintain that temperature at first, gradually lowering it to room temperature over the next few days.

Artificial heating is required to keep water temperatures at 24 to 27°C (75 to 80°F) for bettas, guppies, and other species of tropical fish.

SETTING UP THE AQUARIUM. Wash coarse, dark sand and gravel in a large dishpan by running hot water over the mixture until the water runs off clear when the sand is stirred vigorously. Pile the sand 4 cm deep at the back and slope it to 1 cm at the front. (Sediment and detritus will work down to the front where they can be siphoned off without disturbing the aquarium.) Place a piece of cardboard or two sheets of paper on top of the sand and slowly add water until the aquarium is one-third full, then remove the cardboard or paper. Check the tank for leaks.

Set in some aquatic plants, not only to add beauty but to absorb carbon dioxide from the water, give off oxygen, and provide food for vegetarian fish and refuge for young fish. Suitable plants are *Vallisneria, Elodea, Myriophyllum, Cabomba,* dwarf *Sagittaria,* and *Nitella.* Wash the plants well in running water to remove predacious microscopic organisms; the *Hydra* species and larvae of aquatic insects will prey upon aquarium fish and hinder breeding. Place tall plants at the back and smaller ones in front. Most plants can be tucked into the gravel at the bottom of the tank; push stray roots under the gravel with a small stick. (Do not cover the crown or the leaves.) *Elodea* and *Cabomba* can be left floating. Do not include too many plants; and resist the temptation to use ceramic castles, mermaids, or plastic plants which provide lodging places for debris that fouls the water. Smooth sandstone or granite rocks are acceptable.

Fill the tank with water to within 2.5 cm of the top. Again, check for leaks. Cover the tank and let it stand for several days, preferably a week or more, until all suspended matter has settled and the temperature has become stable.

Determine the number of fish the tank can hold (See Table 9-1), and do not exceed that number. When fish are to be transferred to the aquarium, adjust the water temperature, with an artificial heating device if necessary, until no more than 1°C variance exists between the temperature of the water in which the fish had been living and that of the new aquarium. Or, float a half-filled container with the fish in it in the aquarium for some time (about one-half hour) to allow the temperatures to equalize. Then gently tip the floating container and allow the fish to swim out. (This also will avoid frightening the fish.)

SNAILS. Opinions vary about adding snails to an aquarium. It is probably best not to add them unless they are to be studied. They should *not* be present if fish are to breed—they will eat young fish.

If you decide to add snails, you will find *Planorbis*, the "mystery snail," and other suitable pond snails in pet stores. Add only one snail for each gallon of water. Snails breed readily, and any above the concentration suggested must be removed. A snail that lies motionless on the bottom of the tank for several hours is probably dead and should be removed, or it will foul the water.

CLEANING THE AQUARIUM. An aquarium that is properly set up does not require much cleaning. A 6-mm, hollow glass tube longer than the depth of the water is useful as a dip tube for removing excess food and debris. Place a finger firmly on one end of the tube to seal it. Dip the tube into the water above the debris, release your finger, and the debris will be sucked into the tube. Reseal and remove the tube.

Another cleaning method is to use a piece of rubber tubing (10 mm in diameter and about a meter long) as a siphon. To start the water flowing, immerse the tube in a bowl of water, then close both ends with your fingers. Dip one end into the aquarium and let the other hang into a pail which is lower than the tank. Remove both fingers from the ends of the tube and the water will run out of the tank into the pail. Another, more hazardous method to start the water flowing is to suck on one end of the tube—stopping before you get a mouthful!

Whether or not to change the water, and if so, how often, is debatable. Under normal conditions replacing all the water is inadvisable.

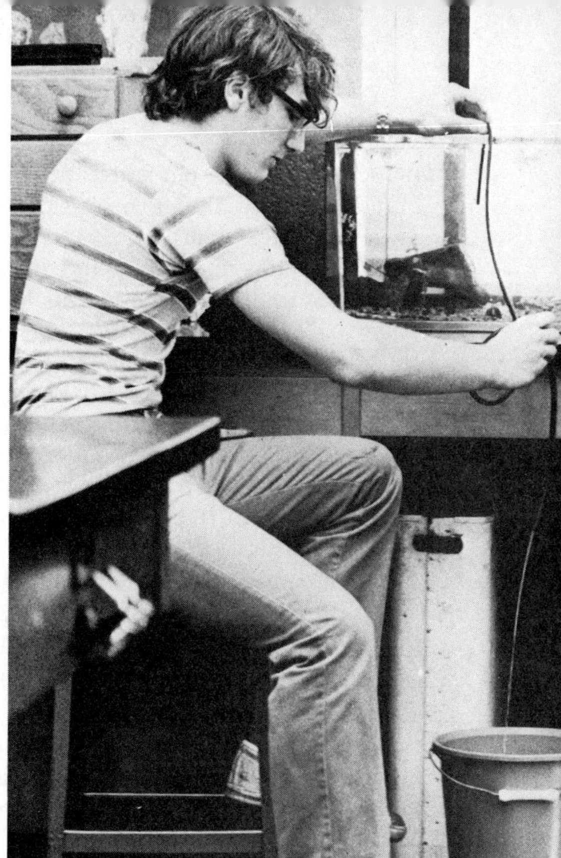

Figure 9-8. Siphoning off water.

Siphon off about one quarter of the water and replace it with suitable water, brought to room temperature by standing for one or two days. Siphoning water is less likely to injure the fish or stir up the bottom than pouring, or dipping with a pitcher. Some experienced aquarium keepers find that they can keep certain species of fish healthy for years without changing the water. They use distilled water (which prevents mineral build-up in the tank) to replace water lost by evaporation.

A regular routine to remove bottom debris, and an uncrowded tank, will reduce the need for major cleaning.

CLASSROOM CARE

Feeding

ADULT FISH. Fish thrive on a variety of foods—depending on their species. Omnivorous species, such as guppies, goldfish, and white cloud mountain fish, eat both animal and vegetable food. A variety of food will produce healthier fish. Purchase three or four brands of prepared food from a pet store and mix them together, or feed a different brand each day, thus averting possible nutritional deficiencies.

In contrast, carnivorous species, such as sticklebacks, paradise fish, and bettas, must have live or fresh-frozen food every day. Suitable live foods include white worms as the most highly recommended (see page 71), *Daphnia* (page 95), earthworms (page 65), mealworm larvae (page 144), freshly hatched or frozen brine shrimp (page 101), wingless fruit fly larvae (page 140), *Tubifex* worms, and *Anguilla silusia* (page 58). *Paramecium, Euglena,* and *Chilomonas* cultures (pages 19, 22, and 29) are easily grown. These protozoa are beneficial for adult fish and essential for young fish. There is now good evidence that many, if not all, fish species belong to the small group of animals which requires a dietary source of vitamin C. The use of live food is particularly valuable in avoiding dietary deficiencies.

Feed the fish each day. It is better if they are fed sparingly three times a day, although one feeding will do. Only one person should feed them to ensure that the schedule is followed. Feed live food in portions about the size of two rice grains. If the fish eat all of it within the next few minutes, give them additional portions until they are satisfied. Experience will show the correct amount of food. As a general rule, remove uneaten food—except for live organisms such as *Daphnia* species, which may be left to survive.

Many people find it difficult to scale down their generosity to fit the needs of small animals like fish, so the aquarium becomes polluted with decaying matter. The presence of decaying food diminishes the amount of vital oxygen and will eventually kill the fish. Continuously cloudy water may indicate overfeeding. (However, a cloudy condition can occur after changing water, but this should clear up in a day or two.)

YOUNG FISH. The feeding of young fish is essentially the same for all species. Newly emerged "fry" (young fish) require tiny food particles such as *Euglena, Paramecium,* or *Chilomonas* species. Use a protozoa culture at its peak concentration; stir it and empty half into the fish tank. Restore the culture to its original volume with distilled water, add a grain of rice or wheat or a slip of hay, and leave it at room temperature to mature. By preparing successive cultures, you can maintain a continuous supply of live food for the fish.

If these cultures are not available, beef scrapings and sieved hard-boiled egg are suitable substitutes. Mix a piece of egg the size of a pea in 30 ml of water and add a *few* drops to the tank with a medicine dropper several times a day. The egg must be freshly mixed each day.

Do not overfeed, because uneaten portions of egg decompose rapidly and are extremely poisonous to fry.

Feeding the fry five or six times a day is ideal; but three times will do. Once a day is not satisfactory. Feed them as much as they can eat each time. Increase the size of the food particles until they can accept the same as adult fish. The rate of increase depends on the rate of growth—some species, like guppies, mature very quickly; others, like goldfish, mature slowly. Guppies will eat newly hatched brine shrimp, *Artemia salina*, and fine tropical fish food after the first week; goldfish are a month old before such food is acceptable. After the fry begin to accept larger food, you may gradually reduce the number of feedings to once a day, if necessary. Goldfish fry need to be fed at least three times a day for three months. Guppy fry are simplest to feed, because they quickly accept prepared foods.

Table 9–1. Number of Fish to Keep in a Tank

Capacity of Tank (gal.)	*Dimensions of Tank (in.)*	*Number of 1″ Fish*
10	20×10×12	8*
15	24×12×12	12
20	30×14×14	17
25	32×18×15	24
50	50×22×15	46

*A 10-gallon tank is suitable for no more than eight 1-inch fish or four 2-inch fish, etc.

Daily Care

Daily care for a properly set up aquarium is minimal: feed the fish, add distilled water if necessary, and remove dead plants or animals. Also remove excess plants and snails.

Water that is green or yellow, often from algal growth, does not necessarily need to be changed. A moderate amount of algae is beneficial, because algae increase the oxygen supply in the water. If a green scum forms, scrape the sides of the tank with a *dull* straightedge blade on a stick and siphon off the debris. Introduce *Daphnia* species to feed on the algae, and reduce the amount of light on the tank. Floating plants which form a raft will effectively inhibit the light source, but these do have to be trimmed from time to time.

Vacation Care

Fish living in a well-established aquarium that contains some plants will survive weekends without feeding. However, they should never be left untended for more than two days. Since fish tanks are not easy to move, arrange for someone to come into school to feed the fish during longer vacations. Written instructions are helpful for a person inexperienced in feeding fish. To avoid problems, make up small packets containing the right amounts of food for a single daily feeding and label each with the date it is to be added to the aquarium. Explain that these small amounts are quite adequate and insist that no additional foods be added.

At the end of the school year it may be necessary to remove the fish. It is not necessary to remove snails; simply move the tank into the darkest corner of a north room. In September, the aquarium can be set up again with new fish.

Handling

Use slow, careful movements when handling fish. A frightened fish can receive skin abrasions that may become infected. If fish are to be moved from one container to another, be sure the temperature is the same in both. Never touch a fish with dry hands—use only a wet net, or nets. Hold a hand over the net to prevent the fish from flipping out. Do *not* handle any fish if your hands are cut or injured; a disease similar to tuberculosis has been spread to humans in this way.

Diseases

Fish usually will not become diseased if you purchase clean animals from reliable sources and provide optimum living conditions—do not crowd the tank or overfeed the fish. Provide the right variety and amount of food for all species.

Occasionally, fish will get sick even when well cared for. Symptoms of poor health are: persistent swimming near the surface or on the bottom of the aquarium, excessive sluggishness, drooping fins, or white or gray patches on fins and scales. Sick fish should be isolated immediately in another container to inhibit spread of any disease; be sure the water temperature is the same.

One common fish disease is called ich (pronounced "ick" or "itch"). It is caused by the external parasite, *Ichthyophthyrius*, and shows up as white spots on fins and scales. It is highly contagious among the fish and can be fatal if untreated. Effective remedies include quinine sulfate or acriflavine, which are available from pet stores. Other diseases, such as white fungus (which commonly attacks goldfish and looks like cottony scum on the lips of the fish), or fin rot (in which the fins become ragged and rot away), can be treated with tetracycline antibiotics which are also available from pet stores. These diseases are easy to recognize and treat. Only the worst neglect will result in fatalities.

Disposal of Fish

Sticklebacks are the only fish discussed in this chapter that can be returned to their natural habitat. Do this in early spring or in the fall. Never release tropical or other exotic species into local waters. They may harm the ecosystem if they survive and reproduce. Find suitable homes for them (some pet stores will accept them) or euthanize them.

EUTHANASIA. A diseased or unwanted fish can be rapidly and painlessly killed by placing it in a temporary container and bubbling carbon dioxide from a compressed cylinder into the water. Continue this procedure until the fish stops breathing. Or isolate the fish in a container with some aquarium water and place it in a refrigerator for several hours to lower the temperature, then transfer it to a freezer. Dead fish should be incinerated.

BREEDING

Guppies

Guppies are prolific live-bearing fish that multiply rapidly; they will breed in comparatively small (10–gallon) aquariums. They start to reproduce when only a few months old; and, unlike many other aquarium fish, they will not eat their young if the tank is not crowded. To prevent or control breeding, separate the sexes from a new batch of young as soon as sex can be distinguished. The distance between the anal and pelvic fins is shorter in males than in females.

SELECTIVE BREEDING. Select males and females from the same brood with the desired characteristics and breed them to study inheritance. Crosses of fish from different broods can introduce new fin shapes and color intensities.

To determine what color the female guppies will contribute to their sons, expose them to the male hormone, testosterone.* Testosterone must be handled with care and under the supervision of an adult. Prepare the following formula: in a quart bottle dissolve 0.1 gm of methyl testosterone in 100 ml of 70 percent alcohol; fill the bottle with water and shake well. This is the stock solution, approximately 3 gamma testosterone per liter of water. Add no more than two drops of stock solution to each gallon of aquarium water in which females are to be treated (higher concentrations will cause sterility). Continue adding two drops per gallon every other day. In two to four weeks the solution will bring out the hidden color in half-grown females; treat adult females for six weeks. Before mating, allow all the females to return to their normal color in untreated aquarium water.

Observe the courtship behavior of guppies in a small 2–gallon tank. Paint the sides and back of the aquarium with an opaque blue-white enamel. Fill it with water from the community tank and maintain it at about 24°C (75°F). Cover the bottom with gravel, but use no plants. Place a shaded low-wattage lamp directly above the aquarium to aid in close observation.

Place the male in the tank first. Some hours later, or the next day, introduce a gravid female swollen with ripe eggs. Courtship should begin as soon as the female is placed in the tank and will continue for about ten minutes. Guppy courtship behavior includes swinging and thrusting the gonopodium (the modified, rodlike anal fin of mature males), body curving and quivering, and finally mating when the tip of the male's gonopodium is inserted into the female's genitalia where fertilization occurs. When mating is completed, the two fish should be returned to their aquariums. The female will retain the eggs and the young will be born live. Remove the young guppies as soon as they start to grow—before the tank becomes crowded.

White Cloud Mountain Fish and Goldfish

Successful breeding of egg-laying species such as white cloud mountain fish and goldfish requires more care and attention than guppy breeding. Use a 20-gallon tank. To breed goldfish the temperature should be 16 to 21°C (60 to 70°F). Use the normal aquarium temperature, 21 to 30°C (70 to 86°F) for white cloud mountain fish. The female deposits her eggs on leaves and roots of aquatic plants (*Myriophyllum* and water hyacinth are recommended). The male follows her and fertilizes the tiny eggs. No parental care is given.

---

*Available from major biological supply houses.

Figure 9-9. *Students examining baby goldfish.*

White cloud mountain fish will not eat their own eggs if the adults are properly fed. The parents can be left with the eggs and can remain in the aquarium until the fry mature. Newly hatched fish hang onto plants and sides of the tank. Attached to each fish is a yolk sac which provides about three days' nourishment. After the yolk sac is gone, the fry subsist on microscopic organisms (see FEEDING, Young Fish, page 172).

Remove sprigs of vegetation bearing goldfish eggs and place them in an enamel pan with shallow water of the same temperature. Put the pan where the sun will strike the eggs for an hour or two each day; keep the water surface free from dust. Two black spots will soon appear in each egg; these are the eyes of the embryo. In two to three days the embryo bodies can be distinguished under slight magnification. Eggs that turn white and fluffy and in which no embryos appear should be removed.

Do not attempt to raise more than about a dozen of the goldfish fry in a small container. Euthanize the remainder by freezing or use them as food for other animals. As the fry grow, divide them among additional containers to prevent crowding.

Paradise Fish and Bettas

The same procedures can be used for breeding both species, but paradise fish are easier to breed than bettas. It is essential to provide space for the elaborate courtship display necessary for successful breeding. Use a 15– to 20–gallon aquarium with a removable opaque Plexiglas® partition down the center to separate the male from the female. Secure a large clump of plants in one corner to provide shelter for the female. Place a male on one side of the partition and a female on the other. In both species, the males are larger and have longer dorsal

Figure 9-10. Male and female bettas in nuptual embrace.

fins. Male bettas are very colorful (red, blue, green, black); male paradise fish change to intense hues during the breeding period.

Both paradise fish and bettas build bubble nests. Keep the male and female housed in their separate compartments at 24°C (75°F) for one month; then gradually raise the temperature to 27°C (80°F). The male should begin to build a nest. He will rise to the surface, take a gulp of air, and blow it out with a mucous secretion. The bubbles will form a cluster, creating a frothy mound. The male is then ready to perform his courtship display for a receptive gravid female. Gravid females can be identified by their swollen bodies. Raise the partition, being careful not to disturb the fragile nest, and allow the two fish to meet. Watch carefully. Be ready to replace the partition to separate them if there is any sign of fighting. (The female will attack the male if she is not ready to mate. Bettas can be particularly unpredictable in their mating—a change of mate is often the answer.) The courtship display makes a fascinating spectacle, which ends with the male wrapping his body around the female as the eggs are laid and fertilized. As the thin stream of eggs falls to the bottom, the male gathers them in his mouth and blows them into the nest, which is floating on the surface. Several mating embraces and spawnings follow at intervals for several hours until the female has laid all her eggs. Female bettas (but not paradise fish) must be removed at this point to prevent the male from killing the female. If you have observed the courting behavior carefully, you should have no trouble deciding when to separate bettas. Gently replace the partition and lift a female betta out, with as little agitation as possible; house her in a separate tank. Female paradise fish, on the other hand, can be left in the tank if there is no sign of aggression—they help care for the eggs.

The male guards the nest for the next several days until the eggs are hatched. He ensures that they get adequate oxygen by fanning them with his fins. Without oxygen the eggs will not hatch. The male will retrieve the newly hatched fry at first, but they soon slip away to live on their own. He may eat some of the eggs; but the instructional value of watching this parental behavior is worth the risk.

The bubble nest gradually becomes shallower, and by the time the young have absorbed the yolk sac which nourishes them during their early stages, the nest will have almost disintegrated. The male will continue to care for the fry for about a week. He can then be removed. Beginning fish breeders often have trouble maintaining the young fish beyond two weeks of age, usually because of inadequate food and a crowded tank.

Sticklebacks

Sticklebacks lay eggs and build nests. However, they may prove difficult to breed. Sticklebacks normally mate early in the spring, for they require 16 to 20 hours of light each day to reach the breeding stage. Females are olive with brown blotches and measure about 6 cm; males are gray-black and are somewhat smaller. Females can be housed in groups of four to ten in a 20-gallon tank. This tank size is also recommended for *each male*.

Isolate individual males to allow them to build their nests. Some species of stickleback build nests in depressions in the sand; others on a twig or stout plant stem. (Insert a stick down through the plants growing in the tank as a useful addition.) In many respects the nest resembles a bird's nest; it is about 2 cm in diameter with a hole in one side. During nest-building, the male changes color to a bright red underside and bluish-white back. He loses these colors immediately after mating.

Select a gravid female and place her in the male's tank. Watch carefully, for the whole courtship and egg-laying ritual is completed quickly. The male swims to the female. Then, swimming erratically, he leads her to the nest. After she enters, he prods her with his snout and she lays 50 to 100 eggs. When this is done, she swims out, and the male swims into the nest to fertilize them. After the eggs are fertilized, he chases the female away; she must be removed to save her life. The parental behavior of male sticklebacks is similar to that of the bubble-nest builders, and the care described for those species can be followed.

EXPERIMENTS WITH FISH

Conduct experiments with fish to study the adaptations necessary for life in the water—breathing, osmotic balance, development, and blood circulation. Standard textbooks usually cover these topics, but additional studies can be undertaken.

Development Studies

Make daily microscopic examinations of eggs of paradise fish, white cloud mountain fish, bettas, sticklebacks, or goldfish for studies of cleavage stages, circulation of blood through the yolk, and the order in which different structures develop (see FILMS, Development, page 189.) Guppies are ideal for studying the development of live-bearing fish. Observe fry daily to study their growth.

Mini-Habitats

Try to duplicate the natural habitat of a particular fish species. Keep a record of all the organisms present at one time or another in the aquarium. Try to identify species of fish, snails, worms, crustaceans, protozoa, algae, and plants. Keep records of the shifts in populations—these will be especially noticeable in protozoa and algae. Study the influence of environmental factors on these populations. Where possible, record the number of offspring and the disappearances of various organisms, and try to account for any changes that may take place in the flora and fauna.

Determine the feeding habits of some organisms; study the predator-prey relationships; work out a food chain and make a diagram of a food pyramid which includes all the organisms for which you have any data on food habits.

Behavior

REPRODUCTIVE BEHAVIOR. Many experiments can be performed with guppies on mating, courtship, and the attitude of females toward courting males.[2] Isolate male guppies, each in a tank with a peephole on one side for your use in observing them. Expose these males to various stimuli, such as females and models of females. Record a positive response only when you observe vibrating of the dorsal fins and maneuvering of the gonopodium. From this experimental design, determine the greatest distance at which a female stimulus elicits a positive response from the male. Does vision alone account for the sexual response of guppies, or could chemical responses be involved?[3] Do guppies or other fish show sexual activity at night?

Observe and analyze the elaborate courtship displays of guppies,[2] paradise fish, bettas,[4] and sticklebacks. A number of studies can be made of the nest-building activities of sticklebacks.[5a, 6] Similar studies can be devised with paradise fish and bettas. (See FILMS, Reproduction, page 189.) Observe the territorial defense by a male and the response of males to models of other males. To investigate the reaction of breeding males of a particular species to various colors, make a number of rough models of that species and paint them different colors (red, silver, blue, and green). Mount the models on wires and, holding them against the outside of the tank (keeping your hand hidden), present them one by one to the breeding males. Which colors provoke the most hostility?

AGGRESSIVE BEHAVIOR. Use a paradise fish, betta, or other fish as a test fish in one of two glass aquariums placed side by side. Place another fish of the same species in the other aquarium. Use fish of the same color and fish of different colors; observe the aggressive responses of the test fish. Devise a quantitative method of scoring aggressive behavior in order to collect the data. A simple system of allotting points is as follows: 1–approach, 2–spread fins, 3–raised gill covers, 4–tail beat, 5–ram.[7a] Run several trials for each stimulus and calculate the average aggression score.

How do fish react to their own mirror image? Cover part of a mirror with tape and gradually increase the covered surface to determine how much of its own image it takes to make a fish respond with aggressive behavior. The stimulus should not be kept in view for long; fatigue will occur and the fish will fail to respond. To enhance the effect, keep the fish in visual isolation for a week before testing.

Habituation can be studied by repeating a visual stimulus for a fixed duration.[5b] How long does it take for aggressive response to decrease? How long does habituation last? What is the function of habituation in the natural behavior of the animals? Does temperature affect these responses? Use 2°C (5°F) intervals between 18 and 30°C (64 and 86°F). Is color important? Will bettas respond to drawings and models of fish?

EXPLORATORY BEHAVIOR. Present a novel stimulus, such as a clean piece of colored glass or plastic, to make quantitative assessments of the exploratory behavior of, for example, goldfish.[5c] Observe the nature, frequency, and duration of response to the foreign object. Include swimming forward or backward, remaining motionless, attacking, and mouthing the object. Does the exploratory response change if this experiment is repeated every day for a week? Does the presence of other fish affect the behavior?

SCHOOLING. Fish exhibit an extreme form of social organization. A school typically consists of fish of the same species and size, without a hierarchy, forming a closely knit group moving at a uniform pace. Most of the members are usually engaged in the same activity at the same time. Brook and three-spined sticklebacks are suitable species for observing this phenomenon in the classroom. Does aggressive behavior occur in a school of fish? What is the density of the school, and under what conditions, if any, does it vary?

Perform a simple experiment with nine fish of the same species using two screw-top jars. Put six fish in one jar and two in the other; place the jars at opposite ends of an aquarium. Release the ninth fish to swim freely in the center of the aquarium, and observe where this test fish spends the most time. Repeat the experiment using a new test fish and an equal number of fish in each jar. Does the test fish tend to associate with the larger or with the smaller school? Make quantitative records of responses and analyze them statistically.[5d]

Effects of Light

Does continuous high-intensity light affect the color of male guppies? Shine the light through two glass tanks filled with water so the second tank, the guppy aquarium, will not overheat.

Some reports show that light induces sterility in male guppies. Try to repeat these experiments, then gradually lower the light intensity until it no longer induces male sterility. Does light also affect the ability of females to lay eggs? In contrast, certain lighting conditions are reported to stimulate reproduction in some fish.[8] The brood intervals of guppies kept under different lighting conditions may vary. Constant light was found to reduce the brood interval from the usual 30 days or more to 21 days. Can reports that light has a stimulatory and a deleterious effect on reproduction both be true? Is the intensity or the duration of light, or a combination of these, the determining factor?

Does light also influence the development of fertilized eggs? Use eggs from any species to study the developmental effects under different light intensities. Compare the rates of development of eggs maintained under fluorescent light, incandescent light, and daylight. Vary only one factor at a time; if fluorescent and incandescent light are to be compared, they should be of about equal intensities. Conversely, if light intensities are to be compared, the type of source should be the same (for example, two incandescent bulbs of different wattage).

Effects of Temperature

Many rewarding studies can be made of the effects of temperature on the respiration of fish.[7b, 9a] Take precautions not to harm the fish when raising or lowering water temperatures. Since goldfish and

Figure 9-11. Timing the respiration of goldfish. A sandwich bag confines the fish for easier observation. The operculum movement rate is measured with the aid of a stopwatch. A thermometer is submerged in the water so that water temperature can be determined. Different water temperatures can be tested and related to rate of respiration.

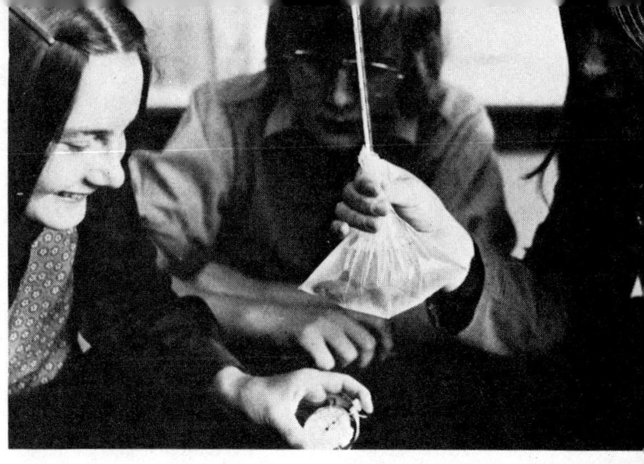

paradise fish can withstand temperature changes better than most other aquarium fish, they are the preferred species for this experiment. How many times do the gills beat when the water temperature is 21°C (70°F)? By slowly adding and stirring in warmer water (take 15 to 30 minutes to do this), you can raise the water temperature to 24°C (75°F) without shocking the fish. Remember—the warmer the water, the less dissolved oxygen it contains. Fish swimming near the top of the water are suffering from lack of oxygen. The maximum temperature to which these fish should be exposed is 30°C (85°F); the minimum is 14°C (55°F). Record the respiratory rates at every 2°C (5°F) temperature change as you raise or lower the temperature.

Over the course of several months, count the number of male and female offspring produced by guppies maintained at different, but constant, aquarium temperatures.[9b]

Carbon Dioxide Metabolism

Measure carbon dioxide metabolism of fish using the method described by Beyers.[10] Compare CO_2 metabolism at various stages of growth in a single species, or between mature fish of different species.

Hormones

The color changes which can be induced by exposing female guppies to testosterone were discussed on page 176.[11,12] Do estrogenic substances have similar effects on immature and mature male guppies? Do estrogens prevent the development of secondary sexual characteristics and cause immature male guppies to assume female characteristics?[13] What are the effects of other endocrine substances, such as adrenaline, on goldfish skin-color patterns?[14] How are activity and body weight of goldfish affected by feeding them ground-up testicular substances for ten weeks.[15]

Different Colored Background

Apart from skin-color changes that can be effected with hormones and light intensity, color change in some fish occurs according to the background in which they live—a camouflage effect. To investigate this characteristic, keep minnows, sticklebacks, or other species for several months in aquariums with walls of different colors—one with pale blue walls, another gray, another brown,—and determine if any skin-color changes occur.

Some fish show preference for certain backgrounds. Obtain yellow and gray goldfish and introduce them one by one to a fish tank which is painted half yellow and half gray (try to match the paint to the fish). Immediately after each fish is put in the tank, make 200 observations, at five-second intervals, of which half of the tank the fish is in. Values over 100 indicates a color preference.[16]

Genetics

Because of their color, guppies, paradise fish, and bettas are particularly useful for studies of inherited characteristics. Guppies and paradise fish can be studied for the inheritance of albinism;[17] bettas, for inheritance of blue and red.[18]

Learning

You can condition fish to come to a certain corner of the tank when you blow a whistle. Blow the whistle once, for about two seconds, just before you feed the fish. Whistle before they see you, or they may become conditioned to your approach. Try to whistle in the same way each time, and always feed them in the same corner. Do not overfeed the fish (they will learn faster if they are a little hungry). During training, do not give the signal without feeding them, and never feed them without first blowing the whistle. Soon they will learn to come to the corner in response to the whistle. This is a conditioned response. Similar responses can be evoked when a bell is rung, a light is flashed, or the side of the tank is tapped gently. How long does it take to train the fish? Do some species learn more quickly than others? How soon do they forget? With goldfish and paradise fish (they can withstand moderate temperature changes), does temperature of the aquarium water affect learning rate? Are the offspring of trained fish quicker to learn the response than those of untrained fish?

Many species, including goldfish, can learn to swim mazes; tests commonly used on mice can be adapted for fish. Goldfish can learn to select and discriminate among objects of different shapes, sizes, and colors.[19,20] Bettas can be trained to display aggressive behavior (fin erection and undulating movements) in response to a red light,[21] or to swim through a hoop to display their aggression to mirror images or models.[22] Some of these learning experiments require considerable time and patience and are therefore more suitable for advanced students.

Enzyme Systems

Since enzyme function and other biochemical actions are influenced by temperature, the problems of how these systems work in fish is of particular interest. Fish are poikilothermic animals—unlike warmblooded vertebrates, they adopt the temperature of their environment, which may vary from 0 to 37°C (32 to 99°F). Do the pathways of intermediary carbohydrate, fat, or protein metabolism vary according to the body temperature of the fish?

In warmblooded animals, enzyme systems work best at body temperature, 37°C (99°F), but what systems are utilized in fish that do not maintain these body temperatures? For a review of recent work in this field, see Tarr.[23]

Vitamin Requirements

Only recently, scientists have come to realize that vitamins are important for maintaining the health of fish. An account of recent work and a description of how fish can be used in studies of vitamin deficiency is given in Halver.[24]

REFERENCES

1. *Aquarium Construction in the Home Workshop.* 1962. Leaflet FL-315. U. S. Dept. of Interior, Fish and Wildlife Ser., Div. of Fish Hatcheries, Washington, D. C.
2. Breder, C. M., Jr. and C. W. Coats. 1935. Sex Recognition in the Guppy, *Lebistes reticulatus* Peters. *Zoologica* 19(5) :187–207. (Advanced)
3. Goldstein, P. and J. Metzner. 1971. *Experiments with Microscopic Animals.* Doubleday & Co., Garden City, N.Y. pp. 114–15.
4. Kuhn, D. J. 1970. Experiments with Display Patterns in the Siamese Fighting Fish. *Amer. Biol. Teacher* 32(2) :102–104.

5. Stokes, A. W., ed. 1968. *Animal Behavior in Laboratory and Field.* W. H. Freeman & Co., San Francisco.

a. Muller-Schwarze, D. Reproductive Behavior of the Three-Spined Stickleback. pp. 93–97. Available from the publisher as Separate No. 816.

b. Marler, P. Response of Male Fighting Fish to Visual Stimuli: A Study of Habituation. pp. 171–73. Separate No. 832.

c. Delorge, J. O. Exploratory Behavior in Goldfish. pp. 167–70. Separate No. 831. (Advanced)

d. Keenleyside, M. H. A. Schooling Behavior in Fish. pp. 35–38. Separate No. 803. (Advanced)

6. Tinbergen, N. 1952. The Curious Behavior of the Stickleback. *Sci. Amer.* 187(6) :22–26. Offprint 414, W. H. Freeman & Co., San Francisco.

7. Pringle, L., ed. 1970. *Discovering Nature Indoors: A Nature and Science Guide to Investigation with Small Animals.* Natural History Press, Doubleday & Co., Garden City, N.Y. a. pp. 41–45, b. pp. 46–48. (Intermediate)

8. Scrimshaw, N. S. 1944. Superfetation in Poeciliid Fishes. *Copeia* 3:180–83.

9. Davis, H. T. 1969. *Projects in Biology.* Science Publications, Normal, Ill. 61761. a. pp. 16–18; b. pp. 112–14.

10. Beyers, R. J. and B. Gillespie. 1964. Measuring the Carbon Dioxide Metabolism of Aquatic Organisms. *Amer. Biol. Teacher* 26(7) :499–510.

11. Eversole, W. J. 1939. The Effects of Androgens upon the Fish (*Lebistes reticulatus*). *Endocrinology* 25:328–30. (Advanced)

12. Eversole, W. J. 1940. The Effects of Pregneninolone and Related Steroids on Sexual Development of Fish (*Lebistes reticulatus*). *Endocrinology* 28:603–10. (Advanced)

13. Berkowitz, P. 1938. The Effects of Estrogenic Substances in *Lebistes reticulatus. Anat. Rec.* 71:160–70. (Advanced)

14. Goodrich, H. B. and P. O. Anderson. 1939. Variation of Color Pattern in Hybrids of the Goldfish, *Carassius auratus. Biol. Bull.* 77:184–91.

15. Stanley, L. L. and G. L. Tescher. 1932. Weight of Goldfish Influenced by Testicular Substance Diet. *Endocrinology* 16:153–54. (Advanced)

16. Breder, C. M., Jr. and F. Halpern. 1946. Innate and Acquired Behavior Affecting the Aggregation of Fishes. *Physiol. Zool.* 19(2) :154–90. (Advanced)

17. Gordon, M. 1955. *Guppies . . . as Pets.* T.F.H. Publications, Jersey City, N. J. p. 20 *et seq.*

18. Goodrich, H. B. and R. N. Mercer. 1943. Genetics and Colors of the Siamese Fighting Fish, *Betta splendens. Science* 79:318–19.

19. MUNTZ, W. R. A. and J. R. CONLY-DILLON. 1966. Color Discrimination by Goldfish. *Anim. Behav.* 14:351–55.

20. MACKINTOSH, J. and N. S. SUTHERLAND. 1963. Visual Discrimination by the Goldfish: The Orientation of Rectangles. *Anim. Behav.* 11:135–41. (Advanced)

21. THOMPSON, T. I. and T. STURM. 1965. Classical Conditioning of Aggressive Display in Siamese Fighting Fish. *J. Exp. Anal. Behav.* 8:397–403. (Advanced)

22. THOMPSON, T. I. 1963. Visual Reinforcement in Siamese Fighting Fish. *Science* 141:55–57. (Advanced)

23. TARR, H. K. A. 1969. Contrast between Fish and Warmblooded Vertebrates in Enzyme Systems of Intermediary Metabolism. O. W. Neuhaus and J. E. Halver, eds. *Fish in Research.* Academic Press, New York. pp. 155–74. (Advanced)

24. HALVER, J. E. 1969. Vitamin Requirements. O. W. Neuhaus and J. E. Halver, eds. *Fish in Research.* Academic Press, New York. pp. 209–32. (Advanced)

FURTHER READING

AXELROD, H. R. 1969. *Tropical Fish as a Hobby.* rev. ed. McGraw-Hill Book Co., New York.

AXELROD, H. R. and R. BADER. 1966. The Educational Aquarium for Native and Exotic Fishes. T.F.H. Publications, Jersey City, N.J.

BROWN, M. E., ed. 1957. *Physiology of Fishes.* Two vol. Academic Press, New York.

Care of Goldfish. 1965. Leaflet FL-57. U. S. Dept. of Interior, Fish and Wildlife Ser., Washington, D. C.

Care of Tropical Aquarium Fishes. 1965. Leaflet FL-411. U. S. Dept. of Interior, Fish and Wildlife Ser., Washington, D. C.

CONROY, D. A. and R. L. HERMAN. 1970. *Textbook of Fish Disease.* T.F.H. Publications, Jersey City, N.J.

EDDY, S. 1970. *How to Know the Freshwater Fishes.* 2nd. ed. W. C. Brown Co., Dubuque, Iowa.

HOKE, J. 1975. *Aquariums.* Franklin Watts, Inc., New York.

INNES, W. T. 1964. *Exotic Aquarium Fishes.* 19th rev. ed. E. P. Dutton & Co., New York.

LEWIS, W. M. 1963. *Maintaining Fishes for Experimental and Instructional Purposes.* Southern Illinois University Press, Carbondale, Ill.

MEYERRIECKS, A. J. 1962. *Courtship in Animals.* BSCS Pamphlet No. 3. Educational Programs Improvement Corp., P. O. Box 3406, Boulder, Colo. 80303.

NEEDHAM, J. G. and P. R. NEEDHAM. 1962. *A Guide to the Study of Fresh-Water Biology.* 5th ed. Holden-Day, San Francisco.

PINCKNEY, G. A. and L. E. ANDERSON. 1967. *Rearing Conditions and Sociability in* Lebistes reticulatus. *Psychonomic Sci.* 9:591–92.

SWENSON, W., BARMAN, C. and KOCH, R. 1976. *Aquaria on a Classroom Budget.* The Science Teacher, Vol. 43, No. 3, March, pp. 35–36.

VILLIARD, P. 1971. *Exotic Fish as Pets.* Doubleday & Co., Garden City, N. Y.

WAINWRIGHT, N. 1970. *Tropical Aquariums, Plants and Fishes.* Frederick Warne & Co., New York.

Marine Animals

DIEHL, F. A., J. B. FEELEY and D. G. GIBSON. *Experiments Using Marine Animals.* Aquarium Systems, Inc., 33208 Lakeland Blvd., Eastlake, Ohio 44094.

MARISCAL, R., Ed. 1974. *Experimental Marine Biology.* Academic Press, New York.

MCCONNAUGHEY, B. H. 1970. *Introduction to Marine Biology*. C. V. Mosby Co., St. Louis, Mo.

MILNE, L. and M. MILNE. 1970. *When the Tide Goes Far Out.* Atheneum Publishers, New York.

O'CONNELL, R. F. 1969. *The Marine Aquarium.* Great Outdoors Publishing Co., St. Petersburg, Florida.

STRAUGHAN, R. P. 1969. *The Salt-Water Aquarium in the Home.* rev. 2nd ed. A. S. Barnes & Co., Cranbury, N. J.

VALENTI, R. J. 1968. *The Salt Water Aquarium Manual.* Aquarium Stock Co., New York.

WATERS, B. and J. WATERS. 1967. *Salt Water Aquariums.* Holiday House, New York. (Intermediate)

FILMS

General

Among Fish. 16 mm, color, 11 min. National Film Board of Canada, 680 Fifth Ave., New York, NY 10019; or contact local Canadian Consulate General.

Aquarium Construction. (Overhead transparencies, overlays to show how to set up a balanced aquarium.) Hubbard Scientific Co., Dept. B-3, Box 105, Northbrook, Ill 60062.

The Betta Fish. Filmloop, super 8 mm, color, 3 min. 40 sec. Ealing Film Loops, Cambridge, Mass 02140

Bubble Nest Builder (Southeast Asian Fighting Fish). Film loop, super 8 mm, cartridge, color. Encyclopaedia Britannica Films, 1150 Wilmette Ave., Wilmette, Ill 60091.

Characteristics of Bony Fish. Film loop, super 8 mm, color. BFA Educational Media, 2211 Michigan Ave., Santa Monica, Ca 90404.

Fish and Their Characteristics. 16 mm, b/w or color, 11 min. Coronet Films, 65 E. South Water St., Chicago, Ill 60601.

Fishes. (Includes goldfish.) Film loop, super 8 mm, cartridge, color, 3 min. 40 sec. Oceanography Unlimited, Inc., 91 Delaware Ave., Paterson, NJ 07503.

Looking at Fishes. 16 mm, color or b/w, 10 min 30 sec. Encyclopaedia Britannica Education Corp., 425 North Michigan Ave, Chicago, Ill 60611.

Maintaining Biological Specimens. (Includes how to make an aquarium.) Set of 6 color filmstrips, avg. 50 frames each. NASCO, Ft. Atkinson, Wisc 53538.

Making a Balanced Aquarium. 16 mm, color or b/w, 11 min. Coronet Films, 65 E. South Water St., Chicago, Ill 60601.

Siamese Fighting Fish. 16 mm, sound, color, 10 min. Wonders of Wildlife Series. Fleetwood Films, Inc., 10 Fiske Place, Mount Vernon, NY 10550.

Story of a Goldfish. 16 mm, sound, color, 18 min. Fleetwood Films, Inc., 10 Fiske Place, Mount Vernon, NY 10550.

Trout Hatchery (Life Cycle of Trout). 16 mm, color, silent, 15 min. ACI Films, Inc., 35 West 45 St., New York, NY 10036.

Development

Development of the Ovum, Fish. Super 8 mm, cartridge, silent, color, 4 min. Encyclopaedia Britannica Films, 1150 Wilmette Ave., Wilmette, Ill 60091.

Embryonic Development of Fish. (common Zebra) 16 mm, color, 27 min. National Film Board of Canada, 680 Fifth Ave., New York 10019 (or contact local Canadian Consulate General)

Fish Embryo from Fertilization to Hatching. 16 mm, color, 11 min. 36 sec. Encyclopaedia Britannica Films, 425 North Michigan Ave, Chicago, Ill 60611.

Reproduction Cycle of Angel Fish. 16 mm, 10 min. International Film Bureau, Inc., 332 S. Michigan Ave., Chicago 60604.

Reproduction–Fish Eggs Hatching. Filmloop, super 8 mm, silent, 1 min. 41 sec. Doubleday and Co., Inc., Garden City, NY 11530.

Reproduction

Courtship Behavior of the Stickleback. Filmloop, super 8 mm, cartridge, color, 4 min. Oceanography Unlimited, Inc., 91 Delaware Ave., Paterson, NJ 07503.

Courtship Ritual of Stickleback. Filmloop, super 8 mm, 4 min. Walt Disney Film. Doubleday and Co., Inc., Garden City, NY 11530.

Stickleback: Experiments with Models. Filmloop, super 8 mm, cartridge, color, 4 min. Oceanography Unlimited, Inc., 91 Delaware Ave., Paterson, NJ 07503.

Territorial Behavoir: Fish. Super 8 mm, cartridge, color, 4 min. 10 sec. Oceanography Unlimited, Inc., 91 Delaware Ave., Paterson, NJ 07503.

10

Amphibians

The clever men at Oxford
Know all that there is to be knowed
But none of them know one half as much
As intelligent Mr. Toad.

Kenneth Grahame (1859-1932)

Amphibians are popular for studies of capillary blood flow and characteristics of nerves and muscles, and their eggs are widely used for investigations of growth and development. The animals themselves are simple to care for. Most amphibians lay eggs that hatch into small dark tadpoles (polliwogs) with fat bodies and long tails. The tadpoles live in water and breathe with gills. In time, they develop legs and lungs, lose their tails, and become adults that live in water or on land. Adult amphibians have three-chambered hearts and usually have moist skin without scales. Among the species described in this chapter are the African clawed toad *Xenopus laevis*; the leopard frog *Rana pipiens* and other *Rana* species; tree frogs of the *Hyla* species; salamanders of *Ambystoma* species; the red-spotted newt *Notophthalmus viridescens;* and toads, *Bufo* species.

Feeding amphibians may or may not present problems. If you select a species (such as *Rana*) that eats live foods, you will need to culture insects or worms. It is much simpler to use a species such as *Xenopus* that eats dead foods. *Xenopus* also is much hardier than *Rana* species, can withstand temperature fluctuations better, and is easier to maintain. The use of *Xenopus* for study would help check the serious depletion of native *Rana* species.[1] It is difficult to reconcile teaching conservation with continued heavy reliance on *Rana pipiens* for biological study.

The eggs most recommended for classroom use are *Xenopus* eggs, followed by those of the frogs *Rana pipiens, Rana sylvaticus* (the wood frog), and tree frogs. *Xenopus* eggs are ideal for observation because they are comparatively large and develop rapidly. With hormone injections, a *Xenopus* toad will produce eggs at any time of the year.* By scheduling successive injections, you can obtain eggs at close intervals and observe all stages of development at one time. This procedure is not satisfactory for *Rana clamitans* (the green frog) or *Rana catesbeiana* (the bullfrog) because they take too long to mature.

Xenopus also can be used for dissection.[2]

Native frogs, toads, and salamanders live in ponds, brooks, and shallow streams where aquatic vegetation is thick, or in nearby woods. Frogs and toads consume millions of common pests, including inchworms and ticks, and are highly beneficial to man. Many states have laws to prevent uncontrolled collecting of toads and frogs. It is illegal to collect hibernating frogs in many areas; New York State, among others, prohibits collection of eggs and tadpoles until after mid-June. These measures help to assure continuance of thriving populations. Check local conservation laws before taking any amphibians from the wild. Do not take adults, and collect only as many eggs or tadpoles as you can house without crowding. Leave the rest in the pond.

Choose very small tadpoles—"inchlings." Leave the larger ones. A very large one, around 9 cm long, is almost sure to be a slowly developing bullfrog.

The eggs are usually attached to sticks and grass in marshes and pools in early spring. Collect them with a fine mesh net or in solid containers, and take home an extra supply of pond water. Frog eggs occur in masses of jelly; toad eggs occur in single rows in long strands of jelly. Small frogs lay 400 to 500 eggs, but the larger ones may lay up to 20,000 eggs at one time. Select clumps of eggs that are 8 to 12 cm across. The eggs of the smaller frogs (leopard frogs, spring peepers, pickerel frogs) develop into adults within one to three months, but larger species (green frogs and bullfrogs) may take up to three years.

Table 10–1 on page 209 lists commercial suppliers of amphibians. *Xenopus* eggs are not sold because they develop so rapidly. *Rana* eggs are available from October until early April. You can order tadpoles in the spring.

A company that does its own collecting from the wild can supply healthier adult animals. To keep shipping distance at a minimum, select the dealer closest to you. (If the weather is hot when the frogs arrive, they will be very active and hard to handle. Place them in a deep sink and sprinkle them with a stream of cool water until they slow down.)

---

*For induction of ovulation, see page 206.

DESCRIPTION OF SPECIES

The three types of housing noted below as I (aquatic), II (semi-aquatic and some terrestrial), and III (terrestrial) are described on pages 196–198. General feeding instructions are given below. In general, native toads are less satisfactory than frogs as classroom animals; they have poisonous skin secretions and tend to be more nocturnal.

AFRICAN CLAWED TOAD (*Xenopus laevis*). Highly recommended. Aquatic, requiring an aquarium (I). The toad's natural home is in lakes, ponds, and swamps over a wide area of South Africa. *Xenopus* toads will feed only in water. They have black claws on the three inner toes of each hind foot. On land, they move forward in awkward jerks, but in water they are skillful swimmers. The female is about 10 cm long and the male 7 cm. The skin is normally brown with a mottled pattern on the back and pale yellow to white on the underside, but *Xenopus* can change to a variety of shades from pale yellow to dark brown. The internal anatomy is basically like that of the common frog, except that *Xenopus* do not have tongues. Although *Xenopus* may take three to four years to reach maximum size, sexual maturity is attained within two years. The reliability with which females lay eggs in response to injections of chorionic gonadotropin has been helpful, in the past, in human pregnancy tests.

Feed the adult *Xenopus laevis* thin strips of beef liver or beef heart, or use horse meat, earthworms, tadpoles, or white worms. They have insatiable appetites. During the early stages of development, when the mouth and glottis are small, provide scrapings of beef or liver, white worms, and earthworms; or try fragments of fat free steak or finely

Figure 10-1. Xenopus, *the African clawed toad. Female, on left, has cloacal flaps which look like a tail. Male, on right, has thicker forelegs than female and the male has swollen thumb pads on front limbs.*

Figure 10-2. Leopard frog. (Courtesy Carolina Biological Supply House)

shredded heart or liver. Allow the young to feed to capacity. Include both meat and live food in their diet.

LEOPARD FROG (*Rana pipiens*). Recommended. Terrestrial (II). These frogs are most commonly used for dissection, although it would be better to substitute *Xenopus*. *Rana pipiens* range from Canada to Central America and have been harvested in the United States for use as laboratory animals and as bait to such an extent that conservationists are advocating artificial breeding. The leopard frog has a beautiful green body heavily blotched with dark, creamy yellow spots. The underparts of the body are white. Leopard frogs emerge from hibernation in the spring and lay eggs in the water. They spend the summer in swamps or fields, and in the fall return to deep water to hibernate for the winter.

WOOD FROG (*Rana sylvatica*) Recommended. Terrestrial (III). This alert species has reddish-brown coloring which looks like the dead leaves littering a forest. The wood frog can change its appearance; it may lose all of its spots or shift from dark to light hue in less than 30 minutes. It ranges from Quebec to South Carolina and westward to the Great Plains. It is even more terrestrial than *R. pipiens*.

PICKEREL FROG (*Rana palustris*). Terrestrial (III). Pickerel frogs are similar in appearance to leopard frogs, except that they are more gray in color with yellow legs, and their spots are more rectangular and regular. Pickerel frogs range only in the eastern United States. They have an unpleasant-smelling, irritating skin secretion. They should not be housed with other species, as this secretion can be fatal to other animals.

GREEN FROG (*Rana clamitans*). Almost entirely aquatic (II). The bright green animals of this species are often confused with the larger bullfrogs. Green frogs occur in the eastern United States. Adults can be kept in the classroom, but their eggs and tadpoles are not recommended for observation, as the tadpoles do not metamorphose until the second summer. In nature, the adults have solitary habits, so they should not be crowded in captivity. They usually eat aquatic insects such as mayflies, backswimmers, and whirligigs, but will accept almost any insect or worm.

BULLFROG (*Rana catesbeiana*). Bullfrogs are too large to be used as classroom animals, and they take two to three years from egg-laying to complete their metamorphosis from tadpoles to adults. They range widely in the United States.

TREE FROG (*Hyla* species). Recommended. Terrestrial (III). Although members of this genus are widespread throughout the United States, they are seldom seen by a casual observer. They are very secretive and are well camouflaged. Some species can be heard frequently, however, especially in early spring. Tree frogs can be tamed, and all species are recommended for the classroom. Most are active and attractive. As the name suggests, tree frogs live in trees and are excellent climbers; they can even walk along the underside of a tree branch. Keep them in tall containers with twigs the diameter of a pencil or with growing plants that have strong stems, such as *Sagittaria*, marsh marigold, and sedges. Sprinkle the plants or twigs daily; tree frogs lap up the drops for drinking water. It may be difficult to get some of these frogs to accept raw

Figure 10-3. Tree frog.

Figure 10-4. Housing for newt in the adult aquatic stage. (Courtesy Carolina Biological Supply House)

meat, but all of them will eat other recommended live foods, particularly flies.

SALAMANDER (*Ambystoma* species). Recommended. Terrestrial (III). Certain *Ambystoma* species are very hardy and adapt well to the classroom. Recommended species are the eastern spotted salamander *A. maculatum*; the blue-spotted or Jefferson's salamander *A. laterale*; and the tiger salamander *A. tigrinum*. These animals may burrow beneath the moss and earth in your terrarium unless you create crevices with rocks and small branches. They climb well, so be sure the lid fits tightly. Usually they can be trained to accept dead meat; they quickly learn to come to a certain spot to be fed, and will eventually learn to eat from a dish. They can run mazes well and are easily tamed.

RED-SPOTTED NEWT (*Notophthalmus viridescens* [Older names are *Diemictylus viridescens* and *Triturus viridescens*]). Recommended. This animal is called the red eft in the terrestrial phase, and the water newt or green water lizard in the adult aquatic stage. House in a terrarium (III) or aquarium (I), according to the animal's stage of development. Of all salamanders, the harmless red-spotted newts are the hardiest and most attractive. They are found all over the northern and eastern United States. After a normal larval stage in the water, red-spotted newts usually live on land, sometimes far from their native waters. These woodland adolescents are called efts and are about 5 cm long. In some localities, such as Long Island, the newt larvae change directly into the swimming adult form. In most regions, the red eft returns to the water for breeding and assumes a different coloration and different habits. When fully grown, red-spotted newts are 7.5 to 10 cm long. In both phases, they have two rows of scarlet spots rimmed with black running down their backs.

If the animals are in the olive-green water phase (larval), keep them in an aquarium. In this stage, they usually eat more readily and are, therefore, simpler to care for than in the red eft stage. Feed them finely cut meat and liver three times a week.

The attractive red eft makes a good addition to a damp moss-covered terrarium. Offer these small animals only small food. They can be difficult to feed, but may accept white worms, fruit flies, or very small earthworms. They will usually not accept dead meat.

TOAD (*Bufo* species). Terrestrial (III). *Bufo americanus*, the American toad found in eastern states, and the similar *B. terrestris*, native to southern states, are satisfactory classroom animals if large food supplies are available. However, they may not survive the winter months in captivity, so keep them only for short periods in the spring or summer, and release them where you found them well before the end of the summer. These species have large vocal pouches which they inflate. Their care is similar to that of terrestrial frogs.

HOUSING FOR ADULT AMPHIBIANS

Some toads secrete a poison that can be harmful to other species; do not house them with other amphibians. Also, if animals of greatly varying sizes are housed together, the larger will eat the smaller.

The three types of housing described here are those noted by number in the preceding species list.

I. HOUSING FOR AQUATIC SPECIES (*Xenopus* and water phase of newts). *Xenopus* species can be kept in any kind of large tank; a toughened polyethylene container is best, because it is strong, light, and unbreakable. Purchase a container 60 × 40 × 17 cm for five pairs of toads. A suitable substitute is a plastic vegetable crisper, although it will house fewer animals because it is smaller. These containers are stackable.

Another possible arrangement is in a laundry sink. Water should be about 10 cm deep and must be dechlorinated. Let the water stand 24 hours before using it.

Change standing water three times a week, and wash the container once a week. If you can provide constant running water that does not contain chlorine, you will not need to clean the tank or sink. Stones or weeds are desirable but not necessary.

Toads can easily leap from the water, so closely fitting lids are necessary. Cut transparent plastic sheeting (from hardware stores) 5 cm larger than the tank and bend it over the rim. Cut four small holes in the top for air. If the tanks are stacked, you will need a lid only for the top tank; enough air will enter through the imperfect seal between tanks. Fine-mesh wire screen, perforated stainless steel, or zinc lids are also

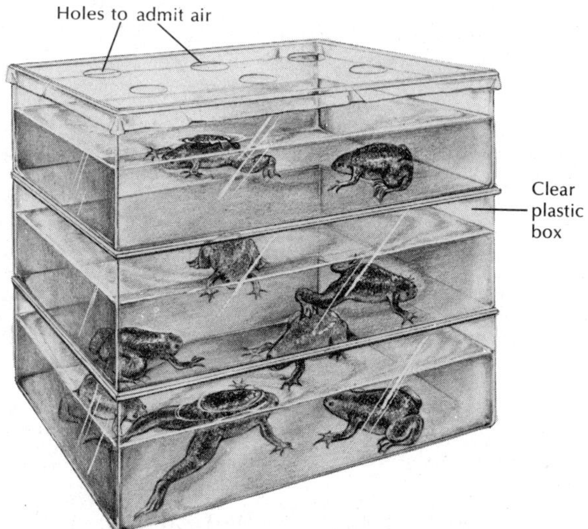

Figure 10-5. Housing for aquatic species such as Xenopus. *Each box is covered with plastic sheeting with holes in it for air.*

suitable. Allow a space between the lid and the water level, so the animals can come up to breathe.

II. HOUSING FOR SEMIAQUATIC SPECIES AND SOME TERRESTRIAL SPECIES. House leopard frogs and green frogs in plastic vegetable crispers with only enough water to half cover the frogs. Chlorinated tap water can be used for these animals. Up to about eight medium-sized frogs can be housed in a crisper 35 × 25 × 11 cm inches. Some provision must be made for the animals to leave the water. A smaller opaque crisper, with one end removed, placed upside down in the larger crisper, will provide a land area and a hiding place. Fit some netting over the smaller crisper, so the animals will not have direct contact with the plastic. (This roof area can be used for feeding them.) Add broken pieces of clay pots as additional hiding places for these normally secretive animals. Keep the tank covered to prevent escape. Change the water three times a week and wash the container once a week.

III. HOUSING FOR TERRESTRIAL SPECIES (*Rana, Hyla,* and *Bufo*). Wood frogs and tree frogs are best housed in a woodland terrarium made from an aquarium or other container with solid sides. (Details for setting up a terrarium can be found on page 225.) A screened container will not retain enough humidity. A glass cover is ideal, but it should not fit tightly. Allow air to enter by supporting the lid on several small pieces

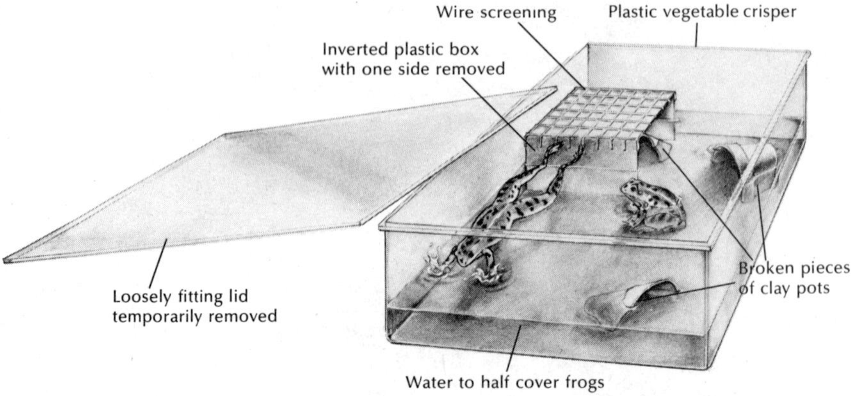

Figure 10-6. Housing for semiaquatic species such as the leopard frogs shown.

of cork glued to the top edges of the terrarium. Use damp (not wet) earth, sphagnum moss, and plant ferns. Tree frogs need taller containers and branches to climb on. Include a sunken dish of water as a necessary part of the environment. If their skin respiration stops due to lack of moisture, your frogs will die.

CARE OF EGGS AND TADPOLES

Cut a mass of eggs into groups of about ten and keep each clump in at least 100 ml of dechlorinated water. A large surface area is more important than a large volume of water (the surface area determines the amount of oxygen exchange between water and air). Plastic half-gallon ice cream containers are large enough for hatching eggs and for raising the tadpoles. Crowding eggs or tadpoles stunts their growth and may be lethal.

Try to maintain the temperature as near 20°C (68°F) as possible, but keep the container away from artificial heat. If you can, set it in direct sunlight near an open window for part of the day, but watch the temperature. A lid is not necessary during the egg and early tadpole stages. Do not mix species of eggs or tadpoles, and do not house tadpoles with adult frogs. Do not hatch more than you need or can care for.

Healthy eggs gradually turn dark as the number of pigmented cells increases. Discard egg masses that stay white; these are either unfertilized or dead. After a few days, when enough eggs have hatched, return the remaining egg mass to the pond from which you collected it.

At first, about ten tadpoles can be kept in each liter of water, but they should be thinned to one per liter when they are grown. (The other tadpoles could be used as food for adult frogs, crayfish, or turtles. Alternatively, euthanize them by freezing.)

Check daily for strands of fecal matter in the tadpoles' water. When these appear, it is time to start adding food. For *Xenopus*, this is about five days after the time of fertilization; for the leopard frog, about ten days. At this stage, tadpoles are swimming around freely. Development time varies. Under classroom conditions, adequately fed, *Xenopus*, leopard, and tree frogs, will transform into juveniles in one to three months.

Water is important. Dechlorinate tap water by letting it stand in an open container for one to two days before use. Chlorine interferes with oxygen exchange through the gills. Pond or spring water needs no special treatment. Change the water three times per week; pour off most of it and add fresh water to the original volume. But if the water becomes cloudy, change it immediately.

Feeding Tadpoles

Tadpoles should be fed twice a week. Finely ground nettle powder,* dry pea soup, or yeast are best for *Xenopus* tadpoles. Place nettle or pea soup powder in a small bag of muslin; submerge the bag in the water and squeeze it. Discard powder that does not pass through the bag. If fresh nettles are available, liquify them in a blender. To feed the tadpoles dry yeast, simply sprinkle a few grains on the surface of the water.

Rana, *Hyla*, and *Bufo* species will flourish on lettuce. Boil the leaves for ten minutes and cool them. Add 2.5 or 5 square cm of lettuce for each liter of water containing tadpoles. Freeze remaining boiled lettuce in aluminum foil to be used later.

The water should become clear between feedings. Cloudy water or mold growth indicates too much food. If tadpoles become sluggish and float on the surface, the water is foul; clean the tank and continue with much smaller feedings. A good schedule is to feed the tadpoles on Tuesday and Thursday and change the water on Monday, Wednesday, and Friday.

The needs of tadpoles change as they mature, so watch development carefully. Hind legs develop slowly, but front legs emerge abruptly, having been hidden by a flap of skin. By the time the front legs emerge, the tadpoles have developed lungs and must come out of the water for air. Arrange some sloping twigs or a slanting shelf half-submerged in the water so the animals can climb part of the way out.

---

*If you cannot find a local source, order from Wunderlich-Diez Corp., State Hwy. 17, Hasbrouck Hts., N.J. 07604.

Figure 10-7. Tadpoles feeding on lettuce.

Unless this is done, the animals will drown—even though they still have tails and can swim. Because the animals will soon be jumping, now is the time also to provide a loose-fitting but secure lid for the container.

After the front legs emerge, stop feeding temporarily. The digestive system undergoes profound changes between the time the front legs appear and the time the tail is resorbed; during this stage, the animals are changing from herbivorous to carnivorous creatures. When the tail has been almost resorbed, expect carnivorous needs and offer scrapings of beef, liver, or chopped earthworms. The animals will soon be ready to accept an adult diet of insects and other foods. As they assume adult habits, house them appropriately; or, better still, release young native frogs (not *Xenopus*) into a pond or swamp. Since *Xenopus* are native to South Africa, under no circumstances should these frogs be released in the United States. Try to find good homes for them as pets.

CARE OF ADULT AMPHIBIANS

Feeding

As a general rule, feed frogs, toads, and salamanders three or four times a week. All amphibians will eat live insects or worms, but some species accept dead food, which usually is easier to provide. *Xenopus* species and aquatic salamanders are among the few species that accept meat such as beef liver (which is ideal food), beef heart, or horse meat. Some other species (see DESCRIPTION OF SPECIES, page 192) can be trained to accept it. Trim fat from liver or meat and slice it into wormlike strips while still frozen (for easier cutting). A fully grown member of *Xenopus* species requires about 8 gm of raw food at each feeding. Merely distribute food in the tank. For species, especially frogs, that have to be trained to eat dead food—hold the food on the end of a broom straw or toothpick and drag it over the ground so the animal can see or hear it.

For other species of amphibians, provide food that is alive and moving, such as sowbugs (highly recommended, page 106), earthworms (page 65), crickets (page 134), mealworms (page 144), houseflies (page 142), fruit flies (page 140), moths, and caterpillars (page 131) —in fact, almost any sort of live insect—and tadpoles. A varied diet is of greater value than a diet based on a single food. As a very temporary measure, insects can be caught alive in traps. For longer maintenance, culture two or three food species. A medium-sized frog will eat the equivalent of up to 15 adult crickets every two days.

It may be advisable to provide vitamins and calcium, especially for long-term care. Sprinkle bonemeal, cod liver oil, or a powdered vitamin A and D supplement* onto the food just before it is offered to the animals.

Handling

Handle amphibians as little as possible, and always wash your hands thoroughly after touching them.

To pick up a frog or a toad, grasp it gently but firmly from above, curling your fingers around its body. Or, place the palm of your hand over its back with your fingers extended to the rear. With your index finger between its hind legs, grip the body gently with your thumb and other fingers. Pick up a salamander or newt by placing your thumb on one side of its skull and your index finger on the other; curl your remaining fingers around its body. Hold the animal firmly without squeezing it. Never pick up newts or salamanders by the tail. If a frog leaps to the floor, drop a damp towel over the animal and recapture it.

Do not pick up toads, especially of the *Bufo* species, and pickerel frogs unnecessarily; their skin secretes a poison (a protection against enemies) that causes irritation and smarting if it contacts human eyes or lips. If this happens, rinse with water immediately.

Identification of Sex

Sex differences vary among species. In *Xenopus* species, the female has a flap of tissue on each side of the cloaca that looks like a tiny tail. This is absent in the male. In leopard frogs, the male has a

---

*Pervinal®, from Thayer Laboratories, Inc., Pet Product Div., Metuchen, N.J. 08840, or Vionate®, from E. R. Squibb & Sons, Inc., 909 Third Ave., New York 10022, or similar products from pet stores.

Figure 10-8. How to pick up a toad or frog. (Xenopus *is shown here).*

swelling, called a *thumb pad*, on the first toe of each front foot and thicker forelegs than the female. Tree frogs do not have thumb pads, but the underside of the male's throat looks discolored because of the deflated vocal sac.

Native toads are difficult to sex. Although the male does develop thumb pads in the breeding season, this trait is not conspicuous the rest of the year.

Diseases

The most common disease in frogs is "red leg," resulting from heavy bacterial infection. This condition in newly shipped animals is usually initiated by skin irritation from contact with dry surfaces. Red leg that appears at other times can quickly kill all the frogs in a colony. Consult a veterinarian for treatment with antibiotics (chloromycetin or tetracycline), or isolate and painlessly kill a badly infected animal. If administered in time, antiobiotics not only cure red leg but can be injected into other frogs to prevent the disease from developing.

Xenopus species and salamanders are subject to fungus diseases characterized by patches of fuzzy white thread on the tail or over the entire body. Isolate infected animals; most will not recover. To discourage fungal growth, keep the water clean and well aerated. Add a few ml of saturated solution of synthetic sea salts* each time you change static water.

---

*Synthetic sea salts, sold under trade names such as Instant Ocean®, Rila Salt Mix,®, and others are available from pet stores and biological supply houses that deal in marine organisms.

Vacation Care

Tadpoles may be left untended for up to a week if the water is clean, the temperature does not fall to freezing, and some light is provided each day. Pond plants will help the tadpoles survive. Cover the container loosely with plastic wrap or thin polyethylene sheeting to retard evaporation. For periods longer than a week, ask students to take the tadpoles home and care for them.

In adult housing systems without running water, change the water on Friday afternoon and Monday morning. Water must be changed after three days. The animals may be left in a reliable running-water system for longer periods, but do not leave them for more than a week without food.

Leopard frogs and *Xenopus* toads may be stored up to three weeks (but no longer) in a quiescent state in a refrigerator. Place the animals in a large covered jar (such as a gallon mayonnaise jar) with a piece of wet absorbent cotton, and punch a few air holes in the lid. Replace the absorbent cotton each week and let a few drops of cold water drip from a spoon over the animals' backs to keep them moist.

EXCEPTIONAL EXPERIMENTS WITH AMPHIBIANS

Anesthesia

On rare occasions, it may be deemed justifiable that students observe frogs that are either pithed or recently dead (see Guiding Principles for Use of Animals, Chapter 1, pp. 4–5). Before either pithing or painlessly killing a frog, the animal should be anesthetized. All of these procedures require considerable skill and should be performed, if at all, by the teacher, and not by secondary school students. Humane procedures for administering anesthesia, pithing, and painless killing are given below.

Check your state laws on animal treatment and experimentation before undertaking such procedures as pithing or injecting. If such procedures are permitted by law and the studies involving them are to be made, anesthetize adult amphibians by chilling them in a refrigerator until they are relaxed; or immerse them for about 15 minutes in ice water. This is effective for all coldblooded animals such as amphibians, fish, and reptiles. Reduce body temperature to about 4°C (39°F) to render the animals insensitive to pain. They will become completely motionless and can be handled with ease.

You can also anesthetize an adult frog by completely immersing it in 0.2 percent chloretone solution for four to eight minutes, depending upon the size and activity of the animal. Maintain anesthesia by wrapping the frog in cotton that has been soaked in chloretone solution and wrung out.

Pithing

For dissection studies, frogs and toads may be killed by pithing if laws permit. High school teachers and other trained biologists should learn these procedures from an experienced technician, and should consult anatomical texts. Pithing should not be performed by secondary school students, and it is best if the students are not even present during pithing procedures.

Do not try these techniques merely by following written instructions. You should understand thoroughly the anatomy of the parts involved before you attempt pithing. If the procedure is bungled, the animal will suffer considerably. Remember that the nervous system of an amphibian is similar to that of a human being.

The object of single pithing is to destroy the brain (and thereby all conscious sensation). The object of double pithing is to destroy both the brain and the nerves in the spinal column. Destroying the spinal column nerves before destroying the brain will cause extreme suffering. The order of the procedure *must* be as follows: Anesthetize, then stun the animal; destroy the brain; and, if double pithing is required, destroy the nerves in the spinal column.

Practice on *dead* animals, as follows. Wrap a piece of toweling around a dead animal, leaving only the head exposed. With a rapid flip of your wrist, strike the back of the animal's head sharply against the edge of a table—hard enough to stun it if it were alive. Press the tip of the nose downward with your left index finger, making a bend at the occipito-vertebral junction. You can feel a gap where the skull joins the vertebral column. Carefully locate the junction and insert a sharp dissecting needle. Move the point quickly from side to side, cutting across the medulla. (As soon as this is done, a live animal feels no pain.) Then push the point of the needle forward into the brain cavity and, with a stirring movement, destroy the brain. When a live animal is used, you can test for destruction of the brain by gently touching the eyeball with a blunt instrument to check the eye-closing reflex. If the eyelids move, you must repeat the procedure until there is no discernible movement. This completes single pithing. Spinal reflexes still function.

For double pithing, reinsert the needle through the same hole but backward down into the spinal column and, with stirring movements, destroy the spinal column. When spinal reflexes are destroyed, the animal becomes flaccid; however, many of the physiological functions remain unimpaired and can be studied without interference from impulses that would normally come from the brain (see FILMS, *Pithing the Frog*, p. 212).

Practice stunning and pithing many times on dead animals until you gain complete familiarity with the anatomy and confidence in performing the procedure. Then anesthetize a live animal by cooling and proceed with pithing.

At the completion of observations, a pithed animal can be disposed of directly since death of all organs and tissues is inevitable after destruction of the brain.

Painless Killing (Euthanasia)

If no alternative is available, the teacher may need to dispose of an unwanted or sick animal. Euthanasia is a word derived from the Greek, *eu* meaning good, and *thanos* meaning death—to kill painlessly. Unless this procedure is performed expertly, the animal may suffer. If in doubt about your proficiency or technique, give the animal to a veterinarian for disposal.

To be performed humanely, the following procedures require skill. Euthanasia techniques should be learned under the supervision of someone experienced in these procedures. Euthanasia should not be performed by secondary school students.

To painlessly kill frogs and other amphibians, first render them insensitive to pain; chill them to about 4°C (39°F) in a refrigerator or immerse them in ice water. When an animal is completely motionless, rap the back of its head sharply on the edge of a sink. Immediately decapitate it with extremely sharp scissors, or pith it, as required by the planned experiment.

To kill salamanders, first immobilize them with TMS* (1:1000 to 1:5000 aqueous solution), then remove the animals to a tin containing cotton soaked in chloroform and leave them for several hours. Amphibians may recover from doses of anesthesia thought to be lethal. Always take the precaution of decapitating or pithing the animal.

Do not kill adult amphibians by freezing; it may cause pain.

Do not kill any native amphibians merely because they are no longer wanted; instead, release them to their natural habitat near a suitable source of water. But do not release *Xenopus* toads, as they are not native to the United States or Canada. If suitable homes cannot be found for *Xenopus*, they must be killed.

---

*You can obtain TMS from Crescent Research Chemicals, Inc., 7050 Fifth Ave., Scottsdale, AZ 85251, and, under the trade name of Finquel®, from Ayerst Laboratories, Veterinary Medical Div., 685 Third Ave., New York 10017.

EXPERIMENTS WITH AMPHIBIANS

One of the best books for detailed descriptions of many experiments using toads or frogs is *The African Clawed Toad* by A. L. Brown.[2] Teachers and students will find it invaluable.

You may need to identify individual animals for certain experiments. The skin patterns of leopard frogs can be coded to tell them from one another. House other animals individually in labeled containers.

REPRODUCTION—INDUCTION OF OVULATION. Frogs and toads are ideal for demonstrating development in vertebrate animals. As noted earlier, ovulation in *Xenopus* species can be induced with hormones. *Rana* species also can be used, but more complicated techniques are involved.

To induce ovulation in members of *Xenopus* species, anesthetize the animals by chilling (page 203), then inject 250 International Units of human chorionic gonadotropin* into one male and one female late in the afternoon.[2a, 3] The ideal site for injection is in the dorsal midline about 6 mm above and to the side of the cloacal opening. The injection is made subcutaneously (just beneath the skin). (See FILMS, *Inducing Ovulation*, page 213.) Keep the animals together overnight in an aquarium in a quiet darkened environment. A platform of ½–inch mesh held in place with rubber suction cups is useful in the spawning tank. Eggs fall through the mesh to the bottom of the tank where they cannot be eaten or damaged by the parents. Spawning occurs in the early morning and may last 24 to 48 hours. Do not remove or disturb the animals until spawning is complete and the eggs are laid and fertilized. You may use the same animals again once a month throughout the year.

Inducing ovulation in *Rana* species requires removal of the pituitary gland and artificial insemination.[3, 4, 5] During the winter months keep females used for these studies in artificial hibernation in a refrigerator, 0 to 4°C (32 to 39°F), or they will catabolize their eggs. In these species, such studies must be made between October and April.

GROWTH AND DEVELOPMENT. Detailed descriptions of normal growth and development of amphibian eggs are encountered frequently in biology books.[6, 7, 8] (See also FILMS, Development, p. 213.) You can devise many experiments to determine the role of environmental factors such as temperature, water, light, oxygen, and availability of food and inorganic salts on egg development.[2b] To successfully study these factors,

---

*Available as Antuitrin S® from Parke Davis & Co., P. O. Box 118, Detroit, Mich. 43232.

keep test and control groups of the same number of eggs or tadpoles in comparable volumes of water, and subject them to the same amount of handling.

To induce precocious metamorphosis (again check your state laws and review your reasons for this study), use thyroxin in varying concentrations of 1:1,000,000; 1:10,000,000; and 1:1,000,000,000; and iodine in concentrations of 1:10,000 and 1:100,000. Over a period of weeks, record changes in tail, hind legs, front legs, and head and body shape.

POPULATION CONTROL.[9, 10] If one or two large tadpoles are placed with a group of smaller tadpoles, the smaller animals are overcome by a strange and fatal loss of appetite. Though offered plenty of food, they will stop feeding and die. Since this event also happens if some of the water from the larger tadpoles' tank is poured into the smaller ones' tank, the effect must be due to a chemical secretion. Investigate this phenomenon and devise methods for determining the strength of the inhibiting agent. Does boiling the water containing the secretion destroy its inhibitory power? What other chemical tests could be made to determine the identity of this secretion?

Consider the meaning of this phenomenon in nature when there is not enough food for all the tadpoles.

RESPIRATION. Simple measurements of respiration rate can be made with the aid of a stopwatch. To demonstrate gaseous exchange in a small frog or toad, place it in a bottle with a carbon dioxide absorbent and connect the bottle to a manometer. A fall in water level shown on the manometer indicates a change in air pressure due to oxygen consumption by the animal.

Figure 10-9. The frog is temporarily confined to a beaker for easier observation. One student measures time on a stopwatch as another counts the respirations.

Try this procedure at different temperatures to demonstrate that, in coldblooded animals, metabolic rate is dependent on external temperature.

PERCEPTION OF MOTION. Motion experiments are best conducted on the common American toad *Bufo terrestris,* because this species responds only to moving food. Other species such as leopard frogs also could be tried. Drag the food along the ground at different measured rates to determine the toad's or frog's threshold for perception of motion. Is this threshold dependent on light intensity?[11]

INTERNAL PARASITES. Make a microscopic inspection of the contents of the stomach and intestine of a frog if dissection studies have taken place. Try to determine the presence and identity of internal parasites.[2c] (See FILMS, *Studying Frog: Internal Parasites,* p. 212.)

ISOLATED ORGAN TECHNIQUES. Frogs and toads are valuable sources of material for a study of tissue suspended in Ringer's solution and for other experiments on various tissues. From an animal that has been humanely killed or pithed (page 204), immediately remove the required tissue. One animal can provide enough material for many students. Use the following tissues: voluntary muscles (the muscles of the leg are most suitable);[12a] nerve-muscle preparations, such as the gastrocnemius muscle and sciatic nerve;[2d, 12b, 13] one-inch lengths of intestine;[14] or heart muscle.[2e, 13,*] Attach the muscles to a kymograph to record contraction and relaxation; then test the effects of electrical stimulation, drugs, and environmental changes.

Study salt transport across membranes in abdominal skin sections. Use liver, pancreas, spleen, and intestine for tissue culture,[12c] biochemical or histological investigations.

VARIATION OF SKIN COLOR. Color change in *Xenopus* species is caused by contraction or expansion of the melanophores of the skin. The skin gradually becomes darker when the toad is placed on a dark background and lighter on a light background. A hormone produced by the pituitary gland is believed to be important in controlling these changes. Color and the ability to change color vary among individuals.

To demonstrate the variations in skin color, raise members of *Xenopus* species from metamorphosis to full size in tanks with different background colors. For instance, use one tank with a substratum of sand, thickly planted with weeds, and use another devoid of sub-

*Also see FILMS, *Isolated Organ Techniques,* page 213.

stratum or weeds. In which environment do the animals develop a darker skin color?

What roles do temperature and light have in the production of skin color? By excluding light from the tank for a few days, is it possible to induce color changes in adult *Xenopus*?

FIELD STUDIES. In the spring, study the breeding behavior in various species of wild frogs and toads in nearby ponds and streams. Try to determine the significance of vocal communication among frogs and toads.[15] How far do their calls carry? How long do they last? Does one male's call affect the calls of other males? Do the males find the females, or do the females find the males? For help in identifying calls, listen to recordings. (See RECORDINGS, page 213.)

TABLE 10–1. Sources of Amphibians*

Supplier	*Xenopus* Toad	*Rana* Frog	*Hyla* Frog	*Bufo* Toad	Red-Spotted Newt	*Ambystoma* Salamander
Bico Scientific Co. 2325 S. Michigan Ave. Chicago, Ill. 60616		•		•	•	
R. F. Carle Co. P.O. Box 1010 Chico, Cal. 95926		•				
CCM: General Bio- logical, Inc. 8200 S. Hoyne Ave. Chicago, Ill. 60620		•	•		•	•
Connecticut Valley Biological Supply** Valley Road Southampton, Mass. 01073		•	•	•	•	•
Charles W. Fletcher P.O. Box 98 Glen Burnie, Md. 21061	•					
Hacienda Aquatics P.O. Box 218 La Puente, Cal. 91747	•					
Hermosa Reptile Inc. P.O. Box 182 Hermosa Beach, Cal. 90254		•	•		•	•

TABLE 10–1. Sources of Amphibians*—(Continued)

Supplier	*Xenopus* Toad	*Rana* Frog	*Hyla* Frog	*Bufo* Toad	Red-Spotted Newt	*Ambystoma* Salamander
Lake Champlain Frog Farms** Alburg, Vt. 05440		•				
Mogul-Ed** P.O. Box 482 Oshkosh, Wis. 54901	•	•	•	•	•	•
Nasco/Steinhilber** Janesville Ave. Ft. Atkinson, Wis. 53538	•	•		•	•	•
Snake Farm P.O. Box 96 Laplace, La. 70068		•	•			
Southwestern Scientific Supply Co.** P.O. Box 17222 Tucson, Ariz. 85710		•	•	•		

**See also Nace, G. W., J. K. Waage and C. M. Richards. 1971. Sources of Amphibians for Research. *BioScience* 21(14):768–73.

**Obtain many of their animals directly from the wild near their place of business.

REFERENCES

1. GIBBS, E. L., G. W. NACE and M. B. EMMONS. 1971. The Live Frog Is Almost Dead. *BioScience* 21(20):1027–34.
2. BROWN, A. L. 1970. *The African Clawed Toad.* Butterworths, London. a. pp. 70–79; b. pp. 83–85, 111–12; c. pp. 54–67; d. pp. 45–47, gastrocnemius; pp. 47–49, heart.
3. Rugh, R. 1962. *Experimental Embryology: Techniques and Procedures.* Burgess Publishing Co., Minneapolis, Minn. pp. 91–96, both *R. pipiens* and *Xenopus* methods. (Advanced)
4. RICHARDS, C. M. 1971. Amphibia. *Proc. Biol. Teachers' Workshop in Classroom Animal Science.* New York Branch of Amer. Assoc. for Lab. Animal Science, P. O. Box 10, Joliet, Ill. 60434.
5. WILT, F. H. and N. K. WESSELS, eds. 1967. *Methods in Developmental Biology.* Thomas Y. Crowell, New York. pp. 75–84, Xenopus; pp. 53–74, Rana species. (Advanced)

6. Etkin, W. 1966. How a Tadpole Becomes a Frog. *Sci. Amer.* 214:78–88. Reprint No. 1042, W. H. Freeman & Co., 660 Market St., San Francisco, Cal. 94101.

7. New, D. A. T. 1966. *The Culture of Vertebrate Embryos.* Academic Press, London. p. 120, *et seq.*

8. Hechtlinger, A. 1971. *Handbook of Modern Experiments for High School Biology.* Parker Publishing Co., Inc., West Nyack, New York. pp. 160–163.

9. Macan, T. T. 1965. Self-Controls on Population Size. *New Scientist* 28:801–803.

10. Rose, S. M. 1959. Failure of Survival of Slowly Growing Members of a Population. *Science* 129(3355):1026.

11. Kaess, W. 1976. Perception of Motion in the Common Toad. *Research Problems in Biology,* Series 3. Second Ed. Biological Sciences Curriculum Study. Oxford University Press, New York. p. 11–15.

12. Dunn, A. S. and J. Arditti. 1968. *Experimental Physiology: Experiments in Cellular, General and Plant Physiology.* Holt, Rinehart & Winston, New York 10017.
    a. The Intact Muscle. Exp. 6–4, pp. 85–88.
    b. Action Potential of Skeletal Muscle. Exp. 5–4, pp. 72–73.
    c. Transport of Sodium Ions through Frog Skin. Exp. 4–4, 52–54.

13. Hake, J. C., J. J. W. Baker and G. E. Allen. 1971. *Twelve Problems in Biology.* Open-ended experiments for introductory college biology. Addison-Wesley Publishing Co., Reading, Mass.

14. Kimbrough, T. D. and G. C. Llewellyn. 1972. A Simplified System for Studying Digestive Function and Responses. *Amer. Biol. Teacher* 34:138–42.

15. Carpenter, C. D. 1968. Behavior Patterns of Breeding Frogs and Toads. Stokes, A. W., ed. *Animal Behavior in Laboratory and Field.* W. H. Freeman & Co., San Francisco. Exp. 23, pp. 105–107. Available as Separate No. 818 from the publisher.

FURTHER READING

Amphibians: Guidelines for the breeding, care, and management of laboratory animals. 1974. National Academy of Sciences, Washington D.C.

Aronson, L. R. 1944. Breeding *Xenopus laevis. Amer. Nat.* 78:131–41.

Billet, F. S. and Wild, A. E. 1975. *Practical Studies of Animal Development.* Halsted Press, New York.

Cameron, S. B. 1947. Successful Breeding of *Xenopus laevis,* the South African Clawed Toad-Frog. *Amer. J. Med. Tech.* 13:120–26.

Case, M. T. 1971. *Look What I Found: The Young Conservationist's Guide to Care and Feeding of Small Wildlife.* Chatham Press, Riverside, Conn. (Intermediate)

CONANT, R. 1975. *A Field Guide to Reptiles and Amphibians.* Houghton Mifflin Co., Boston.

FRAZER, J. F. D. 1972. Anura (Frogs and Toads). *The UFAW Handbood on the Care and Management of Laboratory Animals.* 4th ed. Churchill Livingstone, London. pp. 511–19. Published in the U. S. by Williams & Wilkins, Baltimore.

FRAZER, J. F. D. 1973. *Amphibians.* Sykeham Publications, London, and Springer Verlag, New York.

NACE, G. W. and C. M. RICHARDS. 1972. Living Frogs: 1. Adults; 2. Care; 3. Tadpoles. *Carolina Tips* 35(10, 11 & 12). Carolina Biological Supply Co., Burlington, N. C. 27215.

STEBBINS, R. C. 1966. *A Field Guide to Western Reptiles and Amphibians.* Peterson Field Guide Series. Houghton Mifflin Co., Boston.

Xenopus laevis *(African Clawed Frog).* NASCO, Ft. Atkinson, Wisc. 53538.

ZAPPLER, G. and L. ZAPPLER. 1973. *Amphibians as Pets.* Doubleday & Co., New York.

FILMS

Amphibians. 16 mm, color or b/w, 11 min. Coronet Films, 65 E. South Water St., Chicago, Ill 60601.

Frogs and Toads. (Includes spring peeper, green frog, American toad and Cuban tree toad.) Set of 20 color slides. Educational Images, P. O. Box 261, Lyons Falls, NY 13368.

Frogs, Toads and Salamanders of the United States. Filmstrip, 8 frames, color. NASCO, Ft. Atkinson, Wisc 53538.

Leopard Frog. Film loop, super 8 mm, cartridge, color or b/w, approx. 4 min. BFA Educational Media, 2211 Michigan Ave., Santa Monica, Ca 90404.

Maintaining Biological Specimens. (Includes "How to Make a Terrarium.") Series of 6 filmstrips, avg. 50 frames, color. NASCO, Ft. Atkinson, Wisc 53538.

Pithing the Frog. Film loop, super 8 mm, cartridge, silent, color. BFA Educational Media, 2211 Michigan Ave., Santa Monica, Ca 90404.

Reptiles and Amphibians. 16 mm, color, 52 mins. McGraw-Hill Films, 330 W. 42 St., New York 10036.

Salamanders. Film loop, super 8 mm, color. BFA Educational Media, 2211 Michigan Ave., Santa Monica, Ca 90404.

Salamanders. (Includes newt, tree salamander and mud puppy.) Film loop, super 8 mm, color, 3 min. 30 sec. NASCO, Ft. Atkinson, Wisc 53538.

Studying Frog: Internal Parasites. Film loop, super 8 mm, color or b/w, approx. 4 min. BFA Educational Media, 2211 Michigan Ave., Santa Monica, Ca 90404.

Toads Feeding. Film loop, super 8 mm, 3 min. International Communications Films, NASCO, Ft. Atkinson, Wisc 53538.

What Is an Amphibian? 16 mm, color or b/w, 11 min. Encyclopaedia Britannica Educ. Corp., 425 N. Michigan Ave., Chicago, Ill 60611.

World in a Marsh. 16 mm, color, 22 min. McGraw-Hill Films, 330 W. 42 St., New York 10036.

Inducing Ovulation

Inducing Ovulation in Frogs. Film loop, super 8 mm, color, 2 min. 52 sec. Thorne Films, 1229 University Ave., Boulder, Colo 80302.

Technique of Subcutaneous Injection. Film loop, super 8 mm, cartridge, silent, 1 min. BFA Educational Media, 2211 Michigan Ave., Santa Monica, Ca 90404.

Development

Amphibian Embryo. (Frog, toad and salamander.) 16 mm, color or b/w, 16 min. Encyclopaedia Britannica Educ. Corp., 425 N. Mich. Ave., Chicago, Ill 60611.

Frog Development: Fertilization to Hatching (12 min.) and *Frog Development: Hatching through Metamorphosis* (9 min. 30 sec.) 16 mm films, also available as super 8 mm film loops, color, silent. BFA Educational Media, 2211 Michigan Ave., Santa Monica, Ca 90404.

Tadpole to Toad. Film loop, super 8 mm, 2 min. 45 sec. International Communication Films, NASCO, Ft. Atkinson, Wisc 53538.

Isolated Organ Techniques

Frog Heartbeat. Film loop, super 8 mm, color, Part 1, 3 min. 45 sec., Part II, 4 min. 55 sec. Thorne Films, 1229 University Ave., Boulder, Colo 80302.

Frog Skeletal Muscle Response. Film loop, super 8 mm, color, 4 min. 55 sec. Thorne Films, 1229 University Ave., Boulder, Colo 80302.

Work versus Load in Frog Skeletal Muscle. Film loop, super 8 mm, color, 4 min. 45 sec. Thorne Films, 1229 University Ave., Boulder, Colo 80302.

RECORDINGS

"Amphibians." (Frogs and toads.) 7 inch, 45 rpm. Available from Animals, 21 & 22 Great Castle Street, London W1, England.

"Voices of the Night." (Calls of most frogs, toads and tree frogs found in the eastern United States.) 12-inch LP record. Houghton Mifflin Co., Boston.

11

Reptiles

A survey of school children's attitudes showed that reptiles in general, and snakes in particular, evoke more aversion than any other animals. Biology teachers face a real challenge in introduing students to the positive values of reptiles. An understanding of these values is essential for conservation reasons.

Tales of monsters, dragons, dinosaurs, and sea serpents have created misconceptions about snakes, lizards, and, to a lesser degree, turtles. Reptile fossils, from the carnivorous *Tyrannosaurus rex* to the awesome flying *Pterosaurus*, provide a rich source of evolutionary information. Turtles are useful in studies of alarm reactions, and lizards for studies of courtship behavior. Although snakes are the least useful for experimentation, they are of interest for type study and observations of skin shedding.

LIZARDS

A lizard ran out on a rock and looked up,
listening . . .
And what a dandy fellow! the right toss of a
chin for you
and swirl of a tail!

D. H. Lawrence (1885–1930)

The care of American chameleons is described here in detail. Fence lizards also are highly recommended for classroom use and require the same care. Some modifications in housing and care are needed for other species.

The American chameleon (pronounced ka me' lee un), *Anolis carolinensis*, is commonly sold at circuses, carnivals, and pet shops

Figure 11-1. American chameleon. (Courtesy Carolina Biological Supply House)

throughout the United States. They have a remarkable ability to change color rapidly. However, these are not true chameleons (*Chamaeleo,* which are native to Africa) but belong to a class of animals called anoles. Their life span is about three or four years if they are well housed and cared for; yet each year poor care dooms millions of these creatures to but a few months' meager subsistence in captivity.

American chameleons (hereafter called chameleons) are found in the southeastern United States on trees, shrubs, vines, fences, and wooden buildings. Their principal enemies are snakes, birds, small mammals, and man. They are alert, hairless, slender creatures with a maximum length of about 18 cm. Skin colors range from green to yellow to brown. Chameleons turn green in darkness or when excited, brown in cold temperatures or bright light. The change from green to brown takes less than five minutes. (However, their color-changing abilities are inferior compared to the true chameleons of Africa.)

A male chameleon has loose skin at its throat which can be distended by a rod of cartilage to form a red or pink throat fan (dewlap). This display is used to threaten a rival or to excite a mate. Females are usually smaller and have only a rudimentary throat fan. Males frequently fight among themselves during the courting season in April and May.

Chameleons, fence lizards, and other native lizards can be collected from the wild. The easiest way to capture a wild lizard is to drop a strong noose over its head. Several species are available from pet stores or biological supply houses.* Select lizards up to 15 cm long that are free from mites, common pests which are hard to eradicate. Wild specimens are often infested. Under no circumstances should poisonous species of lizard be allowed in the classroom. Large-sized species are also undesirable for classroom care.

Unless otherwise stated, the following lizards require the same type of housing and food as chameleons. They are listed in approximate order of their desirability for classroom care.

---

*See Reptile Suppliers, page 240.

Figure 11-2. Fence lizard.

FENCE LIZARDS (*Sceloporus* species, also called Spiny Lizards or Swifts). Fence lizards thrive more readily in captivity than chameleons; any local species is suitable. They are widely distributed in the Great Plains, lower Rockies, British Columbia, California, and throughout the South. Western species are called "blue-bellies" because of the bright blue marking the males have along their sides and on their throats. They require a temperature of 27°C (80°F) for at least part of each day.

ALLIGATOR LIZARDS (*Gerrhonotus* species). These lizards range in color from yellowish- to reddish-brown, with broken irregular lines across the back or tail. They are found in the Texas area. This very hardy species eats well in captivity, even to the extent of eating smaller lizards, so house them separately. Provide hiding places and a moderate amount of sunlight.

SKINKS (family Scincidae). These extremely fast, active lizards forage by day but hide under stones or debris at night or during cold weather. Cover two-thirds of the cage floor with rotted leaf mold, peat moss, bark, and rotten wood deep enough to permit burrowing. Cover the remaining area with sand for feeding and sunbathing. Handle them carefully; skinks' tails break off very easily.

GREAT PLAINS SKINK (*Eumeces obsoletus,* also called Desert Skink). These skinks require more arid conditions, more sand and fewer plants. Burrowing species need sand at least 15 cm deep. Desert skinks are very secretive, so be sure to provide rocks under which they can hide. Skinks will bite if provoked. Feed them a mixture of beaten egg and chopped meat twice a week, in addition to regular feedings of live insects.

The following species are *not* recommended for reasons of conservation. Some of these species are fast disappearing over much of their former range; others are delicate and have such a high attrition rate in captivity that keeping them in the classroom cannot be justified.

CHUCKWALLA (*Sauromalus obesus*).

COLLARED LIZARD (*Crotaphytus collaris*).

DESERT IGUANA (*Dipsosaurus dorsalis,* also called Crested Desert Lizard).

GECKOS (*Phyllodactylus* and *Coleonyx* species).

HORNED LIZARD (*Phrynosoma* species, also erroneously called Horned Toad).

The only venomous lizard native to the United States is the Gila monster, *Heloderma suspectum,* which inhabits the southwest desert regions of the United States and parts of Mexico. Its bite can be fatal to man.

Classroom Care

HANDLING. Gently grasp a lizard from above and curl your fingers under it. Do not pick up a lizard by the tail; its tail may break off. If this happens, bathe the wound with a mild disinfectant. A new but inferior tail will slowly replace the original one.

TRANSPORTING. For short journeys, transport lizards in cloth bags. They will usually escape from cardboard boxes. Avoid transporting them in winter months; but if they must be moved in cold weather, provide a hot water bottle wrapped in a towel and keep the animal warm through the entire journey.

HOUSING. Generally, only lizards of the same species should be housed together. A large wooden box (at least 45 × 60 × 45 cm), or a 20-gallon aquarium, makes a good home for one or two chameleons or other small lizards. As with other territorial animals, provide enough space for each chameleon to stake out and protect its living area. The larger the cage, the more active the lizards will be. Crowding is very harmful.

You can make an inexpensive cage from four pieces of glass or Lucite® (two pieces each, 45 × 45 cm and 45 × 60 cm), with a piece of plywood (45 × 60 cm) for the base. Seal the edges with cloth or plastic tape. An overlapping screen lid will prevent escape. Do not use a glass cover. It will make the environment too humid. Cages with screen floors or walls damage the animals' noses and feet.

Use an overhead lamp, if necessary, to maintain the temperature at 22 to 27°C (72 to 80°F) for most species, and from 26 to 29°C (79 to 85°F) for desert species. Try incandescent bulbs of different wattages at varying distances to attain the proper temperature. Keep a thermometer in

Figure 11-3. Spacious terrarium with climbing surfaces for a fence lizard.

the cage and check the temperature often. Maintain the same temperature at night and during weekends. Do not place the cage on a radiator or in direct sunlight; high temperatures are detrimental to the animals. (Higher temperatures also soften the sealing on aquariums, so they will not remain waterproof.)

Add sand, gravel, and rocks, as well as branches to climb on. The depth of the sand depends on the burrowing habits of the lizards. Plants help maintain correct humidity and provide drinking surfaces and hiding places. Set small ferns, sedums, trailing vines, and other low potted plants in the sand. Keep the cage clean and the sand dry.

FEEDING. Suitable foods include fruit flies (see page 140), houseflies (page 142), white worms (page 71), mealworms (page 144), crickets (page 134), waxworm larvae and adults (page 152), caterpillars (page 131), spiders (page 118), sowbugs (page 106), and earthworms (page 65). Vessels of flying prey may be uncovered in tightly closed lizard cages. Culture two or three different insects to provide a continuous and varied supply. A variety of insects is essential for winter care. If lizards are to be kept for only short periods during summer months, capture wild insects in nets or traps.

Feed lizards three or four times a week, although skipping a meal now and then will do no harm. Feed them a little extra on Friday if they are not fed over the weekend. Lizards are slow eaters—be patient. Do not mistake their slow habits for poor appetites. They depend mainly on sight for food information, so live prey or a semblance of movement is essential.

WATER. Chameleons do not drink from pans of water; they only lap drops of water from moistened surfaces. Keep a moistened piece of sponge the size of a walnut in an overhead wire rack. Or, spray the plants and the screen lid with water at least once a day. Chameleons will dehydrate within 24 hours if water is not provided. Do not give them sugared water.

MOLTING. Depending on the species, lizards may shed their skins as often as twice a month or as seldom as once a year. Young lizards molt more often than adults. Provide a pan of shallow water for them to soak in, and wet the animal frequently just before it sheds its skin and also while it is shedding. Some lizards need to rub against a large stone to free themselves of their old skins.

BREEDING. Lizards generally will not breed in captivity. However, if spacious living conditions are provided (for instance, living freely in a greenhouse), chameleons and other lizards may court, mate, and lay eggs. Hatching of the eggs and rearing of the young also may be difficult. Place lizard, turtle, or snake eggs on a moist (not wet) paper towel or filter paper. Then, to hatch the eggs, enclose the paper in a sealed plastic bag.[1]

VACATION CARE. For vacation periods longer than a few days, send lizards home with a student or make other arrangements for their care.

EXPERIMENTS WITH LIZARDS

When several lizards are housed together and individuals cannot be recognized by appearance, you may want to mark them for identification. Place tiny spots of nontoxic enamel paint of different colors on different parts of the animals' bodies. These markings will, of course, be lost at each molting.

SOCIAL STRUCTURES. Using chameleons or fence lizards, observe social relationships such as aggression, subordination, and courtship. Build an enclosure providing at least 3½ to 6 square feet of floor space (or use a 25– or 50–gallon aquarium). The enclosure should be used as the animals' normal living quarters (see page 217). Place three to five males and two or three females of the same species in the cage, or use animals of the same sex. The individuals should be identifiable. Observe social behavior daily, preferably in the morning.

SOCIAL HIERARCHY.[2a] Social structure in a group of lizards is established in about five days. Is there a dominant lizard? Is there a dominant member of each sex? Is there any type of behavior peculiar to subordinate lizards?

Determine if there is any correlation between dominance and body weight.[3] House together a group of males and observe which animal defeats all others when challenged. Call this animal *A*; catch and weigh it, and place it in another cage. Continue your observations of the remaining animals. After several days another animal will establish dominance. Label it *B*; remove and weigh it. Continue until the hierarchy for the entire group is determined. Make a graph, plotting body weight against the order (*A*, *B*, *C*, . . .) in which the animals became dominant. Does the largest animal rank first in dominance?

DISPLAY PATTERNS.[2a, 4, 5] How does a male court a female? What movements and postures constitute a display? From what sites in the enclosure does a lizard display? How does the female react?

COLOR CHANGES—CAMOUFLAGE. Test varying light intensities, background colors, states of excitement, and temperatures[6] (test only within the range of 18 to 38°C (64 to 100°F) to determine what factors cause color change in chameleons.

THERMOREGULATION.[7] What is the range of body temperatures of lizards kept under normal conditions? Insert a thermocouple or a thermometer into the vents of specimens of several species. Record the body temperature, sex, and body weight of each animal. Also record the temperature of the soil and the air, and the time of day. Take 50 to 100 readings for each lizard. Determine statistically if there are significant differences between the mean body temperatures of different species of lizards. Does the body temperature correlate with that of the air or the soil? Do animals of different body weights show similar ranges in body temperature?

TURTLES

Tiny bright-eye
Slow one
To take your first solitary bite
and move your slow, solitary hunt.
Your bright, dark little eye,
Your eye of a dark disturbed night
Under its slow lid, tiny baby tortoise,
So indomitable.

D. H. Lawrence (1885–1930)

In the United States, the designation of "turtle" is applied to aquatic species, semiaquatic species (terrapins), and terrestrial species (tortoises). Over sixty varieties inhabit the United States, most of which are semiaquatic.

Turtles, the oldest of all reptiles, are the only vertebrate animals with backbones that will not bend. Their shells are built on a framework of vertebrae and ribs. They have lungs and the aquatic species must come to the surface of the water to breathe. Man, large fish, some birds, skunks, and raccoons are the turtles' natural enemies. Most turtles sold as pets are hatchlings from turtle farms in Mississippi and Louisiana. These farms produce 13.5 million turtles annually. Because of inadequate care at the farms, almost all of them will die within a few weeks or months after they are sold. Under natural conditions, or when properly cared for in captivity, a turtle will live for many years. Some species can live as long as 100 years.

Some turtles can be captured from the wild. They also are available from pet stores, variety stores, biological supply houses, and other commercial sources.* Recently captured turtles may lay eggs in captivity, but breeding is usually not successful in a classroom. Hatching procedures are similar to those described on page 219 for lizards. (Also, see REFERENCES, page 238.)

Suitable classroom species include box and Blanding's turtles (land species) and painted and red-eared turtles (aquatic species). Like most turtles, these are docile and harmless. Aquatic and terrestrial turtles can be distinguished from each other by obvious external features. Aquatic turtles have flattened shells and webbed feet, both adaptations for swimming. In contrast, land and semiaquatic species have high-domed shells and feet adapted for walking.

Choose turtles less than 15 cm long. Hatchlings are usually an inch long; a healthy specimen, two to three years old, is about 5 to 10 cm long. The age of some turtles can be roughly assessed by counting the ridges around one of the plates of the shell; one ridge is approximately equal to each year of the turtle's life. However, the growth ridges become obscured long before old age is reached.

Several species of native turtles are considered endangered in many localities and should not be used as classroom animals. Select a species with care, and only purchase those reliably identified. The following species are recommended:

---

*See Reptile Suppliers, page 240.

Figure 11-4. *Box turtle.*

Figure 11-5. *Box turtle underside view showing tightly closed shell.*

BOX TURTLE (*Terrapene* species). Terrestrial. A box turtle's lower shell is hinged transversely near the center. When alarmed, the turtle can close up so tightly that a fingernail cannot be inserted between the two shells. Box turtles are found in wooded areas from Maine to Texas and from Arizona to Colorado. They are omnivorous—eating fruits, berries, and raw meat.

BLANDING'S TURTLE (*Emydoidea blandingi*). Terrestrial. These omnivorous turtles live in wooded areas near water and eat both fruit and meat. They are easily recognized by their bright yellow chin or throat. However, in some locations they are almost extinct. You may be able to arrange for a short-term loan of this turtle from a local zoo.

PAINTED TURTLE (*Chrysemys* species, also called Pond Turtle). Aquatic. From coast to coast, pond turtles can be found sunbathing on offshore logs or on rocks in ponds, marshes, or sluggish streams where aquatic vegetation is profuse and the bottom is soft and muddy. These handsome animals may be 20 cm in diameter when fully grown. They have broad, dark, flattened shells marked at the edges with red; the underside shell (plastron) is yellow. Their heads are streaked with red and yellow. Like most turtles, they eat while underwater and are omnivorous—eating fruits, berries, and raw meat.

RED-EARED TURTLE (*Pseudemys scripta elegans*, also called Cumberland or Elegant Terrapin). Aquatic. These omnivorous turtles have grass-green shells and bright red patches that look like ears behind their eyes. They are the most common variety sold in pet stores. Large adults lose their characteristic coloring, which is replaced by big black splotches on the shell. Only very small individuals are suitable for classroom study. Red-eared turtles live in quiet water with a muddy bottom and dense vegetation.

MUD TURTLE (*Kinosternon* species). Aquatic. Mud turtles, related to Musk Turtles, give off a stale musky odor when handled. They have a hinged lower shell, like the box turtle, and are found throughout the southern half of the United States. These gentle animals adapt well to captivity. Mud turtles are almost exclusively carnivorous.

The future outlook for conservation of some turtle species is not good. The following species should *not* be captured from the wild, since their numbers already have been dangerously depleted. (For different reasons, some other species are not recommended.)

DESERT TORTOISE *Gopherus* species, also called Gopher Tortoises.

DIAMONDBACK TERRAPIN *Malaclemys terrapin.*

MAP TURTLE *Graptemys* species, also called Geographic Turtle.

SPOTTED TURTLE *Clemmys guttata.*

WOOD TURTLE *Clemmys insculpta.*

Figure 11-6. Painted turtle, top and underside views.

SNAPPING TURTLE (*Chelydra serpentina*). Almost wholly aquatic. These turtles live up to their name—some can inflict severe wounds. The young can be kept satisfactorily. However, they grow very rapidly, and the problem of disposal soon arises. (A full-grown adult may weigh 15 kilos and has a shell 45 cm in diameter.) They cannot be housed with other turtles.

MUSK TURTLE (*Sternothaerus odoratus,* also called Stinkpot Turtle). Aquatic. These turtles have a disagreeable musky odor which is even stronger than that of the mud turtle, and they may be vicious. Musk turtles prefer slow-moving, shallow bodies of water. The algae that grows on their shells sometimes makes them look like rocks.

Legislation Involving Turtles

STATE LAWS ON KEEPING TURTLES. The food value of some turtles and increased pollution have reduced the numbers of many native species and jeoparadized their existence. It is illegal to keep certain sizes of diamondback turtles in New Jersey and some other states. In New York, the native wood turtle *Clemmys insculpta* and the Easter box turtle may not be captured. Some states forbid collection of desert turtles and other species. Before capturing any turtles from the wild, contact local wildlife officials. Permission to keep protected turtles must be obtained from your state's Wildlife Agency.*

FEDERAL LAWS BECAUSE OF HAZARDS TO HUMANS. Turtles present a particular human health problem. The U.S. Public Health Service has estimated that half of all pet turtles convey salmonellosis, a transmittable bacterial disease that causes nausea and diarrhea in humans. Since 1972, federal regulations have required that all turtles shipped in interstate commerce be certified free from salmonella and Arizona bacteria. Just prior to shipment, however, turtle breeders use copper sulfate to *temporarily* rid the turtles of the bacteria. The U. S. Center for Disease Control has declared that turtles are inherently contaminated and that the bacteria cannot be permanently eliminated. More restrictive legislation was therefore enacted in June, 1975 which banned completely the shipment of live turtles with a shell length of less than 4 inches and of viable turtle eggs.

Since young people are most likely to be among the 300,000 cases of salmonellosis (from various causes) which still occur annually, strict hygiene in handling turtles in the classroom is essential. Follow these

*For the address, see Appendix D, page 357.

two simple rules. Wash your hands *immediately* after handling turtles. Do *not* allow turtle food dishes in areas where human food is prepared.

Housing

Housing for turtles falls roughly into two types. Land and semiaquatic species require land with a water supply for drinking and bathing; fully aquatic species need an aquarium with a few rocks as landing places. Otherwise, care of all turtles is basically the same. As a general rule, do not house turtles with other animals.

The small plastic or glass tanks for turtles sold in pet stores are hopelessly inadequate for even one turtle. Allow at least 30 square cm of floor space for every inch of turtle. Crowded and improper housing conditions have killed many of these creatures. Turtles thrive at temperatures of 21 to 27°C (70 to 80°F). If the room temperature falls during winter nights or on weekends, provide an overhead incandescent lamp (40 or 60 watts) for heat—do not use water heaters with turtles. Shade a part of the enclosure from the lamp, so the turtles can escape the heat. Normally, turtles hibernate during the winter, but warm indoor temperatures prevent them from doing so.

WOODLAND TERRARIUM FOR LAND AND SEMIAQUATIC SPECIES. An old aquarium or wooden box with one glass side can be made into a woodland terrarium. A 10-gallon aquarium 45 × 25 × 30 cm is suitable for one or two hatchling turtles (2.5 cm long); a 20-gallon size 60 × 30 × 40 cm will house one or two turtles 5 cm long. The larger the enclosure, the more content the animals will be. No lid is required.

Start with a layer of broken charcoal or pebbles on the bottom of the container for drainage. Add 5 to 8 cm of earth or sawdust. At one end, sink a flat crock, enamel pan, or bowl for drinking water. The vessel should be removable for cleaning without disturbing the land area. A flat stepping-stone will allow the turtles easy access to the water. Change the water each day and keep the container clean.

Provide a varied terrain. The major area can be earth with plants, but include some flat stones and bark or wood chips. Most greenhouse plants (ferns, liverworts, lichens, and mosses) will grow in a terrarium. You may have to replace the plants often; but without them, soil will stick to the turtles' feet and muddy the water.

FOR AQUATIC SPECIES. Use a 10- or 20-gallon aquarium for two turtles 5 to 8 cm long. Since your turtles will need to get out of the water at times to get completely dry, build an island of large flat rocks (not pebbles and small stones, which shift easily). Then add water to a depth of 10 to

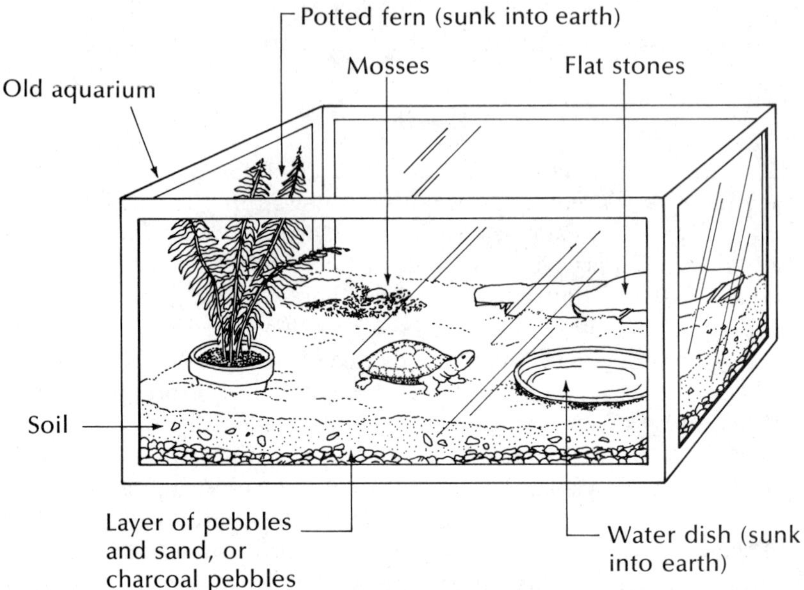

Figure 11-7. Terrarium for land and semiaquatic turtles.

15 cm. Water plants are desirable but will eventually be eaten. Include a lump of plaster of Paris to provide calcium for good shell growth. No lid is required. Round turtle and fish bowls commonly sold at pet stores should not be used.

Situate the aquarium near a window where it will receive two to three hours of sun each day. Open the window—sunshine filtered through glass is inadequate. Since overexposure to sun will kill turtles, you must provide a shaded area, such as a cove.

When the water needs changing, let tap water stand for a day or two to be sure the new water is the same temperature as the old. Major temperature changes may cause shock. Remove the animals; then clean and refill the container.

Classroom Care

FEEDING. Land and semiaquatic turtles are mostly vegetarian although some will eat meat; aquatic turtles are usually carnivorous but sometimes will eat plant food. Fruit, melons, berries, and lettuce are recommended for vegetarian species. For carnivorous species, feed earthworms (page 65), white worms (page 71), larval and adult meal-

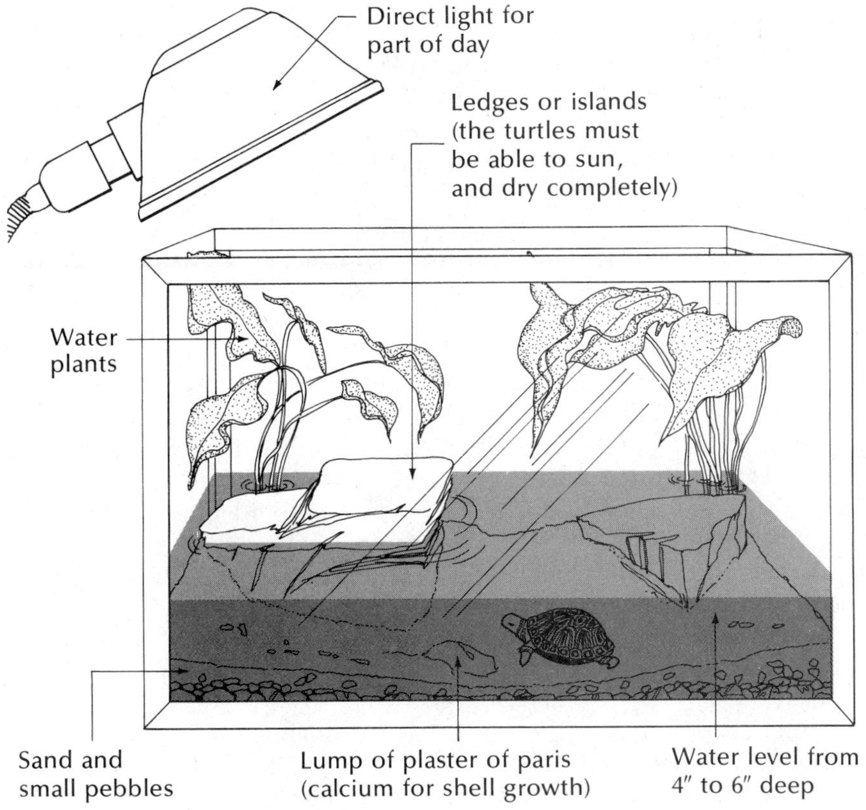

Figure 11-8. Aquarium for water turtles.

worms (page 144), other small insects, small crustaceans, tadpoles, slugs, raw fish, canned dog food, and bite-size pieces of raw lean beef or liver—but not fatty foods, such as pork, ham, or hamburger. Feeding requirements for recommended species are found on pages 222 to 224. Three times a week, place two or three kinds of food near the water's edge, or float it on the water on a lettuce scrap. Your turtles may learn to come to you and accept food from your hand. Allow them to eat all they want in one feeding. Most turtles place their heads underwater to swallow. They can be messy eaters, so you may want to feed them in a separate container (with water) to keep their regular enclosure clean. Remove uneaten food from the tank, or return the animal to its regular home after about one half hour.

About once a month, mix a little high-calcium food with their normal diet for good shell growth. This can be supplied in the form of bone dust (from a butcher), bonemeal (from variety and hardware stores), or cuttlefish bone, such as is used for canaries (from pet stores).

As a substitute for sunlight (especially during the winter), mix a drop of cod liver oil or other vitamin D substance into the food about once a week. A good combination of calcium and vitamin D is provided by feeding Turtle Shell Hardner.®*

"Ant eggs" and other turtle food sold in pet shops cause slow death by starvation and blindness and should *never* be used. Use natural foods exclusively.

DISEASES. A healthy turtle lifts its body off the ground when it walks. Its shell is firm and free from sores or blemishes and external parasites. Undernourished turtles have inflamed eyes and their eyelids stick together. This condition invariably arises if "ant eggs" are used as food but is rapidly cured if fresh natural foods are provided.

You can cure shell maladies by keeping the enclosure scrupulously clean, and providing plenty of sunshine and calcium. White or grey spots around the eyes or on the feet are caused by a fungus. Control the disease by swabbing affected areas with full-strength tropical fish fungus remedy twice a day. Vitamin D and sunshine will prevent fungus attacks.

Internal parasites will cause a loss of appetite with no apparent reason, or a ravenous appetite. These conditions should be treated by a veterinarian. For external parasites or pneumonia refer to page 237. Turtles normally molt at irregular intervals; no special treatment is necessary.

Some stores sell small turtles with painted backs. This inhumane practice prevents normal growth and is now illegal in some states. If such an unfortunate animal is brought into the classroom, gently flake off the paint with your fingernail or very carefully with a sharp knife. If this fails, apply a drop or two of nail polish remover or lacquer thinner with cotton. Be sure to keep such substances away from the animal's eyes and skin. Wash the shell thoroughly with water afterward. Removing the paint may allow proper growth and save the animal's life.

VACATION CARE. Turtles can go without food for a week or two, but someone should observe them every three to four days to make sure

---

*From Lambert-Kay, Div. Carter-Wallace, Inc., 3628 Crenshaw Blvd., Los Angeles, Cal. 90016.

their other needs are met. Keep turtles in the classroom for relatively short periods of time; find good homes for them or, as a last resort, euthanize them before long vacations (see page 238).

EXPERIMENTS WITH TURTLES

To identify individual turtles, put small strips of waterproof adhesive tape on their backs or use *small* dots of nail polish (large painted areas cause shell deformities).

VISUAL ALARM REACTIONS. In response to a rapidly approaching object, turtles will withdraw into their shells, a behavior important for the animals' survival. To study this reaction, shine a narrow shaft of light on a screen. Move an opaque disk 1 cm in diameter between the light and the screen so shadows of varying diameters are formed on the screen. Place a turtle in front of the screen, so it can see the shadow with both eyes. When it sees the shadow, does the animal withdraw its head into its shell?[2b] Does the turtle's response vary with the rapidity with which the shadow changes size? Must the disk's shadow become larger, simulating approach, in order to elicit a response, or will the animal respond to any change in shadow size? Does the animal become habituated to the stimulus with repeated testing? Carefully cover one of its eyes. How does the turtle respond?

HEARING. Turtles have well-developed middle ears—suggesting they can hear well. They quickly perceive slight vibrations transmitted through solids to the skin or shell. However, no one has proved that turtles respond to sound waves carried by the air. Design experiments using tuning forks of different frequencies to test their hearing abilities.

LOCOMOTION. How fast can a land turtle go? Compare turtles, snails, and ants in their pulling power and in their ability to climb and to navigate obstacle courses.

GROWTH. A healthy turtle grows continuously; a very young turtle may double in size in one year. Record the weight and size of a turtle every two weeks. Can you determine the growth rate?

FOOD AND NUTRITION. Do turtles show a preference for foods of different colors? Try offering raw fish colored with vegetable dyes to aquatic turtles.

CONSERVATION. Has a survey of turtles been made in your area? Collect information from local natural history museums and zoos about recent population counts of local native turtles. If the populations are declining, what factors have contributed? What must we do to conserve our native turtles? What is the effect of commercial and pet trade on rare and endangered species? Are conservation laws needed in your area? Are local laws that protect certain species being enforced?

SNAKES

I had an aunt in Yucatan
Who bought a Python from a man
And kept it for a pet.
She died, because she never knew
These simple little rules and few:-
The Snake is living yet.

Hillaire Belloc (1870-1953)

There are about 130 species of snakes native to the United States. Of these, only four are venomous—rattlesnakes, copperheads, water moccasins (cottonmouths), and coral snakes. Indiscriminate killing of any snake encountered in the wild is completely unjustified. Harmless wild snakes should be left undisturbed; they help reduce populations of rodent and insect pests.

Suitable harmless species for the classroom include garter and ribbon snakes, and DeKay's brown snake. Unlike many captive snakes, these species are mainly insectivorous and do not present feeding problems. Do not keep snakes that require hard-to-obtain or expensive foods, such as dead mammals. Under no circumstances should live poisonous snakes be permitted in the classroom. In areas where native snakes are poisonous, students should learn to identify them from pictures and models, and by visits to the zoo. Boa constrictors and other exotic imported snakes are not recommended.

As with all other living creatures, check state and federal regulations before bringing any snakes into the classroom.

The following species are listed in approximate order of desirability for classroom care:

GARTER AND RIBBON SNAKES (*Thamnophis* species, also called Striped Adders or Garden Snakes). These hardy species are easy to acquire and to keep in captivity. When a wild garter snake is picked up, it may emit a foul-smelling secretion from musk glands at the base of its tail.

Figure 11-9. Garter snake.

This is an alarm reaction that will soon be lost with gentle handling. They feed well in captivity and will eat large earthworms, insects, pieces of raw fish, or chopped raw liver. Their natural foods include frogs, toads, salamanders, fish, and tadpoles. Garter snakes (but usually not ribbon snakes) may be induced to eat raw hamburger by first mixing it with earthworms and then slowly reducing the amount of earthworms until the snakes are eating only the raw meat. Garter and ribbon snakes often soak themselves in water—an adequate supply must be provided. Pregnant females collected from the wild in the spring will bear live young which feed on small earthworms and insects.

BROWN SNAKE (*Storeria dekayi,* also called DeKay's snake). Brown snakes are seldom more than a foot long and have two parallel rows of blackish spots down their backs. These "city snakes" are frequently found in parks, cemeteries and under trash in vacant lots in even the largest urban centers. Provide hiding places in their enclosure—they are very secretive animals. Feed them earthworms, slugs, and soft-bodied insect larvae. They will live in harmony in a terrarium with full-grown toads.

The following species are *not* recommended for reasons of conservation:

SMOOTH GREEN SNAKE, *Opheodrys vernalis,* also known as Grass Snake.

HOG-NOSE SNAKE, *Heterodon* species.

Because of the extensive use of insecticides, smooth green snakes and hog-nose snakes are seriously threatened. Overharvesting for the pet trade has added to problems of survival. These species should be protected.

The following species also are *not* recommended:

WATER SNAKE, (*Natrix* species). They are nervous, unpredictable, and emit an offensive odor when frightened. Although nonpoisonous, they are sometimes confused with poisonous water moccasins.

RACERS AND WHIPSNAKES, (*Coluber* and *Masticophis* species). These snakes are nervous and aggressive and present a feeding problem in captivity.

Do not collect snakes from the wild or purchase them from pet stores unless you are an expert in identifying species. (Pet stores often misidentify snakes.) Snakes obtained from reliable sources are correctly identified and guaranteed free from disease. You may be able to obtain small native snakes, which often are not available commercially, from a nearby zoo, natural history museum, or herpetological society. (See REFERENCES, Reptile and Amphibian Societies, page 240.) These organizations may also provide specimens on short-term loan. Biological supply houses and commercial suppliers are the second best sources.*

Do not allow unidentified snakes in the classroom. If a student has a pet snake, be sure it is accurately identified *before* it is allowed in school. Take animals to the zoo for proper identification—a reptile expert cannot identify a snake from a description given over the phone. To be bitten by an unidentified or misidentified snake can be very dangerous.

CLASSROOM CARE

TRANSPORTING. For short journeys, place the snake in a slightly dampened cloth bag with a rubber band wound tightly around the top. A sock knotted at the top is fine for small snakes. They usually escape from cardboard boxes. Avoid transporting snakes during winter months. If they must be moved in cold weather, provide a hot water bottle wrapped in a towel and keep the bottle warm throughout the journey.

HANDLING. Be sure a snake is awake before attempting to pick it up. If it is startled, it will be irritable. It is difficult to tell when a snake is

*See Reptile Suppliers, page 240.

Figure 11-10. Calm handling does not alarm the snake. At the back of the cage, note the resting box which provides a dark hiding place which the snake likes.

asleep, however, because it has no eyelids to close. Try to make the snake aware of your presence by some movement or sound. Then grasp it gently but firmly near the head with one hand and support its body with the other; be careful not to squeeze it. The snake will squirm at first, but if you remain calm, the warmth from your hands will soon quiet it. Hold a snake loosely and give it freedom to move from hand to hand. Rapid movements alarm snakes. Most snakes soon become tame when handled every day.

If you are afraid of snakes, do not handle them in front of students. You may transmit your own fear or reinforce a student's aversion. No one should be forced to handle a snake. However, if a competent person holds a snake so that it will not thrash, most people will at least touch it and learn that a snake's body is cool and dry, not wet and slimy as they may have believed it to be. The darting, forked tongue of the snake does not sting—it is soft and harmless and serves as a supplementary organ for detecting odors. The tongue has nothing to do with fangs or venom.

Snakes should not be handled when they are shedding. Do not permit snakes to be teased or enduced to strike the sides of the cage. It is unfair to goad an animal confined to a cage; there is real danger that the animal will injure itself.

HOUSING. Garter, ribbon, and DeKay's brown snakes can be kept in well-drained woodland terrariums such as those described on page 225. Use a lid. Provide hiding places. Snakes are likely to hurt their noses or develop mouth rot if kept in wire mesh or barred cages, and these cages are not escapeproof for smaller species. An enclosure 45 × 30 cm will house one or two snakes up to 60 cm long. An ideal cage has a floor and three sides of wood or Formica®, one glass side, and a lid which provides some ventilation. Paint the wood surfaces. The lid should fit tightly to prevent escape—weight it down if necessary. A large door, preferably on top, will allow you easy access to the animal.

Figure 11-11. Housing for garter or other small snake, shown from top view.

Do not house together snakes of different sizes—the larger may eat the smaller. To keep the cage clean, cover the bottom with sheets of newspaper, blotting paper, or cardboard. Do not use sand, sawdust, or peat moss, which get into the animals' mouths.

It is interesting to watch snakes move—give them a variety of climbing places such as rocks and a few dead branches. A resting shelf and a rod fastened across the cage are possible embellishments. Snakes tend to be secretive and will need hiding places. A resealed cereal box with a small opening cut out at one end will serve. Hiding places are essential in enclosures with four transparent sides. Replace the cereal box when it becomes soiled.

As a general rule, keep the temperature at 24 to 30°C (75 to 86°F). To simulate natural conditions, you could allow the temperature to fall at night, but not below 21 to 24°C (70 to 75°F). Incandescent lamps will provide the required heat; adjust wattage and distance of the bulb from the cage to obtain the desired temperature. Keep a thermometer in the cage to obtain the desired temperature. Keep a thermometer in the cage to check the temperature. Be sure that adequate shaded areas are provided.

Remove the paper bedding each day or whenever soiled. Sanitation is very important to protect snakes from external parasites. Most snakes will defecate two or three days after feeding; urine is passed out with the feces.

FEEDING. All snakes are carnivorous and swallow their food without chewing it. They should be fed about once a week but can live on much less frequent feedings. Suitable foods include earthworms (see page 65); beef heart; liver; frozen or fresh fish, such as smelt; small amphibians, such as tadpoles (page 198); and salamanders (page 195). They also will eat insects such as crickets (page 134), grasshoppers, houseflies (page 142), or waxworm larvae (page 152). Supplement the snakes' diets by sprinkling a small amount of Vionate®* on the food at each feeding.

---

*A vitamin-mineral powder obtainable from E. R. Squibb and Sons, Inc., 909 Third Ave., New York 10022.

For convenience, food can be packaged and frozen. Kill small salamanders and tadpoles by placing them in plastic containers in a refrigerator until anesthetized, then in a freezer for 24 hours. Place several one-meal portions between two sheets of plastic wrap and staple, as shown in Figure 11–12. Store the sheets of food in a freezer; cut off sections and thaw as needed. Since dehydration often accompanies freezing, make the food more appetizing by thawing it in a container of water.

Place food close to the snake's mouth. If it shows no interest, dangle the food on a thread or drag it along the ground to simulate life, or try holding the food with blunt forceps. Be persistent. Snakes have a tendency to disgorge food, so do not handle the animals for several days after feeding.

There is no cause for alarm if a snake refuses food for several weeks. They differ markedly in their dispositions and food requirements, not only among species but also among individuals of the same species. Treat each snake as an individual. Sometimes overhandling may prevent a snake from eating. A fast may sometimes be terminated by raising or lowering the temperature of the cage, by giving the snake a warm bath, or by repeatedly presenting different types of food in

Figure 11-12. Preparation of frozen food for snakes. Previously killed small salamanders, tadpoles, or any other foods are placed between two sheets of plastic wrap and stapled as shown. Store in freezer and cut sections as required.

various ways. However, if a snake fasts for several months, consult a reptile expert for help.

Cloudy eyes usually indicate skin shedding; do not coax the snake to eat (however, it will be extremely hungry immediately after shedding). Leave it alone during this period.

WATER. A bowl of water large enough to hold the animal for bathing and drinking should be provided. Use a flat-bottomed crock or enamel container that cannot be turned over. Always keep the water clean. Water should be deep enough to cover the snake's head.

SHEDDING. Shedding is a normal process for all snakes. For captive snakes it is the most trying time for their survival. Shedding occurs at regular intervals, varying in frequency according to species and age of the individual animal. The snake's eyes become opaque milky-white, its vision is imperfect, and its skin appears rough, milky-blue, and lusterless. Most snakes will soak in water a great deal for two or three days. Provide warm water. A day or two before the actual shedding, the eyes clear up and the snake can see again; the skin pattern looks almost normal. Provide large rocks and branches against which the snake can rub to loosen the outer skin. Finally, the snake crawls out of its old covering—leaving behind the inside-out cast skin, or *exuvia*. Do not disturb the animal during any part of this period, which may last from 5 to 14 days.

REPRODUCTION. Some snakes bear live young and some lay eggs; however, breeding snakes in the classroom usually is not successful. If eggs are laid or young are born, consult reference books about their care.

VACATION CARE. For absences longer than three or four days, arrange to have someone clean the cages and feed the snakes. Keep snakes in the classroom for short periods of time only.

Snake Studies

The body of a snake always follows the path that the head has chosen. As a snake winds its way among rocks, its body always moves in the chosen path—even if the rocks are removed once the head has passed them. What possible explanations are there for this behavior? Can it be related to survival?

Record a snake's feeding schedule and daily activities. In evaluating this information, remember that a captive snake's behavior may be quite different from that of an animal living in nature.

Learn to identify local species of snakes, their normal foods, their usefulness in controlling pests, and their role in the ecosystem. Observe snakes in the wild with binoculars and spotting scopes as you would birds. Contact your local herpetological society to arrange field trips.

ADDITIONAL INFORMATION ON REPTILES

Diseases

Healthy reptiles eat regularly, are alert, and their skin is unblemished. Mites look like chalky white deposits around the vents, eyes, in the folds of the chin and neck, and, with lizards and turtles, at the joints of the legs. To check for mites, shine a flashlight quickly on suspected areas. These parasites must be removed to ensure the animal's good health. Place a small piece of No Pest Strip®* in the cage where the animal will not come in contact with it (for example, under the water dish). Leave the strip for 10 to 15 hours; repeat as necessary every two weeks to eliminate hatching mites which may have escaped the first exposure. Use of the No Pest Strip® effectively kills all ticks and mites. Physical contact is unnecessary, and no ill effects to the reptiles have been reported.

Symptoms of pneumonia and spontaneous tuberculosis are running or bubbly nose and gasping. Keep the sick animals in well-constructed, uniformly heated enclosures. Provide an overhead lamp 24 hours a day to maintain the temperature at 30°C (86°F). Remember to provide some shaded area. Continue treatment until all signs of disease disappear.

Mouth rot is frequently fatal within a few weeks. It is very hard to treat and can be contagious to other reptiles. To check for mouth rot, gently lift a snake's upper lip or pull the lower lip down to expose the gums. Normal snakes have clear pink, bluish, or white gums; afflicted snakes show bloody areas and cheeselike deposits on their gums. Warm baths, rinsing the affected parts with antibiotics, exposure to ultraviolet light, and use of vitamins are recommended treatments. Consult a veterinarian, zoo or herpetological society for help.

Disposal and Euthanasia

Release native animals into the wild at least a month before freezing weather sets in. Do not release animals that are *not* native to the

---

*A flat 25 cm strip of hard material impregnated with an insecticide, Vapona®. Manufactured by Shell Oil Company and available at Shell gasoline stations.

area. Unwanted animals may be accepted by a zoo or by other schools. Failing that, the animals may have to be disposed of.

EUTHANASIA. Placing reptiles and amphibians in the freezer to kill them may cause slow suffering for the animals. Perhaps the best method for killing a reptile in a high school situation is to give an overdose of an inhalant anesthetic—ether or chloroform—which will first anesthetize and then kill. Euthanasia should be undertaken only by adults experienced in these techniques, not by students. Turtles are best killed with an overdose of ether; for lizards and snakes use chloroform. Do not use chloroform in rooms where other animals are kept. (**Caution:** Handle both ether and chloroform with extreme care. Keep them away from all open flames.)

In order to keep liquid ether or chloroform from coming into contact with the animal's skin (causing intense irritation and pain) use an airtight container which has two compartments, such as a dessicator. Place a generous wad of absorbent cotton soaked in ether or chloroform in the lower compartment and place the animal in the upper compartment. Close the lid. About 60 ml of chloroform may be sufficient to kill a small lizard—but better to add too much than too little.

REFERENCES

1. KERN, A. R. 1972. Incubation and Hatching of Snake Eggs. *The Sci. Teacher* 39(3):68–69.
2. STOKES, A. W., ed. 1968. *Animal Behavior in Laboratory and Field.* W. H. Freeman & Co., San Francisco. (Advanced)
   a. CARPENTER, C. C. Social Structure and Display Patterns of Iguanid Lizards. pp. 109–112. Available from the publisher as Separate No. 819.
   b. HAYES, W. N. Visual Alarm Reactions. pp. 49–51. Separate No. 806.
3. EVANS, L. T. 1936. A Study of a Social Hierarchy in the Lizard, *Anolis carolinensis. J. Genet. Psychol.* 48:88–111. (Advanced)
4. EVANS, L. T. 1938. Courtship Behavior and Sexual Selection in *Anolis. J. Comp. Psychol.* 26:475–98. (Advanced)
5. GREENBERG, B. and G. K. NOBLE. 1944. Social Behavior of the American Chameleon (*Anolis carolinensis Voigt*). *Physiol. Zool.* 17:392–439. (Advanced)
6. WARING, H. 1963. *Color Change Mechanisms of Cold Blooded Vertebrates.* Academic Press, New York. (Advanced)
7. BOGERT, C. M. 1976. Behavioral Thermoregulation in Reptiles. *Research Problems in Biology.* Series 3, Second Ed. Biological Sciences Curriculum Study. Oxford University Press, New York. p. 1–4.

FURTHER READING

Allen, R. 1971. *How to Keep Snakes in Captivity.* Great Outdoors Publishing Co., St. Petersburg, Fla.

Babcock, H. L. 1971. Turtles of the Northeastern United States. Dover Publications, New York.

Cochran, D. M. and C. J. Goin. 1970. *New Field Book of Reptiles and Amphibians.* G. P. Putnam's Sons, New York.

Ernst, C. H. and Barbour, R. W. 1973. *Turtles of the United States.* University Press of Kentucky, Lexington, Ky.

Goin, C. J. and O. B. Goin. 1971. *Introduction to Herpetology.* 2nd ed. W. H. Freeman & Co., San Francisco.

Harrison, H. H. 1971. *The World of the Snake.* J. B. Lippincott Co., Philadelphia.

Headstrom, R. 1971. *Lizards as Pets.* J. B. Lippincott Co., Philadelphia.

Hoke, J. 1970. *First Book of Turtles and Their Care.* Franklin Watts, New York.

Morris, P. A. 1974. *An Introduction to the Reptiles and Amphibians of the United States.* Dover Publications, Inc., New York.

Reidman, S. R. and Witham, R. 1974. *Turtles: Extinction or Survival.* Abelard-Schuman, New York.

Reeves, M. E. 1975, *The Total Turtle.* Thomas Y. Crowell Publishing Co., New York.

Simon, H. 1973. *Snakes—The Facts and the Folklore.* The Viking Press, New York.

Turtles in the Home Aquarium. 1970. Leaflet No. FL 91. Fish & Wildlife Service, U.S. Dept. of the Interior, Washington, D.C. 20240.

White, W. Jr. 1973. *A Turtle is Born.* Sterling Publishing Co., Inc., New York.

FILMS

The Chameleon. 16 mm, color, 8 min. Living Science Films Series, No. 9. International Film Bureau, 332 S. Michigan Ave., Chicago, Ill 60604.

Chameleons. Film loop, super 8 mm, 3 min. 7 sec. Doubleday & Co., Garden City, NY 11530.

Life Story of a Snake. 16 mm, color or b/w, 11 min. Encyclopaedia Britannica Films, 1150 Wilmette Ave., Wilmette, Ill 60091.

Lizards (in the Sonoran desert). Film loop, super 8 mm, color or b/w. Hubbard Scientific Co., P. O. Box 105, Northbrook, Ill 60062.

Nature's Camouflage. (Includes chameleons and others.) 16 mm, color, 13 min. ACI Films, 35 W. 45 St., New York 10036.

Non-Poisonous Snakes: Garter Snake. Film loop, super 8 mm, color or b/w. Hubbard Scientific Co., P. O. Box 105, Northbrook, Ill 60062.

Reptiles and Amphibians. 16 mm, color, 52 min. McGraw-Hill Films, 330 W. 42 St., New York 10036.

Temperature and Activity in Reptiles. BSCS Single Topic Film. Rand McNally & Co., Chicago, Ill 60680.

The Terrarium—Classroom Science. 16 mm, sound, color, 12 min. Film Assoc. of California, 11559 Santa Monica Blvd., Los Angeles 90025.

Turtles, The Care of a Pet. 16 mm, sound, color, 8 min. Film Assoc. of California, 11559 Santa Monica Blvd., Los Angeles 90025.

Turtles. (Includes box and gopher turtles.) Super 8 mm, cartridge, silent, color, 4 min. Popular Science Publishing Co., 239 W. Fair View Blvd., Inglewood, Ca 90302.

REPTILE SUPPLIERS

R. F. Carle Co. Inc., P. O. Box 3155, Chico, Ca 95926 (Chameleons)

Carolina Biological Supply Co., Main Office, Burlington, NC 27215 (Box and painted turtles, chameleons)

CCM: General Biological, Inc., 8200 S. Hoyne Ave., Chicago, Ill 60620 (Box turtles, chameleons, and fence lizards)

Hermosa Reptile, Inc., P. O. Box 182, 219 Pacific Hwy., Hermosa Beach, Ca 90254 (Blanding's turtles, chameleons, fence lizards, and skinks)

Midwest Reptile Sales, P. O. Box 6119, Ft. Wayne, Ind 46806 (Painted turtles)

Mogul-Ed, P. O. Box 482, Oshkosh, Wis. 54901 (Box, Blanding's, red-eared and painted turtles; chameleons; garter snakes)

Nasco/Steinhilber, Janesville Ave., Ft. Atkinson, Wisc 53538 (Box turtles, chameleons, garter snakes)

Snake Farm, P. O. Box 96, Laplace, La 70068 (Box and painted turtles; chameleons and fence lizards; ribbon snakes)

Southwestern Herpetological Research & Sales, P. O. Box 282, Calimesa, Ca 92320 (Skinks and fence lizards)

REPTILE AND AMPHIBIAN SOCIETIES

Information on local herpetological societies can be obtained from zoos or natural history museums. If they are unable to help, contact one of the two big national societies listed below.

American Society of Icthyologists and Herpetologists (ASIH)
Publishes *Copeia* quarterly. Contact ASIH, c/o Div. of Fishes, National Museum of Natural History, Washington, DC 20560.

Herpetologists' League
Publishes *Herpetologica* quarterly. Contact Dr. Philip A. Medica, Secretary-Treasurer, P. O. Box 495, UCLA, Mercury, Nevada 89023.

Other societies are:

California Turtle and Tortoise Club, Royland D. Lewis, 3245 Military Avenue, Los Angeles, Ca 90034.

Connecticut Herpetological Society, Mr. George T. Vesper, Bakos Road, RFD 2, Tolland, Conn 06084.

New York Herpetological Society, P. O. Box 3946, Grand Central Station, New York 10017.

Society for the Study of Amphibians and Reptiles, Dr. Stephen R. Edwards, Association of Systematics Collections, Museum of Natural History, University of Kansas, Lawrence, Kansas 66045. Publishes *The Journal of Herpetology* and annually a directory of all regional, national, and international herpetological societies in the *Herpetological Review.*

12

Gerbils

"Animals are such agreeable friends–they ask no questions, they pass no criticisms."

George Eliot (1819–1880).

Gerbils are friendly, easy to care for, clean and odorless. Since they are not nocturnal, as hamsters and mice are, their activities can be observed during the school day. The animals' normal activity cycles, eating patterns, body movements, and sleeping postures, and their exploratory behavior and response to affection, all make suitable topics for serious scientific investigations.

Only two of the fourteen known species of gerbils are suitable as classroom animals or pets; other gerbil species may carry plague or rabies. The Mongolian species *Meriones unguiculatus*, introduced to this country in 1954, has become a common household pet. The other acceptable species is the Libyan gerbil, sometimes called the North African desert rat, *Meriones libycus*. The Mongolian species, native to northeast China and Mongolia, is more readily available and is described here.

Gerbils are light brown or agouti colored (with hairs that are brown at the base and yellow at the tip). They are dark on the back and lighter underneath. They have long, furry tails. Adults are about 10 cm long and weigh 70 to 90 gm. They sit up a great deal of the time and prefer to eat this way, manipulating food in their forepaws with considerable dexterity. Their intense curiosity about new situations makes them particularly attractive to observe.

Fossil remains show that gerbils have existed in the arid regions of Asia, Africa, and eastern Europe for 60,000 years. Wild gerbils live in colonies; their social life is similar to that of the prairie dog. The colony home is a tunnel burrowed underground for about 2.5 meters, with multiple entrances and branch tunnels. Side chambers serve as nesting sites and storage rooms for grain and plants collected from the scrub regions. Gerbils escape the extreme day and night temperatures of the desert in these underground homes.

White mice and rats, golden hamsters, and guinea pigs are also affectionate and make good classroom animals, but they develop offensive odors and their cages need more frequent cleaning. Because rabbits are larger and require more space, they should be kept outdoors. Guinea pigs can be housed outdoors if extreme temperatures are avoided. On the whole, gerbils, mice, and rats, which must be housed indoors, are the best mammals for the classroom.

Small rodents are notoriously prolific; consider fertility when selecting species. Animals can be prevented from breeding simply by housing the sexes separately. The gestation period for hamsters is the shortest; consequently, they produce more litters per year. Guinea pigs are least prolific; not only is the gestation period longer (ten weeks, compared to two or three weeks for other species), but the size of the litter is small (two or three). If your prime purpose in keeping classroom mammals is to demonstrate their life cycle, you might prefer to

Figure 12-1. Mongolian gerbils.

Figure 12-2. Mongolian gerbils in simulated natural habitat.

borrow a pair of rodents, keep them through the birth and raising of one litter, and return them to their owner. Provisions must be made to prevent overpopulation of animals that are to be kept longer.

Gerbils usually can be borrowed from students or purchased at local pet stores. Try to obtain them locally; shipping can be traumatic for them. Before obtaining the animals, become familiar with their needs and how to care for them, then make the necessary housing and food ready for them.

The care described here for gerbils is also appropriate for other small mammals. Special needs or variations are noted in subsequent chapters on mice, rats, hamsters, guinea pigs, and rabbits.

STATE LAWS PROHIBITING GERBILS In states where there are no natural deserts there is no ecological risk in keeping gerbils. California prohibits importation of gerbils, because they may escape into the desert and multiply, becoming a pest due to the lack of a natural predator. In Nevada, an importation permit is required, but this can be obtained upon request from the Nevada Fish and Game Department. As of 1974, all other states permitted importation of gerbils. However, the U. S. Department of Agriculture cautions against taking gerbils to western Texas, Arizona, or New Mexico.

HOUSING

If wild animals are to adapt well to domestication, their classroom houses should closely resemble their natural homes. Gerbils should have a well-ventilated, warm, quiet environment with plenty of room to burrow. Do not place the cage in direct sunlight; excess heat is more

Figure 12-3. A spacious cage with thick bedding and egg cartons and sticks to gnaw on make a comfortable home for gerbils.

Figure 12-4. A home-made, two-tiered small mammal cage with a mesh ramp and plenty of interesting places to explore. Leave no jagged edges of wire exposed which would hurt the animals.

dangerous than cold. Maintain the temperature at 21 to 24°C (70 to 75°F).

Cages should be 25 cm tall or higher, as the animals need room to sit up. Allow at least 50 square centimeters of floor area for each pair of animals. Cages with glass, plastic or metal sides, 25 × 30 cm or larger, will house one or two gerbils. A 10-gallon aquarium is excellent for a pair of gerbils. (Because aquariums are rather heavy to handle, they are not satisfactory for other small rodents that require more frequent bedding changes.)

Plastic boxes are best for all species of small mammals.* Mesh lids provide essential ventilation. The housing should have solid floors (mesh floors hurt the animals' feet and noses), solid walls (bedding material is not scattered during burrowing and young animals do not fall out), and should prevent drafts. Plastic boxes are easy to clean, lightweight, and inexpensive. Select a box large enough to ensure plenty of space for exercise.

To construct a lid for an aquarium or plastic box, cover a well-fitting heavy wooden frame (which cannot be knocked off easily) with ½-inch hardwire. Be sure there are no jagged edges.

Wooden cages cannot be properly cleaned, and in time gerbils will gnaw through them. If you use metal barred cages, line the floor and the lower 12 cm of the side walls with Formica® or metal sheeting. Cages with mesh floors may be used only for non-breeding mice, rats,

---

*You can obtain plastic sweater boxes inexpensively from local department stores (you will need to make mesh lids). Plastic animal cages can be purchased separately or with fitted stainless steel lids from such suppliers as: Ancare Corp., 47 Manhasset Ave., Manhasset, Long Island, New York 11030; Interex Corp., 66 Woerd Ave., Waltham, Mass. 02154; or Research Equipment Co., Inc., Box 1151, Bryan, Texas 77801.

and rabbits (but not for gerbils, hamsters, or guinea pigs). Breeding cages for *all* species must have solid floors. Tiny mouse cages are not satisfactory for larger animals like gerbils.

If your students take the gerbils home for weekends or vacations, the cage lid must be secured against dogs and cats. The door of a metal cage can be fastened tightly with a key chain—the type that has a loop that clips over a hook is ideal. Also, the door of the room in which a gerbil's cage is placed should be kept closed.

BEDDING. For caged gerbils and other small rodents, provide plenty of bedding for insulation and to absorb body wastes. Put 8 to 12 cm of bedding in the cage for gerbils and 3 or 5 cm for other small rodents. Use coarse pine sawdust; pine, cedar, basswood, and poplar shavings; hardwood chips; crushed corn cobs; beet pulp; dry husks; Vermiculite®, Kitty Litter®, or other commercial litter. (Wood products often are available free from lumber yards, but do not accept highly resinous woods.) Do not use newspaper.

For gerbils, heap the bedding about 20 cm deep at one end, and slope it down to 8 cm at the other. They will burrow in the deep bedding, and you can see the burrows through the glass. Mature gerbils chew up cardboard, which helps wear down their constantly growing teeth. If you put cardboard in the cage regularly, they will make their own bedding. Remove excess shredded material when it reaches 20 to 25 cm in depth. Bedding stays unusually clean; gerbils, being desert animals, produce only two or three drops of urine and some tiny feces each day.

For gerbils only, bedding should be changed every four to six weeks (more often for other small rodents). Put the animals in a large, clean wastebasket or other container with some bedding material under which to hide. Wash and dry the cages thoroughly before adding new bedding. Do not change the bedding in breeding cages after the young are born. Wait until they are separated from their parents (at about one month).

BOXES AND SHELVES. Include in the cage a metal, wooden, or cardboard nesting box, large enough to hold an animal comfortably. Nest boxes are especially necessary if light enters the cage from all sides. Use an inverted box about 15 cm square, with a smooth arched entrance large enough to admit a pregnant female. Build a wooden or metal shelf about 8 cm above the bedding.

GNAWING. Gnawing, a major activity for gerbils, occupies them for many hours every day. Mice, rats, hamsters, guinea pigs, and rabbits

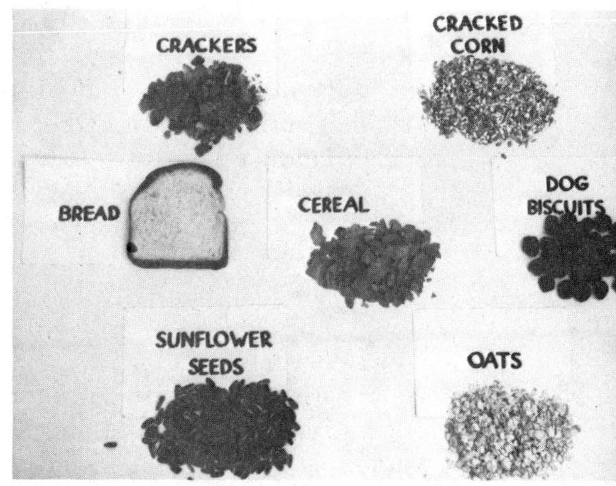

Figure 12-5. Make a mixture of these suitable foods for gerbils.

gnaw decidedly less. All rodents should have a constant supply of twigs and fresh branches or hardwood blocks to gnaw on. Gerbils also should have a constant supply of cardboard egg cartons, boxes, or tubes (which also constitute ready-made tunnels) to help wear down their continuously growing front teeth. (It is a sure sign of pregnancy when the consumption of cardboard soars, as both parents shred it for bedding and nesting material.)

EXERCISE. Gerbils enjoy an exercise wheel, either the inclined-disk or ferris wheel type. However, because gerbils are constantly burrowing, the wheels get choked with bedding unless a separate exercise room is available. With spacious quarters and enough bedding and cardboard, gerbils will exercise naturally by burrowing and gnawing. Wheels of either type are especially welcomed by mice, hamsters, and rats, however, and are described on page 264.

FEEDING

Small rodents eat sunflower seeds, oats, unsweetened breakfast cereals, uncooked oatmeal, wild-bird seed, canary seed, dry dog food, crackers, bread crusts, corn chips, shelled peanuts, wheat, and similar items—about one tablespoon per animal per day. You may purchase laboratory chow from agricultural supply stores, pet shops, or laboratory supply houses,* but animals prefer a varied diet, and it is much

---

*Ralston Purina Co., Checkerboard Square, St. Louis, Mo. 63188. Feed gerbils and hamsters Purina Formulab Chow. Special chows are available for mice, rats and guinea pigs. (Some biological supply houses and pet stores offer a smaller selection at high prices.)

cheaper if you and the students prepare the diet. For a large and convenient supply, mix together several of the foods listed above to provide a *balanced* diet. See how many different types of food you can find. Inexpensive brewer's yeast tablets are an excellent dietary supplement.

Since dry food should always be available in the animal's cage, check the food supply daily; see that the container is full and has not been upset or covered with bedding.

For all rodents, include an ample supply of nuts or other hard food to help wear down their continuously growing front teeth. Provide sunflower seeds in moderation; they are the gerbils' favorite food but are fattening and can impair fertility. Use them to train gerbils to eat from your hand.

Hoppers are convenient for dispensing food, but any small metal or glass dish will do. (Gerbils will gnaw on wood containers.) Small containers from children's kitchen sets make excellent food dishes. If possible, suspend the dish from the roof or wall above the bedding. Empty and clean the containers every few days. Hoppers should permit the animals easy access to the food but should be designed to prevent food spillage without the risk of entrapping the animals' heads. The openings for slatted hoppers should be between 6 and 7 mm for gerbils and mice, 9 to 12 mm for rats and larger animals. Food should not be strewn on the floor.

GREENS. In addition to dry food, include greens, fruit, or vegetables every day or two. These are a most important source of water; but gerbils also drink from their water bottle. Fresh greens such as lettuce, spinach, plantain, or dandelion leaves, and kitchen scraps such as potato, carrot, or apple peel are most acceptable (but not soft fruit or cooked food). Wash this food first, because diseases can be caused in gerbils if the food has been contaminated by wild rodents or birds. Remove leftover greens each day to keep the bedding clean. (Guinea pigs' special requirements for greens are described on page 292.)

WATER. Fresh, clean water should always be available for all animals. An ideal drinking bottle consists of a hollow glass or metal tube inserted into the rubber stopper of an inverted glass bottle. Water bottles should be transparent to show water level and cleanliness. Because the gerbils will gnaw on hard plastic bottles, these must be suspended outside of a mesh or barred cage with the metal or glass spout protruding to the inside. Bottle stoppers can be protected with a metal plate, if necessary.

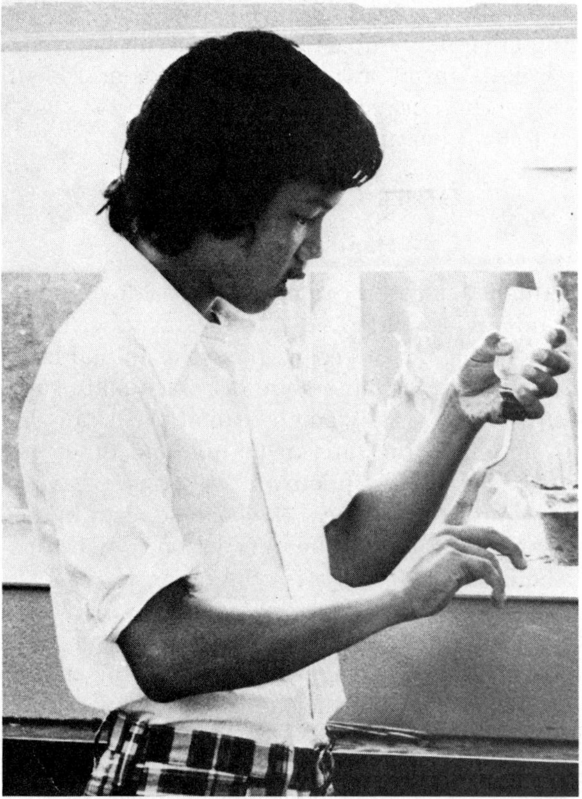

Figure 12-6. Releasing trapped air from a water bottle spout.

To make your own water bottle, insert a 15 cm length of 6-mm glass tubing, straight or bent, through the stopper of a 200 to 300 ml bottle. Reduce the protruding end to 3 mm by melting it slightly in a flame—rotating the tube so it will not crack. The size of the nozzle is important; if the hole is too large, it will leak; if it is too small, water flow will be inadequate. Fill the water bottle, be sure the stopper fits well, then release any trapped air in the spout by inverting the bottle and tapping the tube gently until the water accumulates in the spout; attach the inverted bottle to the cage. Be sure the water spout is easily accessible to the animal but does not touch the bedding (or the water will run out). After a few hours, check whether the tube is still filled with water and that the bedding beneath it is dry. Stainless steel tubes with steel balls at the lower end reduce leakage.* Pans of water placed on the bedding are quickly upset and should not be used.

Every few days, throw away all the old water and fill the bottle with fresh water. The normal daily water intake for a gerbil on a dry diet is from 2 to 6 ml per animal.

OTHER CLASSROOM CARE

Handling Gerbils

When frightened, a gerbil can nip sharply. Move calmly when you approach it, and advise students not to make sudden movements that will frighten it. To pick up a gerbil, grasp the animal from above, but not too tightly. Your other hand should immediately support its feet. Do not pick up a gerbil or any small animal by its tail. (Veterinarians often have to amputate the tails of gerbils and other small animals because the skin has been ripped off.) After you have picked up a gerbil, you may grasp the tail, *near the base*, to restrain the animal and to avoid dropping it. Support the gerbil's body with one hand, and gently hold the base of the tail with the other. (For picking up other mammalian species, see the appropriate chapters.)

Gerbils can struggle violently, and an inexperienced handler may drop the animal. Hold a gerbil about 5 cm above the bedding until it is securely in your grasp. Such a short fall will not hurt it. As you lift the animal to be nestled in your arms, keep its head pointing toward you; you can more easily control the gerbil this way. Do not allow very young children to lift the gerbil. They may squeeze a gerbil too hard or drop it, and may accidentally kill it. Do not let a gerbil get free in a room; it can be difficult to catch!

Inevitably, a few bites will occur, but these are no more serious than any other small wound. The famous naturalist, Robert Snedigar, has said, "When animals bite or otherwise offend, it is almost always because from their point of view it is the right thing to do. The animal owner's attitude, if he is to succeed, must be one of patience, calm and willingness to understand."

Children of all ages, and adults, usually enjoy gently stroking these friendly animals. Hold sunflower seeds in your outstretched hand, be very still and patient; soon curiosity will overcome the shyest gerbil and it will eat from your hand. You can train it to run to greet you if you make a habit of offering it some favorite tidbit. Small rodents should be handled frequently if they are to remain tame; preferably, the same

---

*Such as Atco Ball Waterers®, from Ancare Corp., 47 Manhasset Ave., Manhasset, L.I., N.Y. 11030.

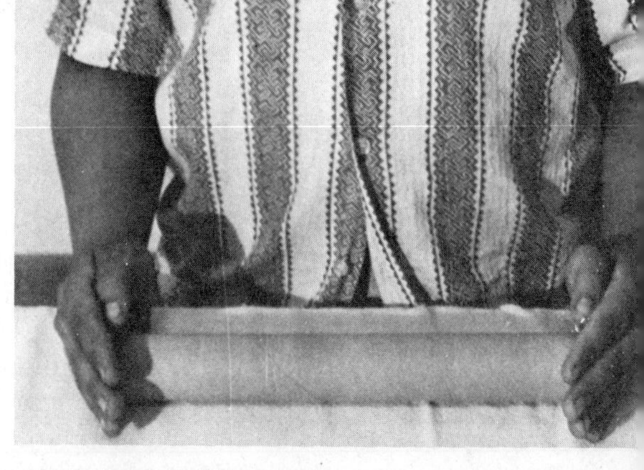

Figure 12-7. Try enticing an escaped animal into a cardboard roll. If you succeed, seal the ends quickly and transfer the animal back to its cage.

Figure 12-8. How to succeed with a coffee can to catch an escaped animal. Not shown is the point at which the can is inverted over the animal. Be sure not to hit the animal with the can.

persons should handle them every day. Do not attempt to pick them up until they are thoroughly accustomed to you. Avoid tight restraint that may cause an animal to struggle and hurt itself. If you proceed gradually and patiently, you can train a gerbil to run up your arm.

ESCAPE. Gerbils will not try to escape if they are properly housed. Should a gerbil or other small rodent get loose, close the door to the room and stop up any gap underneath. Keep calm and wait until the gerbil has finished exploring. Several methods can be used to catch an escaped animal. Try holding a cardboard roll close to the animal. Seal the end furthest away with your hand. If the animal enters, quickly seal off the end where it entered. Another method, to be used if the animal is tame, is to entice it to your hand with sunflower seeds or into a 2-pound coffee can. Hold the can very still, then invert it quickly over the animal—taking care not to hit its head or trap its tail. Slide your hand under the can and turn it rightside up. Another method is to place the cage on the floor and construct a tunnel or ramp into it. Leave the cage this way overnight; the gerbil's homing instinct should lead back.

Weekend and Vacation Care

The care of gerbils and other small mammals on weekends is not difficult, but you must supply adequate water and meet temperature and ventilation requirements. Because they are desert animals, gerbils require less water than other species, so one 200 to 300 ml water bottle per cage should last all weekend. For all other small mammals, two or three bottles of water per cage may be needed. Provide plenty of food. Cages should be cleaned before the weekend.

For longer periods, you must arrange for someone to care for the animals' needs daily, or at least every two days. If this care cannot be provided by school personnel, it may be necessary to ask students to care for the animals at home. Request written approval of parents so their cooperation is assured. On the whole, it may be preferable not to board small mammals in homes where there are cats or dogs.

PAIRING AND BREEDING

Compatibility

When strange gerbils or hamsters are to be paired, either a breeding pair or two of the same sex, wash a cage thoroughly and use entirely fresh bedding, new food, a clean water bottle, and fresh twigs. The two gerbils will meet in territory which neither can claim as its own, and neither will be likely to defend. Watch carefully for fifteen minutes or so and separate them at once if they fight; try again under the same conditions the next day. Success is usually achieved on the first occasion, but in some cases a few days of brief meetings may be needed before a pair can be housed together permanently. If fighting persists, find another mate or companion.

Mice and rats get along better than do gerbils or hamsters. However, all animals newly housed together must be watched carefully for any signs of aggression. Young animals of the same species will be more compatible than sexually mature ones. Sexually mature male rabbits will usually attempt to emasculate each other, so house them separately. Immature rabbits do not present this problem. For mating mice, rats, and rabbits, the female *must* be taken to the male's cage. The additional precautions described for gerbils and hamsters are not usually necessary.

BREEDING

Caring for a litter is more difficult and involves greater responsibility than looking after a non-breeding pair. Normally, a female gerbil will

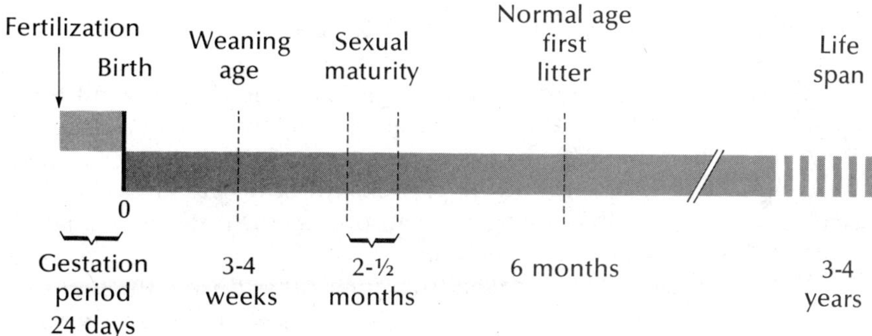

Figure 12-9. Gerbil life cycle.

produce about 40 young during her life span of three or four years. Homes will have to be found for all these gerbils if unrestricted breeding is allowed. You may prefer to prevent pregnancy or to permit a female to have only one litter.

Gerbils reach sexual maturity at two and a half months and the sexes must be separated by this time to prevent breeding. It is wise to wait until the animals are six months old before breeding them. Unlike other small captive rodents, gerbils are strictly monogamous, so keep the same pair together all their lives. The male helps to look after the offspring and (unlike other caged rodents) need not be separated from the female except to prevent subsequent breeding. In this case, separate the parents before a litter is born, because female gerbils can become pregnant again within hours thereafter. Breeding cages must have solid floors, and at least the bottom 8 cm of the sides should be solid to prevent the young from falling out. Barred or mesh sides can be covered with metal sheeting or Formica®.

Mating usually occurs in the late afternoon or night, and gestation lasts approximately 24 days. A nest box is not as essential as with other small animals, since gerbils will make nests in one of their tunnels. For all gestating animals, provide cotton, soft rags, toweling or tissue, which the parents will shred for the nest.* The female should receive extra milk and greens during the last week of pregnancy (when she is noticeably fatter and will probably not want to be picked up), and when she is nursing her "pups."

Parents may hide the pups in tunnels, and you may not know that they have arrived until you hear a faint chirruping. Litter size for ger-

---

**Small squares of compressed material which the animals shred for nests are available from some pet stores and, as Anipads®*, from Ancare Corp., 47 Manhasset Ave., Manhasset, Long Island, N. Y. 11030.

bils ranges from one to ten. Note the date of birth, so the pups can be separated from the parents when they are about one month old.

Gerbils are born blind, deaf, and hairless. The parents tend them closely until they can look after themselves. The first three weeks of life are critical; be sure they have enough food and are not disturbed. Week-old pups totter around quite well but still cannot see; at two weeks, they have teeth and begin to eat solid food. At two and a half to three weeks, the pups' eyes are open.

If they are picked up or taken from their cages during the first two weeks, they may die from too much handling or be eaten by their parents. If enough space, food, and privacy are provided, however, the parents will not cannibalize their young. Do not have an exercise wheel in the cage; the pups may get trapped or hurt.

When the pups are three to four weeks old, transfer them to a separate cage. Take them away from the female in the morning. During that day, give them regular adult food and small pieces of apple or potato. Return them to the female's cage for the night. The next day, take away the pups in the morning and transfer them permanently to their own cage.

SEXING AND PAIRING. After the young gerbils are weaned, you may house the litter mates together until just before they are sexually mature. If adequate floor space is available, weanlings from several litters may be housed together, but they must be about the same age; the sexes should be separated when mature (three to four months). Ages of sexual maturity and breeding vary with species; see individual chapters for other small mammals.

Figure 12-10. Sex differences of newborn gerbils. Female on left, male on right. The ano-genital distance is smaller in the female than in the male.

Figure 12-11. Sex differences of adult gerbils. Female on left, male on right. Although somewhat masked by fur, the ano-genital distance can be seen to be smaller in the female than in the male.

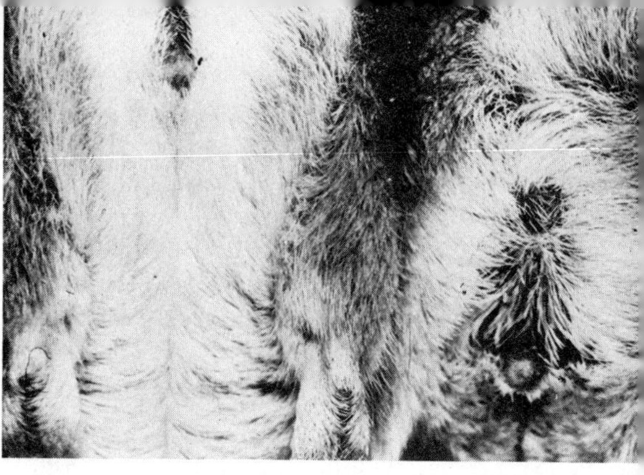

To prevent crowding and fighting, provide separate housing for each mature gerbil or pair. A pair can be either two of the same sex (litter mates or from different families) or a breeding pair (preferably from different stocks). Only one pair should be housed together. Two friendly gerbils of the same sex can often be kept happily together for life, but a single animal should be given special attention and extra playthings.

With experience, you will be able to differentiate the sexes before the pups are weaned; but it is easier to do at weaning time, and easiest when they are adults. Males are usually larger and have a dark tufted contour (the scrotum) near the base of the tail. The female's rear is rounder and lighter in color, and the vagina and anus are about 3 mm apart. In a male of comparable age the penis and anus are about 12 mm apart.

OVERPOPULATION. If you start with a single gerbil or two of the same sex, you will avoid overpopulation worries. Taking care of the many offspring a single breeding pair can produce may become a real problem, even though gerbils are not as prolific as rats or mice.

After a pair has produced one litter, either remove the male and house it separately from females, or have it castrated by a veterinarian. (This operation should not be done in the classroom.) Schedule the castration when a litter has just been weaned. Keep the male separated from the female for one day after the operation. Just before returning him to the cage, bathe his hind quarters to remove antiseptic and other foreign smells which might antagonize the female. Prepare a fresh clean cage with new bedding and reintroduce the gerbils, following the instructions under COMPATIBILITY. Usually no problems arise, and the two live out their lives harmoniously.

Identification

Often, labeling the cage will serve to identify an animal. However, individuals can be temporarily marked by carefully clipping the hair or by marking spots on the back of the head with trypan blue, fuchsin, gentian violet, or other safe water soluble dyes applied with a felt marking pen. Make sure the marking fluids do not go in or near the eyes. Renew the marks every few days.

Health

Gerbils are healthy animals; they have almost no diseases of their own. They are so clean that they are normally free from fleas or mites. Eye injuries sometimes occur, and noses may sometimes be hurt on the side of a mesh cage. Veterinarians recommend bathing such injuries with a strong solution of tea or holding a lukewarm tea bag over the injury for one to five minutes. The tannic acid in the tea is a mild astringent.

If a gerbil does become sick, it should be separated from the others and should receive professional veterinary care when appropriate. If an animal dies, wash its cage and food containers with an antiseptic (such as Lysol®), detergent and warm water, and then rinse well; boil water bottles, sipping tubes, and feeding dishes for ten minutes in water; and install clean bedding. Some diseased states can be mistaken for death. Do not assume that an animal is dead until rigor mortis is established. For sanitary disposal, place the dead animal in a tightly sealed plastic bag and incinerate it.

If you suspect an infectious disease that might endanger other animals, submit the dead animal to the state or provincial veterinary laboratories for proper diagnosis and advice.

Disposing of Unwanted Animals

The teacher is responsible for the disposition of classroom animals at the end of the school term. You should not breed more gerbils than you can provide with good homes. Should overbreeding occur, take the animals to the Humane Society for placement or to a veterinarian who can painlessly kill them. Do not set unwanted animals free; they will die or become pests. If animals must be killed because of severe illness or other reasons, students should not be present. Procedures for painlessly killing small animals are given in Appendix E.

As a general rule, animals should not be offered to the students; but if a student requests one, make sure the person has a genuine interest in caring for the animal, has a large enough cage and other necessary equipment, and understands that he or she must not do any experiments that will harm the animal.

FURTHER READING

Gerbils

Arrington, L. R. and C. B. Ammerman. 1969. Water Requirements of Gerbils. *Lab. Animal Care* 19:503.

Glickman, S. E., L. Fried and B. S. Morrison. 1967. Shredding of Nesting Material in the Mongolian Gerbil. *Percept. Motor Skills* 24(2) :473–74. (Advanced)

Glickman, S. E. and K. E. Hartz. 1964. Exploratory Behavior in Several Species of Rodents. *J. Comp. Physiol. & Psychol.* 58(1) :101–104. (Advanced)

Marston, J. H. 1972. The Mongolian Gerbil. *The UFAW Handbook on the Care and Management of Laboratory Animals.* 4th ed. Churchill Livingston, London and Williams and Wilkins, Baltimore, Md. pp. 257–68. (Advanced)

Thiessen D. D. 1968. The Roots of Territorial Marking in the Mongolian Gerbil: A Problem of Species Common Topography. *Beh. Res. Meth. & Instr.* 1(1) :70–76. (Advanced)

FILM

Caring for Gerbils. Super 8 mm, color, 17 min., taped sound 7-½ rpm. Rent from F. B. Orlans, 7035 Wilson Lane, Bethesda, Md 20034.

13

Mice and Rats

I think mice
Are rather nice
Their tails are long,
Their faces small,
They haven't any
Chins at all.
Their eyes are pink,
Their teeth are white.
They run about
The house all night.
They nibble things
They shouldn't touch,
And no one seems
To like them much.
But I think mice
Are nice.

Rose Fyleman (1877–1957)

General care of all small rodents was described in the previous chapter on gerbils. Those aspects of care that are different for mice and rats are described here.

See Chapter 1 for guidelines on humane treatment of experimental animals. In Chapter 16 there are suggestions and references for mammalian experiments which are suitable for high school students to perform, are within the laws of most states, and satisfy humane requirements.

The safest and easiest way to obtain mice and rats is from pupils or other schools in your community. Some youngsters may be reluctant to donate or lend well-loved pets unless thay can be assured that no harm will befall them. Mice and rats from commercial breeders are expensive, and those found in pet stores are often diseased and from poor stock. Wild rodents should not be kept; not only are they difficult to tame, but they may carry dangerous diseases that can be transmitted to humans. Among the undesirable domesticated strains are those which produce spontaneous tumors, are susceptible to leukemia, or exhibit neurotic tendencies such as waltzing gait. Under *no* circumstances should diseased or cancerous animals be allowed in the classroom.

MICE

For more than 10,000 years, common house mice *Mus musculus* have been members of human beings' immediate environments. From the grain-producing areas of northern Asia, they have spread to all parts of the world. Doubtless, they traveled on the first European ships to America.

Although found wherever man lives, mice are not dependent upon man for their survival. At times, they may be a significant factor in controlling insect populations, but the damage they do to grain crops and storage areas classifies them as pests.

Mice can be white, brown, black, or agouti (with hairs that are black or brown at the base and yellow at the tip). The familiar albino mouse is uniformly white with soft fur, a long tail, pink eyes, and large round ears. In many parts of the world, color varieties of mice are bred and reared as a hobby. An adult mouse is 12 to 20 cm long from its nose to the tip of its tail and weighs about 20 gm.

RATS

Some of the common domesticated types of rats (*Rattus* species) are pure white (albino), black, black-hooded, red (a light auburn), and red-hooded. Most highly recommended are two albino strains—Wistar and Sprague-Dawley. Another recommended strain is the black-hooded rat, a particularly attractive animal with black eyes, a black stripe on its head and back, and a white body. Wistar, Sprague-Dawley, and black-hooded rats, developed from the wild Norway rat *Rattus norvegicus*, are available from commercial suppliers.

A rat's tail is about as long as its body. At maturity they weigh 200 to 500 gm. Adult males are larger than females. Their claws are quite sharp, and they use their strong front legs for scratching and burrowing.

Domesticated strains of rats have been developed from the two major species of wild rats—the brown rat (Norway rat) and the black rat (*Rattus rattus*). The brown Norway rat is a native of eastern Asia, and

Figure 13-1. Rats can be very gentle if you tame them. This one is enjoying being stroked.

Figure 13-2. A spacious, interesting cage complete with a box with cotton inside for a nest, thick bedding, a cardboard tunnel, a block for gnawing, hard food pellets, and a lettuce leaf. The water bottle, shown at left, fits through a hole of the lid (shown at back). The lid and bottle have been temporarily removed to show the contents of the cage.

Figure 13-3. A rat with a good home. Note that the lower parts of the cage have solid sides to prevent bedding from falling out.

normally inhabits stream banks and watery places. Great migrations must have occurred in ancient times, for there are descriptions of them "making periodical visits in infinite multitudes to the countries bordering the Caspian Sea and swimming boldly over the rivers holding by one another's tails."*

Albino forms of the Norway rat were noted in England in 1822, when rats were trapped and held in large numbers for the sport of rat baiting (subsequently outlawed as inhumane). It is very likely that the first person to use albino rats in a laboratory was Philipeaux (1856) in Paris. Considerable changes have occurred during the process of domestication of the albino rat; their fertility has increased and they have lost much of their viciousness and fear of man. A fascinating account of the changes due to domestication of wild animals can be found in Hediger's classic books (see REFERENCES, page 317).

The black rats, south Asian rats, were introduced into Europe by returning caravans during the 11th and 12th centuries. They were probably the Pied Piper's rats. They became formidable pests and spread typhus, the black plague, and the plague of London in 1664.

Wild rat burrows can sometimes be seen near sidewalks or in the foundations of buildings. Their nests are bowl shaped, about 20 cm in diameter, and lined with soft material such as cloth or paper. They eat most grains and a variety of vegetation, birds' eggs, and even marine debris.

CLASSROOM CARE

Housing

Because they are sensitive to drafts and to respiratory infections, mice and rats flourish best in warm dark boxes rather than in open wire cages. Solid sides also retain bedding and young rodents. Provide plenty of room for exercise. For one or two mice, use a large sweater box, vegetable storage box, plastic dishpan, or commercial opaque plastic cage (highly recommended)** which provides a floor area of at least 25 × 25 cm with sides at least 15 cm high. (Most cages sold for mice in pet shops are too small.) For one or two rats, provide a floor area of at least 45 × 45 cm with 30 cm sides. Try to select as large an

*Barrett-Hamilton, G.E.H. and Hinton, M.A.L. 1916. *A History of British Mammals.* Gurney & Jackson, London, England. p. 608.

**For sources of supply see footnote, page 245.

enclosure as possible. Giving animals extra space is beneficial. Securely fasten a mesh lid on top to permit ventilation and to prevent escape.

Another good type of cage has a solid floor (of hard plastic, galvanized sheet metal, or stainless steel), wire mesh or barred sides with the lower 8 to 10 cm covered with sheet metal, and a hinged roof. (Rats can gnaw through wood, most plastics, aluminum, and even cinder block; cages made of these materials will not remain escapeproof.) Metal cages are usually more expensive than the more satisfactory and versatile plastic boxes. Glass cages are satisfactory, but heavy; wood cages absorb urine and soon begin to smell; aluminum cages are noisy, poor insulators, and will be gnawed.

Breeding cages must always have solid sides at least halfway up, and solid floors, so young animals are protected from injury. Rats must have a cage with a solid floor or they will develop decubitus (literally, "lying down") ulcers on their elbows and hocks. Do not keep rats in a metabolism cage with a mesh floor for more than a few weeks (maximum, eight).

Room temperature of 21 to 23°C (70 to 74°F) is suitable for mice and rats. Keep them away from drafts and direct sunlight. Even brief exposure to strong sunlight may kill them. If room temperature drops at night, you must provide nest boxes.

Preferably, house two mice or rats of the same sex together (to avoid breeding). Watch for signs of fighting, and separate incompatible animals. A larger box with proportionately more floor space is needed for more than two (never more than ten mice together or six rats together). More space also will be needed for an exercise wheel—additional floor space for inclined disk wheels; a cage 30 cm high for ferris wheels. You can use a ferris wheel in a 10-gallon aquarium covered with a mesh lid for two mice. House breeding mice or rats in single pairs, not in groups.

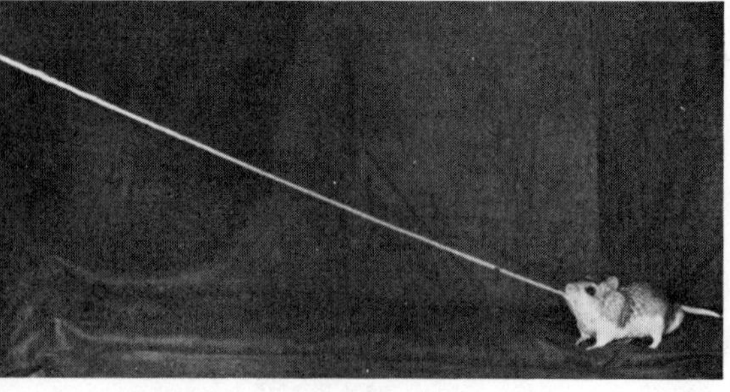

Figure 13-4. Mice are playful. Here is one pulling on a piece of string.

If pupils with pet cats take mice or rats home for weekends, they must keep the animals in rooms with closed doors.

BEDDING. Mice and rats need 3 to 5 cm of dry bedding. Be generous. Use cedar chips, coarse white pine sawdust or shavings, or commercial granulated cellulose; crushed corn cobs are acceptable, but they may contain insects. To any of these, a small amount of cotton or shredded paper can be added. (Newspaper is toxic and is not acceptable.)

Mice and rats make nests just like birds. They must be given the material with which to follow their natural instincts. In addition to plenty of bedding, provide cotton, soft clean rags, or shredded tissue which these animals will use to line a scooped out, hollow nest.

Change the bedding every few days to keep the cage clean and dry and to minimize odors (but do not disturb nursing pups until they are ten days old). Dispose of used bedding by emptying it into a plastic garbage bag. At least once a week, wash cages and floor pans thoroughly with soap or detergent and hot water, and immerse them for at least ten minutes in a mild disinfectant. (Do not use strong disinfectants such as hypochlorites, cresols, and phenol which are very corrosive to human and animal skin.) After disinfecting the cage, rinse it well with clean water and dry it before reintroducing the animals. Always disinfect cages to be used for new mice or rats.

BOXES AND SHELVES. See Chapter 12, GERBILS, page 246. Mice and rats will hide in small boxes with arched doorways made of cardboard, wood, or other suitable material. A pregnant mouse or rat will use a small box as a nest in which to nurse its young.

GNAWING. Mice and rats do not gnaw as much as gerbils and do not require daily supplies of cardboard for shredding. However, since all rodents have continuously growing front teeth, some hard foods are desirable and a few blocks of wood or cardboard are a welcome addition to the cage. Mice and rats also will keep their claws worn down by scratching on wood blocks or branches.

EXERCISE. One of the greatest problems of keeping captive animals is painfully evident in some zoos—in the wild, a considerable portion of the day is spent searching for food, but in captivity other forms of activity must be provided. Exercise is of vital importance to the health and well-being of caged animals.

Every few days, try to offer some new playthings to your animals, such as old socks, walnuts, toy ladders, doll furniture, empty cans, and

Figure 13-5. Inclined disk exercise wheel. The underside view provides some details for construction.

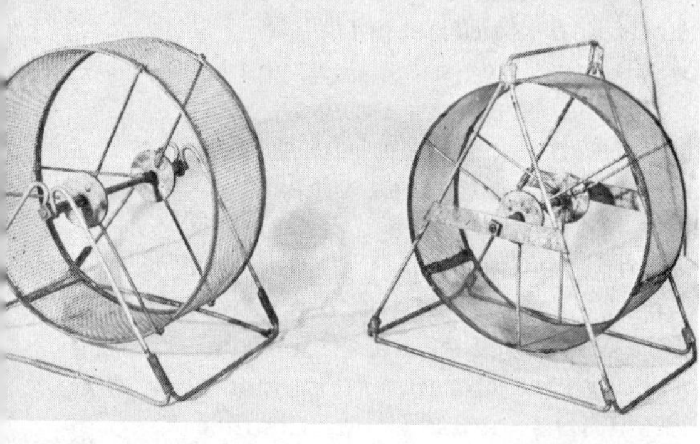

Figure 13-6. Ferris-type exercise wheel.

Figure 13-7. Mice using an inclined disk exercise wheel.

wooden reels. (Check carefully for sharp edges or toxic substances before you give them an object.) Rats, especially young ones, are very playful. They will chase a walnut tossed into the cage, or use an old sock, cut off at the toe, as a hiding place or a tunnel. Of course, the sock will be chewed up after awhile, and you will need to replace it.

There are two types of exercise wheels—the inclined disk and the ferris wheel. Both provide much needed exercise for mice, rats, and hamsters, and contribute to the animals' health and longevity. The inclined disk type is easy to make, and the ferris wheel is available from most pet stores.

To build an inclined disk you will need:

- A flat disk, 10 to 15 inches in diameter, of 1/8-inch Masonite®, plywood, or other rigid material that is easy to clean.
- A piece of sheet metal about an inch square.
- A block of wood 2 inches square and 1 1/4 inch thick.
- A wooden base at least 6 inches square and 1 inch thick.
- A metal rod 1/4-inch in diameter and about 2 1/2 inches long.

Drill a 3/16-inch hole in the center of the base and a 5/16-inch hole in the center of the block of wood. (The metal rod should fit snugly in the base and smoothly in the block.) Drive the rod into the hole in the base. Glue the piece of sheet metal to the center of the disk (to keep the rod from wearing through), then glue the block of wood over this. Reinforce this joint with small nails through the disk into the block. Fit the wooden block over the rod in the base, bend the rod slightly near the base so the disk pivots easily on this axle and at a slight angle. Dr. Ernest Walker, noted mammalogist, warns, "The wheel must run very easily, as you will have only one mouse-power to run it."

The ferris wheel type, similar to a drum without heads, should have a diameter about three times the length of the animal. A mouse that is 8 cm from the tip of its nose to the base of its tail should have a wheel about 24 cm in diameter. Larger animals need larger wheels. An exercise wheel that is too small may injure an animal's back.

Feeding

Mice eat the same food as gerbils (page 247). Mix a variety of these, including both seeds and cereals, for a balanced diet, and feed the animals *ad lib*, or purchase laboratory chow prepared especially for mice and rats.* An adult mouse eats about 5 gm of food per day; however, provide more than the daily requirement. Suspend food containers (page 248) 2 to 3 cm above the bedding for easy access and minimum spilling.

Rats are omnivorous. Suitable foods include oats, cracked corn, wheat, peanuts, acorns, pecans, walnuts, hickory nuts, lentils, beans, linseed, mixed parrot seed, cottage cheese, and hard-boiled eggs. Offer a selection of these foods and vary the menu frequently, or purchase laboratory chow especially prepared for rats. (See GERBILS, page 247, for discussion of diet.) An adult rat consumes about 28 gm of dry food per day, but provide food in excess of the daily requirement. Some

---

*For sources of supply see footnote, page 247.

authorities recommend occasionally sprinkling a little salt and two to three drops of cod liver oil over the food every few weeks. Supply ground meat twice a week and extra proteins during pregnancy.

Be sure the food is clean. Discard soiled food.

GREENS AND WATER. Mice and rats need greens (such as lettuce and cabbage) every day or two and an ample supply of fresh water. (See GERBILS, page 248.) They have relatively small stomachs, so an abundant supply of water is essential at all times. An adult mouse on a dry diet drinks about 6 ml of water daily, an adult rat drinks about 35 ml (over one fluid ounce of water per day). Use a large water bottle or more than one. A nursing female needs an extra water supply. Pay particular attention to her weekend water supply. If it is not possible to check her water and food each day, provide three or more bottles on Friday afternoon.

Handling

The more a mouse or rat is handled, the quieter and tamer it gets; and a quiet animal is likely to grow more quickly and breed better than a nervous one. They are intelligent animals and respond favorably to kind and sympathetic treatment. Stroke a mouse or rat whenever it is to be picked up. (If you feel any repugnance toward doing this, it is better to keep another type of animal.)

Nervous animals may urinate or defecate when first picked up, but this will not happen with tame animals that are not frightened. The time and trouble you take in learning how to handle them will be repaid. With training, they will learn quickly to eat from your hand and nestle in your arms.

To pick up a mouse, scoop it gently into your hand without sudden or abrupt movements. In the wild, such animals as cats, terrier dogs, foxes, and owls attack mice by pouncing on them from above. Any sudden downward movement of your hand may cause fear and a resurgence of the "fight or flight" instinct. Always hold the animal gently and firmly a few centimeters above the bedding until it is calm.

There are several methods for picking up rats. Grasp the animal gently but firmly around the head and forefeet, with your palm over its back, and support its hind legs on your other hand. To restrain an animal that is frightened or difficult to handle, carefully grasp the tail *near its base* with your left hand (for a right-handed person). Sudden movements will alarm it still further. Then circle your right hand around the animal's back with your thumb under its forelegs. With your thumb, gently fold the forelegs under the animal's throat to pre-

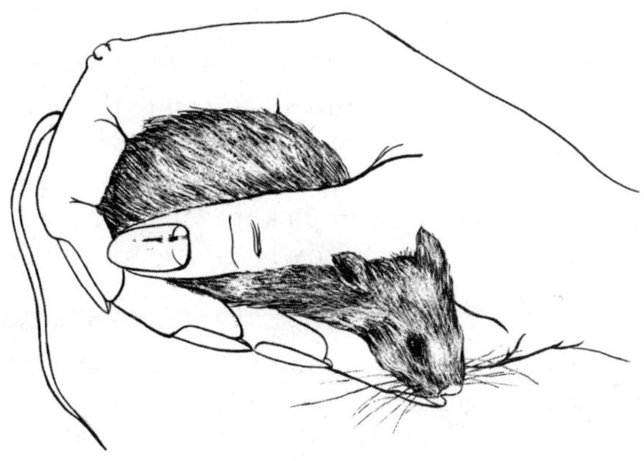

Figure 13-8. A good way to hold a mouse.

Figure 13-9. How to pick up a rat.

vent biting. (Do not press hard or squeeze the animal's throat.) Slip your left hand under the animal to support its hind feet.

Never secure a mouse or rat by the tip of its tail. If a rat is picked up by its tail, it will be so alarmed that it will curl around and bite very hard; and the skin of the tail may rip off. Do not pick it up by its ears. With experience, you will be able to pick up tame rats with one hand, but always have your other hand ready to give extra support.

Wearing gloves for handling rats will result in savage animals. Learn to handle the animals properly. Uncertainty in humans provokes fear and uncertainty in animals. An angry rat will use whipping motions of its tail; a frightened rat will avoid human contact; a tame one will immediately come to your hand for food. If a rat does bite, try to determine what provoked a normally docile animal to aggressive behavior.

Dr. W. R. Reugamer conducted an instructive experiment that can be modified for the classroom. He showed that petting individual weanling rats for ten minutes each day improved their growth and utilization of food over that of unhandled rats. The petted rats also exhibited more activity and curiosity and showed general benefit from the affectionate treatment (see Chapter 16, Enriched Living Conditions, p. 299).

ESCAPE. The procedures for catching escaped mice and rats are the same as those described for gerbils on page 251.

Weekend and Vacation Care

See page 252.

Compatibility

Never mix species. Do not place a mouse (or rat) with gerbils, hamsters, or other animals. Sexually mature male mice (or rats) usually will fight unless they have been housed together before attaining sexual maturity (five to six weeks for mice, six to ten for rats). Do not house two or more male mice (or rats) together after they are six weeks old. Adult females, on the other hand, can usually be housed together without problems. Immediately separate any animals that fight and house them permanently in separate cages.

For mating, mice and rats present fewer problems of compatibility than gerbils. An adult male and female can be housed together with little chance of fighting if there is plenty of space.

Breeding

If you decide to breed mice or rats, wait until they are at least two to three months old. (Up until that age, the sexes should be kept separately.) Do not breed them at all unless good homes can be found for all the young. The life span of mice is about two years; rats will live for three years. The gestation period is about 22 to 29 days. Unless the animals are separated, the first three litters will usually follow in quick succession, and subsequent litters will be somewhat unpredictably spaced. The most productive period is from three months until the end of the first year.

Use a breeding cage with solid walls and floor and provide a nest box. Place the male in the cage first, then the female, or fighting may occur. Always observe the animals for the first 15 minutes, then check periodically to see that no aggression occurs. Remove the female if they fight, and find another mate. The male can be left with the female throughout their lives, but they will usually mate again immediately after the birth of a litter. It is a good idea to keep the same pair together if successive breeding is desired, but this is not essential.

Figure 13-10. Life cycle of mouse.

Fertilization
Birth
Weaning age
Sexual maturity
Normal age first litter
Life span
0
Gestation period 19-21 days
3-4 weeks
5-7 weeks
2-3 months
About 2 years

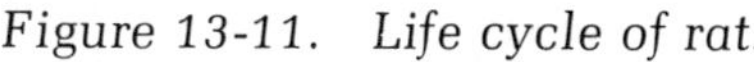

Figure 13-11. Life cycle of rat.

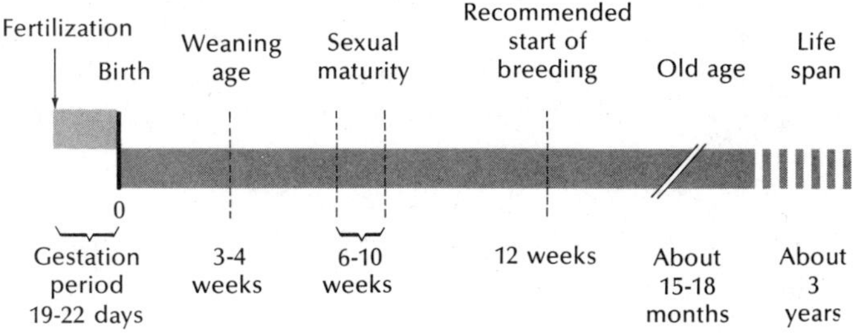

Several special provisions must be made during the breeding period. Supply extra greens and bread soaked in milk (and ground meat, cheese, and hard-boiled eggs for rats) during pregnancy and lactation. During the last week of pregnancy provide cotton, shredded paper, toweling or other soft material* for the nest and remove exercise wheels. Remove the male from the cage in the last week of pregnancy or as soon as the young are born. The female can become pregnant again within 20 hours after the birth of a litter, which is bad for her health. Several weeks should elapse before a female is permitted to become pregnant again. However, in a classroom, it may be preferable to breed only once, if at all.

Do not disturb the female and her young or clean the cage for ten days after the birth. Before removing the young to clean the cage, rub your hands through the bedding to pick up the smell of the female. If this precaution is not observed, human odor will be transferred to the pups, and the female may kill them when they are returned to the nest. (This precaution also may inhibit the female from biting you.) Any major disruption may result in the female eating her young; but this will probably not happen if she receives good care. If the female is accustomed to being stroked frequently and has confidence in you, she may not object to your picking up her young when they are two or three days old. Be careful! She will be very protective and may be more aggressive than she normally is. If she does object, leave them alone.

The average litter size is six to nine for mice, and eight to twelve for rats. The young are usually born at night and are deaf, blind, and hairless. Keep them very quiet and undisturbed. Note the birth date, so you can determine the dates of weaning and sexual maturity. They can hear at about 11 days, open their eyes at 14 days and begin to nibble on solid food—provide extra food for them. Separate them from the female at three to four weeks (see page 269), and separate the sexes. Litter mates of the same sex can be housed together in groups if the cages are large enough.

DETERMINING SEX. Bend a mouse's or a rat's tail backwards (gently) to measure the distance between the anus and the genital tracts. In female mice, this distance is 0.7 to 1.5 mm; in male mice, it is 1.6 to 2.2 mm and the genital protruberance is swollen. Male mice have hair between the urinary papilla and the anus; females do not. With experience, you will be able to differentiate between the sexes when males are about six

---

*You can obtain small squares of compressed materials, which the animals will use for nesting material, from some pet stores; or purchase Anipads® from Ancare Corp., 47 Manhasset Ave., Manhasset, L.I., N.Y. 11030.

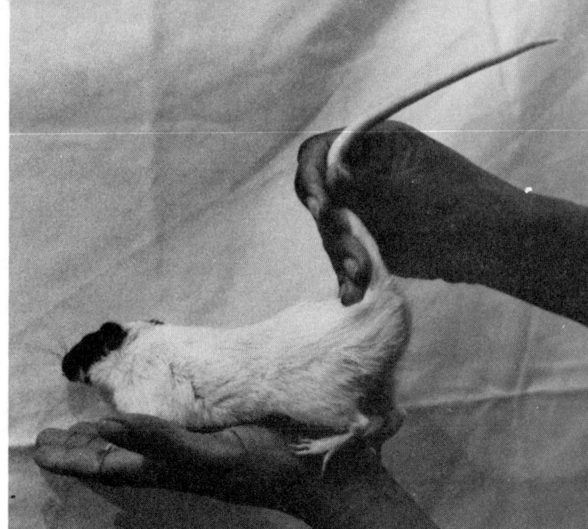

Figure 13-12. Hold a rat on your palm and lift its tail to look at the anogenital distance to determine its sex.

days old and females are 12 days old; but it is easier when they are a few weeks old.

To determine the sex of a rat, measure the anogenital distance and compare it with Table 13-1.

Table 13–1. Anogenital Distance in Young Albino Rats*

	AVERAGE ANOGENITAL DISTANCE (mm)	
Age	*Male*	*Female*
Newborn	2.8	1.2
7 days	4.2	2.7
14 days	8.2	4.9
20 days	12.0	7.0
42–50 days	21.0	13.0

*Reprinted with permission from Farris, E. J. 1950. "The Rat as an Experimental Animal." *The Care and Breeding of Laboratory Animals.* John Wiley & Sons, New York. p. 63.

OVERPOPULATION. With unrestricted breeding, one pair of mice or rats may produce as many as eight litters, 40 to 60 young, during the first year. To prevent breeding, separate the sexes after they are weaned and before they reach sexual maturity. House them singly, or house two females together, or two males that have grown up in the same cage since weaning. It is sometimes possible to keep them together for life.

Identification

Usually, labeling an animal's cage will suffice. However, to mark individual animals for identification, make spots on their backs or heads with any safe dye, ink, or marking pen. Be sure that marking fluids do not go in or near the eyes.

Health

With good management and care, you should have no problems in maintaining healthy mice and rats.

Do not use chloroform in any room where mice are housed; they are extremely sensitive to it and can die from the vapor.

Signs of ill health in rats and mice include: inactivity, excitability, circling, disordered gait, loss of appetite, loss of hair, sore eyes, and holding the head to one side. If any of these symptoms occur, house the sick animal in a separate cage and consult a veterinarian. Keep the animal isolated until it recovers completely. Handlers should wash their hands immediately after touching sick animals. Attention to cleanliness will help control the spread of a disease. If an animal dies, disinfect the cage and equipment before using them again.

Lice and fleas should not be a problem if you observe hygienic routine. However, if you suspect that these pests have intruded, make microscopic examination of hairs removed from the neck or belly regions and mounted in 10 percent potassium hydroxide. Lice and eggs in various stages of development can be seen under a low power lens. If a positive diagnosis is made, dust the animals with 0.5 to 1 percent pyrethrin* from the neck to the middle of the back. Every week or two add one ounce of this dusting powder to each pound of bedding material *unless* nursing young are in the cage. Do not get the powder in the food—it can be poisonous.

Disposing of Unwanted Animals

See Appendix E, page 360.

FILMS

Handling Laboratory Animals—The Mouse. Super 8 mm, cartridge, silent, color, 3 min. Encyclopedia Britannica Educational Corp., 425 N. Michigan Ave., Chicago, Ill 60611.

---

*If you do not find this powder at a pet shop, order Omni-Dust® from Superior Chemical Products, Inc., 3942 Frankfort Ave., Philadelphia, Penn. 19124.

Handling Laboratory Animals—The Rat (how to pick up, sex, palpate for pregnancy). Super 8 mm, cartridge, silent, color, 3 min. Encyclopaedia Britannica Educational Corp., 425 N. Michigan Ave., Chicago, Ill 60611.

The Laboratory Animal Technician—A Career in Care. 16 mm, sound, 22 min. Academic Communications Facility, Royce Hall 152, Univ. of California, Los Angeles, Cal 90024.

Ratopolis. 16 mm, 57 min. color, National Film Board of Canada, 16th Floor, 1251 Avenue of the Americas, New York 10020.

14

Hamsters

". . . if we look closely into the habits of animals that live with us, . . . we shall have occasion to discover facts as wonderful as those we gather from foreign countries and remote ages. It is one same Nature that rolls its course."

Michel de Montaigne (1553–1592)

Hamsters are widely distributed in both Europe and Asia, but there are no true hamsters native to North America. The wild golden hamsters, also called Syrian hamsters, live in a manner similar to that of gerbils. They form colonies and inhabit extensive underground tunnels with multiple entrances. Their characteristics were first described in 1839 to the London Zoological Society. Almost a hundred years later, a litter was obtained from the Syrian desert and maintained at the Hebrew University of Jerusalem. It is believed that all domesticated golden hamsters have been developed from this one litter. Hamsters were first introduced in the United States in 1938.

Only golden hamsters *Mesocricetus auratus* are recommended for classroom study. Their care is quite similar to that of gerbils, and this chapter will, in general, describe only those aspects of care which are different from those described in Chapter 12 for gerbils.

Golden hamsters usually are available from students or local pet stores. Shipping costs are high, so try local sources first. The special strains needed for genetic studies can be purchased from commercial breeders. Species to be avoided because they are pugnacious and unsuitable for classroom study are the European hamster *Cricetus cricetus* (also called the common hamster) and the gray hamster *Cricetulus barbensis* (also called Chinese or striped hamster).

Studies of normal physiology, reproductive biology, learning, and observations of special senses and many other suggestions for hamster experiments are described in Chapter 16. Hamsters are well suited to studies of normal behavior; because of their cheek pouches, they are particularly suited to studies of food hoarding behavior. Males are better suited for many behavioral studies than females, because they are more readily tamed. Hamsters do present problems of compatibility, and they have sharp teeth; so be well informed about their care before undertaking to keep them.

Hamsters have the disadvantage of being nocturnal, so you will usually see them fast asleep during classroom hours. With care, however, you can shift the cycle of daily activity to the daytime. Hamsters may be quite nervous unless handled frequently and gently each day, preferably by the same person. When they are raised from infancy in close contact with humans, they become affectionate animals.

A golden hamster has long soft fur that is a deep golden color on its back and gray on its underside. Its ears are gold with white inside, and its eyes are black. A hamster has a stubby tail and quite large cheek pouches.

Figure 14-1. Golden hamsters are affectionate animals.

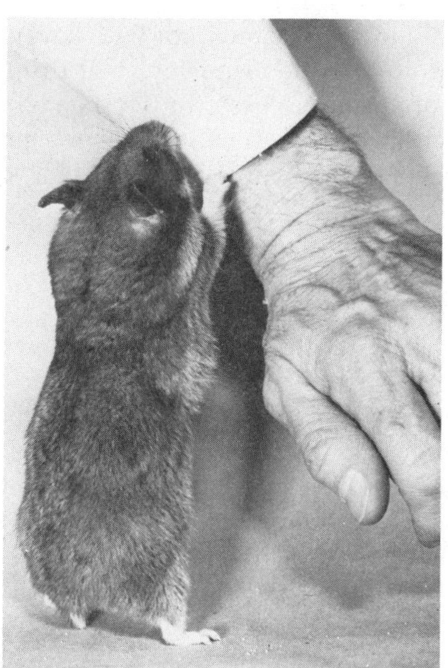

Figure 14-2. They are also great climbers.

Mutant strains and inbred lines of golden hamsters include albino, cream, brown, and agouti colored animals and are available from commercial dealers. Eye color variations include red, ruby, and pink. These color variations are useful for genetic studies.

When fully grown, a hamster is about 15 cm long and weighs about 150 gms. Unlike the guinea pigs and rats, the female hamsters are slightly larger than the males. Hamsters have a life span of two to four years.

There are no known studies of what foods they eat in their native habitats, although they are omnivorous. There is a great opportunity to investigate the food preferences of hamsters.

CLASSROOM CARE

Housing

Hamsters are very sensitive to changes in environment. Strange noises or odors or even a new type of bedding material can disturb them. Keep them in a quiet place, away from environmental changes.

Translucent or clear plastic boxes with mesh lids make the best houses for hamsters.* You may prefer to pay a little more for the clear plastic cage, so you can observe the animals more easily.

The floors of all hamster cages must be solid, because the animals move their food around. Cover a metal mesh or barred floor with a solid piece of wood or plastic. Hamsters produce little urine and their droppings are dry in comparison to those of rats or mice, so wood floors will remain relatively fresh. Hamsters will gnaw on them, however, and wood floors or sides must be replaced before the animals have gnawed through.

Walls can be solid, mesh, or barred. A glass-sided cage or a 10-gallon, or larger, aquarium is satisfactory. If the cage you select has four solid sides, a removable mesh lid will serve as a door and will provide ventilation. Weight the lid at the edges to prevent escape. Hinged doors are dangerous; animals sometimes get trapped in them.

A cage for two adult hamsters or a female and her litter should be at least 30 × 60 cm. A slightly smaller cage may be used for a single animal, but never less than 23 × 35 cm. Commercial mouse cages are inadequate for hamsters. Cages must be at least 18 cm high, because hamsters like to sit up on their haunches, especially to eat. Exercise wheels, either inclined disks or ferris wheels, are highly recommended, but additional space will be needed to accommodate them.

---

*For sources of supply see footnote, page 245.

Figure 14-3. Hamsters are notorious for running away—even from a good home.

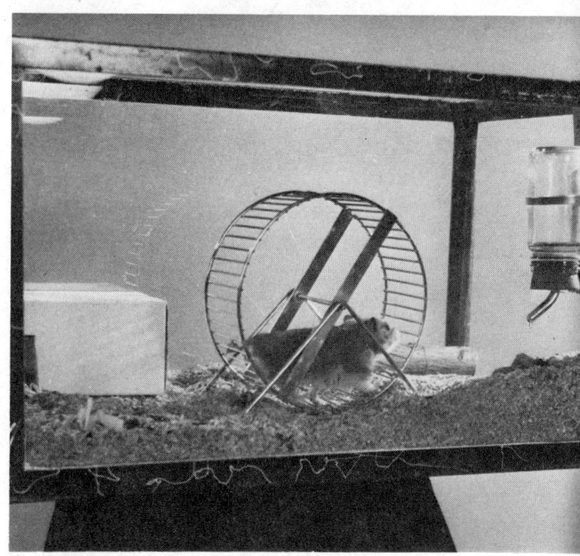

Figure 14-4. If a glass-sided enclosure is used, it is particularly important to provide a nesting box. This gives the animal a dark hiding place to escape from public view from time to time.

If possible, house hamsters in pairs; keep two litter mates of the same sex together to prevent breeding. Keeping more than two hamsters in a container is not recommended. If you mix hamsters from two different litters, they may fight. Breeding pairs will become incompatible and cannot be housed together indefinitely.

Keep the room temperature well above 9°C (48°F) to prevent hibernation. In the wild, hamsters hibernate at temperatures below this, and their bodies become quite rigid. If the temperature is allowed to fall, the more active captive animals may kill their lethargic or comatose cagemates, and females may consume their litters. Keep the temperature between 21 and 23°C (70 and 74°F). Fluctuations in temperature induce drowsiness, so try to avoid temperature changes of more than 1°C (2°F).

If an animal does go into hibernation, place it in a separate cage and raise the temperature *slowly* until it awakens. Do not subject a hibernating animal to direct heat.

Hamsters have no physiological mechanisms for adjusting to temperatures over 27°C (80°F). Do not place the cage in direct sunlight. If the room temperature is likely to rise above this limit in summer months, house the animals in a cooler room, perhaps in the basement. If air conditioning is turned off on weekends, find alternative weekend housing. In their underground burrows, hamsters in the wild are used to moist environments; keep the relative humidity for captive hamsters between 40 and 60 percent.

Include nest boxes made of cardboard, wood, or other suitable material, with arched doorways cut in one side. Such boxes are essential for females with young.

BEDDING. This should be at least 5 cm deep. Hamsters burrow, like gerbils, and they should be able to make tunnels. So be generous. Sawdust, wood shavings, such as cedar chips, and even earth or sand (although these are heavy) can be used. Do not use vermiculite or dried sugarcane, because they will injure the animals' cheek pouches.

Hamsters are very clean animals and will excrete in a corner of the cage. Usually, bedding should be changed once a week, or more frequently if it becomes soiled or wet. However, litters should not be disturbed until the young are at least ten days old. Retain part of the old

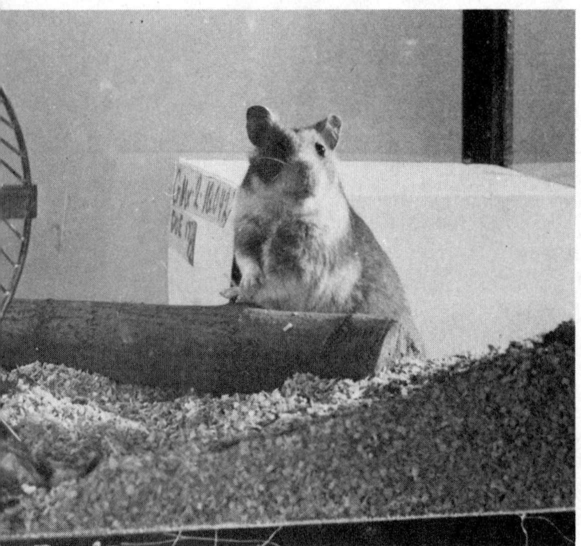

Figure 14-5. A branch provides for good dental care.

bedding and nesting materials and add new bedding and plenty of new materials so the nest can be repaired.

See page 246 for instructions in washing the cage and general comments on bedding.

EXERCISE. Exercise wheels, such as those described on page 264, are highly recommended for hamsters. Hamsters have been reported to voluntarily run the equivalent of 13 miles in 24 hours in a ferris wheel. A real marathon! They make good use of whatever space and materials are provided for exercising. Toys, such as an old sock, a toy ladder, or doll's furniture, also will keep the hamsters active and entertaining.

GNAWING. Hamsters need to gnaw; so cardboard, twigs, and other wood should be available at all times. Their continuously growing front teeth must be worn down by gnawing, or the hamsters will be unable to eat properly.

Feeding

Because of their cheek pouches, hamsters have special feeding habits and needs. They will not overeat, but they do fill up their cheek pouches with favorite foods, which they hide in corners and tunnels. An adult hamster eats up to 8 gm of food per day, but considerably more than this must be provided if hamsters are to pursue their normal food habits. Provide water in drinking bottles (see page 248).

Hamsters will eat the same dry foods as gerbils—wheat, sunflower seeds, bran, uncooked oatmeal, unsweetened breakfast cereal, dry dog or cat food, corn chips, shelled peanuts, and other cereals and seeds. In order to provide a balanced diet, a selection of these foods is needed. A variety can be premixed. Place open dishes of this mixture (or use hamster laboratory chow*) in the cage, as hamsters have difficulty removing food from overhead hoppers.

The size of food seems to be as important as the chemical composition. Young animals feed better on small pieces of food; break laboratory chow into small pieces when feeding small animals.

Give your hamsters fresh fruits or vegetables such as apples, carrots, kale, lettuce, or cabbage each day. Place the fresh food in the cage at the beginning of the hamsters' daytime period, so it will not wilt or dry out before it is eaten. Too many greens will cause diarrhea. If this happens, offer greens only two or three times a week and provide extra water, as diarrhea causes abnormal water loss from the body. Put a few

---

*For sources of supply see footnote, page 247.

drops of cod liver oil on dry food every month or two. Occasionally, provide milk, either in a bottle or poured over bread, especially during pregnancy and lactation.

Too much dry food and too little water can cause constipation and death. It is important to effect the correct balance between dry and moist food. If you offer an ample supply of both fresh fruits and dry foods, the hamsters will select the proper foods to maintain good health.

The extent to which hamsters need animal protein is not known, but given the opportunity, hamsters will eat insects and small pieces of meat. However, it is generally not considered essential to provide these.

Reversing Day and Night

Hamsters are nocturnal animals, but it is possible to effect a 12-hour time shift so the animals will be active during classroom hours. House your hamsters where normal daylight will not intrude. Use a bright light with an automatic timing device to turn it on and off. A photographic darkroom safe light or a 25-watt bulb will provide night light. Initially, set the timer to coincide with normal day and night. Provide artificial bright light for 13 hours out of every 24. Reset the timer to switch on the bright lights 30 minutes later each day until they are turned on at about 8 o'clock each evening and off at 9 o'clock each morning. During this period, the hamsters will sleep. They will awaken when the dim lighting comes on each morning.

Do not place the bright lights too near the animals. Incandescent light will overheat the cage, and fluorescent light produces harmful ozone.

Handling

Hamsters are quick to respond to good or bad handling—a gentle person will have a docile friendly animal.

Unless you have reversed the hamsters' day and night periods, you may have to awaken them before handling. Talk to them and gently tap the side of the cage. Then coax them with choice seeds. If a sleeping hamster is awakened suddenly it will bite.

Hamsters must be trained from infancy if they are to become tame, and males are easier to tame than females. At first, stroke a young animal's back without trying to pick it up. Offer bits of its favorite food in your hand, and remain quite still until it comes out of hiding and sits on your palm. Only when you have gained a hamster's confidence should you attempt to pick it up.

To transport a hamster, you can coax it easily into a tin can. This also is a good way to recover a hamster that has escaped. When returning a hamster to its cage, set it down carefully—not suddenly.

There are three ways to pick up a hamster. To hold the animal with one hand, grasp it loosely with your hand over its back (a tight hold will make the animal struggle). Aim for the region just above the hips—the hamster's head should be under your wrist. When this way of handling is done correctly, as you pick up the animal, it will hang on to your fingers with its hind legs—rather than try to escape.

Another method, using both hands, is to "cup" a hamster. Keep your fingers close together so nothing is exposed for the animal to bite. Use one hand as a platform and the other as a roof across the animal's

Figure 14-6. Picking up a hamster with one hand.

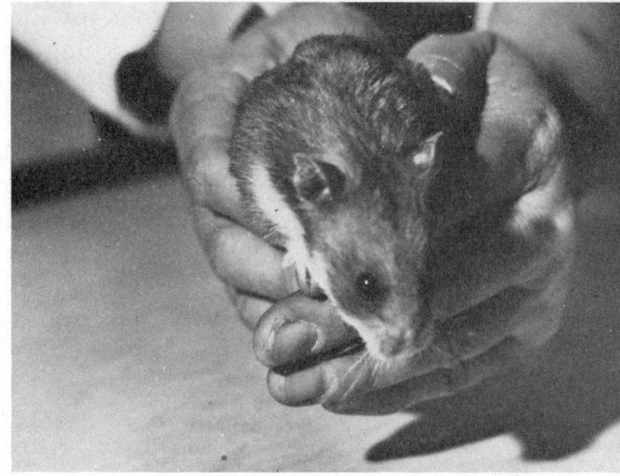

Figure 14-7. Two-handed cupping method of picking up a hamster.

Figure 14-8. Picking up a hamster by gently grasping the scruff of the neck.

back. Do not clamp the animal tightly, but form a frame with your hands around it.

You also can pick up a hamster by gently grasping the scruff of its neck just as a cat manages her kittens. A hamster's neck skin is very loose and provides a good hold in a region which precludes biting.

Watch a hamster's eyes; it will usually close them just before it bites you. At first, hold the hamster a few centimeters above the bedding; if it does struggle free, it will not have a long fall. Learn to hold a hamster properly before carrying it away from its cage; the animal may die of concussion from a half a meter drop onto a hard surface.

ESCAPE. Hamsters are remarkably skillful in opening latches or pushing open cage doors. They are excellent climbers and usually take every opportunity for escape. Females in heat are particularly likely to escape in order to find mates. Cages with tight and firmly secured lids are essential.

The procedures for catching escaped hamsters are the same as those described for gerbils (page 251). The coffee can method is especially successful with hamsters. The U.S. Department of Agriculture warns that hamster owners "should be aware of the dangers of escapes, and make every effort to prevent the establishment of a wild colony....

Release of hamsters under favorable conditions could create a serious rodent problem, since they are destructive to growing crops, gardens and other agricultural enterprises."

Weekend and Vacation Care

See page 252.

Compatibility

Hamsters do present problems of compatibility. When placing two strangers together, all the necessary precautions to prevent territorial defense (a clean cage, new bedding, fresh food, and water) must be followed scrupulously. For full details of these procedures, see page 252.

No more than two mature hamsters should be housed together. After hamsters are one month old, they must be housed singly, in pairs of the same sex, or in breeding pairs. Take special precautions, at mating time, to control a female's aggression toward a male. Watch her closely and separate the two if harm seems likely.

If hamsters become injured, sick or weakened due to fighting, standards of care are grossly inadequate. An injured animal must be isolated immediately, because the other hamsters may kill it.

Breeding

One pair of hamsters can produce as many as 50 young in one year. Think ahead, plan wisely, and avoid problems of overpopulation. Wait until hamsters are 12 weeks old before pairing them for breeding. Females become sterile at 11 to 19 months, but males usually breed until they are two years old. A large breeding cage, at least 30 × 60 cm,

Figure 14-9. Life cycle of hamster.

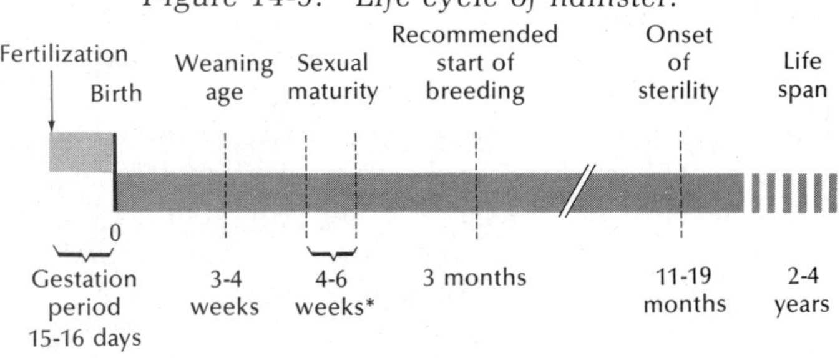

promotes healthy litters. Hamsters do not breed well if housed in a room where there are rats.

Because of compatibility problems, use caution when pairing hamsters for breeding. Select a docile female, and always place the male in the breeding cage *first.* As an extra precaution, wash the cage and put in clean bedding before introducing the female. Observe the animals together for half an hour to ensure that they do not fight. Remove the female immediately if she harrasses the male. She can injure him quite badly.

There is a 12-hour period that occurs every four days during which a female hamster is sexually receptive. This is called *estrus* and is the only time that breeding is possible. Either house the male and female together for five to seven days, or determine the estrous cycle and mate the animals during the 12-hour period. Stages of estrus can be determined by use of an activity wheel (page 306). Another relatively simple method is to examine the female hamster for postovulatory discharge every morning between 8 and 9 o'clock (for animals on a normal lighting schedule). Every four days a creamy white discharge appears in the lower vagina. If gently touched with a toothpick, the discharge can be drawn out into a long thread. When this discharge is observed, successful breeding will occur in the evening three days later. (If you have reversed day and night for your hamsters, the discharge will be observed in the evening and you should place the hamsters together on the third morning after this.) Because of the time lapse, these procedures may involve weekend work. Remove the male after breeding and do not place the two together unless you plan to breed them again.

Hamsters are the fastest-developing mammals so far known; the gestation period is only 15 to 16 days. When pregnancy becomes obvious, remove the exercise wheel, add a nesting box (if not already provided), and plenty of soft bedding and nesting materials, such as cotton or paper towels. The female should receive extra milk and greens during the last week of pregnancy and when she is nursing her young. Handle a pregnant hamster, but with great care, to keep it tame.

Litter sizes range up to 22, but the average is 6 to 8 for the first litter, and 10 to 11 for the second and third litters. The female carries the young in her cheek pouches after they are born, and it may be difficult to count them. If a female has a small litter, 4 or fewer, she may be in poor physical condition and is very likely to kill her young. Give her special attention and nourishing, tempting food. A healthy female may have as many as seven to eight litters within the first year unless breeding is restricted. If rebreeding is planned, allow a rest period of several weeks between weaning and remating.

The young weigh about 1 gm when they are born. They are helpless, although they do have teeth, unlike newborn gerbils. Record the date of birth, so you can determine the ages of weaning and sexual maturity. Females reach sexual maturity as early as four weeks; males in about six weeks. Separate the sexes at weaning, or not later than four weeks, to prevent breeding.

Young hamsters require careful treatment. Do not disturb the female or the young, or clean the cage, for about ten days. Premature disturbance or handling, or even a noisy environment may prompt the female to eat her young. When you clean the cage, remove the female before removing the young, or she may attack you; return the young to the nest first.

By the third day, the young hamsters will have hair. They can hear within five days, and can see after two weeks. They will begin to eat solid food when they are only eight days old. Provide extra food, placing some of it in the bedding so it will be readily available. Hamsters grow rapidly and are ready to be weaned by the third or fourth week.

Determine sex in hamsters after weaning; the anogenital distance in males is approximately double that in females of the same age. In females, the vaginal opening can usually be seen between the urinary opening and the anus. The more tapered body contour of the male also is an indication in distinguishing the sexes.

Wait a week or two before rebreeding the female, or keep her permanently by herself to prevent overpopulation.

Figure 14-10. Rear view of female hamster showing short ano-genital distance.

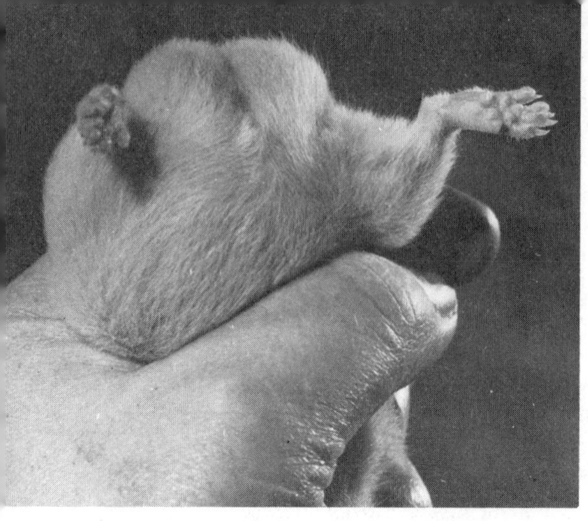

Figure 14-11. Rear view of male hamster showing ano-genital distance which is longer than that of a female.

OVERPOPULATION. To prevent overbreeding, either house the sexes separately or have the males castrated by a veterinarian (page 255). Unwanted hamsters should never be set free; they could become serious crop pests. If you cannot find good homes for them, give them to a pet shop or have a veterinarian dispose of them.

Identification

If your hamsters are housed separately, simply labeling their cages should serve to identify them. Individuals can be marked with spots on their heads or backs—using felt marking pens containing a safe dye. Make sure marking fluids do not go in or near the animal's eyes. Renew the marks every few days.

Health

Hamsters are among the healthiest of classroom animals. With good care, they should present very few disease problems. Like gerbils, hamsters are resistant to most common diseases. Unlike rats and mice, hamsters do not have chronic respiratory infections, but a sudden chill can cause pneumonia and can kill hamsters within three days.

If lacerations form on cheek pouches, change to a softer bedding or nesting material. Mesh flooring may cause ulceration of the feet.

"Wet tail" is the only common disease of hamsters. The area around the anus becomes wet and discolored as if they are suffering from diarrhea. The disease can be serious; unfortunately, there is no medical cure. Isolate sick animals and thoroughly disinfect all cages and watering devices to control the spread of the disease. Some authorities have suggested that wet tail may be the response of a wild animal to the stress of an artificial environment. If the condition occurs, provide a larger cage and more bedding and decrease the fat content in the diet—be imaginative and think up new foods within the categories of grain, fruit, and first-class proteins. Avoid overcrowding; this is a prime factor predisposing captive animals to ill health. If the disease continues to spread, consult a veterinarian.

External parasites, such as mites, usually occur when hamsters are kept in unsanitary cages. Hamsters spend a great deal of time grooming themselves; this is a natural trait and not an indication of external parasites. If mites should occur, treat them with a miticidal agent (page 237).

Disposing of Unwanted Animals

See Appendix E, page 360.

FURTHER READING

BOND, C. R. 1945. The Golden Hamster (*Cricetus auratus*) Care, Breeding, and Growth. *Physiol. Zool.* 18:52–59.

GUMMA, M. R., F. E. SOUTH and J. N. ALLEN. 1967. Temperature Preference in Golden Hamsters. *Animal Beh.* 15:534–37.

Hamster Raising. Leaflet 250, U. S. Dept. of Agriculture. Supt. of Documents, U. S. Government Printing Office, Washington, D. C. 20402.

MAGALHAES, H. 1968. Housing, Care and Breeding. Hoffman, R. A., P. F. Robinson and H. Magalhaes, eds. *The Golden Hamster.* Iowa State Univ. Press, Ames, Iowa 50010.

MAGALHAES, H. 1967. The Golden Hamster. *The UFAW Handbook on the Care and Management of Laboratory Animals.* 3rd ed. Sec. 2. Available as a separate from Universities Fdn. for Animal Welfare, 230 High St., Potters Bar, Hertsfordshire, England.

RICHARDS, M.P.M. 1966. Activity Measured by Running Wheels and Observations during the Oestrus Cycle, Pregnancy and Psuedopregnancy in the Golden Hamster. *Animal Beh.* 14:450–58.

FILM

Handling Laboratory Animals—The Hamster (includes how to pick up, how to sex, how to palpate for pregnancy). Film loop, super 8 mm, cartridge, silent, color, 3 min. Encyclopaedia Britannica Educational Corp., 425 N. Michigan Ave., Chicago, Ill 60611.

15

Guinea Pigs and Rabbits

I think I could turn and live with animals, they
are so placid and self-contain'd
I stand and look at them long and long.
They do not sweat and whine about their
condition, . . .
Not one is dissatisfied, not one is demented
with the mania of owning things, . . .
Not one is respectable or unhappy over the
whole earth.

Walt Whitman (1819-1892)

GUINEA PIGS

About 20 species of guinea pigs have been found in South America from Colombia and Venezuela to Brazil and northern Argentina. They live in rocky regions, savannahs, the edges of forests, and in swamps. Domestic strains of guinea pigs were developed from *Cavia porcellus*. These animals are diurnal and completely vegetarian. They have been introduced in many countries throughout the world, and since 1870 scientists such as Pasteur and Koch have used them for biological investigations.

Guinea pigs have excellent dispositions; they are gentle animals and rarely bite. Their bodies are short and stocky, they have small ears, short legs, and no tail. They weigh between 700 and 1,600 gm. They are noisy; they squeak and grunt and will squeal loudly when alarmed.

Several varieties make suitable classroom animals. The most common English (or Bolivian) type has short smooth hair and is white, black, agouti, sandy red, chocolate, cream, or a combination of two or three of these colors. The Abyssinian guinea pig has a short rough coat arranged in about six rossettes and is found in the same wide range of colors. The shaggy Peruvian guinea pig is not a good choice for the classroom, unless you do not mind brushing its long silky hair each day.

Because of their size, guinea pigs need larger cages than gerbils or hamsters. They can be housed outdoors in temperate climates, and because they neither jump nor climb, they are easy to contain. Care of guinea pigs is similar to that of gerbils, described in Chapter 12.

Select a healthy alert guinea pig whose coat is clean. It should have no discharge from its eyes or ears, and its breathing should be regular and noiseless. Guinea pigs are usually available from students, other nearby schools, or pet stores. If you purchase guinea pigs, secure them from licensed dealers only. Guinea pigs and rabbits are protected by federal laws which require humane housing, care and transportation. (See Appendix A for federal and state animal welfare laws, page 341.)

Figure 15-1. Short-haired guinea pig.

Figure 15-2. Rough-haired guinea pig.

RABBITS

Domestic strains of rabbits have been developed from the wild rabbit *Oryctolagus cuniculus*. Many special strains are used in genetic and nutritional studies and as laboratory experimental animals. The American Rabbit Breeders Association recognizes at least 66 breeds and varieties. Colors range from white to black and many mixtures of colors. Some varieties have very long fur.

Rabbits are not often kept in classrooms because of sanitation problems and space requirements. They are susceptible to snuffles (nasal discharge) and develop more digestive disorders from soiling their cages and food than other animals do. If frightened by improper handling, they may break their backs by kicking with their immensely strong back legs. They are easily injured by the fumes of chloroform and certain other volatile products and should never be housed in science rooms that contain such chemicals.

If it is not feasible for you to raise rabbits for your class to study, you may find a rabbit breeder in the area who would be willing to conduct a field trip through these facilities. In the event that spacious outdoor or indoor facilities are available and you do decide to keep rabbits, refer to the excellent UFAW and USDA booklets (see FURTHER READING, page 296). Or contact the American Rabbit Breeders Association, 4323 Murray Avenue, Pittsburgh, Pa. 15214. Specific instruction will not be given in this chapter, but care of rabbits is basically similar to that of guinea pigs.

CLASSROOM CARE

Standards of Care

In a high school classroom, better than minimum standards should be provided for all small mammals. In many cases, instruction in good care of classroom animals can help fulfill the state laws' requirements to provide teaching in "kindness . . . and humane treatment of living animals" (California law). The cage sizes recommended for mammals in this book are spacious enough for complete and maximum comfort of the animals. Cages can always be made larger than the suggested sizes, but they should not be smaller.

Use only those study procedures with guinea pigs and rabbits which would be considered painless if applied to human beings. Do no experiments which adversely affect the animals' health; do not give them poor diets or subject them to any situation which would cause them distress or threaten their lives. Suggestions and references for acceptable mammalian experiments within the laws of most states and humane in their standards are given in Chapter 16. Pertinent laws are given in Appendix A.

Housing for Guinea Pigs

Although guinea pigs can be housed satisfactorily outdoors when the temperature does not fall below 16°C (60°F) or rise above 30°C (86°F), these animals are not acclimated to *sudden* changes in temperature and humidity. They will suffer more from heat than from cold, so select a shaded area. A pen standing on grass allows the animals space for exercise. Construct a weatherproof hutch from wood sealed with varnish, or from sheet asbestos sealed with polyurethane varnish, and extend the roof over any screened wall to protect the animals from rain. Provide protection as well against dogs, cats, wild rats, and foxes, which will kill guinea pigs; the most open wall of the hutch should be secured by heavy-duty screening or close-gauge fencing of the same quality used for chicken coops.

Animals kept outdoors are unlikely to breed during the fall and winter. Otherwise, they are readily available for a wide variety of studies and observations.

Indoor housing for guinea pigs must not be drafty or damp. Purchase metal or plastic cages that are large enough and have solid floors. A piece of hard plastic can be placed over mesh floors. If you construct your own cage, you can house one or two guinea pigs, or a sow and her litter, comfortably in a cage with floor dimensions of 45 × 60 cm. Walls can be solid, mesh or barred, with the lower 12 cm made of wood to keep out drafts and prevent bedding from falling out.

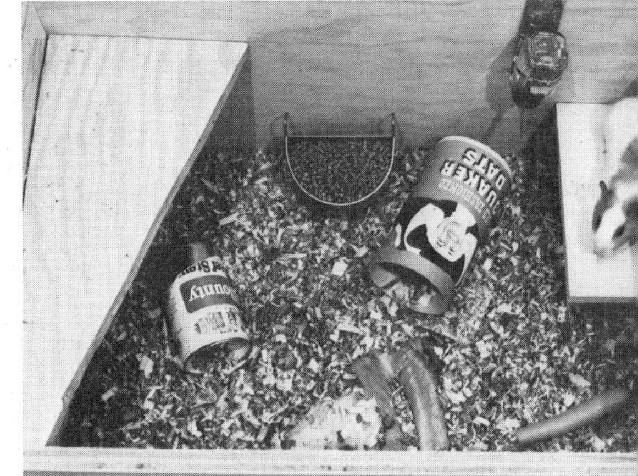

Figure 15-3. A solid-sided guinea pig cage showing two resting boards, tunnels for hiding, and a water bottle. Plenty of green foods are provided and a carrot. Green foods are essential and must supplement the dry food. No lid is required for this cage because the walls are high enough to prevent escape.

If the cage is more than 35 cm high, a lid may be unnecessary; guinea pigs are not good climbers. However, provide a lid to protect the guinea pigs if there are dogs or cats around.

Cages should be escapeproof even though guinea pigs do not tend to escape and are not pests in the wild. If an animal does get free, recapture it by one of the methods described on page 251 for gerbils.

Guinea pigs do not use exercise wheels, so they need spacious cages with room for exercise. They will climb onto low shelves, about 10 cm above the floor. Inverted boxes, large enough to hold the animal and afford comfortable entrance, are a welcome addition.

BEDDING. Straw, hay, or whitewood or cedar shavings are ideal. Do not use sawdust when the guinea pigs are breeding, for it blocks the vagina; but it can be used for nonbreeding animals. Guinea pigs do not burrow in their cages, and even in the wild make only shallow burrows, so 3 to 5 cm of bedding will suffice. Change the bedding about every four days; damp bedding is detrimental to the animals' health. Wash and dry the cage well before adding new bedding.

GNAWING. Guinea pigs do not require special provisions for gnawing; however, a block of wood might be a welcome addition to the cage.

Feeding

Guinea pigs are vegetarians. A mash consisting of two parts crushed oats and one part bran can be fed to them dry or slightly damp. Or, try two parts bran and one part sugar beet pulp.* (Soak the beet overnight, drain off surplus water, add bran, and mix to form a crumbly mass.) Prepare fresh mash each day; a handful will feed one guinea pig. Add powdered skim milk to improve the quality. Commercial guinea pig pellets must be used within 90 days of the milling date and should be stored in a cool area. Essential vitamin C is lost as these pellets deteriorate. You may obtain laboratory chow especially prepared for guinea pigs from pet stores or manufacturers.** Occasionally supplement this diet with bread, milk, and small quantities of brewer's yeast. Salt spools may be suspended to rotate on a wire.

Guinea pigs crunch rather than gnaw their food and, although they do not eat much, they eat often. Average intake for an adult is about 30 to 35 gm per day. Keep food in the cages all the time, either in hoppers

---

*Crushed oats, bran, and sugar beet pulp are available from "Feed Dealers" listed in the yellow pages of your telephone directory.

**For sources of supply see page 247.

or open bowls. Guinea pigs squeal when they think they are going to be fed. If they are very noisy, their ration may be inadequate; provide more nourishing and varied foods. To prevent scurvey, include vitamin C in the daily diet.

GREENS AND HAY. Guinea pigs differ from other mammals (except primates) in requiring large amounts of vitamin C. Vitamin C in the form of fresh greens should be provided daily. Suitable fresh greens include green cabbage, lettuce, kale, lawn clippings, and alfalfa. Wash the greens first; and remove uneaten portions each day.

In addition, provide good quality meadow hay daily. Remove weeds and particularly thistles, which injure the delicate mucosa of the animals' mouths.

WATER. A guinea pig drinks a substantial amount of water each day, usually around 150 ml. Provide large bottles, or more than one, and change the water daily. If you prefer to use vitamin C powder or tablets to prevent deficiency disease, dissolve 5 gm of vitamin C (ascorbic acid) per guinea pig in the drinking water. As the drinking water is changed each day, add the amount of vitamin C for the number of animals using that water. Food bits will be regurgitated occasionally into the sipper tube of the water bottle, so be sure to clean the tubes every other week with a pipe cleaner or test tube brush. Open water dishes are not satisfactory.

Handling

Untamed guinea pigs can be highstrung, so handle them gently. To pick up an animal, place one hand over its shoulders with your thumb behind its foreleg and your fingers well foreward on the opposite side; then lift gently, without squeezing, and slip your other hand under its rump to provide support. Guinea pigs do not usually bite, but they can scratch and will squeal if hurt or frightened. Pregnant females should be handled as little as possible.

Weekend and Vacation Care

See page 252.

Compatibility

Weanlings can be housed with their parents, but do not mix them with other litters or adults. Two strange adult males will not be compatible. Two females may be compatible, but there are exceptions. For

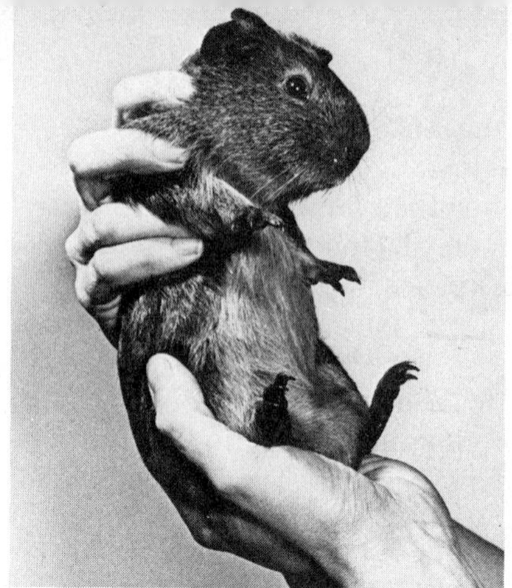
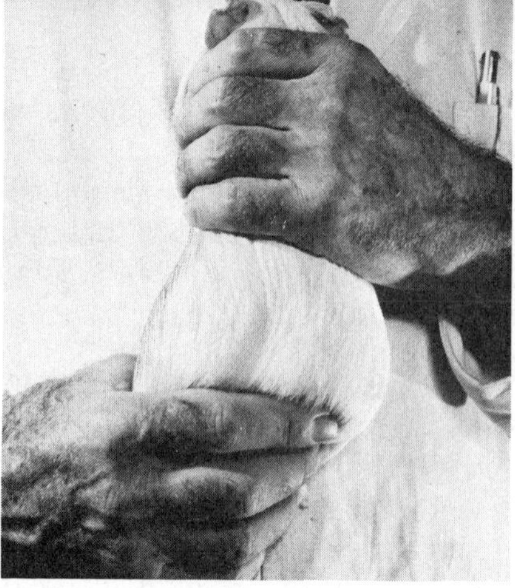

Figure 15-4. Comfortable ways to hold a guinea pig.

companionship, a female can be housed permanently with a daughter or a male with a son. If fighting does occur, separate the animals immediately and house them individually.

Breeding

The estrous cycle in females varies from 16 to 19 days. Within this time, about a ten-hour period occurs when a female will mate. If the male is to remain with the female, the breeding cage should be at least 60 × 68 cm. Place the male in the cage first, then introduce the female. Females may become pregnant within 10 to 12 hours after they give birth. To prevent rebreeding, remove the male before the birth. If rebreeding is desired, the pair can be continuously housed together.

The gestation period is 65 to 70 days. An average litter is three young, but some litters contain five or more. Guinea pigs can reproduce

Figure 15-5. Life cycle of a guinea pig.

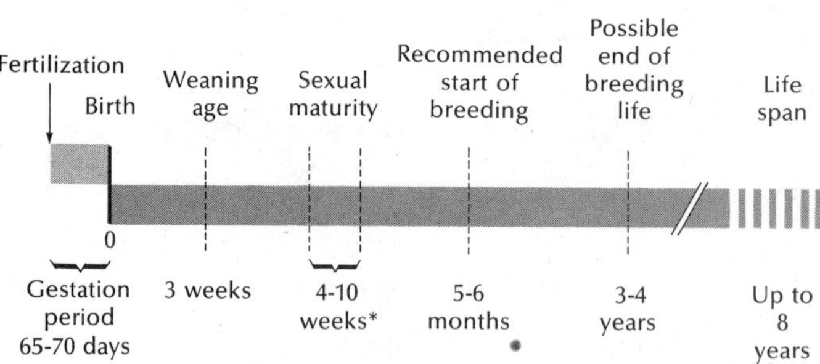

until they are three years old, sometimes longer. They have a life span of several years; the oldest recorded guinea pig was eight years old.

Guinea pigs are exceedingly well developed at birth; they weigh about 100 gm, have a good coat of hair, strong teeth, and open eyes. They will care for themselves very quickly and are able to move about within an hour after birth; within a few hours, they can eat solid food. Although they are still dependent on their mother's milk, extra food and greens should be provided for them. Usually, guinea pigs have only two mammae; large litters of four or more may result in crowding and death of weaklings. The young are weaned at 21 days or when they reach a weight of 200 to 250 gm (7 to 9 ounces).

SEXING AND PAIRING. The genital opening in guinea pigs is the same distance from the anus in both sexes; but in the male it is rounded, while in the female it is a longitudinal slit. To confirm the sex, you can extrude the male organ by gently pressing on the lower abdomen with your thumb.

Sexual maturity is reached at an early age (30 to 45 days for females, 60 days for males). Separate the sexes at weaning time to prevent breeding. Do not breed the animals before they are five to six months old. House together only one of each sex; group breeding is unsatisfactory. A pair kept together continuously may produce up to four litters per year for two years. Guinea pigs will not usually produce as many offspring as will gerbils, hamsters, rats, or mice.

Figure 15-6. A male guinea pig.

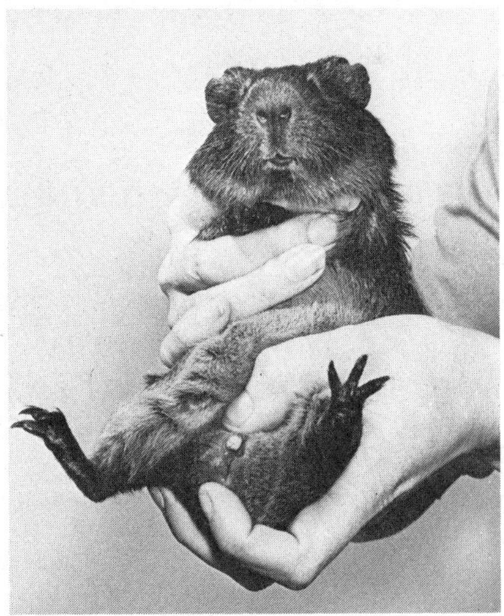

OVERPOPULATION. To prevent overbreeding, house the sexes separately.

Identification

Individual coloring may be sufficient identification, but you may dab spots of safe dye on an animal's head or back if you take care to avoid its eyes. Or simply label the guinea pig's cage.

Health

Guinea pigs can be quite susceptible to a number of diseases, of which pneumonia is the most common. Their diseases are hard to diagnose. Consult a veterinarian if an animal develops a rough coat, lack of appetite, loss of weight, neck swellings, or nasal discharges. Avoid drafts and open windows, as too much temperature fluctuation seems to lower the animals' resistance and predisposes them to pneumonia. Cod liver oil may help a sick animal recover.

If the guinea pigs' housing is unsanitary, they may become infested with lice. Check behind their ears, and dust affected areas with an appropriate parasiticidal agent (see page 272). Improve the standards of sanitation immediately.

Sometimes, after giving birth, females may lose large amounts of hair. Feed such animals plenty of highly nutritious foods until they recover. Do not allow them to become pregnant again.

Disposing of Unwanted Animals

See Appendix E, page 360.

FURTHER READING

Guinea Pigs

Guinea Pigs. UFAW Information Leaflet. Universities Fdn. for Animal Welfare, 230 High St., Potters Bar, Hertfordshire, England.

PATERSON, J. S. 1967. The Guinea-Pig or Cavy. *The UFAW Handbook on the Care and Management of Laboratory Animals.* 3rd ed. Sec. 2. Available as a separate from Universities Fdn. for Animal Welfare, 230 High St., Potters Bar, Hertfordshire, England.

Raising Guinea Pigs. 1970. USDA Leaflet No. 466. Supt. of Documents, U.S. Government Printing Office, Washington, D.C. 20402.

Rabbits

LOCKLEY, R. M. 1974. *The Private Life of the Rabbit.* MacMillan Publishing Co., New York.

PRIDHAM, T. J. *Raising Rabbits.* 1972, January. Publication 210. Veterinary Services Lab., Ministry of Agriculture & Food, Huron Park, Ontario, Canada.

The Rabbit. UFAW Information Leaflet. Universities Fdn. for Animal Welfare, 230 High St., Potters Bar, Hertfordshire, England.

FILMS

Handling Laboratory Animals—The Guinea Pig (how to pick up, sex, palpate for pregnancy). Film loop, super 8 mm, cartridge, silent, color, 3 min. Encyclopaedia Britannica Educational Corp., 425 N. Michigan Ave., Chicago, Ill 60611.

Handling Laboratory Animals—The Rabbit. Super 8 mm, cartridge, silent, color, 5 min. Encyclopaedia Britannica Educational Corp., 425 N. Michigan Ave., Chicago, Ill 60611.

16

Experiments with Mammals

"Humane considerations supercede curiosity."

Henry K. Beecher (b. 1904)

Student studies with mammals should emphasize respect for life along with objective inquiry. *Normal* physiology and *normal* behavior should be investigated; neither area requires the infliction of pain on animals. Chapter 1 includes humane guidelines for student experiments with animals. The legal aspects of experimentation with animals are covered in Appendix A. Conduct class discussions on the social implications of these issues. All humane guidelines are compatible with the thesis that scientific inquiry is necessary and valuable; these guidelines stress *how* it should be conducted.

Student exercises involving small mammals cover many broad topics: studies of normal physiology, reproduction and genetics, learning and behavior, normal nutrition and digestion, respiratory and excretory processes, the senses, biochemical analyses of tissues, and others. Suggested experiments on most of these topics, as prepared by a group of veterinarians, scientists, and high school teachers, are presented in Reference 1, page 316. Other suggestions are given here.

Normal Growth

Observe the normal growth of young animals until adulthood. At regular intervals, measure and record weight, body length, and length of tail; also record the eruption of teeth.[2] Make a graph of the results by plotting measurements on the vertical axis and the ages of the animals on the horizontal axis.

A gerbil's tail is 25 percent of its body length at birth, but at maturity it is 90 percent. Is a similar change in this ratio shown in other mammals?

Determine the average rate of increase in body length in a litter of a particular species at various ages. Record the dates on which you measure the animals so that litters may be compared for seasonal variations in growth.

Measure food and water consumed by a litter of young animals after weaning, and relate this to body growth. (Search the bedding for partially eaten food pellets to ensure accurate assessment of food intake.) Always provide animals with adequate food and water to sustain normal growth.

ENRICHED LIVING CONDITIONS. Many behavioral scientists are investigating the effects of an enriched environment. This has good application to modern human sociological problems. Many captive animals (in zoos, for instance) are kept in conditions that are *minimally* adequate and less than otpimal for maximum growth and health. The adverse effects of poor living conditions are well known, but the beneficial effects of enriched living conditions are not well documented and can provide some challenging ideas for experiments.

Set up two animal cages of the same adequate size—one containing sufficient bedding but no playthings; the other containing deep bedding, an exercise wheel, and playthings. Suitable toys include tunnels, balls, and wooden objects. Place one weanling animal in each of the two cages. (Preferably, use litter mates of the same sex.) Provide identical food and water for both animals throughout the experiment. Measure each animal's rate of growth and ability to learn mazes. Do they differ in growth rate, curiosity and alertness, and ability to learn? (Use response to Novelty, page 313, and Maze Tests, page 315.)

Another similar experiment tests the type of cage an animal will thrive in. Raise one animal in a cage with solid sides; raise the other animal in a cage with mesh sides. Compare the animals' health. Does an extra deep layer of bedding in mesh cages help to compensate for the differences found? Proceed as follows.

Divide weanling litter mates of the same sex into three groups. The members of each group should be about the same body weight. Raise Group A in a roomy plastic box with solid sides and a mesh lid; raise Group B in an open-wire cage of the same size. Raise Group C in a mesh cage with an extra deep layer of bedding and a nest box. (Do not provide nest boxes for Groups A and B.) Bedding levels for groups A and B should be adequate (about 5 cm) but not as generous as that for group C (10 cm). Keep the bedding levels constant throughout the experiment. Assess the growth rate, general health, and activity levels of each group. Which cage conditions produce the healthiest animals? What is

Figure 16-1. To demonstrate the beneficial effects of petting. A baby gerbil is stroked for ten minutes each day for at least three weeks. The body weight is also determined each day. The growth of the petted gerbils (body weight increase) is compared with that of control animals that have not been petted. The petted gerbils usually grow at a greater rate than the control animals.

the relevance of these results to cage requirements of experimental and pet animals?

The harmful effects of sensory deprivation on humans and other animals are well known. However, whether beneficial effects on growth and behavior occur in animals that have been stroked and handled by humans is less well known. The hypothesis suggests useful student projects.

Contrary to instruction in some laboratory manuals that rats and mice should not be handled, scientists have found that (after they are weaned) petting and stroking young rats each day enhanced their growth. To verify these results, divide one or two litters of mice, rats, gerbils, or hamsters into two groups immediately after weaning; the mean weights of both groups should be approximately the same. For the next several weeks, affectionately stroke each of the animals in one group (the test group) for ten minutes each day. Give those in the other (control) group identical food and treatment with one difference, do *not* stroke them. What is the mean body weight of the animals in each group at the end of five weeks? (Periods as short as three weeks can be used.) Is there a significant difference in these weights? Is there a difference between the two groups in the amount of food eaten or water consumed? Count the number of fecal pellets excreted by each group. In laboratory tests, rats that had received extra handling excreted fewer fecal pellets, which indicates better food utilization.

Growth of Hair

When does hair first appear in different species of newborn animals? Compare the skin coverings of different species of adult animals.[3] How many types of hair are there (overhair, underhair, wool, fur, down, lanugo, etc.)? What are their functions?

What are the hair patterns of certain varieties of rodents? The rosettes and whorls of guinea pigs show particularly variable angles of hair slope.

Does a rodent's hair grow continuously? Using a very sharp razor, carefully shave patches, one sq cm in size, from the backs of young and adult animals. With calipers, measure the hair length as it grows back in. Does the young animals' hair grow at the same rate as the adults'?

Environment

Construct a large arena which provides at least four times the area normally acceptable as living space for one animal. Divide the arena into four sections or "rooms," each of which offers a different type of living condition. To construct a suitable arena, simply glue together four identical boxes not less than 38 × 38 cm. (Why do you not use boxes of unequal size?) On each of the inside walls, cut out at least four doorways large enough to allow free passage of the animals from the species to be tested.

Test one variable at a time. For instance, provide different types of bedding (shredded corn cobs, cedar chips, sawdust, ground sugar cane, beet pulp, peat, or clean shredded packing paper) in four rooms which are identical in every other respect. Make the bedding deep, just as it would be in a cage. Avoid harmful materials such as newspaper (the ink is toxic), or highly resinous wood products (which irritate), or straw and other prickly materials (which can damage hamsters' cheek pouches). Place an animal in the arena and, with a stopwatch, measure how long it stays in each of the four sections. After an initial period of exploring all areas, does the animal remain in one? Time the animal for about 15 minutes each day. Is it consistent from day to day in its preference? Are the results influenced by the section in which the animal is placed at the beginning of the observation period?

In the same way, test the animal's preference for darkness or diffuse and bright light from a fluorescent source. Be sure that temperature variations do not interfere with the results. Experimental work has shown that deer mice select moonlight when allowed to press levers to choose the degree of light. Do all species of small mammals prefer dim lighting? Does preference for lighting relate to periods of daily activity?

Floor and wall materials (clear or opaque plastic, wood, glass, sheet metal, various sizes of metal mesh, or metal bars) can be tested in a similar way, although construction of the test apparatus is more complicated. Clear and opaque plastic can be tested with the least trouble. Use an extra large clear plastic box (one half should provide ample living space), and cover half with opaque plastic. Outfit both halves identically and ventilate the box adequately and evenly on both sides, perhaps by boring holes in the plastic. Determine in which part the animals spend most of their time.

Testing preferences for different types of nest boxes also requires extra housing area. Probably only one of several boxes will be used, thus reducing the effective living space. Take this into consideration when determining the floor space to be provided. For a mouse, use an area about 60 cm square (use larger cages for bigger species), containing two nesting boxes, one which is transparent and another which occludes light. Which nest box does the animal choose? Similarly, determine preference for tubular and square boxes, or large and small boxes made of the same material. What is the optimal size of nesting box for a particular species?

Construct two chambers connected by a long tunnel which an animal can traverse freely. Provide *soft* music in only one chamber. Observe and record how much time the animal spends in each chamber, to determine its preference. If you find that the animal prefers music, then go on to supply Mozart or chamber music in one of the two chambers and rock music in the other. Which does the animal prefer?

CONCLUSIONS. If it is shown from the foregoing experiments that, for instance, mice shun sawdust bedding and bright lighting, they should not be kept under such conditions. What general conclusions can be made about adequate housing for captive animals?

Make surveys of students who keep caged animals, and of local pet shops or zoos, to see what proportion of animals in each of these categories has *optimal* housing conditions. In your surveys, consider space versus overcrowding; adequacy of food and water; sanitation; suitability of caging, flooring and bedding materials; lighting; and provisions of nesting boxes, especially for pregnant or nursing females.

Standards of animal care vary in zoos, pet shops, and in homes. Individual owners and zoos provide permanent housing for their animals. Pet shops aim at rapid turnover of animals and, in theory, no animal is kept in its cage for any great length of time. Housing for animals in pet shops is often inadequate and should not be used as a model for keeping animals in school or at home.

Nutrition

To learn what foods make a balanced diet, offer an animal a selection of normal foods and observe its health and development to determine the nutritional value of the foods you selected. You can demonstrate the presence of fat, starch, and water in seeds, vegetables, and cereals, then perform detailed chemical analyses of these and other food constituents.

There is some evidence to show that the size and shape of food plays an important role in nutritional adequacy. Feed weanlings large pieces of laboratory chow which is known to provide a balanced diet, and compare their growth rate with other weanlings raised on the same chow cut up into small pieces. Which group of animals grows best?

Since most rodents gnaw, it is interesting to see what effect the texture of foods has on body growth. Provide one group of animals with food in cubes (a hard surface for gnawing); feed another group the same diet in a powder form; feed a third group the same diet moistened with water to make a mush. Use young growing animals, preferably litter mates. Weigh and measure the animals each day. All groups of animals should receive an adequately nutritious diet. Do the results indicate that the texture of the food does influence growth rate? Fecal and urinary outputs can also be determined in these studies.

In a similar manner, compare the growth rates of animals fed a standard laboratory chow with the growth rates of animals on a high protein diet, and with those of others fed a varied, well-balanced diet of many different kinds of food (include seeds, cereals, and fresh vegetables for the third group). All diets should be fed *ad lib*. Which diet produces maximum growth?

Demonstrate that a small mammal, when allowed to choose freely between suitable and unsuitable foods, will select a balanced diet of correct proportions and amounts. Offer an animal a weighed quantity (25 gm for gerbils, mice, rats, and hamsters, 50 gm for guinea pigs, 300 gm for rabbits) of laboratory chow (suitable food) and any weighed quantity of potato chips or some other snack food (unsuitable food). Offer both types of food to the animal at the same time. At the end of each 24-hour period, weigh the leftovers, including food scattered in the bedding. Does the animal eat *any* of the snack food? If so, does it eat enough to make the total diet unbalanced?

Never force an animal to subsist on an inadequate diet or without ample drinking water. Do not give an animal alcohol or drugs. The well-known results of improper and insufficient feeding can be learned from films. (See FILMS, page 318.)

Metabolism

Determine the basal metabolic rate of an animal. (See FILMS, *Measuring Oxygen Consumption*, page 319.) What effect does the time of day, or a high carbohydrate diet, have on the metabolic rate? How much carbon dioxide does an animal produce in a given period of time. In your experiments, place the animal on a platform, well away from the carbon dioxide-absorbing materials; these are caustic and may cause painful burns.

Chemical Analysis of Tissues and Isolated Organ Techniques

For some studies an animal must be killed; when this is necessary, it should be done quickly and painlessly. Many valuable biochemical or physiological studies can be made of tissues or organs removed from

Figure 16-2. *The metabolic rate of a gerbil is determined by confining the animal temporarily in a closed container. A moving bubble in a capillary tube indicates the pressure (volume) of gas within the container. Oxygen consumption by the animal causes the bubble to move. Students measure the rate of movement of the bubble in a given period of time and can calculate from this the metabolic rate.*

dead animals. Do *not* remove tissues from animals which are merely anesthetized; they must be dead. Mammals should not be killed in the presence of high school students.

Considerable skill is required to humanely kill vertebrate animals. For instructions for killing small mammals, see Appendix E, and for frogs, see page 205.

One animal can provide enough tissue for many students, perhaps for the whole class. For instance, many intestinal segments 2 cm long can be prepared. Useful tissues also can be obtained from the heart, diaphragm, gastrocnemius muscle, and abdominal skin. Of course, biochemical assays can be performed on any body tissue. Liver tissue and fat deposits are ideal for chemical analysis.[4] Advanced students can use liver homogenates to determine biochemical actions of mitochondria,[5a] or they can study active transport of glucose across membranes, using intestinal strips.[5b] Determinations of enzyme activity can be made in liver, kidney, brain, and other tissues.[6] Plan *all* the needed uses of animal tissues before killing an animal, so that others will not have to be sacrificed for tissues that could have been taken from the first one.

One of the best uses of isolated tissue is to study muscular contractions of smooth, cardiac, and voluntary muscles. The range and diversity of such studies are enormous. Remove the muscle preparations from a freshly killed animal, secure them in a bath, and perfuse in oxygenated physiological saline solution to retain their viability. Attach one end of a muscle to a lever which records its responses on a revolving kymograph drum[7] A possible substitute for a kymograph is an event recorder, although this is less satisfactory. Detailed instructions for making an event recorder from an old clock are given in Reference 8. Continuous recordings can be made for many hours—you can, in some cases, store the preparations overnight in a refrigerator and use them again the next day.

Perhaps the most satisfactory isolated preparations for high school students are intestinal strips. You can use these to demonstrate peristalsis and its hormonal control. Add small quantities of neuromuscular transmitting or blocking agents to the bath to demonstrate normal mechanisms of control and basic features of muscular contraction.

Compare the responses of various types of muscles (cardiac and voluntary). Advanced students, adept at dissection, could set up nerve-muscle preparations using phrenic nerve-diaphragm muscle, or sciatic nerve-gastrocnemius muscle preparations. These have the added advantage that the nerves or nerve stumps can be stimulated electrically.

Reproduction

BREEDING. Before using small mammals for breeding experiments, consider carefully the problem of how to dispose of the surplus animals. It may be wise to consider alternative species which avoid this problem. Insects such as fruit flies (page 140), or fish such as guppies or paradise fish (page 175–177), or plants such as corn, tomatoes, and beans can be used most successfully for genetic studies. These species have short life cycles, and are easier and less expensive to keep than small mammals. Furthermore, results with mammals may be very misleading, as Mendel found, because of their comparatively small numbers of offspring. Nevertheless, genetic experiments on small mammals can be highly instructive.[9, 10]

NORMAL SEXUAL BEHAVIOR. Prepare an observation enclosure at least 120 cm square. Mark six females for identification. Place one animal in the enclosure; then add the others, one at a time, at five-minute intervals. Observe and record their interactions, such as sniffing, nibbling and nuzzling, in each five-minute period. If they fight severely or for more than two or three minutes, separate the animals and discontinue the experiment. Is behavior affected by how many other animals are present? Who initiates the investigations, the newcomer or the animals already in the enclosure?

Place two males of the same species together for ten minutes and compare their behavior with that of a male and a female of the same species placed together.[11d]

To determine the effects of the estrous cycle on behavior, compare the social, aggressive, and sexual behavior of a female on different days when placed with a male. The stages of normal estrus can be determined by accepted procedures.

ESTROUS CYCLE. The estrous cycle is the periodic cycle of reproduction in female mammals in which the ovary, uterus, and vagina undergo changes according to hormonal influences. The various stages of the cycle can be determined by several methods. Perhaps the simplest is to use an activity cage which continuously records the amount of movement the animal makes. (See ACTIVITY PATTERNS, page 311.) Records of a solitary female hamster, rat, or mouse in an activity cage will usually show a periodic peak of activity every four or five days. This peak coincides with estrus (heat), the period of sexual receptivity which, in these species, usually lasts about 12 hours.

Another suitable method for rats, mice, and gerbils (but not for hamsters) is to examine vaginal smears each day. During estrus, all or almost all of the epithelial cells have lost their nuclei and are cornified. During diestrus the smear is thinner, and consists of leucocytes and basophilic epithelial cells with practically no cornified cells.[12] Your advanced students may wish to use this method.[13] Attach a 2 mm circular loop of nickel-chromium wire to a handle, heat it in a flame, then dip it in 0.9 percent saline to cool it and to leave a film of saline on the loop. Insert the loop a very short distance into the vagina and rotate it gently to collect loose debris. Smear this debris onto a microscope slide. Dry the smear in air, stain it with methylene blue for one to two minutes, and rinse it in water. Examine the slide under a microscope. (See FILMS, *Estrous Cycle of the Rat,* page 318.)

Once you have mastered the methods for determining normal estrous cycles, you can devise experiments to determine the effects of light and dark on sexual maturation of young animals and on estrous periods of adults. Normally, mice and rats are nocturnal breeders, with estrus always beginning in the evening. How is the estrous cycle affected if the animals are kept in constant light?

SEX RATIO IN A POPULATION. In small rodents, variations in body contour, length and weight, and most reliably, differences in anogenital distance are factors in determining sex. Measure anogenital distance with a *blunt-ended* compass, and read the distance measured on a decimillimetric scale. (See FILMS, *Handling Laboratory Animals—The Hamster;* and *Handling Laboratory Animals—The Rat,* page 319.) Blunt the ends of the compass on a file or sandpaper to ensure that the animal will not get hurt. In certain cases, the two sexes are so similar that careful comparisons between litter mates are needed.

Can the compass method be used reliably with newborn animals? It has been reported that in newborn mice, a tiny blood vessel, which in males is T-shaped but in females is straight and smaller, runs medially along the dorsal side of the genital papilla (see Figure 16-3). Another report showed that, at seven to eight days of age, female mice can be identified by the appearance of the two posterior pairs of thoracic teats.[14] Using statistical methods, compare the reliability of determining sex by (1) the appearance of the genital vascular pattern, (2) by anogenital distance, (3) by body weight, and (4) by appearance of thoracic teats. What is the incidence of the two sexes in successive litters? Does the sex ratio vary for different species?

Effects of Domestication

Domestication profoundly affects the physiology and psychology of animals. Sexual maturity occurs earlier in domesticated animals

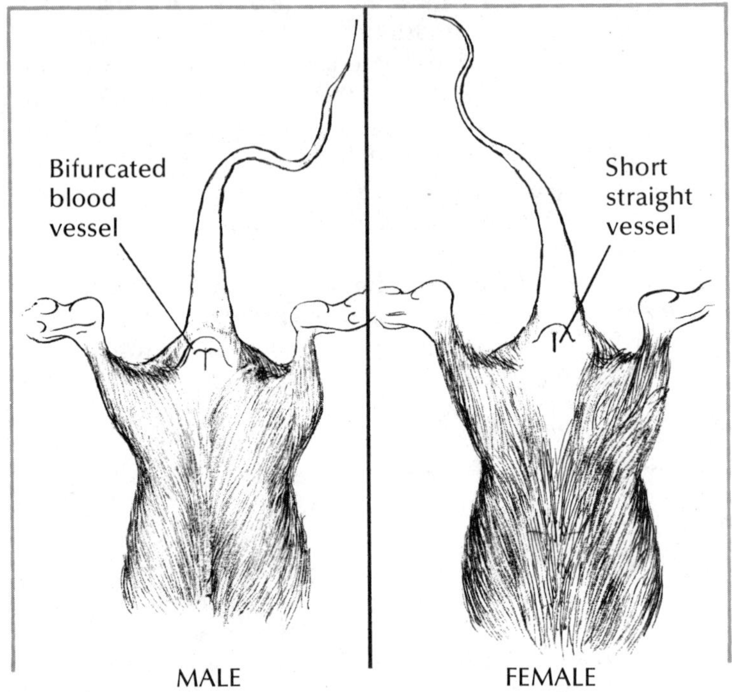

Figure 16-3. Sex can be determined in newborn mice by very careful observation of small differences in the shape of blood vessels supplying the genital region.

than in their undomesticated relatives, and the complicated mating ceremonies of wild animals often are absent. Cross breeds are possible among domesticated animals which would rarely occur among wild animals.[15] The history of the effects of domestication on the physiology and psychology of animals has considerable bearing on the usefulness of present-day laboratory animals as subjects for experimentation. Psychologists, such as Hediger and Lockard, have described domesticated animals as unnatural creatures.[15, 17] Lockard asserts that domestication of laboratory rats has altered these animals to such an extent that their behavior is no longer representative of their species. He criticizes psychologists who rely heavily on studies of laboratory rats, because he believes these are abnormal animals.

An extensive study of fertility and sex ratio of mice was made during the 1920s.[18] Among the 2,000 mice studied, the average litter size was 6.18. Is the average litter size currently the same as it was 50 years ago? Have further years of domestication altered the sexual physiology of laboratory mice? Lockard advocated introducing wild strains into present laboratory stocks to counter, to some extent, the abnormal effects that domestication seems to produce.

The implications of Lockard's proposal are of sufficient importance to merit further study. Request records of litter sizes and sex ratios of breeding colonies in research institutions or commercial breeding farms. Perhaps you could obtain the records of gerbil breeding colonies and compare the figures for 10 or 15 years ago with the current year's. Has the average litter size, or the age of sexual maturity, changed for this species? The effects might be expected to be most pronounced during the early years of the domestication of gerbils.

Special Senses

Can small rodents perceive color? Offer the same food in a variety of colors and see if an animal shows any preference. Use edible food dyes, such as cochineal and others obtainable from grocery stores. Do not use toxic substances, such as paint or ink. Guinea pigs are good subjects for this experiment; they seem to have better color perception than hamsters, mice, or rats.

Test the popular belief that gerbils are colorblind. Cover glass or transparent plastic jars with cellophane of different colors. Place these on their sides in the gerbils' cage as nesting boxes. Do the gerbils consistently choose to sleep in jars of one color?

Keep identically housed animals in two different rooms—one where a tape recording of *soft* music is played for 12 or more hours every day, and another without music. After about two months, use maze tests to determine differences, if any, in learning ability of the animals. Select other psychological or physiological parameters (such as behavior or growth patterns) and test for differences.

Pheromones—Chemical Communication

In the past, research into animal communication systems has been limited to auditory and visual systems, because students of animal behavior have favored species with communication methods similar to those of man. But scientists now realize that the dominant means of communication for many species is through chemical substances called pheromones, which are released by animals and affect the behavior of other animals of the same species. Pheromones play an important role in foraging for food by ants and in the formation of migratory locust swarms. They also influence the sexual behavior of mice and other rodents.

Mammalian endocrinologists have discovered that an odor emanating from male mice modified reproductive physiology in the female. In order to study this phenomenon, advanced students should learn to make vaginal smears and identify the stages of estrus (page 306). Establish the pattern of estrus for a female mouse, housed alone, and then expose this animal to a male, in the same cage or nearby. What effect does this have on the estrous cycle? Is the normal pattern changed? To demonstrate that this effect is transmitted chemically, you must rule out the possibilities of physical or visual stimulation. Repeat the experiment, preventing physical contact. In another test, keep the animals in complete darkness during the experiment to eliminate visual communication.[19] (It has been demonstrated that modification of the estrous cycle can be effected merely by placing male excreta in a female's cage.)

Perhaps an even more remarkable phenomenon is that the odor of a *strange* male can block the pregnancy of a newly impregnated female mouse.[20, 21] The odor of the *original* males leaves the pregnancy undisturbed. For this experiment, mate a pair of mice (successful mating is indicated by the presence of a vaginal plug) and, 24 hours later, house the female with or near a strange male. The effect of blocking pregnancy is most pronounced if the male is of a different strain or is wild. Make daily vaginal smears. If the pregnancy has been blocked, the female will return to estrus within seven days. Although not all pregnancies will be blocked, a significant proportion will be. Bruce found that wild animals caused blockage of pregnancy in 71 percent of the cases.[20]

Recently, it was demonstrated that the presence of a male alters the age of sexual maturity in female mice. If female mice are housed alone, they first ovulate (reach sexual maturity) about 15 days after weaning.[22] In contrast, females housed in the presence of males first ovulate about seven days after weaning. If weanling females are housed alone with bedding material which has been used by males, they ovulate about 13 days after weaning. Apparently, ovulation is stimulated by a pheromone. Students adept in identifying stages of estrus could design an experiment to demonstrate these findings.

*Suitable apparatus is available from Telechron Timers & Motors, General Electric Co., Ashland. Mass. 01721.

Activity Patterns

Demonstrate the variations in activity of small mammals over a 24-hour period in an activity cage (See FILMS, *Temporal Patterns of Animal Activity*, page 319). An activity cage is suspended on springs attached to a writing pen or other recording apparatus that graphically records each joggle of the cage as the animal moves. These cages can be homemade[23, 24] or purchased from biological supply houses. For species that use exercise wheels (rats, mice, and hamsters), attach a counter to a ferris wheel.* Set the counter to trip a lever which marks a graphic record.[25] Place the wheel in the animal's cage but do not force the animal to use it. Record the animal's volitional activity (free choice of activity) in each 24-hour period. At first, animals tend to use an exercise wheel more each day; but after about three weeks, daily activity will stablize. The daily rhythm will show a peak at night. This plateau of activity should be established before you conduct any experiments with varying conditions.

Test the influence of various factors on the daily normal rhythm of activity; for instance, changes in light and dark periods (reversed photoperiods, or extraterrestrial days such as four hours of light and four hours of darkness), or a high protein diet. When two animals are housed together, is the use of an exercise wheel doubled?

Record the activity of animals of different ages, or of the same animal over the course of several months or years, to find out whether volitional activity varies with age.

If the enclosure that houses an animal is large enough (for instance, 60 × 120 cm) to contain a bridge, a hill, an empty box, a cardboard tube, and a wooden block, will the exercise wheel be neglected? From your observations, what can be concluded about the function of an exercise wheel for a captive animal?

Behavior

Konrad Lorenz is well known for his studies of normal behavior in domestic and wild animals, and Jane Van Lawick-Goodall has risen to fame for her remarkable accounts of the behavior of chimpanzees in the wilds of Africa. Making accurate and detailed observations of an animal's activities over long periods is quite difficult.

Comparing the behavior of small caged rodents with that of wild animals will show that caged animals are not in a normal situation, and their behavior may not be typical of their species. Hediger, a noted Swiss professor of animal psychology has said that "the domestic animal, compared with the wild animal, may be characterized as a creature that is not bound by specific ceremonies, and is in particular independent of its environment and of the impulse to avoid enemies. This state of affairs creates a situation of morphological, physiological and psychological degeneration, of distortion that may be grotesque, unbiological, even pathological."[15] Beware of extrapolating from your studies of laboratory animals.

CAGED ANIMALS. The first step is to determine what is to be measured. For caged animals, observe activities and movements for several 15-minute periods each day. Record the amount of time the animals sit still, eat, drink, sleep, dig, sniff, scratch, rear, wag their tails, and groom themselves.[11b–c]

PETS. Record the number of times a dog or cat goes in or out of the house each day. Is this dependent on the weather? What is the barking pattern of a dog? How many times does a dog urinate when taken for a walk? What is the significance of this behavior? How many times a day does a cat or dog seek affection? From whom? What do animals specifically ask for (food, water, for the door to be opened, affection)? Which breeds of dog whine and bay at sirens? What do you think makes a dog bay? Collect accounts from the literature on the baying of dogs before starting an investigation on your own.

How much time each day does a cat or dog spend grooming itself? How much time does it spend sleeping? Make a careful record of the time and duration of sleep. Describe different sleeping, standing, sitting, and lying positions. Are there species variations in these positions?

What is the maternal behavior toward offspring?

GROOMING. Sequence in grooming behavior differs among rats, mice, and hamsters. Record whether front or hind limbs are used first. Which part of the body is cleaned first—face, sides or back of head, or chest? Are there parts the animals cannot reach?

ESCAPE. Can animals learn to escape? Gently place a gerbil, mouse, or other small animal in a flower pot about 10 cm high. With a stopwatch, record (1) when the animal starts to look out of the pot, (2) when it begins to climb out, and (3) the time taken in the climb.[25] Not all animals will try to escape. If an animal escapes, place it back in the pot, and make repeated observations. Does the animal escape more quickly on subsequent tries? Correlate the number of previous attempts with the decrease in time.

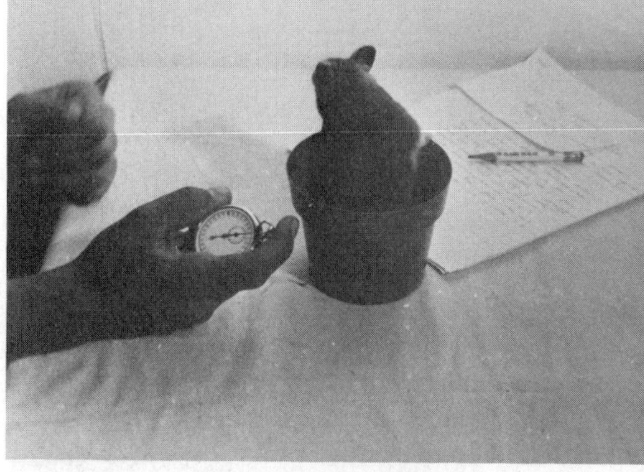

Figure 16-4. A stopwatch is used to time how long it takes for a small mammal to climb out of a flower pot. Conduct repeated trials to determine if the animal learns how to do this more quickly.

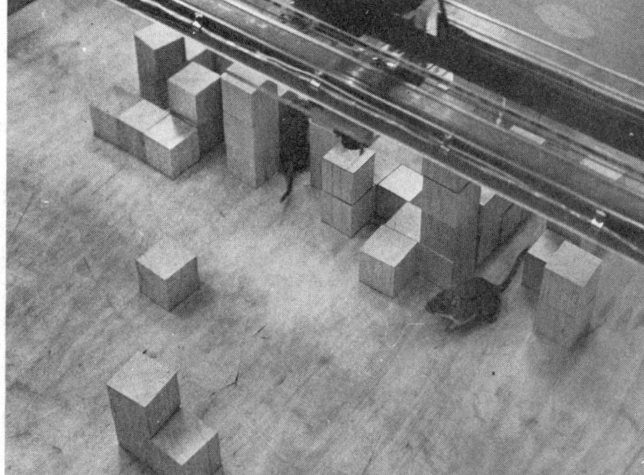

Figure 16-5. Wooden cubes are placed in various configurations in an experiment designed to test patterns of behavior of gerbils in response to new environments.

NOVELTY. To investigate an animal's curiosity, design a strange new environment that includes an exercise wheel, a flower pot lying on its side, a tube, a block, an empty spool, and some paper strewn about. Place a rat, mouse, hamster, or gerbil in the enclosure. Record how long it takes the animal to reach one of the objects. How long does it remain there? Does it manipulate the objects? Record the duration and frequency of visits to an object within a 15-minute period.[25, 26] Record the time taken for "freezing," sniffing, grooming, sitting, lying, and other activities.

Compare the responses of animals to different degrees of novelty by offering first a situation with many new objects, and then with few new objects. Does an animal spend more time sniffing and less time grooming in a situation with a high degree of novelty? What survival value do curiosity and a tendency to explore have in wild species?

Animals frequently defecate when placed in unfamiliar situations, and this can be used as an index of emotionality. Place animals one by one in (1) a large unfamiliar cage (2.5 × 2.5 m), or set them free in a small room; then, (2) place them in their own cage; and finally, (3) in their own cage placed in an unfamiliar room. Record their defecation during five-minute daily trials in each situation. Which situation evokes the greatest emotional response in the animals?

GRAVITY. The influence of gravity upon the orientation and movement of animals is important for survival. In rodents, these responses develop much earlier than do vision, taste, or hearing. The response to gravity is either negative (away from the gravitational force) or positive (toward the pull of gravity). Negative response occurs in such diverse organisms as snails, fruit flies, beetles, crabs, rats, mice, and guinea pigs. However, among rodents some individuals respond positively and others negatively. Since the response is genetically determined, various mouse strains have been inbred so contrasting responses to gravity can be demonstrated. These inbred strains are available commercially,* but any small rodent can be used for these tests.

Plot the movements of an animal as it traverses an inclined plane. Set a board (approximately 60 × 90 cm) on a fulcrum so it can be tipped to any selected angle (from 20 to 70 degrees). Cover the board with a flexible plastic screen so the animal can hang on—even at the steepest angles. The experimenter can trace the path of the animal with a marking brush on a Plexiglas® roof above the board. Full experimental details are given in Reference 11e.

Does the degree of incline affect the animal's orientation? Observe the animal at different degrees down the slope; then test it moving up the slope. What are the results? Place the animal on the slope at different degrees of incline, in no particular order. Are the results different? Thiessen experimented with crossing strains of mice that had contrasting responses.[27]

WALL-SEEKING. If let loose into a room, mice and hamsters will run around the edge by the walls. It is possible to demonstrate quantitatively the wall-hugging or wall-seeking tendencies of these animals by comparing their behavior when subjected to wall (W) and no-wall (NW) conditions. Construct a test box 80 cm square, with removable walls 30 cm high. Mark the floor into a grid of 64 10-cm squares. Place the box on a table top that is smaller than the gridded floor.[11a] (Mice will not jump off this surface when the walls are removed.)

You will need 20 mice. Place each animal in the apparatus individually for five minutes. Test ten with the walls in position and ten with the walls removed. Prepare paper grid replicas on which to record the positions of each mouse. Record your observations every two sec-

*For instance, C57BL/6J and A/J strains, Jackson Laboratory, Bar Harbor, Maine.

onds over a five-minute period (a total of 150 observations for each animal). Clean the floor of the apparatus before testing each new animal to remove confusing odors.

Count the number of times (out of 150) each animal is in one of the 28 peripheral squares of the grid. This is a W score. Count an NW score for the number of times the animal is on an inside square. Tabulate the W and NW scores for all animals and compute the means and standard errors for each test group. Is there a significant difference between the two groups?

CONDITIONED RESPONSE. Feed guinea pigs fresh lettuce or other vegetables each day and ring a bell just before the food is placed in the cage. In time, the animals will associate the sound with the food and will begin squeaking or exhibiting other behavior in anticipation of food when the bell is rung. Be sure that the animals are properly fed after the experimental bell-ringing.

Construct a simple apparatus to train mice and other small animals to obtain food by pulling a wire loop until it rings a bell.[28]

Intelligence

MAZE TESTS. Construct a maze with walls higher than the animal and cover the maze with a transparent lid. A single alternation T-maze with six or seven turns is suitable. Set the entrance of the maze against the open cage door; the animal (rat, mouse, or hamster) will enter out of curiosity. (Gerbils are poor maze-runners, so other species are preferred.) For repeated experiments at short intervals, move the animal's own empty cage to the goal end of the maze. The cage itself is the "reward." Food and water are suitable rewards for experiments to be conducted after longer intervals. (Do not punish animals with electric shocks for wrong decisions.)

The animal's success can be gauged by the time taken to solve the maze and the number of false turns made. Individual animals vary in their problem-solving ability. Some special strains of expert maze-running rats are available from research laboratories. On an average, a rat will require 20 to 50 attempts before it can run a maze without error several times in succession.

How long does a trained animal remember what was learned? Retest a trained animal after a few days, a week, a month, or longer. Compare the record with the original test.[25, 29, 30]

Does age affect problem-solving ability? Do young animals remember how to solve a maze better than older animals?

SHAPE RECOGNITION. Advanced students can demonstrate animals' intelligence by showing that a rat or other small rodent can learn to discriminate between two shapes; for instance, a circle and a square.[25] Place a jumping stand (a square platform on a pedestal) a short distance in front of an upright stand that has a round window and a square one, with a platform behind them. Place a reward of food behind one of the openings. Training the animal to jump to its reward will require much patience and perseverance on the part of the experimenter.

EFFECTS OF HANDLING. Research has shown that animals that have been stroked and petted make fewer errors in a test situation and exhibit more activity and curiosity. Study the effects of extra handling on the ability of animals to learn a maze or on volitional activity.

IMPRINTING. Exposing a very young animal to a certain stimulus produces a continuing preference and attraction to that stimulus. For instance, rats raised with piped-in music of Mozart will continue to prefer that music. The persistence of a preference after exposure during a critical period of development is called *imprinting*. Experiments of imprinting help to explain some adult behavior patterns in animals, including man.

Your students may want to repeat Cross's experiments, in which three groups of rats were raised under different conditions.[31] One group was housed for 52 successive days in a chamber in which music by Mozart was played. Another group lived in a similar enclosure for the same period of time, but they listened exclusively to music by Shoenberg. The third group lived similarly but were deprived of music. (Other types of music may be substituted.) After 52 days, the music was turned off for 15 days. Then, the rats were tested for their musical preference. The animals were placed in a specially constructed enclosure with a floor hinged at the center. The body weight of the animal was enough to lower either side of the floor. Lowering one side activated a microswitch that would turn on Mozart, the other side provided Schoenberg. The rats raised with Mozart chose to live with his music again; those raised with Schoenberg selected Schoenberg.

REFERENCES

1. *Suggestions for Experiments Involving Animals at the Pre-University Level*. Canadian Council on Animal Care, 151 Slater St., Ottawa, Ontario, K1P 5H3, Canada.

2. Norris, M. L. and C. E. Adams. 1972. The Growth of the Mongolian gerbil, *Meriones unguiculatus*, from birth to maturity, *J. Zool.* (Proc. Zool. Soc. Lond.) 166:277–82.

3. Hamilton, J. B. and A. E. Light. 1951. The Growth, Replacement, and Types of Hair. *Ann. N. Y. Acad. Sci.* 53:461–754. p. 493 *et seq.* (Advanced)

4. Berman, W. 1968. *Beginning Biochemistry*. Sentinal Books Publishers, New York.

5. Dunn, A. and J. Arditti. 1969. *Experimental Animal Physiology*. Holt, Rinehart & Winston, New York 10017. a. pp. 23–27, liver homogenates; b. pp. 54–55, glucose transport.

6. Hake, J. C., J. J. W. Baker and G. E. Allen. 1971. Survey of Rat Organs for Alkaline Phosphatase Activity. *Twelve Problems in Biology: Open-Ended Experiments for Introductory College Biology*. Addison-Wesley Publishing Co., Reading, Mass. pp. 65–66, 75–80. (Advanced)

7. Kimbrough, T. D. and G. C. Llewellyn. 1972. A Simplified System for Studying Digestive Function and Responses. *Amer. Biol. Teacher* 34(3):138–42.

8. Callahan, P. 1970. *Insect Behavior.* Four Winds Press, New York. pp. 132–33.

9. Davis, H. T. 1969. *Projects in Biology*. Science Publications, Normal, Ill. 61761. pp. 80–83.

10. Wallace, M. E. *Using Mice for Teaching Genetics.* Reprint. Available from Assoc. Science Education, College Lane, Hatfield, Herts., England.

11. Stokes, A. W., ed. 1968. *Animal Behavior in Laboratory and Field.* W. H. Freeman & Co., San Francisco 94104. (Advanced)
    a. Brubaker, L. L. Wall-Seeking Behavior in Mice. pp. 39–43. Available from the publisher as Separate No. 804.
    b. Calhoun, W. H. The Observation and Comparison of Behavior. pp. 7–10. Separate No. 797.
    c. Marler, P. The Analysis of Behavior. pp. 3–5. Separate No. 796.
    d. McGill, T. E. Sexual Behavior in Male Mice. pp. 141–43. Separate No. 827.
    e. Thiessen, D. D. and G. Lindzey. Negative Geotaxis among Inbred Strains of Mice. pp. 45–48. Separate No. 805.

12. Barfield, M. A. and E. A. Beeman. 1968. The Oestrus Cycle in the Mongolian Gerbil, *Meriones unguiculatus. J. Reprod. and Fert.* 17:147–51. (Advanced)

13. Mandl, A. M. 1951. The Phases of the Oestrus Cycle in the Adult White Rat. *J. Exp. Biol.* 28:576–84. (Advanced)

14. Grove, R. F. 1971. A Note on the Observation of Tests as an Aid to Early Sexing of Mice. *J. Inst. Anim. Tech.* 22(2):93–95.

15. Hediger, H. 1969. *The Psychology and Behaviour of Animals in Zoos and Circuses.* Dover Publications, New York.

16. ———. 1950. *Wild Animals in Captivity.* Dover Publications, New York.

17. LOCKARD, R. B. 1968. The Albino Rat: A Defensible Choice or a Bad Habit? *Amer. Psych.* 23(10):734–42.

18. PARKES, A. S. 1926. Studies on the Sex-Ratio and Related Phenomena. 9. Observations on fertility and sex-ratio in mice, 1922–5. *Brit. J. Exp. Biol.* 4(1):93–104.

19. PARKES, A. S. and H. M. BRUCE. 1961. Olfactory Stimuli in Mammalian Reproduction. *Science* 134:1049–54.

20. BRUCE, H. M. 1969. A Block to Pregnancy in the Mouse Caused by Proximity of Strange Males. *J. Reprod. and Fert.* 1:96–103. (Advanced)

21. BRUCE, H. M. 1969. An Exteroceptive Block to Pregnancy in the Mouse. *Nature* 184:105. (Advanced)

22. VANDENBERGH, J. G., L. C. DRICKAMER and D. R. COLBY. 1972. Social and Dietary Factors in the Sexual Maturation of Female Mice. *J. Reprod. Fert.* 28:397–405. (Advanced)

23. *Activity Wheels—Teacher's Guide for Animal Activity.* 1969. Elementary Science Study. Webster Div., McGraw-Hill Book Co., New York 10017.

24. WESTLING, B. 1971. The Study of Animal Activity. *School Sci. and Math.* 629(6):473–78.

25. HAINSWORTH, M. D. 1967. *Experiments in Animal Behaviour.* Houghton-Mifflin Co., Boston 02107. p. 162–72.

26. BINDRA, D. and N. SPINNER. 1958. Response to Different Degrees of Novelty: The Incidence of Various Activities. *J. Exp. Anal. Behav.* 1:341–50.

27. THIESSEN, D. D. 1970. The Genetic Determination of Behavior. *The Sci. Teacher* 37(4):53–54.

28. PRINGLE, L., ed. 1970. *Discovering Nature Indoors: A Nature and Science Guide to Investigation with Small Animals.* First Ed. Natural History Press, Doubleday & Co., Garden City, N. Y. 11530. pp. 109–12.

29. *Humane Biology Projects.* First Ed. The Animal Welfare Institute, P.O. Box 3650, Washington, D.C. 20007. pp. 18–20.

30. SIMON, S. 1968. *Animals in Field and Laboratory: Science Projects in Animal Behavior.* McGraw-Hill Book Co., New York 10017. pp. 110–14.

31. CROSS, H. A., A. HOLCOMB and C. G. MATTER. 1967. Imprinting or Exposure to Learning in Rats Given Early Auditory Stimulation. *Psychonomic Science* 7:233–34. (Advanced)

FILMS

Estrus Cycle of the Rat (includes how to make vaginal smears). Film loop, super 8 mm, silent, 3 min. 35 sec.; or 16 mm, sound, color, 2 min. 30 sec. A Thorne film. Scott Education, 2385 Lower Westfield Road, Holyoke, Mass 01040.

Foods and Nutrition. 16 mm, b/w, 11 min. Encyclopaedia Britannica Educational Corp., 425 N. Michigan Ave., Chicago, Ill 60611.

Handling Laboratory Animals—The Hamster; and *Handling Laboratory Animals—The Rat.* (Includes how to determine sex.) Super 8 mm, cartridge, silent, color, 3 min. Encyclopaedia Britannica Educational Corp., 425 N. Michigan Ave., Chicago, Ill 60611.

Measuring Oxygen Consumption (in small mammals). Film loop, super 8 mm, color, 4 min. 55 sec. A Thorne Film. NASCO, Ft. Atkinson, Wisc 53538. Also, in 16 mm, color, sound, 6 min. Available for rent from University of Colorado, Bureau of Educational Media, Stadium 348, Boulder, Colo 80302.

Temporal Patterns of Animal Activity. BSCS Single Topic Film. Harcourt Brace Javonovitch, New York.

Vitamins. 16 mm, b/w, sound, 14 min. Medical Motion Pictures, Merck, Sharpe & Dohme, West Point, Penn 19486. (No rental fee.)

Vitamins and Some Deficiency Diseases. 16 mm, color, 35 min. Film Library, Lederle Laboratories, Middletown Road, Pearl River, NY 10965. (No rental fee.)

Vitamins and Your Health. 16 mm, color, 20 min. Eli Lilly Co., P. O. Box 618, Indianapolis, Ind 46206. (No rental fee.)

17

Experiments with Humans

"...to call man 'an animal' is to endow him with a heritage so rich that his potentialities seem hardly less than when he was called the son of God."

Joseph Wood Krutch (1893–1970)

The study of man has much in common with the study of other members of the animal kingdom; the interrelationships and interdependence of man with other animals are inescapable. Although the conditions for physical well-being of human beings (nutrition, health, and so on) are well within the scope of high school biology teaching, they are beyond the scope of this book. A different format will be used for the animal, man; this chapter will consist entirely of suggestions for biological investigations using human beings as subjects.

Using humans as subjects for student investigations has many advantages over using other live animals. The studies often require a minimum of preparation and apparatus, and human subjects are always at hand. They can follow directions and respond verbally to provide data other mammals cannot. Is it not of more value for a student to learn as much as possible by direct study of himself?

Because of the enormous range of biological exercises using human beings as subjects, only a perfunctory coverage can be given in this section. Nevertheless, it is hoped that enough ideas and sources of further information have been presented to indicate the value and potential range of such projects.

"...people do not have to get hurt or in any way [be] demeaned or belittled in Human Physiology, nor in any branch of human inquiry for that matter. There are yet vast fields of inquiry to be searched where no one gets hurt and the investigator retains his full human-ness."

William McBlair

Select projects using human beings as subjects with care. No one should be hurt or embarrassed. Your guiding principle should be to avoid any risk that a prudent parent would not permit. The Association for Science Education in England recommends the following: The teacher should (1) know something about the medical history of the human subject, (2) consult parents if there are any doubts, (3) never press any demonstration to extremes, and (4) consult the school nurse when necessary.

No guidelines have yet been endorsed by any professional organization in the United States or Canada although the American Psychological Association is working on this. The author therefore proposes the following guidelines:

GUIDELINES FOR THE USE OF HUMAN PARTICIPANTS IN EXPERIMENTS CONDUCTED BY HIGH SCHOOL STUDENTS

(1) **All student projects must be meaningfully supervised by a qualified adult.**

After consulting the relevant literature, the student shall write a detailed plan for the proposed project which includes a description of how the rights of the human participants will be protected. This plan shall be approved by a qualified adult supervisor and the school authorities prior to the commencement of experimental work. The supervisor shall meaningfully oversee the conduct of the experiment until its conclusion.

(2) **Procedures must not harm participants physically or mentally.**

High school students shall undertake no procedures involving human participants that could result in physical or mental harm to the participant. These include, among others, procedures involving physical pain (such as electric shock), undue physical stress (such as overexertion), administration of harmful substances (such as drugs), the induction of anxiety or embarrassment, the use of any deception, or even the mildest threat to the participant. Research areas in which some topics could cause mental distress include, but are not limited to, sex, religion, family relations, questions of paternity, physical appearance (body weight, height, skin appearance, attractiveness, etc.), achievement level, and peer acceptance. As a general rule, experimental projects in these areas by high school students should be avoided.

(3) **Agreement to participate must be obtained from all participants.**
The individual conducting the project (the experimenter), must obtain each participant's agreement to participate, based on a full understanding of what that agreement implies. Obtaining agreement involves providing a full explanation of the experimental procedures with special emphasis on aspects of the project likely to affect willingness to participate. All questions asked by any prospective participant must be answered. Even though the procedure will involve no harm, nevertheless, participants who are too young or for other reasons cannot comprehend the project should be excluded, or consent should be obtained from their parents or guardians. A clear and fair agreement must exist between the experimenter and the participant that clarifies the responsibilities of both. All promises and commitments included in that agreement must be honored by the experimenter.

(4) **Participants must have the right to refuse to participate.**
Potential research participants have the right to refuse to participate and the right to withdraw from participation at any time during the course of the experimental procedures. The person conducting the project must explain this right to all potential participants prior to the commencement of the experiment.
Protection of this right requires special vigilance when the experimenter is in a position of influence (such as being in a higher grade) over the participant. Persons who decline to participate in a particular experiment should not be publicly identified. Under no circumstances should potential participants be pressured.

(5) **Undesirable consequences must be removed.**
In the event that a project does result in any unanticipated undesirable consequences for a participant or any other person, the experimenter has the responsibility to detect and remove these consequences and to halt the project if it is still in progress.

(6) **The anonymity of the information gathered must be preserved.**
In certain projects, a participant may not wish the experimenter to disclose the results of the study in a way that individually identifies that participant. This can be achieved simply by not writing down the participant's name when data is being collected. Only with the participant's full agreement can the experimenter disclose identifiable information about that participant to any other individual.

The Special Senses

Classroom experiments on human vision, hearing, touch, and taste are highly practical. There are so many good student exercises to demonstrate function of the human eye that selection is difficult.

Figure 17-1. To determine eye dominance, the person sights a distant object through a hole in a card held at arm's length. The card is then brought slowly toward the face. At a certain point, the person becomes aware that only one eye is being used, and this is the dominant eye.

VISION. Most people have a pronounced eye preference, although few people know it or know which is their preferred eye. To determine eye dominance, the subject, using both eyes, sights a distant object through a 2.5 cm hole in the center of a cardboard sheet which is held at arm's length. (See Figure 17–1.) The subject must hold the card with both hands. Keeping the distant object sighted, the subject gradually moves the card up to the face until only one eye can be used.[2] Which eye was used? Is the same eye always used to keep the object in sight? Is the subject's dominant eye on the same side as the dominant hand? Is this true for others tested? Another way of demonstrating eye dominance is described by McBlair.[3a]

A study of depth perception can be made with a large sheet of white cardboard (60 × 90 cm) and a strip of black paper (about 1 × 30 cm).[4a] Prop the large cardboard sheet in front of the class several feet from the front of the room with the top several inches above the eye level of the subjects.

Trial 1. Hold the black paper 8 cm behind the white sheet with about 5 cm showing above it. Subjects are to judge and record the distance between the large card and the black strip under four conditions:

(a) using one eye, holding head still
(b) using one eye, moving head back and forth
(c) using both eyes, holding head still
(d) using both eyes, moving head back and forth

Trial 2. Repeat the above procedure with the strip 30 cm from the card.

Trial 3. Repeat at 15 cm.

Trial 4. Repeat at 2.5 cm

Next, repeat Trials 1 through 4 using a pencil instead of the strip of black paper. Hold the pencil so that 5 cm of it show above the card, and use the same distances, but change their order.

Have all the subjects record their judgments (16 for the black strip and 16 for the pencil trials). After the trials are completed, tell the subjects the actual distances and ask them to compute their errors. The average error for the whole class can also be computed. Which condition produced the poorest judgments? Which produced the best? What depth cues were available to the subjects under each of the viewing conditions? Were there any differences between the accuracies of the judgments for the black card and for the pencil? Why? Another experiment on depth perception is described in Gregg.[2]

Other high school experiments on human vision can be found in the references, including experiments on locating the blind spot, optical illusion, after-images, and color perception, as well as instructions for measuring chromatic fields, size of the pupil aperature and fields of vision, and studies of eye accommodation, visual accuity, dark adaptation, eye movements, and subject color mixing.[2-9] (See FILMS, *Demonstrations in Perception,* and *The Eyes and Seeing,* page 340.)

HEARING. Determine accuracy in locating sounds by blindfolding a subject and clinking two coins together (or use a snapper "cricket") at varying points approximately 1 meter from the subject's head. Ask the subject to point in the direction s/he thinks the sound is coming from.[4b] Record a score of correct or incorrect for 30 trials on each subject. Do individuals vary in their ability to locate the sound? Can training improve this ability? Do musically talented students, who have learned to listen carefully to sounds, score better than average in this test? Block one of the subject's ears with a plug and repeat the tests. Are sounds located more accurately with both ears than with one? (See FILMS, *The Ears and Hearing,* page 340.) Would you predict that, for people with hearing impairment, two hearing aids would be more beneficial than the more commonly used monaural aids?

TOUCH. Adaptation to touch can be tested by having the subject close her/his eyes and place her/his hands on a table, palms down with fingers spread. Place small corks on the top of one finger between the fingernail and the first joint. Have the subject report when the first

Figure 17-2. The blindfolded subject points in the direction from which she thinks sound is coming. Another student records the number of correct and incorrect answers made.

sensation of touch is felt and the instant the sensation stops. With a stopwatch, measure this duration of sensation. Subjects may report that the cork has been removed, although it is left in place throughout the test. Make five trials. Compare the subject's response to testing of the index finger with the sensations of the little finger or forearm. Is it important that the body be able to adapt to light touch sensations?

What are the limits of man's ability to judge whether two objects are of different weights? Mark one 125 ml Erlenmeyer flask "Test" and another "Control" and fill each with 50 gm water (1 gm = 1 ml). Have a subject hold one of the flasks by the neck in each hand—with eyes closed. Ask the subject if the weights are equal. Then take the flasks from the subject's hands and add 2 ml of water to the "Test" flask and hand the flasks back to the subject. Do this several times, randomly mixing right and left, and each time ask the subject to determine if one of the flasks is heavier. When the subject reports that the test flask feels just perceptively heavier, record the volume of water added. The difference in weight between the test flask and the control flask at this point is the "difference threshold" for 50 gm. Repeat this procedure starting with 100, 200, and 500 gm of water, using larger flasks when necessary. How fine a discrimination can be made in judging weights? Does the difference threshold vary according to the initial weights used? Make a graph plotting the difference threshold against the weight of the control flask. Do the results vary from person to person?

If two touch points are close enough together, they are perceived as a single sensation. Determine how far apart two points must be before they are perceived as two distinct sensations. The ability to perceive two points varies from one part of the body to another according to how sensitive the skin area is (how many nerve endings supply that region). The subject's eyes must be closed while the experimenter sets the points of a compass (or dividers) 10 mm apart and touches them to the skin on the back of the subject's hand, repeating for five trials.[3b, 4c] Each time, ask whether the subject senses two points or one; record the subject's response. Then set the compass for 9 mm and take five more

Figure 17-3. The subject, in center, with eyes closed, holds two flasks of water, a test and a control flask, and judges which is the heavier. Another student, at right, has just added 2 ml of water to the test flask. Throughout the experiment, the volume of water in the "control" flask remains unchanged. Successive 2 ml volumes are added to the test flask until a difference in weight is perceived. The recording student, at left, writes down the responses.

Figure 17-4. The subject, in the center, has his eyes closed and has to say when he can feel two distinct points and when he can feel only one. The experimenter, at left, repeatedly changes the distance between the two points of the calipers before touching the subject's palm. The recorder, at right, writes down the responses.

readings. Continue the experiment, reducing the distance between the two points in steps of 1 mm, until the subject reports that, in three out of five trials for a particular setting, the sensation perceived is a single point. Run a descending and an ascending sequence of distances. Also test other areas such as the forearm, back of neck, and face near the lips. Arrange the areas in decreasing fineness of discrimination for each subject tested. Is this order always the same? Are individuals alike in their thresholds for any one area?

TASTE. Apply a drop of Epsom salt (magnesium sulphate) solution to the tip or edges of the subject's tongue, and then test the taste when applied far back on the tongue. Ask the subject to describe the different sensations. Soak cotton-tipped sticks in various solutions (0.1% quinine sulphate, 5% sugar, 10% common salt [sodium chloride], and 1% acetic acid [vinegar]). Apply each, in turn, to different regions of the tongue (sides, tip and front third, middle third, and back third). After each test, have the subject rinse the mouth with distilled water and dry the tongue with gauze. On a diagram of the tongue, map the regions in which sensations of bitter, sweet, salty, and sour are registered, using different symbols (circle, square, triangle and cross) for each primary taste.[10a]

Repeat the trials, placing a piece of ice or a hot solution on the subject's tongue just before applying each test solution. Ask students to map the taste areas for several members of their families. Are there similarities? Compare these results with tests on several nonrelated persons.

How low a concentration of common salt (NaCl), sugar, saccharine, or acetic acid can be detected by human taste? Do the results comport with those of the scientist who found that subjects could distinguish between as weak a solution as 0.009 M NaCl and distilled water with 100 percent accuracy, if the solutions were boiled and cooled to the same temperature prior to testing.

Demonstrate that sugar can cancel out the taste of salt. To do this, place two teaspoonsful of salt and an equal volume of water into each of six beakers. Add ¼ teaspoon of sugar to one beaker, ½ teaspoon to another, 1 teaspoon to another, and so on. Ask a group of people to taste the mixtures and determine at which point no salt taste is discernable, that is, the point at which the sugar cancels out the salt taste. Is this the same for everyone tested? Do the results vary according to the ages of the subjects? Are the taste buds of a five-year-old child as well developed as those of a young adult? Analyze the results statistically to show the range of response (standard error) in each age group and any differences that exist between age groups.

Another project relating taste to pH is described in the USDA pamphlet *What Makes an Apple Sour?*[11]

SMELL. In several vials, put various substances, such as oil of cloves, peppermint, alcohol, and tincture of camphor. Have your subject close the eyes; then ask the subject to identify the smells of the various vials held, one by one, close to the subject's nose. When this is completed, have the subject block off one nostril and smell the tincture of camphor again until the odor can no longer be detected. Then, using the same nostril, immediately retest the subject's ability to distinguish between oil of cloves and peppermint. Record the results. Repeat the experiment using alcohol instead of camphor.

Properties of Skin and Hair

Make microscopic preparations of human hair, skin scrapings, and cells from the lining of the mouth to demonstrate the cellular properties of these tissues.

Use powdered charcoal to make fingerprints and compare the patterns of different subjects.

Figure 17-5. To determine sweat gland activity, the subject's hand is painted with 1 percent iodine solution. When it is dry, a one-inch square of bond paper is held in close contact with the painted area for thirty seconds. Small blue dots appear on the paper wherever there was an active sweat gland.

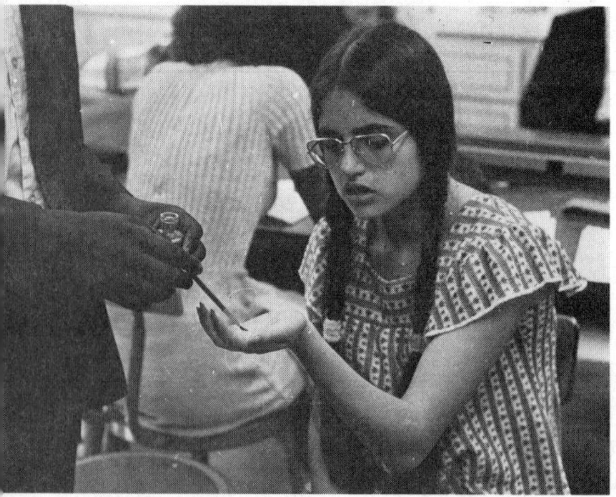

Record variations in electrical resistance of human skin with physical activity.[12]

Map sweat glands on the palm of a subject's hand by painting a 2 cm square with 1 percent iodine solution. Allow it to dry completely. Then hold a 2.5 cm square of bond paper on it for 30 seconds, while the subject rests quietly. Remove the paper and record the number of bluish dots in one square centimeter.[3c] Each bluish dot represents one active sweat gland. Repeat on the palm of the other hand, sole of the foot, back of neck, and underarm. Make this test after the subject has performed light exercise and after the subject has been in a cold room. What conclusions can be drawn regarding the distribution and activity of sweat glands?

Determine at what temperature the forearm hair stands on end.

Study the various types of hair found on a single individual and on different individuals. Compare the diameters of hairs taken from different regions of the body. Are all head hairs from one individual about the same diameter?

What are the chemical changes involved in permanent waving and hair straightening processes?

Measure the rate of growth of head hair. Who can set the class record for fast-growing hair? Is there any sexual or seasonal variation in the rate of hair growth? What is the maximum length to which hair can grow? Does this differ for individuals? What are the patterns of baldness (loss of side hair, loss of top hair)? Is the pattern a family trait?

Skeletal and Muscular Systems

Compare the movements of various joints. What types of joints are there (hinge, ball and socket, gliding)? Which joints give the greatest range of movements? Make models of joints with levers and string to replicate the positions of human bones and muscles.

Have a subject swing a leg in a regular rhythm, and then tell the subject to swing it faster (increase the frequency). The natural tendency is to swing it farther (increase the amplitude) instead, until you point out that this is not what was requested. Does it require greater effort to change the frequency of swing than it does to change the amplitude? Is this effort an indication of the amount of work done?

Study the arches of feet either by making water prints or, for more permanent records, by stepping into powdered charcoal and then onto a sheet of paper. What are the variations in footprints? Do members of the same family tend to have arches of the same shape? Try to obtain a series of footprints over a period of months of someone who is taking remedial treatment for fallen arches. Does this record show any beneficial effects from the treatment? What exercises improve the muscles of the feet?

Muscle fatigue can be tested by continuously opening and closing your hand rapidly and forcefully. Record the number of times this can be done in 20 seconds. Repeat this exercise ten times and record the number of closures per trial. Graph the results by plotting the number of closures against the number of trials. To demonstrate the importance of good blood circulation for muscular activity, repeat this experiment with a tourniquet on the arm to slow down the venous return.

Circulatory System

The rate of heartbeat is an important health sign. Understanding the range of normal heart rate permits recognition of abnormal rates. Determine the heart rate for many individuals, making several determinations for each subject. Take each subject's pulse either in the wrist or in the carotid artery in the neck. Plot the distribution curve by graphing the number of individuals tested on the vertical axis against their heartbeat rates on the horizontal axis.[13] Determine the standard deviation and make other statistical analyses if the sample is large enough.

Make microscopic preparations of blood (See FILMS, *Staining and Observing Blood Cells,* and *Studying Blood: Smear and Stain Techniques,* page 340). Identify the different types of blood cells. Count the number of red blood cells. Make other preparations stained with methylene blue and count the number of white cells. Measure blood pressure, heart and respiration rates of subjects before and after light exercise. (See FILMS, *Blood Pressure Readings,* page 340.) Persons not permitted to participate in ordinary physical education activities should not be subjects for this experiment.

A unique way of obtaining white blood cells is from the mouth. When the mouth is rinsed with a harmless saline solution, leukocytes can be removed easily.[14a] These can be stained and studied microscopically.

Digestive System and Nutrition

Ask a local dentist to save all the teeth he extracts until a full set is acquired. Alternatively, collect "milk" teeth as they fall out from younger members of the family, carefully recording the position from which each tooth came. Store the teeth in 95 percent alcohol or strong formalin to kill harmful germs. Then clean them by brushing well in hydrogen peroxide and mount them in correct sequence and position. (An insect Riker Mount is excellent for this purpose.) Study the anatomy of the mouth and relate the variations in structure of the different types of teeth with their various functions. What are the differences between "milk" and permanent teeth? When do permanent teeth erupt?

Make charts of teeth, tooth decay, and fillings for several members of a family. Do parents with a substantial amount of tooth decay tend to have children with the same problem?

Compare cultures of bacteria taken from the mouths of several persons.

On which side of their mouths do most people chew their food? Or do they use both sides or their mouths? If a person uses mainly one side, is this the same side that is preferred for hand, foot, and eye use?

To demonstrate the process of digestion involving the chemical conversion of starch into sugar by enzyme action, mix saliva with cooked starch solution and test it for the presence of sugar. Initially, such tests (with Benedict's, Lugol's, or Fehling's solution) are negative; but as enzyme action proceeds, these tests become positive, and sugar is formed from the starch.[10b, 14b, 15]

Check the effect of temperature on these reactions to show that the normal human body temperature of 37°C (98.6°F) is optimal for enzyme activity.

Study dietary habits of students. How many students in a class eat special foods (diet foods, organic foods, for example) or take vitamins? Ask students to keep a detailed record of their eating habits and to assess the nutritive value of the food they eat.

Elicit reaction time, decision-making ability, and work ability of a group of students who have regularly omitted breakfast for four weeks; then have them eat a good breakfast and conduct a retest. (A simple standard test is the time taken to sort a deck of cards into suits and rank.) Or, compare simple and choice reaction times (page 332) before and after subjects have had a good breakfast. These tests could be conducted comparing the performance of students who regularly omit breakfast with those who regularly eat breakfast. Your results may agree with professional findings that made use of a variety of tests and showed that students who normally did not eat breakfast took longer to make decisions, had less neuromuscular control, and did less work.

PUBLIC HEALTH MEASURES. What laws regarding food protect the consumer's health? Currently, there are laws governing sanitation, food activities, distribution of free school lunches and other welfare measures, and many others. Determine the purposes of present laws and estimate their value and effectiveness in achieving adequate national standards of nutrition. Are additional laws needed?

Other suggestions for nutritional studies are found in Orlans.[16]

Excretory System

The composition of urine reflects the activity of the kidneys, and, to some extent, the type of diet. Some of the chemical analyses for waste products found in urine are quite simple to do. Tests should be made of specific gravity, pH, the presence of glucose, protein (albumin), and phosphates.[10c]

Microscopic examination of the precipitate from centrifuged urine will show the presence of cell debris (the remains of various body cells) and sometimes crystals of various salts. The chemical characteristics of urine from someone on a high protein or low salt diet could be compared with those from someone on a normal diet.

Nervous System

REACTION TIME. To demonstrate the time lag between stimulus and response (reaction time), the subject stands beside a chalkboard with measured distances marked on it and holds a ruler or meter stick between the thumb and index finger; s/he releases the grip, then, as quickly as possible, tries to grasp the ruler again. Measure the distance the stick travels before it is stopped. Several trials should be made. The average distance the stick travels is a measure of the reaction time. Conduct the test with objects of different weights. Compare the results with several subjects. Have subjects repeat the test after chilling their hands in iced water. What effects does this have on the results, and why?

To demonstrate a *simple* reaction time, have ten students line up in a single column and ask each person to place the left hand on the left shoulder of the person in front. Tell the subjects that each one will be tapped on the shoulder and that they are to respond as quickly as possible by tapping the person in front of each of them on the shoulder. Ask the first person to raise an arm so that it can be readily seen, and tell the first person to drop the arm when the subject's shoulder is tapped. Tap the left shoulder of the last person, and start a stopwatch, stopping it as soon as the first student drops the raised arm. After some practice runs, record the time for ten trials. Average the results and compute the mean time taken for each person to respond—simple reaction time.

To measure *choice* reaction time, have the subjects place both hands on the shoulders of the student next in line. This time ask them

Figure 17-6. Simple reaction time. The teacher has a stopwatch in his hand and will tap the shoulder of the last student in the row.

to respond by tapping the shoulder *opposite* the one on which they received the stimulus. Then, tap either shoulder of the last person in line, and record the time lapse until the first person again drops the raised arm. Make ten trials, varying the shoulder on which the initial stimulus is given, and compare the results with those obtained for simple reaction times. Which reaction time is faster? What are the neural explanations for the differences in the two situations? Give examples of increased efficiency in industrial or other work when a task has been organized to reduce the frequency of choice reaction times. Additional experiments on reaction time can be found in the references.[3d, 4d]

REFLEXES. Demonstrate various reflexes, such as (*a*) the knee jerk, by striking the tendon just below the kneecap as the subject sits with legs crossed; (*b*) sneezing, in response to tickling the lining of the nose with a thread; (*c*) the blink, in response to an object approaching or threatening to touch the eye; (*d*) the light reflex, the change in pupil size in a bright light; and (*e*) the cilio-spinal reflex of change in pupil size when the nape of the neck is pinched.

The blink reflex is useful for demonstrating conditioned responses, in which a subject learns to associate one stimulus with another. The blink is elicited by a puff of air directed at the eye. The subject is seated with an air tube taped to one cheek.[17] An experimenter, working behind the subject, puffs air by pressing the bulb, and another experimenter, facing the subject, notes the eye response. Do both eyes blink, or does just the one which receives the puff of air?

To change this simple reflex into a conditioned response, every time the puff of air is blown, sound a horn simultaneously from behind the subject. Do this 10 to 30 times in succession. Then blow the horn, but do not deliver the air. Does the subject blink? If not, repeat the experiment with more reinforcing trials (horn and air) until the subject does blink when the horn is blown, even though no air is delivered (unreinforced test). To measure the "durability" of the conditioned

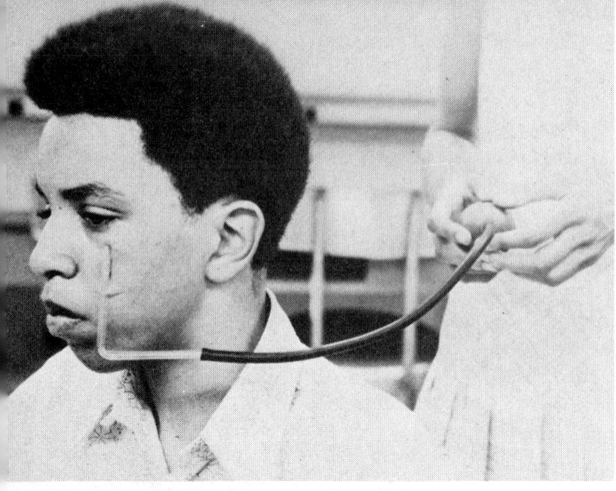

Figure 17-7. A rubber bulb, when pressed, delivers a small puff of air through a tube attached to the cheek of the subject. The eye will blink with each puff.

Figure 17-8. A bell is sounded simultaneously with a puff of air being applied to the subject's eye. After repeated trials, the subject learns to associate the puff of air with the sound of the bell. Eventually, he will respond by blinking his eye when only the bell is rung and no puff of air is delivered.

response, continue to use the horn only until the subject no longer blinks. Compare this durability in several subjects. Comparisons could also be made of the number of trials that were necessary to establish the conditioned response.

Behavior

SLEEP. Conduct a survey of people's sleep habits. Questions might include: How many hours do you sleep each night? Do you usually feel rested when you get up? How many hours of sleep do you think you need?

HUMAN ERROR. The following experiment tests a person's ability to observe accurately and demonstrates the fallibility of the human organism as a reliable measuring instrument. Have the entire class open their textbooks to a particular page and ask them to perform the simple task of counting the number of words on that page in a specified period of time. Instruct them that hyphenated words count as one, and the letter "a" counts as a word. Have them write their answers on a piece of paper and collect the results. Make a frequency distribution graph of the responses. Usually, there is an enormous range of responses.

INFLUENCING OTHERS. To find out whether a person is influenced by what others say, instruct three assistants ahead of time to give certain answers to a question. Bring in a fourth person (the subject) and ask that person to judge the distance a light moves (use a flashlight beam in a dark room). If the three assistants answer first and give high answers (for instance, 4, 5, and 6 m), the subject is more likely to answer in this range too. If the assistants give low estimates (1 or 2 m), once again, the subject's answer is likely to conform to these answers. What are the limits of this suggestibility? If the assistants give answers which are far removed from the truth, does the subject then reject their influence?

Another approach is to study commercial advertising. How effective are advertisements in influencing potential buyers? Conduct a survey to determine students' ractions to TV advertisements in the following categories: soaps and cleaners, antismoking, deodorants and cosmetics, drugs and patent medicines, soft drinks, automobiles, or others. What are the reasons for liking or disliking advertisements (funny, beautiful, interesting, clever or dull, fake, insulting to one's intelligence, bad taste, and so on)? Collect information to assess whether bad advertising stops people from buying those goods.

MEMORY. Which is easiest to memorize: a series of letters, of digits, or a mixture of letters and digits? Test your subjects by reading a list of increasingly larger numbers—asking the subject to repeat each list after you read it. For instance, start off with a short number like 253, and ask the subject to repeat it; then say 7490, and continue the test—making each digit list longer. Record the number of errors made on each trial. Repeat the test with letters instead of numbers. Then determine the errors made when a mixture of letters and numbers is given. Which series results in the least errors? Test many subjects to determine which series most people find easiest to remember.

This test of short term memory has practical application—in dialing a long distance telephone number, it is now necessary to remember ten digits in correct sequence. Although most telephone numbers in the United States are all digits, in England and other countries, long distance dialing schemes use a mixture of letters and digits. Also, US postal zip codes contain only digits, but in Canada, a mixture of letters and digits is used. Based on the results of your experiment, which system would you say is more practical?

For detailed instructions on administering memory tests, see DeBold.[18]

LEARNING. Measure, with a stopwatch, the time it takes for a subject to assemble a small jigsaw puzzle which has been presented in separate, well-mixed pieces. Repeat the test several times until the subject can do it easily. Time each trial. At what point did the subject learn to solve the puzzle? How many trials are necessary before it is possible to complete the puzzle twice in a row without errors? Plot the learning curve on a graph—the number of minutes to complete the puzzle against the

Figure 17-9. Two finger mazes.

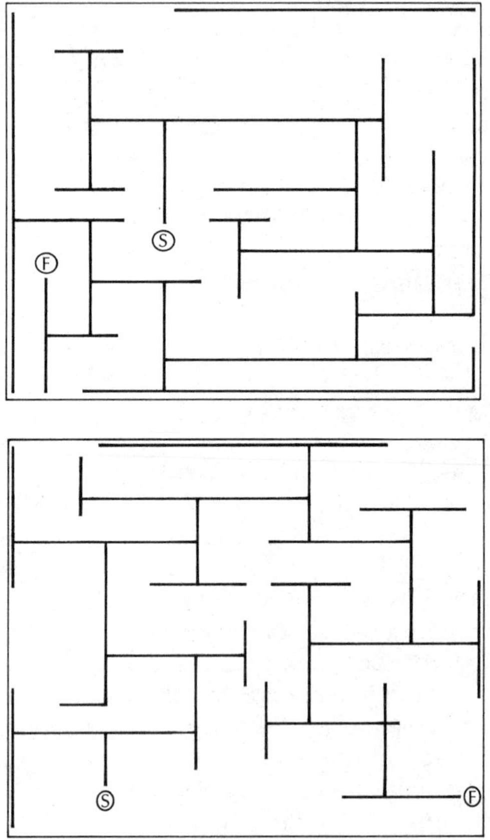

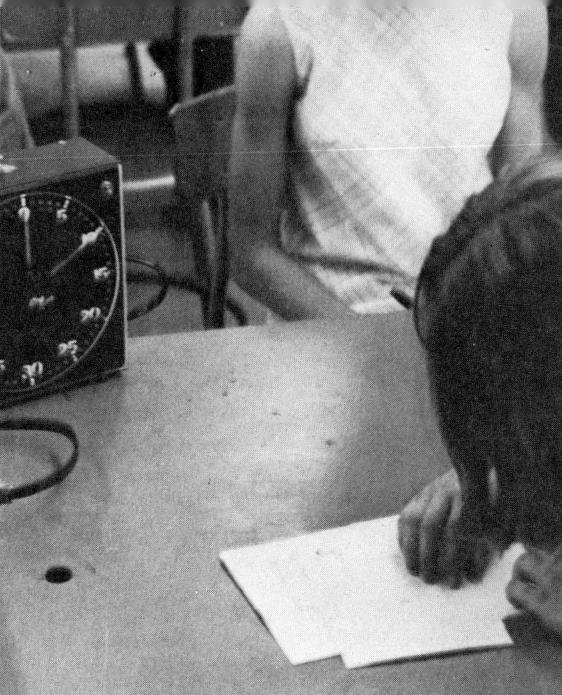

Figure 17-10. The subject is being timed to see how long she takes to complete the finger maze.

number of trials, in sequence. Compare the results of several subjects. Is the learning time improved if rewards are offered? Do all learning curves have the same general shape?

Another learning curve can be determined by using a finger maze. All you need is a card with a 6 mm hole punched in the middle, to act as a shield for the maze, and a stopwatch. Place the card over the maze so the start (marked S) shows through the hole. Instruct the subject that on the word "go," the card must be moved so the maze pathway shows through the hole in the card. If an incorrect path is chosen, the subject must retrace the path and find the correct one instead. If the correct path is chosen, the subject will finally arrive at the end of the maze (marked *F* for finish). Record the time in seconds that the subject takes to complete the maze for each of ten trials.[4e] Continue the tests with maze *A* until the subject completes two errorless trials.

Now have your subject learn another maze (maze *B*.) Then ask the subject to return to maze *A* and learn it again. Does it take more or fewer trials to relearn maze *A* the second time? Other finger mazes are described in Smith.[19]

Instructions for many other experiments on learning and motivation are described in the references.[4]

EFFECTS OF BACKGROUND MUSIC. What are the effects of background music on a student's performance? Ask a subject to perform a set task (sort a deck of cards into suits and rank, or solve arithmetic problems), with and without background music. Compare the results.[20]

Try to assess people's attitudes toward background music by asking every tenth person leaving a public place (restaurant, store, for instance) where background music has been playing, if they liked the music. Repeat the survey in a similar place without background music and ask the subjects if they would have preferred background music. Unless both situations are investigated, misleading results can be obtained.

In class, ask two groups of students to work a set of arithmetic problems. Try to assemble groups of equally proficient students, give them the same problems to work, and provide identical environments. Show one group a chart indicating that student performance is better with background music and show the other group a chart indicating the opposite. Compare the performance of the two groups.

Growth

Collect data on children of different ages and correlate age with height, body weight, length of feet, length of fingers, diameter of head, distance between the eyes, and so on. If enough data is obtained, make graphs plotting the ages of the subjects against the measured characteristic. This represents a normal growth curve. Does the growth curve of each characteristic "level out" at the same age?

Genetics

A survey of family members can be conducted to determine the incidence of inherited characteristics, such as the ability to roll the tongue up from the sides to the middle of the mouth. Construct a family tree showing which members possess the dominant gene (having the ability to roll the tongue) and which members lack it (not having this ability). Other inherited traits which can be studied are the presence of M and N blood types,[21] the ability to bend the thumb backwards (hitchhiker's thumb), the ability to taste PTC,[10d, 14c, 22a] the occurrence of free or attached ear lobes,[22b] or the presence or absence of a widow's peak (a hairline that extends to form a center point on the forehead).[10d, 22b] A good reference book which contains many detailed experiments concerning human genetics is called *Genetics Laboratory Investigations*.[23]

REFERENCES

1. *Biology Teaching in Schools Involving Experiment or Demonstration with Animals or with Pupils.* 1970. Ass'n for Science Education, College Lane, Hatfield, Herts., England.

2. Gregg, J. R. 1966. *Experiments in Visual Science: For Home and School.* Ronald Press Co., New York.

3. McBlair, W. 1965. *Experiments in Physiology.* National Press, Palo Alto, Cal. a. pp. 77–81; b. pp. 59–65; c. pp. 41–44; d. pp. 69–70.

4. Minihan, N. M. 1971. *Experiments on a Shoestring: A Handbook of Experiments and Demonstrations for General Psychology.* University of Illinois, Urbana 61801. a. pp. 15–27; b. pp. 14–15; c. p. 10; d. pp. 4–5; e. p. 49.

5. Davis, H. T. 1969. *Projects in Biology.* Science Publications, Normal Ill. 61761. pp. 146–49.

6. Beeler, N. F. and F. M. Branley. 1951. *Experiments in Optical Illusion.* Thomas Y. Crowell, New York. (Intermediate)

7. Brindley, G. S. 1963. Afterimages. *Sci. Amer.* 209(4):84–90. Separate No. 1089. W. H. Freeman & Co., 660 Market St., San Francisco, Cal. 94104.

8. Day. R. H. 1972. Visual Spatial Illusion: A General Explanation. *Science* 175:1335–40.

9. Land, E. 1959. Experiments in Color Vision. *Sci. Amer.* 200(5):84–101. Separate No. 223. W. H. Freeman & Co., 660 Market St., San Francisco, Cal. 94104.

10. Green, E. R. and K. Bobrowsky. 1968. *Laboratory Investigations in Biology.* Silver Burdett Co., Morristown, N. J. a. pp. 213–16; b. pp. 87–90; c. pp. 131–34; d. pp. 207–12.

11. *What Makes an Apple Sour?* USDA Educational Services, Agricultural Research Service, Beltsville, Md. 20705.

12. Edelberg, R. 1976. The Variation in Electrical Resistance of the Human Skin with Physical Activity. *Research Problems in Biology,* Series 3. Second Ed. BSCS, Oxford University Press, New York. pp. 45–48.

13. Hake, J. C., J. J. W. Baker and G. E. Allen. 1971. *Twelve Problems in Biology: Open-Ended Experiments for Introductory College Biology.* Addison-Wesley Publishing Co., Reading, Mass. pp. 1–6. (Advanced)

14. Stiles, K. A. and R. D. Burns. 1972. *Laboratory Explorations in General Zoology.* 5th ed. Macmillan Co., New York. a. pp. 299–301; b. pp. 274–77; c. pp. 335–36.

15. Chiddix, J. C. and E. Bailey. 1968. *General Science Projects.* Science Publications, Normal, Ill. pp. 117–18.

16. Orlans, F. B. 1970. Better Nutrition Studies. *Amer. Biol. Teacher* 32(8):484–86.

17. Vogel, S. and S. Wainwright. 1969. *A Functional Bestiary: Laboratory Studies about Living Systems.* Addison-Wesley Publishing Co., Reading, Mass. pp. 90–91.

18. DeBold, R. C. 1968. *Manual of Contemporary Experiments in Psychology.* Prentice-Hall, Englewood Cliffs, N.J. 07632. pp. 37–67.

19. Smith, M. L. 1973. Construction and Use of a Human Maze. *Amer. Biol. Teacher* 35(10):415–16.

20. Schlichting, H. E., Jr. and R. V. Brown. 1970. Effect of Background Music on Student Performance. *Amer. Biol. Teacher* 32(9):427–29.

21. Rife, D. C. 1970. A Laboratory Exercise in Human Heredity. *Amer. Biol. Teacher* 32(5):290–91.

22. Schonberger, C. F. 1972. *Laboratory Manual of General Biology*. 3rd ed. W. B. Saunders Co., Philadelphia, Pa. a. pp. 341–46; b. pp. 357–63.

23. Gardner, E. and Mertens, T. 1975. Sixth Ed. *Genetics Laboratory Investigations.* Burgess Publishing Co., Minneapolis, Minn.

FILMS

The Autonomic Nervous System. 16 mm, color, 18 mins. International Film Bureau, Inc., 332 S. Michigan Ave, Chicago, Ill 60604.

Blood Pressure Readings. 16 mm, color, sound, 30 min. National Medical Audio-visual Center Annex, Station K, Atlanta, Ga 30324.

Demonstrations in Perception. 16 mm, b/w, sound, 30 min. U.S. Navy Medical Film Library, Nat'l Naval Medical Center, Betheseda, Md 20014.

The Ears and Hearing. 16 mm, b/w, sound, 11 min. Encyclopaedia Britannica Educational Corp., 425 N. Michigan Ave., Chicago, Ill 60611.

The Eyes and Seeing. 16 mm, color, sound, 20 min. Encyclopaedia Britannica Education Corp., 425 N. Michigan Ave., Chicago, Ill 60611.

Have a Heart. 16 mm, color, 15 min. Pyramid Films, Box 1048, Santa Monica, Ca 90406.

The Heart and Circulatory System. 16 mm, b/w, 16 min. Encyclopaedia Britannica Educational Corp., 425 N. Michigan Ave, Chicago, Ill 60611.

The Skin as a Sense Organ. 16 mm, color, 14 min. International Film Bureau, Inc., 332 S. Michigan Ave, Chicago, Ill 60604.

Staining and Observing Blood Cells. Silver Burdett Co., 250 James St., Morristown, N.J. 07960.

Studying Blood: Smear and Stain Technique. Film loop, super 8 mm, cartridge, color or b/w, approx. 4 min. Holt Rinehart, and Winston, Inc., Box 3670, Grand Central Station, New York, New York 10017.

Appendix A*

PART I: USA STATE LAWS GOVERNING USE OF ANIMALS IN PUBLIC SCHOOLS AND TEACHING OF HUMANE EDUCATION**

Alabama 1960 Title 52, Section 546

20 minutes each week spent in humane education.

Course in humane education to be offered in teacher training institutions.

Monthly report of each school must state that this section has been complied with.

California 1973 section 1, article 2, chapter 5 of division 8 of the Education Code

Humane Treatment of Animals, 10401, states that "In the public elementary and high schools or in public elementary and high school-sponsored activities and classes held elsewhere than on school premises, live vertebrate animals shall not, as part of a scientific experiment or any purpose whatever:

(a) Be experimentally medicated or drugged in a manner to cause painful reactions or induce painful or lethal pathological conditions.

(b) Be injured through any other treatments, including, but not limited to, anesthetization or electric shock.

Live animals on the premises of a public elementary or high school shall be housed and cared for in a humane and safe manner.

The provisions of this section are not intended to prohibit or constrain vocational instruction in the normal practices of animal husbandry."

Also, *California 1951 1671, chapter 1750* requires that the State Department of Public Health shall inspect and register facilities where living animals are kept for educational purposes. Regulations include requirements for "satisfactory shelter, food, sanitation, record keeping, and for the humane treatment of animals. . ." In addition, *California 1943 Education Law 11152* states that the State Board of Education shall include in texts and teachers' manuals, materials

---

*Much of this information is derived from "Animals and Their Legal Rights," 2nd edition, 1970, published by the Animal Welfare Institute, Washington, D.C., to whom grateful acknowledgement is made for their permission to reprint.

**In addition, there are federal and state laws and some local ordinances which restrict the keeping of certain animals such as birds and large reptiles and which govern interstate shipping of mammals and insects. These laws are too many and varied to be listed individually but more information is given in appropriate chapters.

deemed necessary to encourage humane treatment of animals. Education Code, Section 7851, was amended in 1965 to include the following: "Each teacher shall endeavor to impress upon the minds of pupils. . . Kindness toward domestic pets and the humane treatment of living creatures. . . "

Connecticut 1960 Section 10–15

In the public schools shall be taught "instruction in the humane treatment and protection of animals and birds and their economic importance. . ."

Also, the Connecticut State Board of Education policy states that no vertebrate animal shall be "subjected to any experiment or procedure which interferes with its normal health or causes it pain or distress." (Series 1967–68, Circular Letter No. c–13, February 14, 1968. Connecticut State Board of Education, Hartford.)

Florida 231.09

Teach efficiently and faithfully, using books and materials required, the following prescribed courses of study: . . . kindness of animals. . . conservation of natural resources. . .

Georgia 1929 Title 32—1701–2

Public school instruction in bird, animal, fish, forest life, etc., not less than 25 minutes each week—kindness and humane treatment and conservation.

Illinois 1961 122 Section 27–13

In every public school—one half hour each week during whole of each term—teaching the pupil kindness and justice to and humane treatment of birds and animals and the part which they fulfill in the economy of nature.

Also, Illinois revised statutes, 1959, Chapter 122, Section 27–13 (upheld by 1965 legislature): No experiment upon any living animal for the purpose of demonstration in any study shall be made in any public school. No animal provided by or killed in the presence of any pupil of a public school shall be used for dissection in such school, and in no case shall dogs or cats be killed for such purposes. Dissection of dead animals shall be confined to the classroom and shall not be practiced in the presence of any pupil not engaged in the study to be illustrated thereby.

Indiana—Senate Concurrent Resolution No. 13, 1973.

The Senate of the General Assembly and with the House of Representatives concurring resolved that in order to "develop an understanding of life and science as well as to foster respect for life itself, and in the interests of education and scientific inquiry, we urge that all elementary and secondary schools and colleges and universities encourage controlled and humane treatment in the use of live animals."

Louisiana 1962 17.266

Kindness to Dumb Animals: Board of Education may take such steps as it may think necessary and wise to provide for the teaching of kindness in the public schools to dumb animals.

Massachusetts, Annotated Laws
Public Schools, Chapter 71

§33 Vivisection and Dissection Regulated; Penalty.—"No person shall in the presence of a pupil in any public school, practice vivisection, or exhibit a vivisected animal. Dissection of dead animals or any portions thereof in such schools shall be confined to the class room and to the presence of pupils engaged in the study to be promoted thereby, and shall in no case be punished by a fine of not less than ten nor more than fifty dollars." (1894, c. 151; R.L. 1902 c. 42§21)

Maine, 1975, H.P. 457—L.D. 561, Chapter 155

1. Use of animals in elementary schools. No school principal or headmaster shall allow any live vertebrate to be used in grades kindergarten through 8 of any public or private school as part of a scientific experiment or for any other purpose in which said vertebrates are experimentally medicated or drugged in a manner to cause painful reactions or to induce painful or lethal pathological conditions. No live vertebrate shall be used as part of a scientific experiment or for any other purpose in grades kindergarten through 8 in which said vertebrates are injured through any other type of treatment, including but not limited to anesthetization or electric shock. These provisions shall also apply to any activity associated with or sponsored by the school system.
2. Use of animals in secondary schools. No school principal or headmaster shall allow any live mammal, bird or chelonian, excepting bird eggs, to be used in any scientific experiment or for any other purpose in grades 9 through 12 in which said mammals, birds or chelonians are subjected to treatment and conditions prohibited in subsection I. These provisions shall also apply to any activity associated with or sponsored by the school system.
3. Treatment of animals in general, in grades kindergarten through 12. Live animals used as class pets or for purposes not prohibited in section 1055, subsections 1 and 2 in grades kindergarten through 12 shall be housed and cared for in a safe and humane manner. Said animals shall not remain in school over periods when such schools are not in session, unless adequate care is provided at all times.
4. Standards of treatment. Any animal, whose use is permitted under this section, shall be treated in accordance with a set of ethical and humane standards to be promulgated by the Commissioner of Agriculture, Division of Animal Welfare after the consultation with representative groups

in the State having an interest or expertise in the field of animal welfare, biology and education.

5. Enforcement. Enforcement shall be the responsibility of the Commissioner of Agriculture in consultation with the Commissioner of Education and Cultural Services.
6. Penalty for violation. Whoever violates this section shall be punished by a fine of not more than $75.

Also, *Maine Section 144 of Chapter 41:* All teachers in the public schools . . . devote . . . one-half hour of each week to teaching . . . the great principles of humanity as illustrated by kindness to birds and animals. . .

Michigan Act No. 241, P.A. 1947

Requires registration of facilities where animals are kept, inspection of these premises by the State Commissioner of Health, and that "all animal quarters shall be kept in a sanitary condition."

Also, *Michigan 1955 Section 365 Act 269* states that in every public school a portion of time shall be devoted to teaching the pupils thereof kindness and justice to and humane treatment and protection of animals and birds, and the important part they fulfill in the economy of nature.

North Dakota 1943 Sec. 15–3811

Oral instruction in the humane treatment of animals shall be given in each public school.

New Mexico 1953 Public School Laws 73–17–5

Humane Education courses.—Prescribing—

The state board of education shall prescribe and cause to be taught in the public schools in the state of New Mexico a course of humane education and such as in the opinion of said board of education and the superintendent of public instruction as will educate and train the pupils of said schools in the humane treatment of dumb animals and other subjects calculated to develop in the minds of the pupils a spirit of kindness, humanity and tolerance.

New Jersey 1957 Public School Laws 18:14—85.3

Instruction in Humanity

Each board of education may teach, by special courses or by emphasis in appropriate places of the curriculum in a manner adapted to the ages and capabilities of the pupils in the several grades and departments, the principles of humanity as the same apply to kindness and avoidance of cruelty to animals and birds, both wild and domesticated.

New York Education Law, Title 1, Section 809 1953

Weekly instruction in every elementary school in the humane treatment and protection of animals and birds and the importance of the part they play in the economy of nature. School district not entitled to public school money if instruction required is not given therein.

Oregon 1963 336.240

In the regular course of the elementary and secondary public schools, special emphasis shall be given to: . . . Kindness and justice to and humane treatment of animals.

The superintendent of Public Instruction shall prepare an outline with suggestions as in his judgment will best accomplish the purpose of this section, and shall incorporate the same in a course of study for all elementary and secondary schools of the state of Oregon.

Pennsylvania 1961 24 Section 15–1514

Instruction in humane education shall be given to all pupils up to and including 4th grade and need not exceed one-half an hour each week during the whole school term.

Also, *Pennsylvania Education Law* Title 24, Section 15–1514: No cruel experiment on any living creature shall be permitted in any public school in this Commonwealth.

South Dakota 1901 15–3109 (Repeated 1955)

Relating to the Humane Treatment of Animals.

10 minutes each week to be taught in all public schools.

Texas Article 2911 2783 Prescribed Studies. All Public Schools

Suitable instruction shall also be given in the primary grades regarding kindness to animals and the protection of birds and their nests and eggs.

Utah 1953 53–14–3 Bird Day To Be Observed With Lessons

It shall be the duty of the board of education of every school district to cause to be observed in the schools the last Friday in April of each year a Bird Day, with appropriate lessons and exercises relating to the observation, the study, and the value of birds and other forms of animal life, particularly as aids in the extermination of insects, weeds, and other pests.

Washington 1961 28.05.020

Education in Manners and Conduct

Not less than ten minutes each week shall be required to be devoted to the systematic teaching of kindness to all living creatures and particularly to domestic animals.

Also, Washington law, section 16.52.070: Every person who. . . deprives of necessary sustenance . . . or cruelly kills . . . any animal . . . shall be guilty of a misdemeanor.

Wisconsin 1957 40.46, #6.

Animal Life. Each public school teacher shall devote not less than 30 minutes a month to teaching pupil kindness to and the habits, usefulness and importance of animals and birds and the best methods of protecting, preserving and caring for all animal and bird life.

Wyoming 1957 Section 21–267

Humane Treatment of Animals to be Taught

There shall be taught in the public schools of Wyoming, in addition to the other branches of study now prescribed, a system of humane treatment of animals, as embodied in the laws of Wyoming; such instruction to consist of not less than two lessons of ten minutes each per week.

PART II: CANADIAN REGULATIONS GOVERNING USE OF ANIMALS AT THE PRE-UNIVERSITY LEVEL

by HARRY C. ROWSELL, D.V.M.

At the National Level:

Specific legislation governing the use of animals in research, testing and teaching at the national level in Canada is nonexistent. However, in the Criminal Code of Canada, as revised in 1970, section 402 covers cruelty to animals. Although this Criminal Code does not mention specifically the use of animals in education at the pre-university level, it is nevertheless a comprehensive statement respecting cruelty to animals. While it has never been applied to the pre-university use of animals, charges under this section of the Criminal Code could be laid against students who in the opinion of the Crown were causing unnecessary suffering and distress to animals in Science Fair projects. There have been instances where this section of the Criminal Code has been used as a threat, which has resulted in the stopping of the projects. In the majority of such instances, the project had been undertaken in ignorance of the consequences of the effects of the experimental manipulations on the animals.

Students sometimes include in their projects birds protected under the Migratory Birds Convention Act of Canada. This Act originally passed in 1916 is an Act respecting a convention between the Government of Canada and the United States of America for the Protection of Migratory Birds in Canada and the United States. Item 6 of this Act states "No person, without lawful excuse, the proof whereof shall lie on such person, shall buy, sell, or have in his possession any migratory game bird, migratory insectivorous bird, or migratory non-game bird, or the nest or egg of any such bird or any part of any such bird, nest or egg during the time when the capturing, killing or taking of such a bird, nest or egg is prohibited by this Act."

At the national level the Canadian Ministry of Environment has indicated a desire to introduce legislation concerning endangered species and exotic animals. All individuals contemplating using animals should ensure that the species which they contemplate using are not subject to any Federal or Provincial legislation.

At the Provincial Level

Education in Canada is a Provincial jurisdiction; therefore Federal legislation carefully omits any direct reference to matters pertaining to education. Therefore information concerning specific acts and regulations pertaining to the use of animals in schools should be directed towards the Ministry of Education in the specific Province for which the information is required.

In two Provinces legislation exists that is concerned with the use of animals in research and teaching. In 1966 in the Province of Alberta, section 50 of the Universities Act and subsequent regulations (which were amended by Alberta Regulations 333-72) cover housing, care and treatment of animals used for biological or medical purposes. Although directly applicable to universities, these regulations have been used as guidelines concerning the housing, care and treatment of animals used at the pre-university level.

In the Province of Ontario, the Animals for Research Act of 1970 and Regulations promulgated in 1971 apply to the use of animals in the school and in Science Fairs. Research under the Act is defined as "the use of animals in connection with studies, investigation and teaching in any field of knowledge, and, without limiting the generality of the foregoing, includes the use of animals for the performance of tests, diagnosis of disease and the production and testing of preparations intended for use in the diagnosis, prevention and treatment of any disease or conditions." Although the use of animals in schools or at the pre-university level is included in the coverage of the Act, schools and Science Fair sites are exempt from the requirement for registering as research facilities. All regional school boards in Ontario have been requested under the Act to form a regional school board animal care committee, one of whose members shall be a veterinarian. Proposed guidelines for the use of animals have been distributed to the respective school board animal care committees which are similar to those approved by the Canadian Council on Animal Care and the Youth Science Foundation of Canada. Details of these guidelines will be reviewed later. The regional school board animal care committee must approve of any projects involving animals ensuring that the guidelines and the requirements under the Act will be followed.

Canada-Wide Science Fairs

Up until 1968 the Science Fair movement in Canada had no guidelines concerning the care and use of experimental animals. In that year the Canadian

Council on Animal Care and the Youth Science Foundation working together with assistance from the Canadian Veterinary Medical Association established guidelines concerning the use of experimental animals at the pre-university level. Over the next three years the guiding principles were modified as experience was gained. Initially it was considered that in certain instances where fastidious techniques such as surgery, use of radioisotopes, anaesthetics, etc., a qualified supervisor must be obtained. However, it was the experience that students did *not* contact supervisors even when the names of such experts were given to them. The regulations were therefore modified to place stringent restrictions on the use of animals (see Regulations below).

The Animal Care Committee of the Youth Science Foundation (the sponsor of the Canada-wide Science Fair) meets on a regular basis to review the regulations concerning animal experimentation in Science Fairs. Because of this annual review, these regulations should not be interpreted as being in a fixed form.

Each Regional Science Fair affiliating with the Canada-wide Science Fair is responsible for compliance with these regulations. If a project arrives at the Canada-wide Science Fair and does not comply with the regulations, such a project is not allowed to be exhibited.

Regional Science Fairs may or may not have a Regional Science Fair Animal Care Committee to receive and approve projects involving animals. Previously such Regional Animal Care Committees were mandatory. But because the changes in the regulations in 1975-76 now place stringent restrictions on the use of animals, the Regional Animal Care Committees are not now as necessary as they once were. Nevertheless the presence of a Regional Animal Care Committee can serve as an important resource to ensure that regulations are enforced and to give advice and assistance to students wishing to use animals.

The student must sign a declaration which is conveniently placed on the back of the regulations for animal experimentation. This declaration states the student has read the regulations for animal experimentation in Science Fairs and understands them. It states that the project will follow these regulations and that the outline of the project will be available to judges, officials of the Science Fair, or the animal care inspectors in provinces where legislation governing the use of animals exists. The science teacher is required to sign a certification that the student made this declaration.

In Ontario the officers of the Veterinary Service Branch of the Ministry of Agriculture and Food of the Province of Ontario who enforce the Animals for Research Act will accept the declarations as evidence that the projects have been reviewed and fall within the requirements of the Act.

The Animal Care Committee of the Youth Science Foundation will pass judgement on any Science Fair project outline where animals are to be used, and where the Regional Science Fair Committee or the student questions whether or not the project complies with the regulations. In spite of the explicitness of the regulations, there remain a few students each year who wish to do studies that could cause pain in the animal and therefore do not comply with the regulations. However, the requirement to submit such experiments to the Animal Care Committee of the Youth Science Foundation has now ensured that such projects are not carried out.

Regulations for Animal Experimentation in Science Fairs

1. Biological experimentation is essential for an understanding of living processes. Such studies should lead to a respect for all living things. Capable students, anxious to pursue a career in biological sciences must receive the necessary encouragement and direction. *All aspects of the project must be within the comprehensions and capabilities of the student undertaking the study.*
2. Lower orders such as bacteria, fungi, protozoa and insects can reveal much basic biological information. If experiments are to be conducted on living subjects for Science Fair projects then only lower orders of life may be used.
3. *Vertebrate animals are not to be used in experiments for projects for Science Fairs,* with the following exceptions:
   A. Observations of normal living patterns of wild animals in the free living state or in zoological parks, gardens or aquaria.
   B. Observations of normal living patterns of pets, fish or domestic animals.
4. *No living vertebrate animal shall be displayed in exhibits in Science Fairs.*
5. Cells such as red blood cells, other tissue cells, plasma or serum purchased or acquired from biological supply houses or research facilities may be used in Science Fair projects.
6. Observational type studies on only chicken egg embryos may be used in Science Fair projects. If normal egg embryos are to be hatched, satisfactory humane considerations must be made for disposal of the chicks. If such arrangements cannot be made then the chicken embryos must be destroyed on the 19th day of incubation. No eggs capable of hatching may be exhibited in Science Fairs.
7. All experiments shall be carried out under the supervision of a competent science teacher. It shall be the responsibility of the qualified science teacher to ensure the student has the necessary comprehension for the study to be undertaken. Whenever possible specifically qualified experts* in the field shall be consulted.

*For information and names of qualified experts write to:

Canadian Council on Animal Care
151 Slater Street, Suite 1105
Ottawa, Ontario KlP 5H3

Youth Science Foundation
Animal Committee
151 Slater Street, Suite 302
Ottawa, Ontario KlP 5H3

Accepted by Regional Representatives, Canada-Wide Science Fair May 23, 1975.

Various Canadian Agencies Concerned with the Use of Animals in Animal Experimentation

Agricultural Institute of Canada,
Suite 907,
151 Slater St.,
Ottawa, Ontario
KIP 5H4

Canadian Council of 4H Clubs,
185 Somerset St., West,
Ottawa, Ontario
K2P 0J2

Canadian Federation of Biological Societies,
Honorary Secretary,
Dr. D.T. Armstrong,
Dept. of Physiology,
University of Western Ontario
London, Ontario
N6A 3K7

Canadian Federation of Humane Societies,
900 Pinecrest Rd.,
Ottawa, Ontario
K2B 6B3

Canadian Nature Federation,
46 Elgin St.,
Ottawa, Ontario
K1P 5K6

Canadian Teachers' Federation,
110 Argyle St.,
Ottawa, Ontario
K2P 1B4

Canadian Society of Animal Science,
Suite 907,
151 Slater St.,
Ottawa, Ontario
K1P 5H4

Canadian Association for Laboratory Animal Science,
84 Barrie St.,
Kingston, Ontario
K7L 3J8

Canadian Council on Animal Care,
151 Slater St.,
Suite 1105,
Ottawa, Ontario
K1P 5H3

Canadian Veterinary Medical Association,
360 Bronson Ave.,
Ottawa, Ontario
K1R 6J3

Youth Science Foundation,
151 Slater St.,
Suite 302,
Ottawa, Ontario
K1P 5H3

Canadian Society of Environmental Biologists,
Secretary, W.J. Thurlow,
P.O. Box 2292,
Station D,
Ottawa, Ontario
K1P 5K0

Canadian Society of Zoologists,
Secretary, Dr. J.E. Phillips,
Dept. of Zoology,
University of British Columbia,
Vancouver, B.C.

Appendix B

BIBLIOGRAPHY OF TEXTS DESCRIBING HUMANE EXPERIMENTS WITH LIVING ORGANISMS[†]

Listed in three categories as follows: a) Elementary (E), grade K–6, and Intermediate (I), grade 6–8; b) High School (H), grade 9–12; and c) Advanced High School (A), grade 12 and above.

Elementary (K–6) and Intermediate (Grade 6–8) Levels

* 1. *Insects in the Classroom,* John H. Borden and Brian D. Herrin, British Columbia Teachers' Federation, 105–2235 Burrard Street, Vancouver 180, British Columbia, 1972, 147 pp.(E, I)

* 2. *The Curious Mollusks,* Marie Jenkins, Holiday House, New York, 1972. (I)

* 3. *Animals in Field and Laboratory: Science Projects in Animal Behavior,* Seymour Simon, McGraw-Hill Book Company, New York, 1968. (I)

* 4. *Discovering Nature Indoors: A Nature and Science Guide to Investigations with Small Animals,* Ed., Laurence Pringle, The Natural History Press, Garden City, New York, 1970. (E, I)

* 5. *Can Invertebrates Learn?* Barbara Ford, Julian Messner, New York, 1972, 96 pp. (Gr. 5–6)

6. *Adventures with Insects,* Richard Headstrom, J. B. Lippincott Co., Philadelphia, 1963. (Gr. 4 up)

7. *Look What I Found,* Marshal T. Case, The Chatham Press, Inc., Riverside, Connecticut. Distributed by Viking Press, Inc., 625 Madison Avenue, New York 10022, 1971. (E)

8. *Teaching Science in an Outdoor Environment,* P. Gross, and E. P. Railton, University of California Press, Berkeley, 1972, 188 pp. (E)

9. *Experiments in Optical Illusion,* Nelson F. Beeler and Franklyn M. Branley, Thomas Y. Crowell Co., New York, 1951. (Gr. 5–9)

10. *Come with Me to the Edge of the Sea,* William Stephens. Julian Messner, New York, 1972, 80 pp. (Gr. 2–6)

---

†All experiments described in these texts comply with guidelines for the USA and Canada reprinted on pages 4–7.

*Highly recommended.

11. *Life in a Bucket of Soil,* Richard Rhine, Lothrop, Lee and Shephard, New York, 1972, 96 pp. (Gr. 5–6)
12. *Magnify and Find Out Why,* Julius Schwartz. McGraw-Hill Book Company, New York, 1972, 40 pp. (Gr. 2–4)
13. *Track Watching,*David Webster. Franklin Watts, New York, 96 pp. (Gr. 4–6)
14. *Worms,* Lois and Louis Darling. William Morrow, New York, 1972, 64 pp. (Gr. 2–5)

High School Level (grade 9–12)

* 1. *Suggestions for Experiments involving* [small mammalian] Animals at the Pre-University Level. Canadian Council on Animal Care. 151 Slater Street, Ottawa, Ontario KIP 5H3. (H)

* 2. *Experiments in Animal Behavior,* Marguerite D. Hainsworth, Houghton Mifflin Co., Boston, 1967. (H)

* 3. *How to Follow the Adventures of Insects,* Vinson Brown, Little Brown and Co., Boston, 1968. (H)

* 4. *Experiments with Microscopic Animals: Investigations for the Amateur Scientist,* Philip Goldstein and Jerome Metzner. Doubleday and Co., Inc., New York, 1971. (H)

* 5. *Manual of Field Biology and Ecology,* A. H. Benton and W. E. Werner, Jr., Burgess Publishing Co., Minneapolis, 1972, 408 pp. (H)

* 6. *Humane Biology Projects,* Animal Welfare Institute, P. O. Box 3650, Washington, D.C. 20007, 1977, free to teachers. (H)

* 7. *Experiments in Visual Science for Home and School,* James R. Gregg, The Ronald Press Co., New York, 1966. (H)

* 8. *Research Experiences in Plant Physiology: A Laboratory Manual,* Thomas C. Moore, Springer-Verlag, New York, 1974. (H)

* 9. *Investigations with Animals.* Ken Kurs. Ontario Teachers' Federation Science Unit Four. 1973. Ontario Teachers' Federation Science Project, c/o MacDonald School, Colborne Street, Kingston, Ontario K 7K 1E4. (H)

*10. *Handbook of Modern Experiments for High School Biology.* Adelaide Hechtlinger. 1971. Parker Publishing Co.,Inc. West Nyack, New York. (H)

11. *101 Simple Experiments with Insects,* H. Kalmus, Doubleday and Co., New York, 1960. (H)
12. *Human Physiology,* Thomas F. Morrison, Frederick D. Cornett, J. Edward Tether, and Pauline Gratz. Holt Rinehart and Winston, Inc., New York, 1968. (Grades 11–12)
13. *The Curious Mollusks,* Marie M. Jenkins, Holiday House, New York, 1972, 224 pp. (H)

14. *Plants in the Laboratory.* A manual and text for studies of the culture, development, reproduction, cytology, genetics, collection, and identification of the major plant groups. William J. Koch, Macmillan Co., New York, 1973. (H)

Advanced High School Level (grade 12 and above)

* 1. *Drosophila Guide,* M. Demerec and B. P. Kaufmann, 8th Ed., Carnegie Institution of Washington, 1530 P St., N.W., Washington, D.C. 20005. (A)

* 2. *A Manual of Psychological Experimentation on Planarians,* Ed., James V. McConnell, 2nd ed., 1967. Journal of Biological Psychology, Box 644, Ann Arbor, Michigan 48107. (A)

* 3. *Experiments on a Shoestring–A Handbook of Experiments and Demonstrations for General Psychology,* Nancy M. Minahan. Available from Professor Frank Costin, Department of Psychology, University of Illinois, Urbana, Illinois 61801. (A)

* 4. *Experiments in Physiology,* William McBlair, The National Press, Palo Alto, California 1965. (A)

* 5. *Animal Behavior in Laboratory and Field,* Allen W. Stokes, Ed., W. H. Freeman and Co., San Francisco, 1968. Chapters available separately. (A)

Order the following chapters by number and title from the publishers, W. H. Freeman and Co., 660 Market Street, San Francisco, Ca. 94104.

796. The analysis of behavior
797. The observation and comparison of behavior
798. Locomotion in animals
800. Optical orientation in the fly larva
801. Pheromones and trail making in ants
803. Schooling behavior in fish
804. Wall-seeking behavior in mice
805. Negative geotaxis among inbred strains of mice
806. Visual alarm reactions (turtles)
807. Behavior of earthworms
808. Cockroach behavior
809. Cyclic reproductive and feeding behavior in the milkweed bug
810. Food hoarding in rats
813. Mating behavior of Drosophila
814. Reproductive isolation in Drosophila
815. Aggressive, territorial, and sexual behavior of crickets
816. Reproductive behavior of the three-spined stickleback

---

*Highly recommended.

817. Display patterns in Anabantid fish (Paradise fish, Siamese fighting fish)
818. Behavior patterns of breeding frogs and toads
819. Social structure and display patterns of iguanid lizards
831. Exploratory behavior in goldfish

* 6. *Insects in the Classroom*, J. H. Borden, and B. D. Herrin. British Columbia Teachers' Federation, 105–2235 Burrard St., Vancouver 180, British Columbia, 1972, 172 pp. (H)

7. *Laboratory Exercises in Invertebrate Physiology*, J. H. Welsh, R. I. Smith and A. E. Kammer, 3rd Ed., Burgess Publishing Co., Minneapolis, 1968. (A)

8. *Experimental Physiology—Experiments in Cellular, General, and Plant Physiology*. Arnold Dunn and Joseph Arditti. Holt, Rinehart and Winston, Inc., New York, 1968. (A)

9. *Twelve Problems in Biology: Open-ended Experiments for Introductory College Biology*, J. C. Hake, J. J. W. Baker, and G. E. Allen, Addison-Wesley Publishing Co., Reading, Masschusetts, 1971, 191 pp. (A)

Appendix C

MAILING ADDRESSES OF ANIMAL SUPPLIERS AND ABBREVIATIONS USED IN TEXT OF CHAPTERS

AQU—Agua Engineers, Box 1, Ortonville, Michigan 48462

BCC—Bio-Control Company, Route 2, Box 2397, Auburn, California 95603

BIC—Bico Scientific Company, 2325 South Michigan Avenue, Chicago, Illinois 60616

BUB—The Butterfly Breeding Farm, 275 Colwick Road, Rochester, New York 14624

CAR—R. F. Carle Co., Inc., P. O. Box 3155, Chico, California 95926

CBR—California Brine Shrimp, Inc., 711 Hamilton Avenue, Menlo Park, California 94025

CBS—Carolina Biological Supply Co., Main Office, Burlington, North Carolina 27215

CCM—CCM: General Biological, Inc., 8200 South Hoyne Avenue, Chicago, Illinois 60620

CES—Central Scientific Company, 2600 S. Kostner Avenue, Chicago Illinois 60623

CON—Connecticut Valley Biological Supply Co., Inc., Valley Road, Southampton, Massachusetts 01073

CRO—Crop Protection Institute, P. O. Drawer "S", Durham, New Hampshire 03824

CUD—Curator of Drosophila Stocks, Genetics Research Unit, Cold Spring Harbor, New York 11724

CWF—Carter Worm Farm, Plains, Georgia 31780

DBI—Doris Bing, 6419 Palm Drive, Carmichael, California 95608

EVA—Everglades Aquatic Nurseries, Inc., P. O. Box 587–706 Plaza Place, Tampa, Florida 33601

GIA—Giant Ant Farm, Dept. 35, 1238 N. Highland Avenue, Hollywood, California 90038

ILO—Insect Lore Products, P.O. Box 1535, Shafter, California 93262.

INS—Insect Control and Research, Inc., 1330 Dillon Heights Avenue, Baltimore, Maryland 21228

LEV—Dr. Leo Levenbook, Laboratory of Physical Biology, National Institutes of Arthritis and Metabolic Diseases, National Institutes of Health, Bethesda, Maryland 20014

MOG—Mogul-Ed, P. O. Box 482, Oshkosh, Wisconsin 54901

NAS—Nasco/Steinhilber, Janesville Avenue, Fort Atkinson, Wisconsin 53538

PYR—Pyramid Nursery and Flower Shop, Box 5274, Reno, Nevada 89503

RAI—Rainbow Mealworms, 126 East Spruce Street, Compton California 90220

SCH—SCH Corporation, 1 Greentree Place, Greenbelt, Maryland 20770

SEL—Selph's Cricket Ranch, Inc., Box 2123, DeSoto Station, Memphis, Tennessee 38102

TIM—Timco Scientific Co., 18218 Delaware, Detroit, Michigan 48240

VIT—Vitova Co., Inc., Biological Control Division, P. O. Box 475, Rialto, California 92376

WAR—Ward's Natural Science Establishment, Inc., P. O. Box 1712, Rochester, New York 14603

West Coast Branch: Ward's of California, P. O. Box 1749, Monterey, California 93940

Appendix D

STATE WILDLIFE AGENCIES

The laws and regulations issued by the various states governing fishing and hunting license requirements and fees for taking "resident" wildlife (including fishes) and information concerning the wildlife laws of Canada, Mexico and Puerto Rico may be obtained from the following agencies:

Alabama: Director, Dept. of Conservation, 64 N. Union St., Montgomery 36104

Alaska: Commissioner, Dept. of Fish and Game, Subport Bldg., Juneau 99801

Arizona: Director, Game and Fish Dept., 2222 West Greenway Road, Phoenix 85023

Arkansas: Director, Game and Fish Commission, Game & Fish Bldg., Little Rock 72201

California: Director, Dept. of Fish and Game, 1416 9th St., Sacramento 95814

Colorado: Director, Dept. of Game, Fish & Parks, 6060 Broadway, Denver 80216

Connecticut: Director, Dept. Environmental Protection, State Office Bldg., Hartford 06115

Delaware: Director, Div. of Fish and Wildlife, Dept. Natural Resources, Dover 19901

District of Columbia: Chief of Police, 300 Indiana Ave., Washington 20001

Florida: Dir., Game & Fresh Water Fish Commission, 620 S. Meridian, Tallahassee 32304

Georgia: Director, Game and Fish Commission, 270 Washington Street S.W., Atlanta 30334

Hawaii: Dir., Div. of Fish & Game, Dept. of Land & Natural Resources, 1179 Punchbowl St., Honolulu 96813

Idaho: Director, Fish and Game Dept., 600 S. Walnut, P.O. Box 25, Boise 83707

Illinois: Director, Dept. of Conservation, 605 State Office Bldg., 400 South Spring Street, Springfield 62706

Indiana: Director, Dept. of Natural Resources, 607 State Office Bldg., Indianapolis 46204

Iowa: Director, State Conservation Commission, 300 Fourth Street, Des Moines 50319

Kansas: Director, Forestry, Fish and Game Commission, P.O. Box 1028 , Pratt 67124

Kentucky: Com., Dept. of Fish & Wildlife Resources, State Office Bldg. Annex, Frankfort 40601

Louisiana: Director, Wildlife and Fisheries Commission, 400 Royal St., New Orleans 70130

Maine: Commissioner, Dept. of Inland Fisheries and Game, 284 State Street, Augusta 04330

Maryland: Director, Fish and Wildlife Administration, Dept. Natural Resources, Tawes State Office Building, Annapolis 21404

Massachusetts: Director, Division of Fisheries and Game, 100 Cambridge St., Boston 02202

Michigan: Dir., Dept. of Natural Resources, Stevens T. Mason Bldg., Lansing 48926

Minnesota: Commissioner, Dept. of Natural Resources, Centennial Office Bldg., 658 Cedar Street, St. Paul 55155

Mississippi: Director of Conservation, Game and Fish Commission, P. O. Box 451, Jackson 39205

Missouri: Director, Dept. of Conservation, P. O. Box 180, Jefferson City 65101

Montana: Director, Fish & Game Dept., Mitchell Bldg., Helena 59601

Nebraska: Dir., Game and Parks Commission, P. O. Box 30370, Lincoln 68503

*Nevada:*Dir., Dept. Fish & Game, Box 10678, Reno 89510

New Hampshire: Dir., Fish & Game Dept., 34 Bridge St., Concord 03301

New Jersey: Dir., Div. of Fish & Game and Shellfisheries, Dept. Environmental Protection, Box 1809, Trenton 08625

New Mexico: Director, Dept. of Game & Fish, State Capitol, Santa Fe 87501

New York: Director, Fish & Wildlife, Dept. Environmental Conservation, 50 Wolf Road, Albany 12233

North Carolina: Exec. Dir., Wildlife Resources Commission, P. O. Box 2919, Raleigh 27611

North Dakota: Commissioner, Game & Fish Dept., 2121 Lovett Ave., Bismarck 58501

Ohio: Director, Dept. of Natural Resources, Fountain Square, Columbus 43224

Oklahoma: Director, Dept. of Wildlife Consv., P. O. Box 53465, Oklahoma City 73150

Oregon: Director, Wildlife Commission, Box 3503, Portland 97208

Pennsylvania: Executive Director, Fish Commission, P. O. Box 1673, Harrisburg 17120

Rhode Island: Chief, Div. of Fish and Wildlife, Veterans Memorial Bldg., 83 Park St., Providence 02903

South Carolina: Dir., Div. of Game and Freshwater Fisheries, Box 167, Columbia 29202

South Dakota: Secretary, Dept. of Game, Fish & Parks, State Office Bldg., Pierre 57501

Tennessee: Exec. Dir., Wildlife Resources Agency, Ellington Agricultural Center, P. O. Box 40747, Nashville 37204

Texas: Exec. Dir., Parks & Wildlife Dept., John H. Reagan Bldg., Austin 78701

Utah: Director, Div. of Wildlife Resources, 1596 West North Temple, Salt Lake City 84116

Vermont: Com., Fish & Game Dept., 5 Court Street, Montpelier 05602

Virginia: Exec. Dir., Commission of Game & Inland Fisheries, Box 11104 Richmond 23230

Washington: Director, Dept. of Game, 600 North Capitol Way, Olympia 98504

West Virginia: Director, Dept. of Natural Resources, State Office Bldg. 3, Charleston 25305

Wisconsin: Secretary, Dept. of Natural Resources, Box 450, Madison 53701

Wyoming: Director, Game & Fish Dept., P. O. Box 1589, Cheyenne 82001

CANADA (Federal): Chief, Canadian Wildlife Service, Ottawa

CANADA (Provincial Offices):

Alberta: Fish & Wildlife Div., Dept. of Lands and Forests, Edmonton

British Columbia: Chief, Game Mgt., Fish & Game Br., Parliaments Bldg., Victoria

Manitoba: Dir. of Wildlife, Dept. of Mines and Natural Resources, Winnipeg

New Brunswick: Chief, Fish & Wildlife Br., Dept. of Lands and Mines, Fredericton

Newfoundland: Dir. of Wildlife, Dept. of Mines, Agriculture, and Resources, St. Johns

Northwest Territories: Deputy Commissioner of N.W.T., Vimy Bldg., Ottawa

Nova Scotia: Fish & Game Association, P. O. Box 654, Halifax

Ontario: Chief, Fish & Wildlife Br., Dept. of Lands and Forests, Parliaments Bldg., Toronto

Prince Edward Island: Dir. of Fish & Wildlife, Dept. of Industry & Natural Resources, Charlottetown

Quebec: Dir. of Wildlife Div., Dept. of Tourism, Game and Fish, Quebec

Saskatchewan: Dir. of Wildlife, Dept. of Natural Resources, Government Admin. Bldg., Regina

Yukon Territory: Game Dept., Yukon Territory, White Horse

Appendix E

PAINLESS KILLING OF SMALL MAMMALS

Euthanasia is a word derived from the Greek, *eu* meaning good, and *thanatos* meaning death; it means "the humane destruction of an animal accomplished by a method which quickly produces a state of unconsciousness followed by death without visible evidence of pain and anxiety" (as defined by the Laboratory Animal Welfare Act 1971). For certain biological studies it is necessary to obtain tissues, such as the heart, the intestine, or muscle from freshly killed animals.

The taking of a life for any purpose is a repugnant event. Therefore the emotional effects on the biologist of euthanizing small warmblooded animals cannot be lightly dismissed. Unfortunately, some people have quite different attitudes toward the killing of warmblooded animals as compared to coldblood animals, *i.e.*, fish, frogs, snakes. Man's kinship with other mammals causes him to identify with them. The closer the kinship the greater the identification and concern for the animal. However, euthanasia of all species—warmblooded or cold, close kinship with man or not—requires special considerations to ensure that the killing is carried out with care and respect to produce a humane death. Procedures for euthanasia should be carried out by trained adults, preferably in the absence of young students. In some states it is illegal for primary and secondary school students to witness the killing of an animal. It is possible that emotional trauma and psychological harm may be done to sensitive and immature minds. Therefore the presence of young students during the performance of procedures for euthanasia is not recommended.

Euthanasia must be performed expertly, else the animal may suffer. If the teacher has any reservations about proficiency in these techniques, then the procedures should not be attempted by that teacher. A choice of several humane methods are available. However, emphasis will be placed on carbon dioxide because of its known superiority.

Carbon dioxide (CO_2) produces rapid and painless death in small mammals. The 1972 report of the American Veterinary Medical Association Panel on Euthanasia recommends its use and states that "animals do not detect the presence of CO_2 immediately and the depressant action of the gas takes place almost unnoticed".* This method is highly recommended by Humane Societies.**

---

*Journal of the American Veterinary Medical Association, 160(5):761-772, 1972. Reprints available from the AVMA, 600 South Michigan Ave., Chicago, Illinois 60605.

**The method described here is taken from "Humane Killing of Animals". Universities Federation for Animal Welfare, 230 High St., Potters Bar, Hertfordshire, England.

CO_2 Acts by combining with the hemoglobin of the red blood cells to produce fatal anoxemia (lack of oxygen). The brain, lacking sufficient oxygen, is depressed and unconsciousness occurs without pain or appreciable discomfort. Respiratory arrest and death occur with no intervening period of excitement. CO_2 is safe to handle (unlike chloroform), is non-explosive (unlike ether), is inexpensive, and easy to obtain.* It is odorless, however, so the operator must be careful to avoid excessive inadvertent inhalation.

CO_2 is stored as a liquid under pressure in a cylinder. When slowly released, it turns into gas. Most cylinders are supplied with a simple locking device which is replaced by a reducing valve before use. A short length of rubber hose is used to connect the valve outlet with the container holding the animal. The animal is placed in an open mesh cage and allowed time to get accustomed to this new environment. When the animal has settled down, showing no signs of excitement, the cage is placed inside a *clear plastic bag* approximately five times the volume of the cage. The bag is gently pressed close to the sides of the cage in order to ensure that the plastic is not pierced or torn. A clear plastic bag is necessary because one must be able to see the action of the animal in order to take necessary corrective measures (administration of more carbon dioxide) if excitement or distressful action occurs. Additionally, the signs of death, *i.e.*, cessation of breathing, must be visible to the operator. The end of the hose from the CO_2 cylinder is introduced through the mouth of the bag. The operator holds the mouth tightly around the hose with one hand around the hose and with the other turns on a slow flow of gas. CO_2 has the effect of rapidly freezing tissues. By the time the bag becomes half inflated, the animal will have become narcotised or unconscious — with mice this normally takes about 10-20 seconds. When the plastic bag is full of gas, but not under pressure, the nose is withdrawn, the gas turned off, and the mouth of the bag sealed with a rubber band or plastic tie. Continue to observe the animal until *all signs of breathing have ceased.* When this occurs, and if no fresh tissues are needed from the body, then leave the animal in contact with the gas for another 5-10 minutes. Then open the bag, taking care not to breath in the contents of the bag. Even if fresh tissues are needed, the animal should not be removed from the bag for at least one minute after all visible signs of breathing have ceased. The animal is then exsanguinated (drained of blood) by cutting open the throat, being sure that the jugular and carotid vessels are cut. This is done under a stream of cold water. When all blood flow has ceased, the animal can be opened for removal of tissues. Exsanguination is an essential part of the method for collection of fresh tissues because it assures that the animal is dead and not merely unconscious. It is better to practice "overkill" than to have any doubt that the animal is dead. The tissues required should be removed immediately from the body to ensure they remain viable. The appropriate method for handling the tissues must be clearly understood and practiced; otherwise the death of the animal will have no meaning because invalid or poor results will be obtained from the studies.

---

*For local suppliers of carbon dioxide, look in the yellow pages of the telephone directory under "Gas — Industrial and Medical."

As a general principle, animal bodies must not be disposed of by incineration or other methods until *rigor mortis* occurs and the animals are quite stiff. At the completion of the euthanizing procedure, carbon dioxide should be allowed to seep out of the plastic bag, sink to the lowest level available (since it is heavier than air), and become harmless by its dispersal in the atmosphere.

Under certain circumstances, if the preferred carbon dioxide method cannot be used, it may be necessary to administer an overdose of ether or chloroform. There are limitations and disadvantages of using either ether or chloroform. Rabbits react badly to chloroform and should never be killed in this manner. It is preferable to have rabbits destroyed by a veterinarian through an intravenous injection of an overdose of barbiturate.

Ether and chloroform are dangerous substances to handle. Ether is highly flammable and explosive. Chronic exposure to chloroform can cause liver and kidney damage. In a culture where young people often become addicted to inhaling volatile organic compounds, the advisability of using either ether or chloroform in schools must be questioned.

The vapours of these substances have an irritant effect on the mucous membranes, and both agents elicit a considerable amount of excitement in the animal before and after loss of consciousness. The American Veterinary Medical Association state that these agents "are not normally recommended without the prior use of preanesthetic agents or tranquilizers". Drops of mineral oil must be placed in each eye to protect against irritation from the vapors. A two-compartment container such as a dessicator must be used. A pad soaked in either ether or chloroform is placed in the lower compartment, and the animal on the upper level. Under no circumstances should the soaked pad be allowed into contact with the animal's skin. Too great a concentration of chloroform at the outset will cause a sense of suffocation and the animal will struggle, therefore *build up the concentration gradually*. More details for use of these agents in euthanising animals and precautions or their use are given on page 238. Exsanguinate the animal as described on the previous page before removing any body tissues.

Index

Credits

DESIGN: Rick Chafian

ARTWORK: Judith McCarty

PHOTOGRAPHS

Cover: Hulda Magalhaes, Bucknell University, PA; Fig. 2-1 Gabriel A. Cooney; 2-2 John A. Moore; 2-3 and 2-4 Josh Schmidt, Landon School, Bethesda, MD; 2-5 Gabriel A. Cooney; 2-6 from *Freshwater Microscopy* by W. J. Garnett. By permission of Dover Publications Inc. in the US and Constable & Co., Ltd. in Canada; 2-7 Harbrace Photo; 2-8 Gabriel A. Cooney; 2-10 BSCS; 2-11 Harold Orlans

Fig. 4-2 and 4-3 Jeffrey Georgia, Landon School; 4-4 and 4-5 James V. McConnell; 4-7 Eric V. Gravé; 4-8 Gabriel A. Cooney

Fig. 5-1 Josh Schmidt; 5-2 Gabriel A. Cooney; 5-4 Robert Gannon; 5-6 Bergman Associates; 5-7 Robert Gannon

Fig. 6-1 through 6-3 and 6-5 through 6-7 Alvin E. Staffan

Fig. 7-1 Thorne Films Inc.; 7-2 Gabriel A. Cooney; 7-3 W. Robert Stamper and Daryl L. Biser; 7-4 and 7-6 American Museum of Natural History; 7-7 Josh Schmidt; 7-8 through 7-12 Gabriel A. Cooney

Fig. 8-1 Josh Schmidt; 8-4 through 8-6 U.S. Dept. of Agriculture; 8-7 American Museum of Natural History; 8-12 U.S. Dept. of Agriculture; 8-14 Gabriel A. Cooney; 8-15 through 8-20 and 8-22 U.S. Dept. of Agriculture

Fig. 9-1 The Universities Federation of Animal Welfare, Herts, England; 9-2 American Museum of Natural History; 9-3 Braz Walker; 9-4 and 9-5 American Museum of Natural History; 9-7 Jeffrey Georgia; 9-8 Josh Schmidt; 9-9 Jeffrey Georgia; 9-10 American Museum of Natural History; 9-11 Barbara Clark, Houghton High School, Houghton, MI

Fig. 10-1 Amphibian Facility of the University of Michigan; 10-3 John A. Moore; 10-7 and 10-8 Amphibian Facility of the University of Michigan; 10-9 Barbara Clark

Fig. 11-2 American Museum of Natural History; 11-3 Ernest G. Hofman. By permission of Authors' and Publishers' Service, New York; 11-4 through 11-6 American Museum of Natural History; 11-9 George Ancona; 11-10 Boston Museum of Science; 11-11 Lothrop E. Smith, MD.

Fig. 12-1 and 12-2 Victor Schwentker, Tumblebrook Farm Inc., Brant Lake, NY; 12-3 through 12-5 J.A.R. Mead, National Institutes of Health; 12-6 Josh Schmidt; 12-7 Michael Simmonds, Akiba Hebrew Academy, Mercon Station, PA; 12-8 Hulda Magalhaes 12-9 and 12-10 Frank M. Loew, Animal Resources Center, University of Saskatchewan, Saskatoon, Canada

Fig. 13-1 through 13-3 J.A.R. Mead 13-4 through 13-7 Ernest P. Walker; 13-12 J.A.R. Mead

Fig. 14-1 and 14-2 Ernest P. Walker; 14-3 through 14-7 Hulda Magalhaes; 14-8 Produced by Eothen Films International Ltd. Distributed in the USA by Encyclopedia Britannica Educational Corp.; 14-10 and 14-11 Hulda Magalhaes

Fig. 15-1 and 15-2 U.S. Dept. of Agriculture; 15-3 J.A.R. Mead; 15-4a The Universities Federation for Animal Welfare; 15-4b Produced by Eothen Films International Ltd. Distributed in the USA by Encyclopedia Britannica Educational Corp.; 15-6 The Universities Federation for Animal Welfare

Fig. 16-1 Michael Simmonds; 16-2 Barbara Clark; 16-4 Edward M. Spivack, Akiba Hebrew Academy; 16-5 The Architecture Machine Group, Department of Agriculture, Massachusetts Institute of Technology

Fig. 17-1 and 17-2 Michael Simmonds; 17-3 Edward M. Spivack; 17-4 and 17-5 Michael Simmonds; 17-6 and 17-7 Edward M. Spivack; 17-8 and 17-10 Michael Simmonds; 17-9 Derived from Minahan's *Experiments on a Shoestring*